Alex Battler

The Twenty-First Century:

The World Without Russia

Copyright © Alex Battler
Copyright © SCHOLARICA®

No part of this book may be used or reproduced in any manner whatsoever without written permission except in the case of brief quotation embodied in critical articles and reviews.

Inquiries should be addressed to
www.scholarica.com

Alex Battler

The Twenty-First Century: The World Without Russia. Second edition. —Publisher SCHOLARICA, 2020. —416 p.

In this book, Alex Battler questions the assertion of Russia's status as a great power in the acuminate form. The author reveals the contradictions between Russia's real modern potential and its foreign policy objectives formulated by official Moscow.

The author has formulated laws on the Pole, the Center of Power, and Force. Battler introduces some new concepts of the Theory of International Relations: The Foreign Policy Potential of the State and The Law on the Optimal Balance Between the Costs of Domestic and Foreign Policy.

On almost all problems raised by the author, his views do not coincide with generally accepted interpretations and approaches.

The second extended edition of the book "*The Twenty-First Century: The World Without Russia*" includes updated copyright and newly added parts and paragraphs.

ISBN: 978-1-7355989-1-8

SCHOLARICA®
2020

To my wife,

who is the inspiration in my life and work

Contents

Preface for Western Readers

This book was originally published in Russia in late 2001 under my journalistic pen name of Oleg Arin. I then decided to publish it in English, for two reasons. To begin with, the book's topics are as much of interest to the West as they are to Russia; and second, I wanted the Western reader to get a more realistic perspective on Russia's place and role in the world. The latter is particularly important, considering that academic and especially popular literature in the West often presents a distorted picture of Russia; in particular, it tends to exaggerate the achievements of "democratic reforms" in this country.

In this book I cast doubt on the great power status claimed for Russia. Moreover, I was compelled to prove, by drawing on a vast body of material, that Russia has altogether lost the capacity of being a structure-forming subject of international relations. In the process, I uncovered the contradiction between Russia's actual potential and the official foreign policy objectives formulated by Moscow. The book also contains criticism of Russian politicians and scholars of all persuasions, but especially those who rely on wishful thinking rather than facts in their research and prognoses. I label such personages "if-only-ists." Some Western scholars, Americans for the most part, also come in for their share of criticism, even though the quality of their analyses depends on more rigorous standards of research than do the works of Russian political scientists.

In this book, I formulate, among other things, the laws of ***poles***, of ***centers of power***, and of ***power*** and introduce new concepts in The Theory of International Relations: ***A state's Foreign Policy Potential*** and ***The Law of Optimal Proportion Between Expenditures on Domestic and Foreign Policy.***

On almost all issues raised, my views differ from the generally accepted interpretations and approaches prevalent both in the West and in the East.

I want to draw the readers' attention to the fact that although I am a Canadian citizen, I wrote this book from the perspective of a Russian (I am Russian by birth) concerned about Russia's destiny. I have spent most of my life in Russia, worked in its most prestigious scientific centers and schools, and traveled all over the country, rubbing shoulders with both those who govern Russia "from the top" and those who suffer their misrule "below." I am, therefore, free of the illusions entertained by some western scholars and politicians about Russia.

January 2002

Preface

I ask my Russian readers not to panic. I don't mean to say that Russia will disappear from the face of the earth, although that is what many opponents of Russia dream about. But it won't happen, at least not in the twenty-first century. What will happen is that Russia will cease to influence the course of world events; indeed, it has practically ceased already to do so. In geostrategic terms, it means that Russia has lost its superpower status and has ceased to be a "center of power" and world pole determining the structure of world relations. As a consequence, international relations are developing and unfurling without Russia's involvement. From the historical viewpoint, there is nothing special about this because history shows that the course of world events is influenced by a handful of empire-type states fighting for hegemony in the world. All other states usually serve as objects of their policies. Hegemonic states replace one another, but the struggle for power and, ultimately, for hegemony continues. These states have always shaped the regional and global structures of international relations in the geostrategic world, and it is they that determine the course of events.

The Russian state has only twice changed the system and structure of international relations since its emergence. The first occasion was the birth of the Soviet Union after the October Revolution of 1917. The world then split into two camps (those of socialism and capitalism), with the struggle between them after World War II shaping the geostrategic bipolar system with its two centers of power headed by the The Twenty-First Century: The World Without Russia

USA and the USSR. The Soviet Union's defeat in this struggle spelled the end of the Soviet superpower, and the bipolar system was replaced by a monocentric one headed by the USA. The Russian Federation that emerged in the place of the USSR very quickly regressed to the same marginal status that Russia enjoyed prior to 1917. Russia is now way below the world's top ten nations in terms of GNP, and its influence is limited to its territory, which it barely manages to keep from further fragmentation. Thus, the birth and death of the Soviet empire shook the world in the twentieth century and changed the structure of international relations.

I find confirmation for these seemingly self-evident facts all the time, whenever I travel in North America, Western Europe, or East Asia. In whichever country I visit, there is almost no mention of Russia whatsoever, except for the occasional ten-second spot about Chechnya.

Nonetheless, Russia's degradation is most vividly seen and felt by those living in Russia. The country is dying right before our eyes. One must be perfectly blind not to see the mass impoverishment of the majority of the population; the decay of dwellings, villages, towns, and cities; the inability of the authorities to deal with natural disasters or with the catastrophic levels of crime, drug addiction, and other social and physical ills. Most people's minds are fixated on survival. In the provinces, the degradation has reached the stage of early feudalism. The average income has dropped to the levels of poor African countries. I could go on and on.

Against the backdrop of these multiple domestic tragedies, it is bewildering to hear Russia's president, political leaders of all stripes, and scholars of different ideological persuasions talk and write so often about Russia as a great power that plays a role of global proportions. In this regard, I recall the saying of the famous Chinese military thinker, Sun Tsu, from his Art of War: "So it is said that if you know others and know yourself, you will not be imperiled in a hundred battles; if you do not know others but know yourself, you win one and lose one; if you do not know others and do not know yourself, you will be imperiled in every single battle."[1]

I am deeply convinced that the majority, if not all, of those who call Russia a great power belong to the third category of people, i.e., those who do not know Russia or the outside world. It suffices to ask these people some concrete questions, such as: What is the critical mass of a state's weight that qualifies it for the status of a great power? What is the degree of financial commitment required to make the country's "greatness" felt around the world? What is the difference between a state's place in the world and its

1 Sun Tsu, *The Art of War.* Translated by Thomas Cleary (Boston and London: Shambhala, 1988), 82.

role in the world, and how are these categories related to the country's economic potential and the state budget? Ask any politician what sums are allocated for foreign policy in Russia and what sums in, say, the USA. I doubt whether the "great power propagandists" even consider these questions.

I'd like to believe that Russia is a great power. The facts, however, don't support such a view. I was compelled to resort to arguments from the economic, political, and military-strategic areas to prove the opposite, namely: From the moment the capitalist reforms started, Russia lost the status not just of a superpower but even of a great power. It has turned into a regional power whose influence in the world is inferior not just to the G-7 countries of "the golden billion," but also to a number of other countries with a GNP of more than $500 billion.

Therefore, the purpose of the present book is to show Russia's real place and role in the first half of the twenty-first century. For completeness of the picture, I had to use different methods and approaches. One of these consists of taking a look at Russia from the outside; that is, determining Russia's place and role in the strategic doctrines and concepts of the most active subjects of world politics. The latter are represented in this book by the USA. (Japan and China are represented in another book titled The Strategic Contours of East Asia. Russia: Not a Step Forward.) I left out Western Europe, not because it is of little importance in world politics but because it is close to the USA regarding strategic policy toward Russia. Besides, an analysis of the "Russian policies" of the four main powers (Germany, France, Great Britain, and Italy) would greatly inflate the volume of this work.

The other approach is to take a look at Russia from inside Russia itself, i.e., through the official doctrines and concepts of the country's present leadership and through the works of Russian scholars of bourgeois leanings. I consciously avoided using, as far as possible, the political literature of the left-wing or "patriotic" camp because I regard its influence on Russia's foreign policy as being close to zero.

The political science approach had to be complemented by a theory of international relations—a theory to which I introduce three laws (the law of economic mass or "pole," the law of "center of power," and the law of "power"). The theoretical parts of this book are the most difficult to read, but without comprehending or at least perusing them, it is hard to get an understanding of the development of international relations and of everything connected to it.

This book is divided into three parts. Though each of them can be regarded as a whole in a certain way, they are connected through the axis of the main topic—what Russia is and what it will be.

Naturally, for a book of this size, I had to work through a lot of literature and statistical data. I obtained the bulk of my research material through the Internet. In this regard, I want to give a warning to the reader unfamiliar with the Internet system: Some of my references do not indicate pages. This means that the material was presented in HTML format. Pages are indicated only where the material was published in a PDF format. As of the present moment, the rules for making references to material found on the Web showing an Internet (Web site) address are not yet finalized. Therefore, I did the following: Wherever the address-holder is obvious (for example, international organizations, Japan's Foreign Ministry, the CIA, the NSC, the Pentagon, the State Department), I did not indicate the address; in nonobvious cases, I did.

Regarding the language of this book, I am often accused of writing about serious subjects in "nonscientific" terms, which apparently means the academic writing style of Russian scholars. Also, I am accused of using the word "I" too often and criticizing everyone all the time. I use this opportunity to respond to my accusers. First, I don't criticize indiscriminately; I criticize only those who use "scientific" language to write texts that have no relation to science. Second, I use the word "I" simply because it is I who am writing my works, not any sort of "we." "We" is a way of shirking responsibility for what is written. Third, the academic style is the result of a form of depersonification common under the Soviet regime, especially during the period of stagnant socialism. Though I am better disposed toward the Soviet regime than toward the present one, I have no desire to depersonify myself, especially because I am convinced that one should write humorously about serious matters.

In my texts, I put the word "APR" (Asian-Pacific Region) in quotation marks, though abbreviations are not supposed to have quotation marks in the English language. I do this on purpose, for I maintain that the "APR" is a fiction. But when quoting documents or other authors' texts, I am constrained to preserve their spelling and punctuation marks.

I also wish to note that certain paragraphs and small excerpts from this book have been published in certain newspapers, magazines, and collections. No one has criticized me for those texts; on the contrary, many readers have expressed their agreement with me. However, the publication of this book in its full form, under its actual title, is bound to cause some indignation, especially from Russian "if-only-ists," and most certainly will provoke accusations of being anti-Russian. This does not perturb me because I believe the actions of politicians and politically engaged "scientists" cause more harm to Russia than does the truth about it. Nonetheless, should they find and publish any credible counterarguments, I am always prepared to respond, and I would be thankful to anyone who messages to my e-mail address with criticisms or reflections found in the press on my book.

As with my previous works, I never subjected this book to any preliminary discussions, and no one assisted me in writing it, except, of course, my wife, Valentina. As always, she read and edited texts of a nature alien to her. As always, I tested on her the degree to which my writing, especially the theoretical parts, would be accessible to laymen. Because this book was readily understood by an artist-pianist (my wife), I count on it not to be too difficult for those with an interest in foreign policy and international relations.

In my opinion, this book should be of interest not only to instructors and students of international affairs but also to all those who are interested in the theory of international relations and the foreign policies of the world's leading powers.

May 2001

Acronyms and Abbreviations

- **ABM** — Antiballistic Missile (Treaty of 1972)
- **APEC** — Asia-Pacific Economic Cooperation
- **APR** — Asia-Pacific region
- **ASEAN** — Association of South-East Asian Nations
- **CIS/NIS** — Commonwealth of Independent States/New Independent States (the former republics of the USSR)
- **CPSU** — Communist Party of the Soviet Union
- **EA** — East Asia
- **EC** — European Community
- **FDI** — Foreign direct investment
- **EIB** — Export-Import Bank
- **FPP** — Foreign political potential
- **G-7** — Group of seven industrial countries
- **GATT** — General Agreement on Tariffs and Trade
- **GDP** — Gross domestic product
- **GNP** — Gross national product
- **Goskomstat** — States Statistics Committee
- **HDI** — Human Development Index
- **ILO** — International Labor Organization
- **IDV** — Russian acronym for Institute for Far Eastern Studies
- **IMEMO** — Russian acronym for Institute of World Economy and International Relations
- **IMF** — International Monetary Fund
- **MNBs** — Multinational banks
- **MNCs** — Multinational corporations

- **NAFTA** — North American Free Trade Area (Agreement)
- **NEA** — Northeast Asia
- **NGO** — Nongovernmental organization
- **ODA** — Official development assistance
- **OECD** — Organization for Economic Cooperation and Development
- **OSCE** — Organization on Security and Cooperation in Europe
- **PACE** — Parliamentary Assembly of the Council of Europe
- **PPP** — Purchasing power parity
- **R&D** — Research and development
- **RSFSR** — Russian Soviet Federative Socialist Republic
- **SAA** — Strategic attack arms
- **START** — Strategic Arms Reduction Talks
- **TVD** — Russian acronym for theatre of military action
- **TNBs** — Transnational banks
- **TNCs** — Transnational companies (corporations)
- **UN DP** — UN Development Program
- **USSR** — Union of Soviet Socialist Republics (defunct since 1991)
- **WHO** — World Health Organization
- **WMD** — Weapon of mass destruction
- **WTO** — World Trade Organization
- **WTO** — Warsaw Treaty Organization

Should no one like these Thoughts, they are doubtlessly bad; but in my eyes, they would be despicable should they be liked by all.

Diderot

PART I

U.S. Strategy in the Twenty-First Century:

Leadership Through Hegemony

Chapter I

The Concept Apparatus and Research Approaches

Russian scholars, with rare exceptions (E. Pozdnyakov, V. Baranovsky, N. Kosolapov, and a few others), are not concerned about the problem of the concept apparatus of the theory of international relations. They can write quite casually about globalization or integration, while in fact they are describing issues of internationalization; they can talk about a state's power, while in fact they are describing that state's might; they can formulate concepts of national security, while in fact they are describing problems of domestic policy. To them, world relations are identical to international relations, etc. This approach reflects the peculiarity of the Russian mind-set, which rejects rationality for irrationality, which they feel helps them to penetrate "deeper" into the essence of phenomena. I will later demonstrate this with examples, but for now, let us look at American ways of looking at the same problems.

The majority of American international relations scholars and political scientists are not inclined to "theorize." This gives grounds for the authors of the monograph *American National Security* to state: "A chronic source of presidential difficulties with the Congress and, sometimes, the nation at large, is the tendency to use the concept of national The Twenty-First Century: The World Without Russia security overly broadly, invoking it as a cloak to cover various controversial actions."[1]

One has to admit that Americans have been pondering the subject of this conceptual apparatus since the end of World War II,

1 Jordan, Taylor Jr., and Mazarr, *American National Security*, 4.

and in many respects they have achieved impressive results. Nonetheless, the problem persists. Ken Booth demonstrates its urgency in the following fashion: "Many," he writes, "use the word 'peace' in the sense of 'absence of world war,' despite the fact that since World War II, more than 20 million people have been killed in military conflicts.[1] The term 'Third World' is used to mean all underdeveloped countries. But the upper social strata of this 'world' is not any different in its level of well-being from the wealthy in the 'First World.' The term 'power' is used as being synonymous with 'military power,' even though these notions are not identical." Booth draws the following conclusion: "If these and other key words in academic international relations have not been naming things properly, how could the theories they create help us discern the future?" (336)

A confusion regarding concepts is often the result of several fields of science intersecting or overlapping. It is a known fact that in the West, "international relations" is studied as a branch of political science. Booth however says, "It has become increasingly evident that political science can be seriously studied only as a branch of the study of politics on a global scale. ...World politics is the home of political science, not vice versa. Kant was right: political theory has to be international theory." (340)

Here's one more curious reflection from Booth: "Therefore, the goal of international political theory must be the joining of Marxian "science" with the "science" of Morgenthau in the art of utopian realism; the problem of international political science must be the attempt to unify the world through changing it." (347)

Though it's not clear from this sentence what Booth means by "Marxian science" and "Morgenthau's science," the term "utopian realism" reminded me at once of an utterance by Mr. Data the Android, one of the colorful characters in the TV series *Star Trek: The Next Generation*. He remarked once, quite reasonably: "To expect the unexpected is impossible."

To a substantial, if not decisive, degree, the recent wave of theoretical research was caused by the end of the Cold War, when the Berlin Wall crumbled, along with the established clichés and stereotypes of the theory of international relations. To put it simply, this theory used to have two mighty currents: One was completely ideologically engaged (the school of political idealism dom-

1 Booth, and Smith, eds, *International Relations: Theory Today*, 334.

inant in the USSR), explaining all developments in international life through the struggle between "communism" and "capitalism." The other one, called geostrategic (the school of political realism), relies on the concept of power.

Nowadays, when ideology has ceased to play a dominant role (in the opinion of American theorists) and the concept of power has begun to change, the elegant constructs of the past have become outdated. What has emerged instead? This is where debates start, centering in most cases on the following: the current structure of international relations (bipolar, unipolar, or multipolar); the content of the concept of power in today's world; the role of the state in the era of "globalization"; and "national security"—an artificial abstraction or something objectively real?

I will address all these topics in one way or another throughout this book. But for a start, I want to present the views of Messrs. A. Jordan, W. Taylor, and M. Mazarr, the well-known authors of the textbook *National Security of the USA*. Their popularity is evidenced by the fact that their book is already in its fifth edition and is used by students of military academies and universities.

These authors (henceforth referred to as JTM) believe that the Cold War was followed not by simple peace but by a "hot peace." The difficulty lies in describing this peace. Unlike the champions of the concept of U.S. "unipolar hegemony" (such as Charles Krauthammer), JTM believe that what has really emerged is "a complex multipolar international system."

By the way, they remind the reader where the concept of "unipolarity" originated. Back in 1992, a document was prepared in the Pentagon and unfortunately leaked to the world, from which everyone learned of the proposed policy emphasis "on precluding the emergence of any potential future global competitor." (545) This was not directed at an already weakened Russia but rather at the allies of the USA, and formulated in rather harsh phrases, such as: "American defense should be so strong that potential competitors, from Western Europe or Asia, as well as the former Soviet Union, would be deterred from even aspiring to a larger regional or global role." (546)

The authors remind us that apart from the die-hard "unipolarists," there exist proponents of "superpower multipolarity" who champion hegemony by the USA while "allowing" other powers, such as Germany and Japan, to provide a multipolar background. JTM themselves favor a "complex multipolarity," denying hegemonic status to the USA for a number of reasons, among which is the following: The focus of U.S. national strategy has shifted from the global to the regional level. On the global level, there is no other global power; therefore, there is no adversary for a global struggle. On the regional level, the structural aspects vary widely. In Africa a balance of power shapes the structure of relations; in some places, it is defined by bipolarity; in others, by multipolarity. In other words, not one of the "power models" is universal, and none explains the actual reality.

Another cause of "multipolarity" has to do with the fact that several mighty regional powers are capable of ensuring their survival and independence on their own, without help from allies. This argument might appear strange at first, but the authors mean to say there is no hostile power in the world capable of endangering "the survival and independence" of, say, Germany, Great Britain, or Japan.

But the main reason for "multipolarity" is something else, namely, the problem of diffusion of the term "power"—the key term in all concepts of "polarity." "The diffusion of the other non-military elements of power—particularly of economic strength—throughout the international system further refutes this unipolar concept." (8)

In this connection, I want to draw your attention to the following important fact: Power is a key category in the theory of international relations, debated by generation after generation of theorists who have failed to this day to define what it is. JTM acknowledge this fact, adding that the method for calculating power is also absent. That's only natural. If there is no definition, there is nothing to calculate. Because power is an important category, we'll let the authors expound in more detail on this subject.

JTM believe that the enigma of power is that "power is dynamic." They write: "In the simplest terms, it is the ability to get others to do something they would not do of their own volition." The authors clarify: The ability to coerce does not necessarily only mean "physical violence upon an adversary," though that is an important argument of power. Other aspects of power are listed as "bargaining ability" and "persuasion, based on common interests and values." (9) They consider this definition of power sufficient and move on to its estimation.

They write: "Power can be viewed and appraised in several ways. Since it is based upon capabilities, power has certain objective characteristics. But *it also has a highly subjective element,* for the reputation for having and being willing to use power is sufficient to achieve results in many cases, without really applying it. Hobbes rightly wrote, 'Power is what people think it is until tested.'" (Emphasis by the authors, ibid.)

At this point, JTM fall into an elementary logical contradiction. If power is an objective category, it cannot have "a highly subjective element" because only the evaluation of power can be subjective, not power itself. The observer's (analyst's) goal is precisely to have his subjective evaluation coincide with the content of power. (Hegel called this the merging of object and subject.) The multiplicity of interpretations of a single phenomenon means only that the phenomenon is not perceived correctly. Having fallen at this stage into a logical and philosophical trap, JTM are subsequently unable to get out of it.

They write: "*Power is also essentially relative in character*, for its utility depends in part on comparing it with whatever opposes it; when this comparison is made explicit, the resulting calculus is often called *net power*. Further, *power is highly situational*; what may generate power in one set of circumstances may not in another. Such intangibles as the political and technical skills of the key actors, national will and solidarity on the issue, the nature of the issue in question, and the purposes being sought all condition the power a state can bring into play in a given situation." (Emphasis by the authors, ibid.)

If it is impossible to objectively estimate power as such, then it is also impossible to estimate the opposing power, and no kind of comparison will help because in this case two indeterminate values are being compared. JTM are optimists, however.

"If power is dynamic, subjective, relative, and situational, as well as objective in character, can it usefully be defined at all? Despite the caveats and difficulties, the answer is "yes." Particularly if we focus on its objective characteristics (which are, more accurately, measures of 'strength' and may or may not yield influence, as already noted) and qualify it appropriately for time and circumstances, we can say at least a few things useful about power." (ibid.)

They did indeed say a few things, but not about power. Like everyone before them, they confused the concepts of strength and power, and I will return to this topic in the corresponding chapter.

The authors do offer valid criticism of the views held about the category of power by Harold and Margaret Sprout, for: "They suggested a crude equation: power is equal to human resources, plus physical habitat, plus foodstuffs and raw materials, plus tools and skills, plus organization, plus morale and political behavior, plus external conditions and circumstances." (ibid.) Clifford German's writings on the subject are in much the same key, while Ray Cline added "strategic purpose and national will" to those quantifiable characteristics. (10) By the way, the understanding of power by JTM themselves coincides to a large degree with Cline's formulations.

Further, JTM attempt to define the contemporary state of national power, which has been naturally undergoing some changes. "It was not only more fragmented, but at the same time more interdependent. The fragmentation came from the demise of the major bipolar blocs of the Cold War, as well as corresponding release of previously suppressed ethnic or rather tribal nationalism in many nations across the globe." (548) This resulted in national power becoming more diffuse, complicating the effect of one state's influence on another. "'Soft' forms of power, such as the ability to manipulate interdependences, become more important, as does the long-term economic strength of the nation, which is the base for both hard and soft forms of power." (548)

Please note that the authors have started using the terms power and strength as synonyms without even noticing. This is the pit that ensnared all theorists who have ever struggled to define the category of power. Approaching "power" first from one side, then another, they failed to produce a clear definition thereof. They went on to repeat the well-known banality: "Power and the will to use it become the prerequisite for success, even survival. ...*The purpose of power is to overcome resistance in an effort to bring about or secure a preferred order of things.*" (Emphasis by the authors, 13.) The result is this: Instead of defining power, JTM identified two of its functions (both debatable)victory in struggle and securing of order. Power, as such, slipped away from them once again. In other words, the authors realize the treacherous nature of this concept, yet they fail to transcend the framework of views held by all theorists (without exception) who have struggled with this concept since the time of Hans J. Morgenthau.[1]

An even wider circle of theorists is involved in discussions of the category of national security. Heated attacks are mostly directed against the neorealists who represent two schools of thought, ordinarily called paradigms—structural neorealism and neoliberal institutionalism. The attackers are sociologists whose mission is the "innovative unification of research in the areas of sociology and national security." Their views are presented in the monograph The Culture of National Security: Norms and Identity in World Politics, edited by Peter J. Katzenstein, one of the principal ideologues of the sociological approach.[2] To understand their charges against the neorealists, a few words are in order about those people's views.

One of them is Kenneth Waltz, who belongs to the structural neorealists of the second wave (after Hans J. Morgenthau, George F. Kennan, Arnold Wolfers, and others). He identifies three distinctive characteristics in the international system of states: (1) It is decentralized; (2) the most important actors (states) are unitary and functionally undifferentiated; and (3) differences in the distribution of the capabilities of the most important states distinguish bipolar from multipolar state systems. (12)

The well-known theorist Robert O. Keohane is classified as a neoliberal institutionalist. He maintains that after the collapse of hegemony, international politics does not necessarily collapse into uncontrolled power politics that results in anarchy. The international order created in the period of hegemony has the capability to rectify the problems that provoke international anarchy. "The institutional infrastructure of a post-hegemonic system thus can facilitate the coordination of conflicting policies by lowering the transaction costs associated with cooperation." (13)

Sociologists accuse Keohane's theory of not explaining the category of interest, even though it does not deny its existence as an out-

1 For example, see Maruyama, "Thought and Behavior" in *Modern Japanese Politics*), 268–89; Kaizer u. Schwarz, Hrsg., *Weltpolitik. Strukturen – Akteure – Perspektiven*; and Ward, "Structural Power—A Contradiction in Terms?" *Political Studies* 35, no. 4 (1987): 593–610.

2 Katzenstein, ed., *The Culture of National Security: Norms and Identity in World Politics*.

side phenomenon. The category of interest is the sociologist's favorite hobbyhorse. This is recognized to a degree by Keohane himself: "Without a theory of interests, which requires analysis of domestic politics, no theory of international relations can be fully adequate. ... Our weak current theories do not take us very far in understanding the behavior of the United States and European powers at the end of the Cold War. ... More research will have to be undertaken at the level of the state, rather than the international system." (14)

According to P. Katzenstein, the sociologists' research paradigm contains a three-step analysis. "First, there is the specification of a set of constraints. Then comes the stipulation of a set of actors who are assumed to have certain kinds of interests. Finally, the behavior of the actors is observed, and that behavior is related to the constraining conditions in which these actors, with their assumed interests, find themselves." (ibid.)

All this balderdash, meaningless to the uninitiated, really is an exposition of certain elements of behaviorism as directed to the analysis of security problems. Sociologists maintain that only on this basis can one capture such important factors as "prestige and reputation, which neorealists view as 'force effects' rather than as social attributions." (ibid.) In this connection they remember the well-known political economist Robert Gilpin. Katzenstein writes that though Gilpin, being a realist, does recognize sociological approaches, he falls back all the time on economic explanations. This is because for Gilpin "prestige" is the "functional equivalent to the concept of authority in domestic politics and has functional and moral grounding." "Gilpin," Katzenstein writes ironically, "asserts, but does not demonstrate, that 'ultimately' prestige rests on military or economic power." But he writes that "'prestige,' rather than power, is the everyday currency in international relations." (15)

If only American theorists knew Russian (I never met a single one who did), they would have discovered to their surprise that the concept of prestige and authority as a function of several variables was described by the Soviet systemic-economist A.V. Sergiev back in the 1970s and repeated by me in a book published in 1986.[1] Equally naïve is the tendency on the part of American sociologists to view the state as a "social organism" whose self-identification and norms affect national interests; these topics were widely discussed

1 Aliev, *Japan's Foreign Policy, 1970s–80s*, 284–5.

by Soviet political scientists in the 1970s and 1980s.[1]

Be that as it may, the sociological approach to the problem of national security through an analysis of the concept of national interests of the state as a social organism gained widespread acceptance, as evidenced by a monograph written by a group of English sociologists.[2]8 The practical creators of America's security policy prefer for the time being to rely on the neorealist approaches, including those of Jordan, Taylor, and Mazarr (JTM).

The essence of their approach is not complicated and can be summarized as follows: Admitting the elasticity of the term "national security," JTM see a difference nonetheless between the volume of its content before and after World War II. The term itself, in its narrowest sense, means "defense." But prior to World War II, the policy of national security barely connected with foreign policy, or with economic, trade, and environmental policies. After World War II, parts of these three spheres overlapped each other, that is, became interconnected, though other segments of these blocks remained autonomous. (See figure below.)

The overlapping parts have a name of their own, complex national security. This concept was formulated some time ago by the Japanese and played an official role in the late 1970s and early 1980s.[3] It is composed of three components: military security, economic security, and political security.

Few argue in principle with this approach (though some do argue; more about that in the corresponding chapter). More serious debates start with the topic of tying together national and international security. They center on the problem of combining the former with the latter; that is, on ways to ensure that national security (protecting national interests) does not contradict international security (designed to satisfy the interests of the international community). Some believe that this contradiction can be resolved through collective security. JTM remind the reader: "Under such an approach, an attack upon one member is taken as an attack

1 *International Relations, Politics and Personality. Annual of SPSA, 1975*; *Contemporary political systems. Essays*; Pozdnyakov, ed., *National Interests: Theory and Practice. Selected articles.*

2 Chafetz, Spirtas, and Frankel, eds., *The Origins of National Interests.*

3 See Aliev, 148–64.

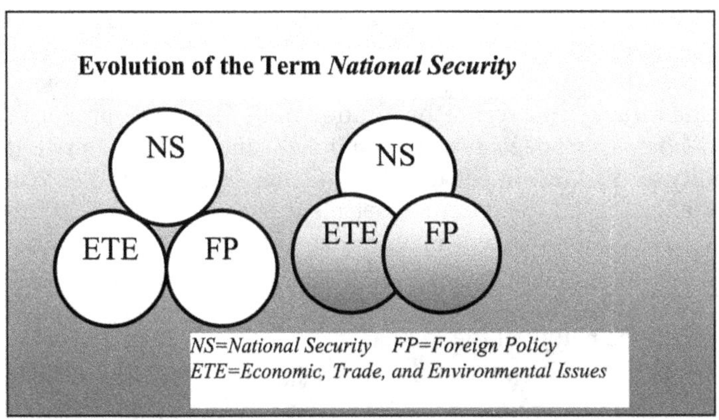

upon all, with the expectation that such a united opposition would deter any would-be aggressor." (14) In actual practice, however, there have never been any such precedents, and the authors believe that there are none at present. That is why: "The result is that collective security in any universal sense does not now exist, nor does it seem likely to come to exist, given the sovereign state system and the inequalities within it." (ibid.)

JTM are quite trustful of alliances and coalitions because these kinds of systems are built on mutual benefit. They pin big hopes, however, on international law, which is known to be treated quite skeptically by many scholars of international affairs. The authors believe that this skepticism is misguided. They write: "Law exists not only to improve the distribution of justice but also to make life predictable by providing all who live under the law with a code of expectations regarding the behavior of others in the system." (16) Besides, there is "mature law," and there is "primitive law." Understandably, the authors hope that in international affairs, "mature law" will be used. The problem is in determining the degree of the law's "maturity." Historical practice shows that the dominant states in the world make these decisions. As the still-relevant Karl Marx once wrote, when two equal rights come into conflict, the conflict is resolved through power. Once again, we're back to this ill-fated concept. JTM themselves indirectly confirm Marx's formula when they write about Russia and China.

For a start, they describe certain parameters of the Russian state: imperial history, vast resources, a strong industrial base, a well-educated population, and an obvious desire to play a significant role in the world arena. The problem is this: "How Russia chooses to engage its neighbors and the rest of the world, whether in the form of an overt reconstitution of its former empire or in a more benign strategic design, will in large measure depend on the ability of the West to engage Moscow effectively. ...The West cannot afford to let this grand experiment collapse." (556–57) There you have it: Everything is made to depend on American intentions to be of use to Russia on the basis of the "mature laws" of democracy and free markets, regardless of whether these laws are compatible with the nature of the Russian state.

It's the same thing with China. JTM see no serious contradictions between the USA and China. They are not much concerned about the modernization of China's armed forces because they are still much inferior to those of the USA; Beijing's relations with Taiwan likewise cause no excessive concern at present. But should events like those in Tiananmen Square happen again, or should the military confrontation in the Taiwan Strait suddenly heat up, then the course of the present positive relations may change. The authors note one other important fact: "The imbalance between Chinese economic development and its lagging authoritarian political system make future bilateral problems highly probable." (558) That is, the methods China's leaders use to resolve their domestic problems (Beijing considers the Taiwan problem a domestic one) do not conform to the standards of the "mature law" of the West. So, to bring the Chinese closer to "civilizational norms," the authors recommend a policy of "engagement" with relation to China, similar to the one adopted with respect to Russia. What they mean is involvement in the Western world, in its standards, which in the minds of Western ideologues are universal.

This conviction about the universality of "mature law" has many times tripped up and will continue to trip up scholars who pounded these kinds of illusions into their heads. I will show later that some of them are beginning to get rid of these clichés. They will be helped along in this process not only by China with its national specifics but also by Russia, whose experience disproves that capitalism enjoys a natural advantage over other systems.

Yet one has to admit that some American scholars, including those mentioned above in this chapter, are now seriously tackling the task of developing a conceptual apparatus, realizing that without it, all pronouncements on foreign policy and international relations are nothing more than empty talk. In this respect, I agree with Ronald Rogowski, who writes: "There is a fundamental failing in the theory that makes definitions uncertain; uncertain definitions make for uncertainty about strategies and measures; and so long as measures remain uncertain, convincing tests of the theory are impossible. The problem lies with the theory. It may be possible to remedy it; but ... it is hard to see how."[1]

Continuing his thought, Michael C. Desch writes: "Without systematic variables, there is no prediction. Prediction, however, is central to the social scientific enterprise not only for theoretical reasons (we need theories to make predictions in order to test the theories) but also for policy analysis (theories that do not make clear predictions are of little use to policymakers)." (153)

The problem has its roots in the absence of a comprehensive science of foreign policy and international relations. What exist are separate areas of research, dedicated to particular segments of world politics. Each of these areas uses its own set of terms, which are only in rare instances defined as concepts, and practically never defined on the level of categories.

Thus, the geostrategic approach uses the terms "bipolarity," "multipolarity," "power centers," "national security," and "national interests"; underlying all these is "power" (though no one has, as yet, managed to determine which kind of power—force, power, might, or strength). The geoeconomic approach exploits the terms "integration," "globalization," "internationalization," etc. The ideological, or class-based, analysis uses yet another set of terms: democracy, dictatorship, and authoritarianism. The geopolitical approach, the civilizational approaches, the system approaches, and others all have their own terminology. One should keep in mind that often one and the same term can have a different meaning depending on the approach taken. For example, the terms "pole," "power," "integration," and others are used in a variety of ways by different scholars.

When an author does not specify in advance the field of his research, it becomes unclear what exactly he is analyzing and prognosticating about—the entire system of international relations or

1 Quoted from Desch, "Culture Clash. Assessing the Importance of Ideas in Security Studies," *International Security* 23, no. 1 (Summer 1998), 151.

just a certain part of it. The ambiguity becomes worse whenever the author doesn't explain the content of a term he uses in his analysis. While at least quite a few American and English scholars strive toward conceptual clarity, the vast majority of Russian research workers ignore such "trifles."

Chapter II

Role and Place of the USA in the Twenty-First Century in the Research of American Political Scientists and Scholars of International Affairs

In this chapter, I summarize the views of some American scholars on the structure of international relations in the twenty-first century, the place and role of the USA in the system of international relations, and ideas about the place and role of Russia in the world. I have no intention of criticizing Americans, though I can't help adding certain comments of my own. The important thing is to let them speak their minds, so that the reader can judge their views for himself. Please don't be put off by the abundance of quotes, for I wanted to preserve the authors' style and avoid glossing over or simplifying their ideas.

Hans Binnendijk: Back to Bipolarity?

It makes sense to start with the works of those authors whose analysis of current events and the future is preceded by a historic overview of structures and systems of international relations. The Twenty-First Century: The World Without Russia

Occupying a prominent place among American scholars of international affairs is Hans Binnendijk, director of the Institute for National Strategic Studies at the National Defense University and editor-in-chief of *Strategic Assessments*. In one of his articles, co-written with Alan Henrikson, he identifies six historic systems of international relations.[1]

The first system functioned in the period between the Treaty of Utrecht (1713) and the battle of Waterloo (1815); Binnendijk defines it as a "loose balance of power" in a multipolar framework.

The second system came into being at the Congress of Vienna (1815) and survived until the Crimean War (1853–55); it, too, was based on a balance of power, but already there was a pronounced anchor, Great Britain, and emerging, informal bipolarities (between Great Britain and France in the West; Russia, Prussia, and Austria in the East).

The third system emerged in the period between the Crimean War and World War I (1914). It started off by being multipolar but ended up by the early 1900s in a rigid bipolar block system (the Entente nations on one side, and the Alliance powers on the other).

The fourth system existed in the period between the World Wars (1918–1939). The authors assign no definite characteristics to that system, which is only natural because it is hard to define from a structural perspective. This period was neither multipolar (the axis-pole of Germany, Italy, and Japan was formed in the middle of this period) nor bipolar (the other "axis" was not well defined until 1941) nor unipolar because neither of the "axes" or powers dominated in the world.

The fifth system corresponded to the Cold War period (1945–1989), manifesting itself at first as "multipolar" and transforming soon into a "fundamental bipolarity." (In reality, there was no such thing as "multipolarity"; there were two victorious powers that regarded each other from the very beginning as ideological and geostrategic rivals.)

The authors draw attention to one important fact: All five systems emerged initially as multipolar and grew into bipolar structures. They also emphasize that "Bipolarity was not the only factor that produced the major conflict, but it provided a structure

1 Binnendijk with Henrikson, "Back to Bipolarity?" *Strategic Forum*, no. 161 (May 1999).

for it and appears to have made conflict more likely." Here they confuse cause and effect, for bipolarity is actually the consequence of a conflict that brews because of deep contradictions between two sides.

Finally, the sixth system came into being after the end of the Cold War (1989). The authors consider it difficult to characterize this system because its long-term trends are not yet defined. In this connection, Stanley Hoffmann, another prominent American theorist of international affairs, wrote that when you are unsure how to name a system, you call it "post-something," such as post-Cold War Era, post-Industrialized Era, post-Communist Era, etc.

The sixth system has five categories of players and four dominant trends that affect the players' behavior in different ways. The democratic players are the market-democracy nations. Their ideology has become global (the authors remind us that of 191 states in the world, 117 embrace democracy). The USA is their leader, and the international system at present is unipolar because America's influence is global in character.

The second group of players is the states in transition from authoritarianism to democracy. Chief among them are China, Russia, and India.

The third category is the "rogue states": Iraq, Iran, North Korea, Libya, Sudan, Cuba, and Serbia. The authors state: "Containment of their activities has become the main task of the U.S. defense policy in the first decade of the sixth system's emergence."

The fourth category is failing states; counted among these are Bosnia, Rwanda, Cambodia, Algiers, Somalia, and Haiti.

The fifth category is nonstate players, an assortment of different kinds of subjects with different structures and goals. For instance, the global corporations (in our terminology these are called transnational companies or transnational banks) promote the globalization of the world economy; this goal is also pursued by international criminal syndicates, while terrorist organizations, on the contrary, work against market democracies.

The authors list the main trends in the world: (1) rapid globalization; (2) democratization; (3) fragmentation (meaning the process of setting-self-apart by a state or group of states); and (4) proliferation of weapons of mass destruction (WMD). What's ironic about the third trend is that it is stimulated by globalization;

groups of states seek out their place in the globalizing world and increase their might on the regional level, i.e., fragment. (The authors here fail to see the contradictory process of interaction between globalization on the one hand and integration or fragmentation on the other.)

The authors believe that these global trends are going in the direction of bipolarity. "A look at recent relations among the major powers tends to confirm this possibility."

They believe that Russia and China are the stimulating factors in this process. In the former case, they mean U.S. disagreements with Russia regarding approaches to NATO, anti-missile defense, proliferation of WMD, the knot of problems around the Caspian region, and also NATO's policy toward Serbia. In the latter case, they note the conflicting positions of the USA and China on the issues of Taiwan, Tibet, those same WMD, human rights, espionage, and economic policy. They write: "As a result, China and Russia are strengthening their security relationship with each other, overcoming countervailing factors which might otherwise prevent a closer collaboration."

In their opinion, it is these common suspicions about the West that prompted Yevgeny Primakov to propose the idea of a wider RussoSino-Indian alliance against Western democracy, an alliance which would inevitably be driven toward cooperation with the rogue states.

Should a new polarization take place in the sixth system, new forms of interaction may emerge, similar to those that existed during the Cold War years, only "based this time on common interests rather than ideology."

Binnendijk and Henrikson prognosticate: "It could be a schism between the technologically advanced haves (the market democracies) and have-nots (the rest). ...This coalition might be more difficult to deal with and deter than our Cold War foes. It is not a future to encourage."

And in summary: "A new bipolar world is not inevitable. History need not repeat itself, but current trends are leading us in that direction." The authors call on politicians to take this scenario into consideration.

The Institute for National Strategic Research: Russia as Geostrategic Ghetto

Let us now take a look at the views of the authors of Strategic Assessments, published annually since 1995 under the aegis of the National Defense University and its associate organization, the Institute for National Strategic Research (INSR). Hans Binnendijk is the editor-in-chief of these collections, and INSR researchers are its principal authors. Prominent scholars from other universities and institutes are sometimes invited to participate. Active politicians, in particular those in the State and Defense departments, sometimes participate in the writing of certain chapters.

It is believed that the ideas put forth in *Strategic Assessments* have a considerable influence on the formulation of official policy. This is not surprising, considering that the authors used to be or still are functionaries (in the Pentagon, the State Department, and various other agencies directly accountable to the president).

In this chapter, I make use of the issues of 1997, 1998, and 1999.[1]

In the 1997[2] annual number, the authors' view of the world system after the Cold War looks like this: First of all, the world system is experiencing three qualitatively new phenomena which the authors designate as "revolutions." The first revolution is the geostrategic one. It is characterized by "a world asymmetrical multipolarity," where one power, the USA, alone has global reach. Other great powers enjoy influence on a regional scale. The authors emphasize that "the world has not become unipolar, as many believed at first after the Cold War."

Another aspect of global geostrategy is "the triumph of the idea of market democracy." From this perspective, the world is

---

1 An analysis of *Strategic Assessment 1996* is contained in my book *Asia-Pacific Region: Myths, Illusions and Reality. Eastern Asia: Economy, Politics, Security*, 220–2.

2 *Strategic Assessment 1997*. Flashpoints and Force Structure.

divided into three categories: (1) the states that have successfully implemented the ideas of market democracy; (2) the states in transition from an authoritarian system to market democracy, where a politicized economy and a partially free political system may yet slow down this process; and (3) the troubled states that are way behind the rest of the world, in many instances struggling with ethnic and religious extremism.

Another revolution is the informational one; it introduces new parameters to the definition of national might.

The third revolution is the change in the role of government, as it apparently "retreats" in the face of regional authorities in many countries (USA, the European Union, Russia, China) and before the might of international business. (This revolution is directly related to the theory and practice of internationalization, which will be discussed separately.)

Prior to giving their evaluation of Russia's place in the world, the authors specify their understanding of the term "major powers." These are "countries with sufficient weight to be major players in several aspects of world affairs." According to this definition, only the USA is a great player at once in the political, economic, and military spheres. "Russia is not among the world's top ten economies, yet it qualifies as a major power because of its military might and the legacy of its days as the core of the Soviet superpower." (Chapter one, *Context*)

The authors draw attention to the gradual decline of Russia's military might. To illustrate, they offer certain data: "No more than 20 percent of the military's manpower perform combat-related jobs. In the Ground Forces, only eight maneuver divisions are judged missioncapable—and four of these are under the peacekeeping command; 70–75 percent of tanks are in need of replacement; modern tanks account for only 2 to 5 percent of the force inventory, with estimates that the proportion will rise to only 30 percent by 2005. Only 60 percent of Air Assault units are judged to be combat ready; in the Naval Forces, between 1990 and 1995, personnel was cut by 50 percent (fleet aviation personnel by 60 percent), ships by 50 percent, and fleet aircraft by 66 percent." (Chapter two: Russia)

Considering the interests of the USA, the authors write that because the future of political reforms in Russia is still questionable, "The hopes for a new strategic partnership between the U.S. and Russia have faded." **(Chapter one: Context)**

At the same time, they note: "For the foreseeable future, Russia will retain the capability to inflict unacceptable damage on the U.S. through use of its nuclear arsenal. Reducing the threat from this nuclear arsenal will remain the principal U.S. interest vis-à-vis Russia." **(Chapter two: Russia)**

Nonetheless, the United States "has encouraged democratic reform in Russia and supported Russia's attempt to establish a market economy through bilateral and international loans and technical-assistance programs." The United States also exerts influence on the IMF, persuading it to give loans to Russia.

The 1998[1] issue of *Strategic Assessments* contains additions and clarifications. The most important one is that ideology, not power, structures the world. Accordingly, the world is divided into four groups of states.

The first group is a core of partner nations—flourishing democracies that are capable of joining the United States in shouldering the burden of this core's security and expansion. This group accounts for about one-fifth of the world's population and four-fifths of the world's economic might.

The second group of states (most prominent among them are China, India, and Russia) is in a state of transition. How this group evolves will determine the degree to which the core is able to expand and guarantee its security in the future. The bigger part of the world's population belongs to this group.

The third group consists of rogue players that reject the core's ideals, universally accepted means, and opportunities. They are capable of doing harm to U.S. interests and the interests of its core partners. The rogue states seek to acquire weapons of mass destruction and other dangerous technologies. Among them are North Korea, Iran, Iraq, Syria, and Libya, as well as all kinds of terrorist organizations.

The fourth group of countries, called failing states or troubled states, is usually subject to coups and wars (for instance, Bosnia, Sudan, Angola, Rwanda, Somalia, and Afghanistan).

1 *Strategic Assessment 1998. Engaging Power for Peace.*

However, the general state of global relations gives the authors satisfaction because: "The enemies of the United States are thus few, isolated, and relatively weak. No global challenger or hostile alliance is on the horizon." (Chapter one: The Global Environment)

The authors emphasize that despite its strength, the United States seeks respect from other countries, not hegemony over them. Possessed of unique capabilities, the United States does not strive for supremacy over others. "Power is not its goal, achievement of supremacy is not its strategy." (Chapter One: The Global Environment)

The United States is mainly interested in strengthening the democratic core, partly through a more even distribution of responsibility between its members; in expanding that core through the addition of transitional states; and in neutralizing the "criminal" states, partly through swinging transitional states to their side on this issue.

At the same time, the United States pursues not only "tangible interests" but also some idealistic objectives, such as the establishment of a system of international norms. The authors emphasize that the establishment of these norms does not mean forcing "Western values" on other states and cultures; rather, it implies growing recognition by lawful governments of basic standards of correct conduct.

The norms of the core are as follows: (a) *Those that bolster international peace* (nonaggression, the right of collective self-defense, the laws of war, arms control, peaceful settlement of disputes, anti-terrorism covenants, respect for the authority of the UN Security Council, and respect for other instruments and institutions that affect directly whether and how conflicts occur); (b) *Those that govern the functioning of the international economy* (self-determination of commerce, law of the sea, access to resources, noninterference with the flow of information, environmental protection, the rules of open multilateral trading, and cooperation in addressing transnational problems; and (c) *Those that bear on the treatment of people by states* (human rights, the rule of law, representative and accountable government, individual liberties, freedom of the press, and other tenets of civil societies and states).

The authors believe that the collapse of communism, the expansion of the core, and the democratization of many underdeveloped nations open up great opportunities "for the acceptance of these norms by almost everyone."

These scholars attach a great importance to China, Russia, and India, emphasizing that "China is the most important transition state, by virtue of its size, aspirations, untapped human potential, prosperous expatriate community (some 150 million strong), and location in the world's most vibrant region."

As for Russia, its present problems are explained by the absence of economic and political liberties for her population throughout history. "Russia is unlikely to emerge as a major threat to the core: The free fall of industrial production, the lack of domestic investment, inhospitable conditions for value-added enterprise, and the country's deteriorating human capital point toward a continued contraction, not a rebound, of Russian power." Russia, however, is capable of not only being a threat to its "near abroad" but also of creating enormous problems for the USA and its partners through supplying dangerous technologies to rogue states.

In future scenarios up to the year 2008, the worst one envisions the expansion of democracy coming to a halt. This can come to pass through increased Chinese hostility because China's energy needs will push it toward closer relations with Iran and other criminal states. Besides, the failure of reform and disenchantment could also push Russia toward spreading WMD technologies.

In chapter six, titled "The New Independent States," where Russia gets much more attention, the general conclusion is that Russia's development is impossible to forecast. Though the authors note that Russia is unlikely to return to the Soviet model, "the question now is what kind of capitalism Russia will create." At the present moment, they see a formation of a system of criminal capitalism in which business, government, and organized crime are merged. In this connection, their recommendation is to continue assisting Russia in its economic reforms over the next ten years, but also give more attention to the countries of the Caspian region, a region that has the potential to move up to fifth or fourth place in the world in terms of fuel production.

The 1999 issue of *Strategic Assessments* is marked by a less optimistic view of the future than the preceding volumes[1]. This is evident even from the subtitle: "Priorities In a Troubled World." A number of events are cited as having negatively impacted upon world relations. These include the Asian economic crisis, the growing belligerence of Iraq and North Korea, tensions with China, failure of reforms in Russia, tests of nuclear weapons and missiles in South Asia, growing fears of WMD proliferation, and the war in the Balkans (xi). Therefore, hopes for a democratization and stabilization of the world, expressed in the 1995 issue of *Strategic Assessments*, are clearly unfulfilled.

The authors list the same four groups of states as key players, describing them in already familiar terms, but impart to them somewhat different characteristics from the perspective of their behavior and their role in the system of international relations.

The market-democracy players retain the biggest influence, though the spreading of democracy is now less obvious than in previous years.

The *transition states* are the same (Russia, China, India), but this time other goals are ascribed to them. "They are pursuing foreign policies anchored in state interests and seek to establish themselves as leading powers on the world scene. Each seeks a revision of the status quo that will increase its influence *at the expense of the United States*. Only China has the potential to become a global power, but Russia and India will remain regionally influential." (*Emphasis mine*; xiv)

The rogue states remain the main causes of conflicts; added now to their list is Serbia.

The "troubled" states are described as extracting unjustifiably large resources from the USA and its allies for the purpose of maintaining internal stability. (The point being, for how much longer they will keep doing that?) Yet this can't be avoided because these countries are the source of transnational players such as terrorists, drug dealers, organized crime, and refugees.

Despite all this, the USA remains the sole superpower, in spite of its inability to solve international problems on its own. The following is a list of potential threats and dangers:

1 *Strategic Assessment 1999: Priorities for a Turbulent World.*

- Aggression by current rogues and emergence of new rogues;
- Increasing ethnic warfare and violence from failed states;
- Accelerating proliferation of weapons of mass destruction and missiles;
- The spreading of terrorism, organized crime, and drug trafficking;
- Military developments that erode U.S. superiority and encourage regional aggression;
- Authoritarian rule in Russia or other major countries, coupled with militarism and imperialism;
- An anti-Western global coalition of rogues and malcontents;
- Clashes over resources, or a global economic collapse that produces widespread frustration and less political cooperation;
- Geopolitical rivalry with Russia and/or China;
- Emergence of a strong Islamic alliance in the Greater Middle East that seriously challenges Western interests;
- Disintegration of the Western Alliance system and renewed nationalism. (7) More specifically, the risks related to Russia and China mean the following: "A bigger risk is that a global coalition of regional rogues and local troublemakers might emerge, perhaps under Russian or Chinese sponsorship, to challenge the United States." (xii)

On the regional level, it is again Russia and its Eurasian neighbors that give concern to the American analysts. The authors lament: "In Russia, reforms aimed at instituting market democracy have fallen short. Russia has adopted some important features of democracy, but its transformation is far from complete, owing to a host of problems. Its economy is in shambles, organized crime has taken hold, its government is not effective, its society is becoming disillusioned, and regional fragmentation is growing." (xii)

Even though the authors of this collection, as well as the previous ones, don't expect a return to "communism" or the establishment of different kinds of extremist ideologies, they forecast that: "The entire region could become an unstable geopolitical ghetto, creating anti-Western attitudes and internal dangers of its own." (xiii) Richard L. Kugler, apparently the author of the term "geopolitical ghetto," warns: "Such regional chaos may be a new menace to Europe, as it would be a natural breeding ground for authoritarianism, even fascism." (5)

Yet it is Asia that remains the biggest question mark for the USA. "In the long term, the emergence of China as a world power and the reactions of Japan and other countries will be the key. If China integrates into the Western community, regional stability will be enhanced. If not, China could become a major security problem and an eventual military threat in ways that affect the entire region, as well as U.S. relationships with key allies." (xiii)

This complicated and uncertain situation in the world arena requires a transformation of security policy, derived from the strategy of *involvement*, based on three central elements: *shape, respond,* and *prepare.*

The essence of this change is described by the well-known principle of the carrot and the stick. This is how it applies to Russia and China:

The carrot in this case is still the USA's willingness to "integrate" (the authors' expression) Russia and China in the Western community. The stick is applied when integration fails: "If this is not possible, the United States should cooperate with them when mutual interests permit, but react firmly when legitimate U.S. interests are opposed by them. At a minimum, U.S. policy should prevent them from becoming adversaries of U.S. interests and leaders of a new anti-Western global coalition." (xvii) For instance, in the Pacific region, China should be treated with a combination of firmness and containment, i.e., frustration of her attempts to destabilize the situation. "A new containment strategy could be needed if a stronger China seeks hegemony in Asia. Conversely, a broader emphasis on collective security may be possible if China becomes a cooperative partner." (xviii) This, of course, is only allowed the USA and, to a lesser degree, Japan.

Transforming Defense. National Security in the 21st Century[1]

The above title belongs to one of the most important papers commissioned by the Pentagon; it was prepared by nine influential military experts and scholars for the purpose of correcting official defense policy for the period up to 2020.[2]

The report's authors identify the dynamics of four key trends that will determine, parallel and in interaction, the structure of international relations in the first quarter of the 21st century.

The first trend is defined as a geopolitical revolution; it has to do with the collapse of the Soviet Union and the emergence of China as a great power on the regional and the global scale.

The second trend is the pressure of demographic and social factors on social systems.

The third trend is the emergence of a global interconnected marketplace that will affect the well-being of practically all states and societies.

Finally, the fourth trend is related to the technical revolution that transforms industrial economies into information economies and affects the revolution in the military area (5).

Within the framework of the geopolitical trend a further changing of the geopolitical landscape is envisioned in Europe, Asia and Africa as a result of racial, religious and political conflicts. At the same time, the roles of non-government players are on the increase: MNCs, criminal groups and narcotics suppliers.

As for new regional developments coming into prominence, the oil-rich Caspian Sea region is mentioned.

---

1 *Transforming Defense. National Security in the 21st Century*. Report of the National Defense Panel.

2 This document is actually a specification/supplement to Pentagon's *Report of Quadrennial Defense Review* /QDR/).

The second trend, connected to demographic and social factors, will bring acceleration of population growth, migration and immigration, chronic unemployment and less-than-full employment, increased competition for resources, in particular, fuel and water.

Economic trends will interact with the demographic and social ones.

The activities of MNCs will have a strong effect on international relations, which will complicate the implementation of policies by nation-states.

Global economic stability is imperiled in the Persian Gulf and the Caspian Sea regions. The wealth gap that exists when resource-abundant areas are controlled by a relatively small number of states can create tensions and presents governments with political and moral challenges.

The technological revolution will produce ever more destructive weapons, which will present threats to nations in the hands of hostile states, terrorist and criminal groups.

All these trends (even without considering unforeseen situations /wild cards/) may result in the following four scenarios in the system of international relations in the years 2010–2020:

The ***First World:*** Shaped Stability. Even in this state certain problems and tensions cannot be prevented, but on the whole global well-being is increasing and spreading around more evenly.

The ***Second World*** scenario extrapolates the current situation: the present uncertainty transforms into increasing rivalry and political diversity of the world. Though the globalization of economy will continue, some countries will find themselves in an unfavorable situation. China becomes the key state in the Pacific ring region, both economically and politically. India's importance increases. Hostile states and non-government players acquire means for spreading WMD. "Although the United States is still the leading world power, its sustained political-economic-military dominance is uncertain." (9)

In the ***Third World*** scenario, the leadership rivalry is still going strong in the shape of a traditional balance of power, in which hostile regional alliances emerge (or possibly individual states) to challenge the United States. In the Far East a Pan-Asian trading block forms. The states of South and South-West Asia form a new alliance, concentrating on counteracting the political, economic and cultural influence of the West.

The ***Fourth World*** scenario means a chronic crisis. Global economic conditions deteriorate, causing the collapse of international institutions. The weakened states, non-government organizations and coalitions fight between themselves for the dwindling resources. Alliances are unreliable, unpredictable and opportunistic. Nationalism and ethnic hatred produce power movements for the independence of Asia, South America and the Middle East. The principal states are in crisis. Drug-dealer states exist in South and South-East Asia. WMD are available everywhere. Mass migration exacerbates chaos in the cities.

Relying on these scenarios, the authors propose a plan for reorganizing the military potential of the USA that will require in the subsequent years an additional $10 billion on top of the current Pentagon plan. I note that the Clinton administration went even further, increasing defense spending in the fiscal year 2000 to $282 billion against $272 billion in 1998.

Hugh De Santis's Mutualism Concept[1]

Hugh De Santis is a former high-ranking official in the State Department. He is currently a professor of international security politics and represents the National War College, part of the National Defense University, whose workers are closely affiliated to the Pentagon. His distinctive vision of American security strategy begins with a criticism of a number of schools of thought in American political science.

The schools. Hugh De Santis identifies several schools of thought that, in his opinion, reflect the existing realities inadequately. One is the neo-Wilsonian school, which expects the rational, educated world to absorb the values of liberal democracy. The realist school maintains that the unequivocal power the United States has at its disposal will force the others, in one way or another, to recognize that country's leadership in the world, the "American Sheriff" standing guard for America's interests in the world. Comprising the so-called neoReaganite school is a group of American nationalists who believe that America has a special mission in creating a peaceful and moral world order. There are also the neoisolationists, some of whom champion the idea that "America is above everything else," while others (the pacifists) are opposed to the political and economic costs of maintaining the American empire.

On the surface, these schools of thought appear to differ. In reality, all of them are variations on the theme of American exclusivity an proceed from similar convictions about the current international situation.

The Mythology of Unipolarity. This relies on two postulates: (1) Despite the spread of liberal democracy, the world proves to be more complex, unpredictable, and dangerous now than during the

1 Santis, "Mutualism: An American Strategy for the Next Century," *Strategic Forum*, no. 162 (May 1999).

Cold War; and (2) "The maintenance of a peaceful and stable international system accordingly depends on the moral and political leadership, if not hegemony, of the United States."

The first of these postulates is absolutely correct. The second one, about the USA being a world "superpower" establishing peace and order, is doubtful. De Santis thinks so. World development cannot be viewed as a process of Americanization, and this is why:

"First, in contrast to its economic dominance following World War II, the United States no longer possesses the resources to fix the world's problems. Despite its recent economic vigor, its current share of world production is somewhere around 20 percent, it suffers from a massive trade imbalance, its gold reserves are roughly half that of the European Union (EU), and it is the world's largest debtor nation. Although there have been gains in worker productivity, the factors that powered the economic boom of the 1990s—corporate downsizing, computerization, reduced healthcare costs, and a strong dollar—are not likely to be sustained. America's ability to police the world, the Clinton administration's belated defense budget buildup notwithstanding, will diminish."

Second, the image of global sheriff has not gone down well with the American public—a hotchpotch of special interest groups. Although there is widespread support for the promotion of liberal-democratic values, NATO, and, as the polls reflected in the 1998 crisis with Iraq, selective military strikes, the public remains generally opposed to American intervention to resolve disputes in faraway places perceived to be removed from the daily concerns of Americans.

Third, in the absence of a global threat to peace, the United States is likely to find it increasingly difficult to marshal international support for its policies. Examples include the opposition of the United Nations and key European allies to Washington's contemplated use of military force against Iraq in 1998 and the initial reluctance of European allies to employ force against Serbia because of its actions in Kosovo.

The Concept of Mutualism. In this connection, De Santis proposes the concept of mutualism, formulated in these words: "Mutualism is an interest-based rather than a norm-centered concept of international relations. It emphasizes regional rather than global approaches to international cooperation, recognizes the continued importance of the nation-state, and is *ipso facto* a nonhegemonic approach to international security." It is obviously attractive to politicians when one considers its applicability to burgeoning trends in the economic, social, cultural, and political-military spheres.

The interdependence between economies of different regions and countries demands more active participation of the state in establishing the "rules of the game" to reduce the frequency of financial crashes and rein in the greed and excesses of an unbridled marketplace. The Eurodollar leads to yet another monetary system. "The emergence of the Euro as an alternative reserve currency will not only help countries that trade with Europe to stabilize their exchange rates, it will also lessen America's burden of being the central banker for the world."

De Santis draws attention to an important element of his concept, *cultural tolerance.* "Social and economic integration," he writes, "cannot be sustained without the constructive participation of the diverse cultures that comprise them. National and international cohesion require sensitivity to different cultural traditions, mores, and values."

"Besides, can Americans be certain that ours is the only path to a free and harmonious society? In a world of 'value pluralism' to use Isaiah Berlin's term, we must all be tolerant of the political choices others make—choices, it should be emphasized, that are not God-given but are products of different cultural traditions and experiences."

The mutualism concept envisions the resolution of regional problems on the basis of security and cooperation without involving the USA or the UN. Only when the regional security institutions are powerless to solve a problem should extra-regional powers be involved. Yet, even in this case the USA should not be in a hurry to get involved in every hot spot on the planet.

Therefore, the mutualism concept of Hugh De Santis is actually a variant of the selective involvement concept championed for the most part by scholars who used to work for the State Department.

Samuel Huntington: The Concept of a Unimultipolar World[1]

Samuel Huntington, the well-known Harvard University professor, presents an original view of the world and the place and role of the USA within it. In many works, he tried to prove the inevitability of a clash of civilizations.[2] Later, he apparently came to the conclusion that purely civilizational differences are not in themselves sufficient for a clash. Instead, he turned his attention to analyzing the geostrategic structure of international relations, the imbalance of which is, at a minimum, an additional source of conflict. He believes that global politics always revolves around power and the struggle for power. In the current situation, there are changes because the emerging structure is very different from the period of bipolarity.

He maintains that although just one superpower exists today, it does not mean that the world is unipolar. He reminds the reader that superpowers have existed even in the past—the Roman Empire is an example. In East Asia, China was the hegemon. The bipolar system was built on the rivalry of two superpowers that headed their respective coalitions and fought for influence on the nonaligned states.

The multipolar system was always based on several great powers of comparable strength that cooperated and competed among themselves, as was the case for centuries in Europe.

The current system does not correspond to any of the previous ones. "It is instead a strange hybrid, a unimultipolar system with one superpower and several major powers. …The United States, of course, is the sole state with preeminence in every domain of power—economic, military, diplomatic, ideological, technological, and cultural—with the reach and capabilities to promote

1 Huntington, "The Lonely Superpower," *Foreign Affairs* 78, no. 2 (March/April 1999).

2 Huntington, *The Clash of Civilizations and the Remaking of World Order.*

its interests in virtually every part of the world." (36) This is the first level.

At a second level, in Huntington's opinion, are major regional powers that are preeminent in certain areas of the world without being able to project their interests and capabilities as globally as the United States. They include Germany and France in Europe, Russia in Eurasia, China and potentially Japan in East Asia, India in South Asia, Iran in Southwest Asia, Brazil in Latin America, and South Africa and Nigeria in Africa. (ibid)

I wish to note that Russia's sphere of influence is essentially confined to its own territory.

At a third level are secondary regional powers whose interests are often in conflict with the more powerful regional states. These include Britain in relation to the German–French combination, Ukraine in relation to Russia, Japan in relation to China, South Korea in relation to Japan, Pakistan in relation to India, Saudi Arabia in relation to Iran, and Argentina in relation to Brazil. (36)

The superpower or hegemon (to Huntington, these words are synonyms) in a unipolar system, lacking any major powers challenging it, is normally able to maintain its dominance over minor states for a long time until it is weakened by internal decay or by forces from outside the system. In Huntington's opinion, the great powers of today strive toward multipolarity because their own interests are often at odds with those of the USA. "Global politics has thus moved from the bipolar system of the Cold War through a unipolar moment—highlighted by the Gulf War—and is now passing through one or two unimultipolar decades before it enters a truly multipolar twenty-first century." "The United States," as Zbigniew Brzezinski has said, "will be the first, last, and only global superpower."(37)

Therefore, Huntington sees the structure of relations as being in evolution: Bipolarity is followed by unipolarity, which is followed by multipolarity. He figures that bipolarity lasted for about forty years, unipolarity will last for about twenty years, and multipolarity will last through the remainder of the twenty-first century. Let us memorize these time frames.

It is necessary to note that Huntington's approach is different from the official approach of Washington that actually presupposes a unipolar world. It is precisely in this connection that Huntington subjects the official policy of the USA to sharp and sarcastic criticism, especially the concept of the "benevolent hegemon." He reminds us of the expression used by Lawrence H. Summers, deputy secretary of the treasury, who called the United States the "first nonimperialist superpower," a claim that manages in three words to exalt American uniqueness, American virtue, and American power. Huntington "confirms" all these sarcastically with the following arguments: "In the past few years, the United States has, among other things, attempted or been perceived as attempting more or less unilaterally to do the following: pressure other countries to adopt American values and practices regarding human rights and democracy; prevent other countries from acquiring military capabilities that could counter American conventional superiority; enforce American law extraterritorially in other societies; grade countries according to their adherence to American standards on human rights, drugs, terrorism, nuclear proliferation, missile proliferation, and now religious freedom; apply sanctions against countries that do not meet American standards on these issues; promote American corporate interests under the slogans of free trade and open markets; shape World Bank and International Monetary Fund policies to serve those same corporate interests; intervene in local conflicts in which it has relatively little direct interest; bludgeon other countries to adopt economic policies and social policies that will benefit American economic interests; promote American arms sales abroad while attempting to prevent comparable sales by other countries; force out one U.N. secretary-general and dictate the appointment of his successor; expand NATO initially to include Poland, Hungary, and the Czech Republic and no one else; undertake military action against Iraq and later maintain harsh economic sanctions against the regime; and categorize certain countries as "rogue states," excluding them from global institutions because they refuse to kowtow to American wishes." (38)

All these things were feasible for a while, but now the situation has changed. The American professor believes the time of all-permissiveness for the USA is over. The instruments of this policy are economic sanctions and military intervention; both have practically stopped working. Moreover, Huntington is justified in noting that the harder the United States tries to punish the "rogue states," the more popular their leaders become in their own countries. Just consider, for instance, Fidel Castro, Saddam Hussein, and even Slobodan Milosevic.[1]This policy of global leadership does not have the support of most Americans. According to Huntington's data, in 1997 public opinion polls, only 13 percent spoke in favor of a supreme role for the USA in world politics, while 74 percent said they wanted the USA to share responsibility for world problems with other countries. (39) Fifty-five percent to 66 percent declared that events in Europe, Asia, Mexico, and Canada don't affect their lives. The foreign-policy elite, however, ignores these attitudes. That's how foreign policy acquires the growing reputation of "hegemony for show." (40)

It is supposed that the USA acts on behalf of "the world community." In reality, it acts mostly on behalf of its Anglo-Saxon brethren (Great Britain, Canada, Australia, New Zealand) on most issues; on behalf of Germany and several smaller European democracies on many issues; on behalf of Israel on some Middle Eastern issues; and on behalf of Japan on the implementation of UN resolutions. (41)

Huntington reminds the reader that between 1993 and 1996, many decisions were made about imposition of economic sanctions. Only rarely did the USA get support from its partners; more often than not, it was forced to act alone. Even though the United States keeps pinning the "rogue" label on different countries, in the eyes of many states it has itself become a rogue superpower. (42)

To support his position, Huntington quotes the Japanese ambassador, Hisashi Owada, who said that after World War II, the USA conducted a policy of "unilateral globalism," and now its policy is "global unilateralism," that is, pursuing its own interests while paying formal attention to the interests of others. (ibid)

Referring to a conference held at Harvard in 1997, Huntington points out that scholars representing two-thirds of humanity (Russia, China, India, Africa, Arabs, and other Moslems) claimed that the USA poses an external threat to their societies. That threat is not military; it has to do with their wholeness, autonomy, ability to flourish, and freedom of action. They called the USA an interventionist, exploitative, hegemonist, hypocritical state, practicing double standards and pursuing policies of "financial imperialism" and "intellectual colonialism."(43)

1 He was mistaken about Milosevic, though.

America's leaders are convinced that world affairs are *their* affairs. In the author's opinion, a unimultipolar world dominated by just one superpower automatically presents a threat to the other major powers.

"The United States rewards countries that follow its leadership with access to the American market, foreign aid, military assistance, exemption from sanctions, silence about deviations from U.S. norms (as with Saudi human rights abuses and Israeli nuclear weapons), support for membership in international organizations, and bribes and White House visits for political leaders." (45)

Yet, despite the criticism of Washington's foreign policy, coordinated counteraction to the USA is absent from this world. In Huntington's opinion, the reason is this: "Global politics is now multicivilizational. France, Russia, and China may well have common interests in challenging U.S. hegemony, but their very different cultures are likely to make it difficult for them to organize an effective coalition."(46) Besides, they would themselves be facing the problem of leadership: Who would be number one in their coalition, and who would be number two? This was one of the reasons behind the Sino-Soviet spat. "Similarly, an obstacle to an anti-U.S. coalition between China and Russia now is Russian reluctance to be the junior partner of a much more populous and economically dynamic China." (ibid) As a result, "The interplay of power and culture will decisively mold patterns of alliance and antagonism among states in the coming years." (ibid)

In Huntington's opinion, U.S. tactics are to support the secondary regional power against the primary regional power. In Europe it means support for Great Britain; in East Asia, for Japan (against China); for Ukraine, against Russia; in Latin America, for Argentina; in the Middle East, for Saudi Arabia; in South Asia, for Pakistan.

What should be America's policy in a unimultipolar world? Huntington formulates the question and answers it in this fashion:

1. First of all, foreign policy should renounce the false notion of the existence of a unipolar world.
2. America's leaders should let go of illusions about a natural coincidence between their interests and the values of the rest of the world.

3. Because the USA is unable to create a unipolar world, it is in its interest to use its superpower status to organize an international order based on cooperation with other countries to solve global problems.
4. The interaction of strength and culture has a special importance in European-American relations. Strength leads to rivalry; similarity of cultures leads to cooperation. Attainment of goals depends on culture prevailing over strength. Europe is the central link in America's policy.

Should these recommendations be heeded, Huntington envisions the emergence of a world satisfactory both to the world community and the USA. He writes: "In the multipolar world of the twenty-first century, the major powers will inevitably compete, clash, and coalesce with each other in various permutations and combinations. Such a world, however, will lack the tension and conflict between the superpower and the major regional powers that are the defining characteristic of a unimultipolar world. For that reason, the United States could find life as a major power in a multipolar world less demanding, less contentious, and more rewarding than it was as the world's only superpower." (49)

I feel like adding: "And then will come the Kingdom of peace on Earth, and the whole world will be united in brotherhood, and the lion will lie down with the lamb." This is but a dream dreamt by all utopians ignorant about the laws of world affairs. Huntington must have been shaken by the criticism of his preceding concept about the clash of civilizations, so he decided to mend his ways and offer a concept of universal brotherhood, leaving the field of science as a result and dropping to the level of "common sense." Apparently, we can soon expect him to take up a religious vocation.

Zbigniew Brzezinski: As Always, Favoring U.S. Hegemony and Status Quo for Russia

Because Zbigniew Brzezinski gets more attention from Russian political scientists, it is worth taking a look at some of his views. His vision of the world is naturally, cardinally different from Huntington's. In an article included in the collection dedicated to the theory of complexity, he analyzes in his conventional traditional manner America's foreign policy, making it clear that his approach has nothing to do with the theory of complexity.[1]

Right away, he attacks the thesis about America defended by many American scholars of international affairs, expressed in the briefest form by the phrase: "It's leadership, stupid!" Brzezinski designates this as an "exit strategy," i.e., a strategy of detachment in all international affairs. He identifies six problems that cannot be resolved through application of that concept, formulating them as six questions: Will a larger and a more secure Europe emerge? Will Russia become a status quo power? Will the Persian Gulf and the Middle Eastern region become more stable? Will the Far East adjust to the nature of the power shift that is now under way? Will we effectively manage nuclear proliferation? Will large-scale social collapse be avoided in some critical parts of the world?

The American expert's answer to all these questions is perfectly obvious: Of course they won't be solved without the U.S. involvement. If somehow they are solved, the solutions won't be satisfactory from the point of view of U.S. national interests. We are interested in the subject of Russia as it figures in his answers. Brzezinski believes that Russia should be helped, but how and in what areas? He writes: "That means creating circumstances in which Russia has no choice but to become a status quo power. That in turn means on the one hand, the expansion of NATO because it does reduce any geopolitical temptations to which Russia at some

1 Brzezinski, "America in the World Today," in *Complexity, Global Politics, and National Security.*

point may aspire and might be able to exercise even from a position of weakness. On the other hand, it also means creating conditions in the space of the former Soviet Union in which the status quo becomes permanent. That means a deliberate policy of matching aid to Russia with simultaneous aid to the newly independent states of the former Soviet Union. For only if they remain sovereign and independent, will Russia be more inclined to accommodate the status quo society."

Here is another of Brzezinski's clarifications that follows his musings about more attention to Ukraine: "My choice, in addition to Ukraine, would be Azerbaijan and Uzbekistan, for reasons that are probably familiar to many of you. Uzbekistan because it is the hard core of an independent Central Asia. It is in our interest to preserve an independent Central Asia, because it helps to make Russia a status quo society. Azerbaijan because it is the cork in the bottle. If Azerbaijan is sealed because of Russian, or Russian and Iranian collusion, there is no access for us to Central Asia. Central Asia would become strategically vulnerable."

Many regard this as no more than leisurely musings of a onceinfluential policy adviser. In point of fact, Brzezinski simply describes the actual policy of the USA in the zone of the former Soviet Union.

In another article[1] based on the concept of "Eurasian wholeness" (the European Union, Russia, China, and Japan), Brzezinski proposes the forming of two triangles—one to include the USA, the EU, and Russia; the other, USA, Japan, and China. This construct seems to him effective for the purpose of "constructive involvement of Russia." So, what is the essence of this proposal?

It is quite simple, actually. To start with, Brzezinski lists a whole bunch of figures illustrating the pitiable state of Russia's economy, the social situation, the weak external ties, etc. He also notes that the current ruling political elite headed by Putin belongs to the third generation of the Soviet class of "apparatchiki", consisting mostly of former KGB persons. This composition of the elite accounts for anti-American attitudes, greater negativity toward the process of NATO expansion, and attempts to instigate rivalries between European states and the USA. At the same time, Russia's leadership developed the conviction about the necessity

1 Brzezinski, "Living With Russia," *The National Interest*, 61 (Fall 2000).

to restore Russia as a powerful state and use that power to subjugate again the entire Commonwealth of Independent States (CIS) space. In Brzezinski's opinion, the Kremlin has been taken over by Leninist ideas about zero-sum political games. It is manifested in the Kremlin leaders' belief that non-Russian regions of the CIS are better off not developing their economies at all than falling under the West's influence. As an example, he cites Moscow's approach toward the Caspian region countries and President Putin's hostility to Ukraine's flirtation with NATO. In other words, these three directions of Russia's policy—the Caucasus region, Ukraine, and Belarus (with the idea of "unification in brotherly Slavic solidarity") and attempts to prevent Baltic countries from joining NATO—do not agree with Brzezinski's ideas about a constructive structure of international relations. Brzezinski is certain, though, that Moscow's present goals are unattainable in principle. For instance, an alliance with China can only result in Russia's subjugation by China "without resolution of her problems." Should Russia continue her present policies, instead of a "Europe stretching to the Urals," the result may well be a devastated, besieged "Russia stretching to the Urals."

This result does not suit the West. Brzezinski proposes that the West, or rather the USA, pursue the same kind of policy toward Russia that the West followed toward Turkey after the collapse of the Ottoman Empire in the time of Kemal Ataturk. Brzezinski thinks that Putin is no Ataturk (because his thinking reflects the thinking of the last generation of the Soviet leadership, rather than the first post-Soviet generation); therefore, he should not be relied on. But the next generation will think differently, having been educated in and viewing themselves as part of the West. In this direction, active measures should be taken, i.e., the number of invitations to study in America should be greatly increased, so that young Russians may digest the fruits of American democracy. This new generation can be convinced that Russia will derive all kinds of benefits from NATO expansion, including not just Russia's neighboring states but Russia herself. At some time in the future, a NATO–Russian Joint Council can be formed. On this permanent basis, the above-mentioned idea of two big triangles can be implemented.

Brzezinski is correct in stating that Russia's current foreign policy is doomed to failure. However, he is dead wrong when he envisions the policy of involving Russia in one of the two triangles as the way to avoid this failure. Such a construct cannot be balanced when one of the three pillars (Russia) is weaker by (at least) an order of magnitude than the other two. We're only talking about economic mass here. The Western mentality of the next generation of leaders will not strengthen the Russian "corner" of the triangle; on the contrary, it will be weakened because the interests of *this* kind of elite can only be pro-Western, not pro-Russian.

Besides, it would be naïve to expect Russians to believe that the inclusion of the Baltic States in NATO can have some kind of strategic benefits for Russia. It is perfectly obvious that the expansion of NATO does not have Russia's interests in mind. By the way, this article by Brzezinski received a response from Stephan Sestanovich, who convincingly showed that a favorable Russian reaction to NATO's expansion and a "Turkish approach" to Russia was not possible.[1]

I would add one more thing regarding Brzezinski's proposal to fit Russia and China in different triangles directed by the same patron. Of course, from Washington's perspective, the implementation of this idea would suit the U.S. strategic interests perfectly; all the "poles" would then be covered and under control. But think: Even the USA's resources would not be enough to form these triangles. To me, President Bush's current approach appears to be more optimal from the perspective of U.S. interests, because it is "point"-oriented and well structured in its priorities. Nevertheless, Brzezinski's proposal is not without merit as a strategic idea.

1 Sestanovich, "Where Does Russia Belong?" *The National Interest*, 62 (Winter 2000/2001).

The Council on Foreign Relations: Russia Invited to Be Part of the West

Prominent among the agents that form U.S. foreign policy is the Council on Foreign Relations, whose projects involve experts from different research institutions. The product of one of these projects is the book *The New Russian Foreign Policy,* written in early 1998 by a group of authors that included Michael Mandelbaum, Leon Aron, Sherman Garnett, Rajan Menon, and Coit Blacker.[1]

Mandelbaum states from the beginning: "Russian foreign policy is difficult to define. It is difficult, even, to detect. What are the international purposes of the new Russian state? Where and how will it seek to achieve them?" These are precisely the questions the authors set out to answer.

Mandelbaum himself sees the main cause of Russia's problems and her foreign policy in the legacy of the Soviet empire that emerged and collapsed in a completely different way from the earlier British, French, Habsburg, and Ottoman empires. Its collapse wasn't caused by a world war but by Gorbachev's *perestroika* and new political thinking, and it was incredibly quick. It was unexpected, even for the USSR's leaders themselves, especially after they encountered the explosion of nationalist sentiment in Central Asia and in the subsequent war in Chechnya. Having fallen victim to their own domestic policy, Russia's leaders were counting on help from the West, especially the USA, and they were taken aback by NATO's expansion to the East at the expense of Central European countries. The populace perceived this expansion by NATO as a campaign of exclusion, isolation, and humiliation directed at the new Russia. As a result, Russia's foreign policy lost its bearings and collapsed.

In Leon Aron's opinion, some Russians in Moscow became convinced that Russia must become a regional superpower, an international great power, and a nuclear superpower. This Russian

1 Mandelbaum, ed., *The New Russian Foreign Policy.* Council on Foreign Relations.

variant of Gaullism can psychologically satisfy a part of the political elite. In fact, the situation is this: "Russia has inherited the Soviet nuclear arsenal, which is, of course, a source of influence. In other ways, however, Russia's presence is scarcely felt beyond its immediate neighborhood." If we look at the ordinary folk rather than the elite, they are sincerely heartbroken by the falling away of the Ukraine, a state with which they were together for three centuries. As for Central Asia and the Caucasus, their feeling is not so much of loss as of fear.

Aron is correct about the attitudes of the greater part of the country's population, but he is wrong about the political "elite." They have no intention of letting go of the Caucasus, as evidenced by the second Chechen war.

One chapter is written by Coit Denis Blacker, a Stanford professor and a leading figure in Russia studies. In his opinion, for most Russians "the world" still means, first and foremost, the West. His argument is "that political and economic integration with the West, the aim of the original foreign policy of *perestroika*, is not only the most desirable goal for post-Soviet foreign policy, it is also the only feasible one."

In this view, the Gaullism of the post–1993 period is to be understood not only as a politically necessary and largely rhetorical response to domestic pressures but also as a tactic designed to improve the terms under which Russia is integrated into the West. The relevant precedents for the new Russia are Germany and Japan after World War II. These states were defeated, democratized, and integrated into the Western security and economic order, of which the United States was the chief architect and most powerful member.

That is the ideal scenario. The reality makes Blacker less optimistic. In his scenarios of the future the place of Russia is as follows: "The Western economic and political order, with Japan, North America, and Western Europe constituting its core, may be seen metaphorically as a magnetic field, pulling other countries toward it. Because this community of free-market democracies is both powerful and successful, other countries seek to join its organizations, observe its norms, and replicate its institutions." In principle, that is.

One reason for Russia's lack of an effective foreign policy is Russia's inability to form an efficient national government. The current trends, should they be amplified, could result in the disintegration of Russia as a unified state. There would be hyperinflation, disintegration of the armed forces, the ascension of politically independent regional authorities; all these trends are already in evidence, although central authority is still far from total collapse. "A historical precedent for a Russia of this kind is the chaos in China in the 1920s and 1930s, when different parts of the country were dominated by military leaders known as warlords who controlled independent armed forces."

Obviously, the realization of this scenario is undesirable because it would mean loss of control over nuclear weapons and, in general, the scattering of Russian armed forces through territories beyond the control of a centralized government. One can envisage other possibilities outside these extreme outcomes. They would manifest themselves in different foreign policies adapted to its three global neighborhoods not only the West and the Middle East but also, by virtue of its border with China and coastline on the Pacific Ocean, the Far East. "The politics and economics of the three regions differ sharply. It would not be surprising, therefore, if Russian policies toward them should turn out to differ from one another."

Russia's proximity to China may play a special role, shaping a third variant of foreign policy that is anti-Western in direction. "Russian neo-Gaullism has elements of such a policy. Russia has displayed a friendlier attitude toward countries that the United States considers "rogue" states than Washington has thought appropriate, although so too have America's Western European allies."

Once again, this is in theory. Having identified the possibility, Blacker "blocks" it right away, pointing out an opposite trend: "Both Russia and China, however, have evinced more interest in joining the Western order than in overturning or boycotting it." Besides, Russia and China are potential rivals for influence in the newly independent countries of Central Asia that were once Soviet republics, which are wedged between them. The tensions can be exacerbated by the issue of the illegal migration of Chinese into Russia caused by the underpopulation of the Russian Far East and the overpopulation in China's Northeast. Therefore: "Of all the possible scenarios for Russian foreign policy, the most desirable remains integration with the West." Russia used to belong to Europe for centuries; yet it remained the least European of nations. Now it has the opportunity to become a European country, both internally and externally. In Blacker's opinion, this is helped by the fact that Russia has ceased to be an empire, thus facilitating her entry into the civilized world. Blacker sincerely wants Russia to become part of Europe.

I used to share these views, naively believing that Russians are closer in spirit and culture to Europe than Asia. But now, having seen all of Europe and Northeast Asia, I have personally come to the conclusion that Russia will never become either European or Asian; it will remain what it always was: Russian.

Strobe Talbott: Historical Optimism about Russia

Former Deputy Secretary of State Strobe Talbott supervised Russia affairs during the Clinton administration. Unlike many Russia experts who became disenchanted with democratic reforms and the prospects for American–Russian relations, Talbott always maintained a steady historical optimism, even during periods of worsening relations with Russia.[1]

Talbot ascribes all the obvious failures of the building of capitalist society in Russia to the legacy of the Soviet dictatorship and leftovers of the Socialist past, all of which, in his opinion, are gradually being overcome. In any event, however problematic Russia's moving into capitalism may be, everything that happens is good for the national interests and security of the United States. At least the two "basic goals" are being accomplished satisfactorily. The first goal includes the strengthening of security, the reduction of Cold War arsenals, the prevention of WMD proliferation, and the strengthening stability of European integration. The second goal directs the USA toward helping Russia in the cause of transforming her political, economic, and social institutions in accordance with the standards of market democracy.[2]

Talbott is particularly inspired by the successes in the realization of the second goal, i.e., the transformation of Russia into a capitalist state. In this connection, he lists as achievements the demolition of the Soviet regime's bureaucratic apparatus, free elections, the replacement of centralized planning with institutions of market economy, etc.

Talbott reports with some pride to the Senate Committee on Foreign Policy on the U.S. contribution to these achievements, in-

1 Talbott, *Russia: Its Current Troubles and Its Ongoing Transformation.* Testimony before the Senate Foreign Relations Committee.

2 See more on this topic in Talbott, "Dealing with Russia in a time of troubles," *The Economist* (November 21, 1998), 50–2.

cluding the Presidential Freedom Support Act. He warns the Senate against cutting the budget for this Act by 25 to 30 percent—an initiative proposed in the aftermath of a money-laundering scandal of those funds through New York banks. In his opinion, such an action would be nearsighted on the senators' part, because this aid is spread over many areas of U.S. activities in Russia—from the financing of mass media to the support of small business, all of which are in the USA's interest.

The essence of Talbott's speeches and writings about Russia is this: Government circles should not panic on account of all the disappointments, be it the financial crisis, the bribe scandal involving high-ranking officials, yet another domestic war, or a surge in anti-Western sentiment. All these are temporary difficulties of the transition from totalitarian communism to democratic capitalism, which will inevitably be completed.

Strobe Talbott's optimism is grounded in at least two reasons. One is his former position. He was responsible for Russia in a previous U.S. administration and cannot be expected to admit the failure of the policy he was actively involved in. The other reason is more substantial. Indeed, a capitalist structure has been created in Russia, and the country's leadership operates within its framework. Even though Talbott understands full well that Russia will never come to resemble any nation of the West, one cannot exclude the chance of its becoming another Brazil or Mexico. America has learned very well to manage these kinds of countries. At the present moment, this is more than enough from the perspective of U.S. interests. Strobe Talbott did his job satisfactorily, and his optimism about Russia can be considered justified—for now.

The Concept of "Engagement" as a Strategic Principle of U.S. Foreign Policy

The Strategy of "Engaging" Russia: An Application of the Carrot-and-Stick Principle (Michael McFaul)

Professor Michael McFaul is one of the more respected Russia experts in the USA, and with good reason. He spent many years in Moscow, both before *perestroika* and after the start of capitalist reforms, so he is in a position to make comparisons.

Unlike all the American Russia experts who talk about "economic reform" or "the third wave" of democratization after the collapse of the Soviet Union, McFaul proclaims straightforwardly that a revolution has taken place in Russia, comparable in scale to the French Revolution of 1789 and the Bolshevik revolution.[1] Proceeding from the classical definitions of a revolution, he shows quite convincingly that Yeltsin's regime demolished the old structure of power and the society's economic organization, and replaced both with a capitalist system. In his opinion, it differs from previous revolutions in that it was accomplished through non-violent means, if one disregards such "trifles" as the shelling of the Parliament in 1993. Another difference, labeled by McFaul as "fundamental," is that the ideologies of those earlier revolutions challenged the established order of the international system of the time. However, the ideology and goals of the current Russian revolution were not directed against the status quo of the contemporary international system. On the contrary, the ideology preached by Yeltsin and his supporters is completely compatible with the economy and politics of the core powers. Moreover, Russia's "revolutionaries" did every-

1 Nation and McFaul, *The United States and Russia into the 21st Century*, 49.

thing they could to join that core. (54)[1]

There is nothing surprising in this, for it is precisely a capitalist revolution that took place, i.e., a society started to form whose content is identical with other capitalist states. It is unclear yet, even for McFaul himself, exactly what kind of capitalism will establish itself in Russia; as of yet, there is no answer.

Despite all this, the professor is convinced that: "Over the long term, Russia's size, natural resources, educated population, and strategic location in Europe and Asia ensure that this country will emerge again as a power in the international system." (66) (Note: He says simply "power" rather than "great power.") The problem is, will this power become part of the Western core, or will it turn into a rogue nation threatening the world community? To a large degree, this depends on the policy that the USA pursues with regard to Russia.

McFaul reminds the reader that in America's political-academic circles, there exist different approaches to the U.S. role in the world after World War II. Mentioned among them are isolationism, neocontainment, and engagement/enlargement. (54)

In McFaul's opinion, the strategy of engagement is the best option as regards Washington's policy toward Russia. In his understanding, this policy should be built on several basic principles. First, the United States must lead by example. A growing market economy and a robust democracy in the United States provide the best arguments for adopting capitalism and democracy in other countries. Second, engagement or enlargement requires a sustained and unwavering commitment to the principles of free markets and democracy. Third, engagement is not always a non-zero-sum game. Sometimes, U.S. foreign policy leaders must be prepared to accept short-term losses (and these are usually economic losses) to win long-term gains regarding enlargement of the "core." A corollary to this principle is that engagement requires the use of both carrots and sticks. Progress regarding the development of market and democratic institutions is not without cost. (55) Fourth, not only must American leaders expend their energies trying to get "bad guys" to do good deeds, but they also must assist "good guys"

1 Curiously, McFaul views the whole international system through the prism of the "core's" ideology, failing to notice the existence of other ideologies in this system, for example the socialist ideology of China.

in performing good deeds, even if such engagement might become complicated. (ibid.)

What McFaul had in mind was a policy designed to stimulate changes in the conduct of authoritarian leaders ("bad guys") while simultaneously sponsoring and supporting new democratic leaders ("good guys"). These general principles are entirely applicable in Russia, too.

In the professor's opinion, American tactics toward Russia don't always fit the strategic goals of the United States. For instance, NATO's eastward expansion contradicts the policy of engagement because it isolates Russia from the core and brings about an anti-Western reaction. This doesn't suit the long-term interests of the USA. On the contrary, Russia must be enticed to join NATO structures. In this same manner, Russia must be included in different international organizations, such as the Paris Club, the World Bank, and the Group of Seven.

A special emphasis should be placed on the forming of market and democratic institutions, giving priority to the latter. McFaul believes it necessary to intensify collaboration with such people as Chubais, Nemtsov, Gaidar, and D. Vasiliev, and not abandoning them in their time of trouble, when they are out of government.

In other words, if the USA wants to see Russia in the core, it must carry out wide-scale work at all levels of political and economic power. McFaul is sincerely convinced that only the capitalist way of development will bring progress and prosperity to Russia.

Craig Nation's Policy of "Limited Engagement"

Another Russian expert is R. Craig Nation, who has written extensively on Soviet and Russian foreign and security policies. He expresses a somewhat different view of Russia. He writes that in the United States, three approaches toward Russia exist. The first reflects hope for a strategic partnership with Russia and implies her association with the West. The second reflects the policy of neo-containment, mentioned also by McFaul. The third corresponds to the policy of limited engagement—precisely the one pursued by the Clinton administration. (32–33)

The latter option is the most realistic one because Russia and the USA agree on some things and differ on others. Besides, a strategic partnership implies parity or near-parity of powers; Russia is currently in decline; therefore, there can be no partnership, and "Russia has no choice but to adapt its aspirations to the realities of its subordinate status." (34) Russia's behavior reflects precisely that kind of status. Appeals to multipolarity, rhetoric with pretensions to a great power status, balancing acts, and alliance-building games are all typical manifestations of a country's weakness. Therefore, the United States should free itself from the illusion of special relationships, avoid cultivating exaggerated notions of a threat, and start working with Russia on a pragmatic basis, concentrating on areas of mutual interest.

This is the approach of a typical pragmatist who fully understands the balance of power and relative strength of states.

The Concept of "Rational Engagement"

As an example, it is worth presenting the views of Congressman Lee Hamilton (D), a member of the Foreign Affairs Committee of the House of Representatives.[1]

Hamilton believes that the world leadership of the USA is historically inevitable for two reasons: (1) The USA is too great a country, too representative, not to be involved in world affairs; and (2) without the USA fulfilling its international role as a superpower, the world would be more unstable and dangerous.

He emphasizes that during the Cold War, the U.S. national interests amounted to containment of communism, while today they amount to the expansion and strengthening of the world community, based on market democracy. In spite of the USA being the sole superpower, it cannot accomplish that task on its own; it will

1 Lecture by Hamilton, "Changes in American Foreign Policy Over the Past Thirty Years," *Institute for the Study of Diplomacy* (November 18, 1998).

need to cooperate with its allies.

Foreign policy must proceed from long-term interests, rather than consist of reactions to current problems and crises.

Hamilton is one of those politicians who opposes isolationism and supports the official course of "engagement." He sees the "international politics" budget, currently standing at 1 percent of the federal budget, as clearly inadequate for discharging international obligations, such as the funding of the UN (the USA owes a large sum of money to this organization), the IMF, and the World Bank. Hamilton is convinced that one cannot aspire to a leadership role without an adequate financial base.

Of course, increased spending on foreign policy presupposes a strong economy, which depends to a large degree on the foreign economic activity of American business.

The leadership of the USA is also supported by a strong military potential. A diplomacy relying on military strength works better than one without such support. In Hamilton's words, "Diplomacy and the threat of force must be orchestrated to achieve U.S. foreign policy goals."

The theme of military intervention remains current to this day. When U.S. vital interests are at stake, the answer is obvious: Intervention must be used as an instrument of policy. "We should intervene, with force if necessary, to defend our borders, to prevent any single power from gaining control over Europe, Japan, Korea, or the Persian Gulf, and to protect ourselves against terrorism or weapons of mass destruction." In the instances when the interests at stake are not vital but merely important, the answer is not so obvious. In such cases, it is better to act together with friends and allies on the basis of collective security.

Finally, foreign policy must be developed with a view to being understood by the American people.

Hamilton is a typical supporter of collectivist hegemony of the Western world, headed by the USA, on the basis of "rational engagement," normally championed by the Democratic Party and American transnational corporation (TNCs).

* * *

Republican Senator Kay Baily Hutchison criticizes the Clinton administration from an unexpected direction[1]. She writes that in the 1980s, Reagan's harsh military policy toward the Soviet Union was called "gunboat diplomacy." "But the Clinton Doctrine of "gunpoint democracy" is much worse," – writes the Senator. Talking constantly about peace, the President sends American troops to sort out political situations that don't threaten the USA or their allies. It started with Somalia, followed by Haiti, Bosnia and now Kosovo. "In the name of restoring democracy and preventing humanitarian chaos, we bombed a sovereign nation that had not attacked us or our allies. That is unprecedented. NATO has been turned into an alliance that starts wars" (3). Hutchison reminds us that the intervention in the Balkans, while having nothing to do with the security of the USA, consumed $25 billion and produced very dubious results. "As noble as that sounds, in practice it means the United States could become involved in civil wars all around the globe, trying to create a utopian American multi-party democracy—at the point of a gun" (2).

The main cause of such an irrational policy, in the Senator's opinion, is this: America *reacts* to events instead of *shaping* them.

She thinks that the policy of the USA as the world's sole superpower should heed two important facts. Firstly, leadership means understanding that war is the last word in politics, not the first. "We should not allow our allies or our enemies to suck us into regional quicksands. This means having the courage not to act" (4). Secondly, the USA must not get involved in civil conflicts that turn them into parties to those conflicts. "Yes, Serbia has a terrible leader, and it is tempting to punish him with military force. But we cannot declare war against every crazed dictator in this world" (ibid.).

The Senator is not opposed to the use of military power in principle, but only in those cases when it comes "naturally." In her view, examples of such cases are the Gulf War of the possible invasion of South Korea by North Korea.

Hutchison's general idea is this: resources should not be expended on peripheral interests, so as not to lose the core – something that happened before to Great Britain and Germany. (I would add: most notably, it happened to the Soviet Union.) This approach

1 Hutchison, "*A Foreign Policy Vision for the Next American Century*," Heritage Foundation Heritage Lectures, no. 639, July 9, 1999.

brings the conservative Senator close to the supporters of "rational engagement." But she differs from the Democrats in that the latter advocate collective engagement together with allies, while the conservatives prefer to manage without allies, using solely the strength of the USA.

U.S. National Security: the Realist Approach

A few years ago, the Strategic Studies Institute (SSI) and Dickinson College's Clarke Center organized a lecture series on U.S. national security in the post-Cold-War period. The speakers were scholars of international affairs and former diplomats, well known in their own country. These lectures were published in 1997 under the aegis of the SSI.[1] The main reason they are of interest is that even though both the Institute and the Center are part of the Department of Defense, their scholars express ideas and views that are substantially different from the U.S. official positions on national security, especially those of the Pentagon. As an example, I picked the lecture by former Ambassador Robert F. Ellsworth, who held high positions in the State Department and other organizations involved in U.S. foreign policy. My other choice is the lecture by Professor Ronald Steel of George Washington University and the University of Southern California, the author of five books on U.S. foreign and domestic policies.

I will start with Ellsworth.[2] He identifies "the twin Transformations" that will substantially change international relations in the twenty-first century. The first of the two forces is the demographic explosion in the underdeveloped regions, the migration from those regions to the wealthy ones, and the globalization of economic relations. Also included in this force is the rivalry between religions and the new self-affirmation of states on an ethnic basis, which development, he thinks, is paradoxically stimulated by nation-states. He sees China as precisely one of the driving forces that promote ethnic "Asianism."(70)

The second force is formed through the influence of technological change, most notably computer systems and biotechnology that give birth to new industries and instruments used in military operations throughout the world.

---

1 *U.S. National Security: Beyond the Cold War.*

2 Ellsworth, "American National Security in the Early Twenty-First Century." In *U.S. National Security: Beyond the Cold War.*

The interaction of these two transnational forces can theoretically produce three results in the system of international relations: chaos, prosperity, or something in between.

To be prepared for any of these eventualities, the national security of the United States in the early twenty-first century must be based on five vital national interests. These vital interests are (1) to prevent, deter, and reduce the threat of nuclear, biological, and chemical weapons attacks on the United States; (2) prevent the emergence of a hostile hegemony in Europe or Asia; (3) prevent the emergence of a hostile major power on U.S. borders or in control of the seas or of space; (4) prevent the catastrophic collapse of major global systems (trade, financial markets, energy, and environment); and (5) ensure the survival of U.S. allies. (72)

A sixth vital interest, entirely up to the United States, will be instrumental to securing the first five; that is, to promote U.S. leadership, military capabilities, and the reputation for adhering to clear U.S. commitments and evenhandedness in dealing with other states and people. (ibid.)

Apart from vital interests, there also exist, in Ellsworth's terminology, twelve "extremely important" national interests, such as preventing and ending major conflicts in important geographic regions and preventing massive uncontrolled immigration across U.S. borders; eleven "just important" ones, such as discouraging massive human rights violations in foreign countries as a matter of official government policy; and five "less important," or secondary ones, such as balancing bilateral trade deficits and enlarging democracy elsewhere for its own sake. (85)

The way the ambassador sees it, the difference between vital and important interests is that the former must be protected by any means, including military force, and alone, if necessary. The latter must be defended—if the issue of using military force arises—"only with a coalition of allies whose vital interests are themselves threatened."(73)

Ellsworth believes that Russia must not be compared to the former Soviet Union, as some researchers are wont to do. He writes: "The government of Russia enjoys only limited political legitimacy at home and, despite the rhetoric of its brilliant foreign minister, lacks the ability to project political, economic, or military power beyond its 'near abroad.' Even in its 'near abroad' Moscow's writ runs weak. "…The proliferation of Russian weapons and skills among criminals, insurgents and terrorists, and rapid military fragmentation, pose a far more immediate international danger than notional Russian military aggression anywhere." (78–79)

Ellsworth emphasizes that Russia's military potential, together with her military-industrial complex, continue to deteriorate, being in a demoralized state since 1991. "Leading Russian politicians count survival as Russia's most pressing national interest, and this will clearly be served by keeping an open U.S. option. Yet the way of thinking of many in the U.S. foreign policy elite is still tinged with nostalgia for the good old Soviet threat." (79)

On the other hand, the ambassador remarks with optimism that Russia is becoming actively involved in the world economy—not just through her usual exports of fossil fuel and mineral resources but also through the export of steel, armaments, and cooperation in outer space, etc. Ellsworth reminds the reader that Russia has on her territory enormous energy resources, exceeding those of the Caspian region; those resources touch in one way or another on the problems of security in the twenty-first century.

The ambassador believes it necessary to encourage Russia's rapprochement with the West, for example, through the strengthening of relations between NATO and Russia, giving the latter a "real voice" in European security. On the general plane, it is necessary to engage Russia in the realization of "three of our own (and many others') national interests: a strong and truly global energy system, in which Russia itself, and the Caspian Sea region, would be copious sources of oil and gas; containment of Islamic militarism; and no hostile hegemony in Europe." (80)

I wish to draw attention to the words I have italicized: our own. The ambassador ponders ways to make Russia an accomplice in the realization of American interests. Do these interests correspond to Russia's interests? Such a silly question doesn't even enter the ambassador's mind. Perhaps that goes with being American. Only Russians worry about how things are going in, say… Ethiopia? Do they need any help over there?

Ellsworth insists decisively on the leading role of the United States in the twenty-first century, meaning that it seeks to solve all international problems in cooperation with its allies and through finding common ground with Russia and China. This approach is characteristic of the supporters of a collective hegemony of the West, headed by the United States. It is unusual for Ellsworth to take this position, considering that he was Senator Robert Dole's adviser on foreign policy issues during the latter's presidential campaign of 1996. It is well known that Dole insisted on a solitary hegemony of the USA in the world with no regard for its allies. Times have changed, apparently, and so has Ellsworth.

Ronald Steel: "Security is Mortals' Chiefest Enemy"

Ronald Steel put it nicely: "The most troublesome concepts are the ones we take for granted. This is not only because they are familiar but also because they are embedded in our way of thinking. They roll off our tongues without our ever stopping to think what they really mean. We come to take them as established truths, like Biblical injunctions."[1]

One of these concepts is "national security." The concept itself emerged in connection with the National Security Act of 1947, which provided the basis for establishing the National Security Council. Somewhat later, the Eberstadt report featured the phrase "national security in terms of world security." The latter term was not explained; its meaning was taken to be "obvious." The implication was that "national security" included "defense." Following the book by Walter Lippmann (1943) that first mentioned the "idea of national security," the term "defense" was understood to mean resistance to an "invading power," while "national security" did not mean just resistance to aggression but also a policy that takes into account potential threats. This understanding of the term connected "security" to "national power." It follows, in Steel's view, that a regional power would have a regional perimeter of security, while a global power would have a global one.

"For this reason, security gets unhinged from its geographical moorings. It becomes a function of power and an aspect of psychology. It becomes internalized. It is not a specific reality, and it does not exist entirely in space. It is a function of definition, and can be defined broadly or narrowly. Small and weak states define security narrowly; large and powerful ones define it broadly. Security, then, is a reflection of a nation's (or at least of a nation's elite's) sense of its power. It is a powerful operating mechanism, and at the same time an abstraction." (41)

1 Steel, "The New Meaning of Security." In *U.S. National Security: Beyond the Cold War*, 40.

In the Americans' minds, the sense of security quickly became transformed into the sense of danger of a global kind, appearing as the threat of the Soviet Union's Communist ideology spreading throughout the world. As a result, there was no place on the globe where real security existed. Even in those places where the Soviet Union's influence was absent, there were Communists or their sympathizers. It was this sense of danger that fed the Truman doctrine.

Steel shows the reader how the concept of national security became filled with ill-defined terms such as "vital," "desirable," "critical" or "peripheral" interests, or "international peace." The interpretation of these terms led to all interests becoming "vital." Later it turned out they were not so "vital" after all, as it happened, for example, with South Vietnam.

Despite all this, all these terms with multiple meanings led to the forming of the concept of "national security," separating it from the concept of "defense." "Defense is precise, national security is diffuse; defense is a condition, national security is a feeling." (43) In other words, defense is tied to the state as the monopolist of military power; national security is tied not just to the state but also to the national state.

In Soviet times, scholars of international affairs criticized the American doctrine of national security for its failure to reflect the interests of the entire nation. It was interpreted as reflecting only the interests of the bourgeois *state* because the nation, i.e., the American people, could not be interested, for example, in the U.S. aggression against Vietnam. In other words, Soviet scholars clearly distinguished national interests from interests of the state as applicable to "imperialist states." It is remarkable that Steel's criticism is similarly developed. How does he apply it to contemporary material?

To begin with, he identifies two facts: (1) After the end of the war, the role of the military factor in international politics became relatively smaller; and (2) the economic processes tied to the internationalization of the world economy are reducing the government's role. (43–44)

Steel reminds the reader that during the Cold War years, the universally accepted paradigm of international relations was the theory of realism, or the theory of power politics, in which the principal subject is the state, providing security to its citizens.[1] He remarks reasonably that at the same time, in some parts of the world, states were falling apart (e.g., in Central Africa), or becoming instruments of "drug lords" and local oligarchies (e.g., in parts of Latin America), or they were ruled by a family or "clan" (as in many countries of the Middle East and the Third World). Therefore, instead of providing security to their citizens, these states actually constituted a threat to them. Steel asks what are the state's obligations in that case and emphasizes that this question is not an abstract one. "In recent years we have seen the disintegration of established states, such as Yugoslavia and the Soviet Union, and the hollowing-out of others that exist only at the convenience of outside forces that sustain their ruling regimes, as in the former African colonies of France. Even in parts of the industrialized world, the state is sometimes incapable of providing security for some of its citizens. One has only to look to the slums of our major cities for confirmation of this sorry fact—or even to affluent areas, with their guarded gates and private police forces, for confirmation." (44)

It doesn't mean, says Steel, that the state is incapable of providing security. It is simply that this function becomes secondary from the perspective of the people's economic life. To the foreground come private economic players who are responsible for investment, jobs, wages, and production. "Within the economic realm, we are approaching the condition described by Karl Marx (albeit under different circumstances) where the state is withering away." (44–45)

In the spirit of certain theorists of globalism, Steel goes on to develop his thesis about the decline of the state's role. "Governments are being reduced to the role of traffic cops, ensuring that everyone follows the regulations that are, of course, written by and for the most powerful corporations." (45)

"In some places this process has gone so far that the state can hardly be said to exist at all. By this I do not mean such 'narco-states' as Colombia, Mexico, Burma, and Pakistan, where drug lords rule independent fiefdoms. Rather, I have in mind Russia, where the new giant corporate entities (themselves former state

1 Note that this theory was founded by H. Morgenthau, A. Wolfers, *et al.* Nonetheless Steel is not quite correct. Paradigms did change during the Cold War; e.g., the "idealist" school dominated during the Johnson and Reagan administrations.

enterprises stolen from the people by their former managers and the new Mafia entrepreneurs) control the government and refuse to pay taxes to a state that they consider, quite understandably, the servant of their ambition. In effect, the role of such a state is to keep the population in line, deflect criticism of commercial operations by engaging in military diversions, such as the war in Chechnya, and keep out competitors." (46)

Though Russia is indeed an obvious example, she is not unique. This is true of the industrial world as well, to a greater or smaller degree. The main point is that national security in its traditional meaning has lost its significance.

To support this thesis, Steel adds examples from the fields of religion and cultural science. The idea here is that people define themselves not only as citizens of a particular country but also as belonging to a certain religion or civilization which transcends state borders. This sometimes leads to situations in which citizens "may view their own state as their enemy." (ibid.) For example, he mentions the situation in Algiers and also reminds the reader of the events in Philadelphia where American police and troops firebombed several city blocks occupied by the MOVE group.

Steel also points out that inside modern societies, there is a war going on between traditionalists and modernists, between those who absorb technological and social change and those who fear and oppose these innovations. He doesn't go as far as identifying the class stratification of society, but he does come very close to understanding how the interests of a particular strata of society may differ from the interests of the state. This topic, by the way, is completely ignored by the contemporary political elite in Russia.

In light of all that was said above, the question arises: What traditional threats to security does the United States face? (Traditional means threats coming from other states.) In other words, which states can threaten America? Steel finds no such states either in the industrial world or the Third World. "Russia is a deeply wounded state that was always weaker than we believed and that will take decades to recover even a semblance of its former power. For a long time it will remain the sick man on the fringes of Europe: a problem but not a threat." (48)

As for China, it is unclear whether she will be a boundless market or an endless problem. Considering the balance of problems and achievements and China's current development, she is not likely to choose the course of aggression unless provoked. (49) In fact, the United States faces "few threats" coming from other states. No one is laying claims to U.S. territory. The USA is not overly dependent on foreign trade. Washington has many allies that "we don't really need." The Pentagon has established a lot of military bases abroad that are not there for the purpose of defense. "Because of its economic and military strength, its physical resources, its loyal population, and its privileged geographical position, the United States can afford to ignore a good deal of the turbulence in much of the rest of the world." (49)

Despite all this, politicians make a long list of potential threats to U.S. security. There is nothing surprising in this, for "that is one of the things they are paid to do." (ibid.) There even exists a class of specialists who are preoccupied with the management of global security. This manifests itself in a large number of political speeches, strategy scenarios, and Pentagon wish lists. The most amazing paper is the one prepared by the Department of Defense in 1992 that argued that the United States must "discourage the advanced industrial nations from challenging our leadership or even aspiring to a larger regional or global role." (ibid.)

But this is precisely something on which both Europeans and Japanese can agree because this approach enables them to spend less on their own defense. The Europeans, for instance, agreed eagerly to expand NATO because that is what the United States wants.

This leadership strategy is an expensive one. NATO expansion alone is scheduled to cost some $100 billion to upgrade East European armed forces. No wonder Wall Street likes it. We continue to spend militarily at Cold War levels. Currently, it costs about $100 billion a year to "reassure" the Europeans against unspecified threats, and another $45 billion or so to provide the same reassurance to the Japanese and Koreans. Today more than 50 percent of all discretionary federal spending is still devoted to national security, even in the absence of an enemy. While other nations invest for production, the United States borrows for consumption—and in the process becomes further indebted to the trade rivals whose interests it seeks to protect. (50)

The time has come to establish a balance between national foreign policy and national security, to make our resources match our obligations. "The American people want the nation to be strong and to stick by its ideals. But they are not interested in grandiose plans of global management." (ibid.) Steel concludes that a national security policy that does not account for these considerations is inadequate, unrealistic, detached from reality, and doomed to failure. (51)

He personally believes that the USA does have "critical" interests, but they are relatively few in number. They amount to the need to protect the country from destruction and preserve the social institutions and the form of government. Secondary interests lie in the sphere of expanding the market-economy core, protecting the environment, and maintaining the peace process in the regions connected to America by cultural and political ties. The third level of interests lies in promoting the spread of democracy, not because it contributes to security in any superficial sense, but because it reflects American values.

Steel concludes that the USA should not wear itself thin with grandiose plans, but rather approach all problems realistically; that is, by proceeding from real needs rather than imagined ones.

Security, after all, is not a condition, but a feeling and a process. It is also an abstraction. We may feel secure while being in danger, and we may be secure while feeling otherwise. Steel quotes Macbeth to make his appeal: "Let's not get to the point where 'Security is mortals' chiefest enemy.'"

I classify Steel as a realist-"isolationist" of the left-liberal persuasion.

Rand Corporation's Forecasts and Future Scenarios to Year 2025[1]

The book *Sources of Conflict in the 21st Century: Regional Futures and U.S. Strategy* was written by associates of the Rand Corporation, an important think-tank that influences the shaping of the foreign and domestic policy of the USA. Commissioned by the U.S. Air Force, this particular book contains forecasts for the period up to 2025. I will analyze one of the more important chapters in that book that deals with problems of interest to us. It was written by the well-known American scholars of international affairs Zalmay Khalilzad and David Shlapak, in cooperation with Ann Flanagan.[2]

The authors set out nine propositions about the state of the world in the next twenty-five years:

1. The United States will remain a globally engaged actor.
2. The global distribution of power will change.
3. Great power relationships will be in flux.
4. Regional divisions will be increasingly blurred.
5. The U.S. homeland will be more exposed to attack.[3]
6. The rise of a "global competitor" is uncertain.
7. Technology, including military technology, will spread rapidly.
8. The spread of nuclear, chemical, and biological (NBC) weapons will remain a major problem.

---

1 Khalilzad, Lesser, eds., *Sources of Conflict in the 21st Century: Regional Futures and U.S. Strategy.*

2 Khalilzad and Shlapak with Flanagan, "Overview of the Future Security Environment" (chapter two) in *Sources of Conflict in the 21st Century.*

3 Unfortunately, this prognosis was too quickly proven correct.

9. The U.S. military will be called upon to respond not only to major regional warfare but also to other crises, and to play a key role in shaping the future security environment. (7–8)

The authors predict that by 2025, three kinds of scenarios might unfold on the world stage: (1) base case, (2) benign, or (3) malignant. They proceed from the assumption that Russia as the "Russian Confederation" fits the first scenario, "Dynamic Russia" fits the second, and "Sick Man of Eurasia" fits the third. The corresponding scenarios for China are called "Assertive," "Liberalizing," and "Hegemonic." (8)

In keeping with the American tradition of prognosticating, the authors hedge their predictions by mentioning wild cards, i.e. unpredictable, random events. Listed among these are deadly viruses, cosmic objects, neo-fascists' ascension to power in nuclear-weapon states, and a new Cold War caused by "civilizational" differences (i.e., Islamic fundamentalism against the West), etc.

The geostrategic context. In this scenario, the USA remains a global power. The authors are certain that this status will be maintained through the early twenty-first century because the entirety of economic, political, military, cultural, and other factors makes the United States the globe's 500-pound gorilla, whether we like it or not. (10) In this connection, by the way, they make a note of U.S. cultural penetration throughout the world, deeper and more important than political ties. They even give this reminder in parenthesis: "Recall that Levis blue jeans were a status symbol in the pre-perestroika USSR." (ibid.)

In the context of a global shift of power (point two of nine), the authors suggest, referring to World Bank data, that China, currently the world's second biggest economy (as measured at PPP), will become the biggest economy by 2020. (12) As for Russia, Ukraine, and other former Soviet republics, they contend that nothing definite can be said about them due to the uncertainty of their current development. (ibid.)

Nonetheless, they do mention two possible variants of Russia's development. The first is called a "Russian miracle," analogous to the examples of Germany and Japan after World War II. The authors remind the reader in this connection how quickly the Soviet Union managed to build up its power and win the war against Germany, just as unexpectedly as Germany and the USA grew in the period 1870–1910. (19–20) The second variant of Russia's future is called "the new sick man of Eurasia." (14) Because both variants are theoretically possible, the USA must be ready for either one.

In connection with point six (uncertainty about increase of "global competition"), the authors write that China is capable of dramatically increasing her strategic weight and her military potential over the next twenty-five years. "China might even attempt to challenge the United States and its interests worldwide." (19)

*In Scenario One, **World I: Evolutionary**,* the authors suppose that Belarus, Ukraine, and the Russian-populated parts of Moldova and Kazakhstan are reunited with Russia proper in a confederation (in Ukraine's case, perhaps loosely so), while the Central Asian and TransCaucasus countries drift away from Russia and into the Asian and Middle Eastern spheres. (26)

*Scenario Two, **World II: Benign**,* describes a peaceful, prosperous world, structurally interconnected and convergent. Naturally, in this world, democratic institutions and market mechanisms are the norm. Here Russia is a dynamic, democratic, market-oriented state, building relations with neighbors on the basis of commerce and investment and not through military mechanisms. (23) Ideal for the USA is the scenario in which Russia becomes a regional power whose influence only extends over part of the borders of the former USSR.

*Scenario Three, **World III: Malignant**,* describes a bad world of power rivalry and frequent conflicts. In Europe, this scenario envisions failures of integration processes, a vacuum of power and influence. Western Europe is unable to enforce stability in Eastern Europe and the Balkans. The vacuum is filled by a mighty Germany and with interstate conflicts, as well as ethnic conflicts. NATO is either paralyzed or split. "Although the Russia of World III is 'authoritarian but weak' in the wake of failed political and economic reform, the overall depressed state of Europe could allow Moscow to reemerge as a potential hegemon, at least over the eastern part of the continent. China tugs on Russia from the east, and Iran and Pakistan from the south. Amidst these tensions, a catastrophic breakdown of a country that still possesses thousands of nuclear weapons is a never-too-distant possibility." (30–31) Considering China's ascension, she may strike an alliance with Russia. In any case, even "a weak Russia relying on its nuclear arsenal to protect itself could pose a constant danger to important U.S. interests worldwide." (32)

Analyzing one official government paper, the authors note one "curious" detail, namely, in the chapter that deals with the "APR" the impact of different countries on the USA, China, Japan, and India are mentioned, but not a word is said about Russia. The same is true of the discussion on the Middle East. The European part of the paper states: "With Russia's military in drastic decline, the United States and its allies will enjoy a decisive technological superiority over potential adversaries in Europe." (41)

Conflicts connected to Russia. A special chapter in this book, dedicated to the sources of conflict in Europe and the former Soviet Union, is written by the Dutch author John Van Oudenaren.[1]

The author posits that the fundamental interest of the USA in the area of security in Europe is to prevent the emergence of a hostile hegemon, or a country aspiring to the status of a hegemon. He indicates Russia as potentially aspiring to such hegemony. Despite Russia's current weakening, her re-emergence as a serious "adequate rival" cannot be ruled out. At least this threat may emerge in the event of strengthening relations within the CIS or some "other grouping," leading to the re-creation of the former Soviet Union. Having thus scared the reader, Van Oudenaren qualifies his statement right away: "However, as will be argued below, no Russian-led state or coalition is likely ever again to achieve the global power position or pose the same threat to the United States that the Soviet Union did in 1945–1990." (233)

He emphasizes that within the framework of the economic and geopolitical shifts throughout the world, and considering the globalization of security issues in a multipolar world from the perspective of the long-term view, the interests of European security constitute for the USA only part of its overall security. He reminds the reader that in the first half of the twentieth century, the USA was supposedly supporting weak Russia against ambitious Japan in the Far East.

1 Oudenaren, "Sources of Conflict in Europe and the Former Soviet Union," chapter five in *Sources of Conflict in the 21st Century.*

Van Oudenaren clearly does not know history: In the geostrategic game in the Far East, the USA was actually provoking Japan against both Tsarist Russia and Soviet Russia; this policy culminated in the joint aggression of Japan and the USA against the Soviet Far Eastern republic in 1918. This lack of knowledge enables the author to suggest that the possibility of supporting contemporary Russia "against an aggressive China or other Asian power cannot be ruled out and follows from the overriding U.S. interest in preventing the emergence of a dominant and hostile power in either Europe or Asia." (233)

The Dutch scholar views Russia's relations with the Baltic countries from the perspective of a military threat proceeding from Russia. The threat can be realized by territorial disputes with Estonia and Latvia, or by some shifts in the status of Kaliningrad, or by a change of Belarus's attitude toward Lithuania. It can also be provoked by the expansion of NATO.

Russia may develop equally difficult relations with Turkey, a NATO member. The conflict may arise on any pretext in connection with economic, political, or geostrategic problems. (237)

"Russia could use levers short of military intervention to destabilize and expand its influence in some of the countries of Central and Eastern Europe. These levers might include economic dependence, espionage, exploitation of contacts and relationships left over from the Soviet period, and military intimidation through deployments and exercises. Russian stresses of this sort may not necessarily lead to overt conflict but could intensify pressures on the United States and its allies to extend security arrangements and guarantees to countries within what traditionally has been Russia's sphere of influence." (238)

Van Oudenaren believes that short of military conflict, Russian political and economic weight in the CIS area poses a latent threat to the independence and maneuvering freedom of other states in the former Soviet Union. Reintegration of Belarus into a Russian-controlled union, particularly military reintegration, would constitute a threat for Poland, Lithuania, and Ukraine.

A threat to the environment also exists. Especially worrisome are the forty-five commercial nuclear reactors built in the Soviet era and still functioning in Russia, Ukraine, and Armenia. (239)

A modified Cold War order. This state of the world envisions a strong Russia/CIS and a relatively weak Western Europe that relies on the United States. In other words, the European structure resembles the structure of the Cold War period. (241)

It is expected that the relative economic potential of some countries (for instance Germany and Italy) will decline somewhat in absolute terms, while other states will experience a modest increase. Germany's population is expected to decline from 81.1 million in 1995 to 77.7 million in 2015 and to 73.4 million in 2030. A number of factors (such as Germany's known political limitations, an aging population, and declining numbers of draft-age recruits) should modify the perception of Germany as a threat to stability on the continent. One must also consider the new population ratio between Russia and her "near abroad." Some experts expect Russia's population to grow from the current 149 million to 153 million in 2015 (an increase of four million). But over that same time, the eight countries of Central Asia and the Caucasus will see their population grow from 72 million to 96 million (an increase of 24 million). (243)

"A similar range of views exists with regard to Russia. Many policy analysts stress the different cultural and political traditions of Russia and conclude that Russia constitutes a permanent geopolitical challenge to its western neighbors; that "enlargement" of the Western community inevitably will stop at Russia's western border (or, in Samuel P. Huntington's view, at the western edge of the entire Orthodox world)." (262)

Other experts believe that Russia will be adjusting to the world in one way or another, in view of the dramatic decline of her status. Still, a weak Russia has a better chance of being integrated into the global system than the stronger Soviet Union used to have.

Russia's military potential. From the military perspective, Russia will remain weak, unlikely in the short or the middle term to present an aggressive threat to other European countries, except the Baltic nations. Her armed forces currently suffer from insufficient funding and are below full strength. Draft evasion is ubiquitous, and officers of all ranks are quitting the armed forces in droves. Those who remain suffer from a serious fall in status and standard of living. Shipments of most types of armaments are virtually nonexistent. The technology gap between Russia and the advanced Western countries, especially the United States, will doubtlessly grow. (278)

Russia's air force is facing myriad problems having to do with obsolete armaments, though several new aircraft models are in the works, including the MiG-33 and the Su-35. Despite the constant emphasis on quality and technology in modernization, one should not expect Russia to make progress in the development of fifth-generation fighter jets. The air force top brass has often proclaimed its desire to acquire a new fighter plane, emphasizing the growing importance of stealth technologies. But competing priorities in the defense administration and the general shortage of funds in the defense budget will most likely prevent the Russian air force from acquiring a new generation of aircraft in the near future. (281)

"In defense as in foreign policy, Russia draws a distinction between what it calls its 'near abroad' and its 'far abroad,' and at least for now is focusing on the former. Russian national security policy places a heavy emphasis on defense integration in the CIS, even though, as has been seen, several key members do not participate in the CIS's military activities.

"Much of what has been concluded at CIS meetings on defense can be discounted as rhetoric." (279)

Contrary to official doctrine, Russia's military planners and political leaders do not rule out the possibility of conflict with countries of the "far abroad." Border clashes are not impossible between Russia and Turkey or China; Russian forces in Tajikistan may clash with guerrillas from Afghanistan supporting the Tajik opposition. "Over the long term," notes the Dutch scholar, "Russia could be especially vulnerable to pressure from China." (280)

Russia and the CIS. For Russia and the CIS, depending on which of the scenarios discussed above comes to dominate, four alternative orders are possible: (1) reconstituted union, (2) muddling along, (3) dynamic Russia, and (4) sick man of Eurasia. (287)

Alternative Developments of the Situation in Europe. The future of the strategic order in Europe depends on which direction the development of each of its subregions takes, and how these subregions interact with each other and with the rest of the world.

"Six such alternative strategic worlds could result: (1) Modified Cold War Order; (2) Atlantic Partnership; (3) European Bipolarity; (4) West European Dominance; (5) Rivalry and Fragmentation; and (6) Pan-European Order." (290)

It is important to keep in mind that the present strategic order is a mix of the Modified Cold War Order (where NATO membership for Central and Eastern European countries is perceived as a defence against Russia) and the Pan-European Order (as evidenced by NATO's efforts to include Russia in the European security structures, even as it expands against Russia's will).

Probabilities and time frames. The current strategic order in Europe can be characterized as an approximation of the Modified Cold War Order, although with a lower threat level, with tendencies toward building a Pan-European Order. A shift toward another strategic order will probably occur as soon as the process of post-Communist transition is over and in response to the long-term trends described earlier in this chapter.

The intensification of rivalry in Europe and its falling apart is the least likely alternative, though even this variant cannot be ruled out in the longer term (2025 and beyond). From the short- and middle-term perspective, it is difficult to imagine Western Europe in the kind of economic and political crisis that could lead to the collapse of the integration that started in the 1950s. (292)

The Pan-European Order is the most desirable trend that may materialize even in the longest term. A political dialogue, as well as the many new and traditional institutions (ESCO, the Founding Act Russia, NATO, etc.), represent useful links in a Pan-European Order. Nonetheless, in the short- and middle-term perspective, an effective implementation of this order is hardly possible because the expansion of NATO and the European Union, as well as objective conditions "on the ground," widen rather than narrow the gap between Russia (Ukraine and other CIS members) and a large part of Central and Eastern Europe.

Yet, the most likely scenarios for Europe in the middle- and longterm perspectives are European bipolarity, West European dominance, or a continuation of the modified Cold War order, in combination with the Atlantic Partnership.

Due to the economic superiority of Western Europe over Russia, West European dominance would appear to be, at first sight, the most likely outcome. But a number of factors, including the reluctance of several West European countries to speed up integration, the difficulties that stem from the acceptance of Central and Eastern European states into the European Union, and the problems of establishing the European currency, make the emergence of such a scenario doubtful. More important problems are the burden of military expenditures and the formulation of a common concept of defense and security policy.

This knot of problems implies that bipolar relations with a weakened Russia will turn out to be the most likely scenario. Keeping in mind U.S. involvement in counteracting Russia's hidden or real threat to Western Europe, this order would turn out to resemble the modified Cold War order. If one considers another group of factors, namely that parts of Central, Eastern, and Southeastern Europe remain an unstable gray zone, not fully integrated into Western Europe though free from Russian domination, then this order fits the rivalry and fragmentation scenario. (293)

The Pan-European Order. This order appears to be the preferable one for the United States. It frees the USA from involvement in internal European conflicts, including those stemming from a containment policy against a reconstituted Russian nuclear threat to other parts of Europe. Stability would be established throughout Europe, and the principal European states, the EU, and Russia would be capable of implementing on their own a policy of maintaining peace on the continent.

John Van Oudenaren draws attention to one important aspect of the Pan-European Order's desirability to the USA, one that Americans themselves prefer not to discuss. It has to do with China. The author reflects that it would be quite important to the USA and Western Europe to support a friendly Russia (and possibly Kazakhstan and other states of Central Asia) in response to China's resurgence. Moreover, "This effort could entail military assistance by the West to Russia, and possibly even the extension of NATO or other security guarantees to Russia (and/or Kazakhstan) at some point in the future." (298)

War between Russia and China. The probability of the above mentioned events is explained by China's ascension and transformation into a global economic and geostrategic power located on Russia's borders. "Regional trends point to the growing importance of China as a global economic power—and the strategic implications for Russia of the geopolitical rise of its eastern neighbor. War between Russia and China would burst the parameters of the alternative strategic worlds outlined above (based on existing regional trends), raising the prospect of an entirely different strategic world coming into being, perhaps built along civilizational lines with Russia allied with the West against China. The position of Japan in such a world would be crucial." (300)

The author doesn't explain the reasons for Russia and China coming to war, but he already outlines in advance the anti-China coalition that might take shape. Van Oudenaren believes that, generally speaking, Russia does have the potential to become a military threat to Western Europe by the period 2015–2025. But this will only happen if Russia's economy gets back on track and/or Russia manages to re-establish her *de facto* or *de jure* hegemony over parts of the former Soviet Union. "It is less likely to resume its role as a peer competitor to the United States. Indeed, Russia is unlikely ever to exercise the kind of global and European role that it did for 45 years after World War II, especially given German reunification, the loss of influence in Eastern Europe, and the rise of China on its eastern flank." (302)

The appendix to Van Oudenaren's book contains a scenario of a possible war between Russia and Ukraine. (I remind the reader that the book was published in 1998.) Here is how it goes:

Russia has evolved its own variant of semi-authoritarian rule based on a strong president and market capitalism dominated by huge quasi-monopolist firms in key sectors. Fears of encirclement by hostile powers—aggravated by NATO's expansion to include Poland, the Czech Republic, Hungary, and Slovakia in 1999 and continued talk in the West about admitting the Baltic states and Ukraine to the alliance—are a growing source of pressure in Moscow's decision making.

By 2005, Ukraine has made substantial progress toward building a bona fide state and a viable national economy, but the country remains poor by European standards and critically vulnerable to Russian pressure from a variety of sources, including dependence on Russian energy supplies, extensive Russian ownership in key economic sectors, penetration of Ukrainian offices by Russian intelligence, and dependence on Russian suppliers for arms and spare parts.

NATO has been weakened by the effects of enlargement and disputes among its members on a variety of issues such as containing Chinese expansion in Asia and deterring Iranian adventurism in the Gulf. Western Europe has established an energy community with Russia, from which it obtains an increasing share of its oil and natural gas.

In 2005, an anti-Western president triumphs in Russia, while Ukraine is suffering from the cyclical effects of a recession, etc. Gripped by anti-Russian sentiment, Western Ukraine is closely intertwined with Poland, Hungary, and Slovakia, while the eastern parts of the country maintain close cultural and economic ties with Russia. Many there believe that their interests are sacrificed in order to develop the Western parts of Ukraine. The problem of the Crimea worsens. In this situation, Moscow believes that Ukraine is allying itself with Turkey against Russia. The pro-Russian part of the population takes to the streets. Demonstrations are suppressed, with many people killed.

Russia then has no choice but to occupy the eastern part of Ukraine and Crimea, using rapid reaction forces. Russia's air force neutralizes Ukraine's air force on the ground and proceeds to attack key military targets.

Ukraine formally appeals for help to NATO, the United States, and the European Union.

The U.S. NSA (National Security Agency) orders the JCS (Joint Chiefs of Staff) to prepare to execute operations aimed at deterring further Russian aggression and restoring the territorial status quo. Once this is accomplished, the outbreak of a major civil war in Ukraine is prevented.

The EU and NATO response to the crisis has been tepid, at best. The German government blames Ukraine for setting off the confrontation. The remainder of Western Europe appears inclined to follow Germany's lead. Within pre-1999 NATO, only the United States, Great Britain, and Turkey are urging a forceful military response.

Poland, the Czech Republic, and Hungary have also called for a strong Western response to defend the Ukraine against Russian aggression. However, Warsaw in particular makes clear that its support is contingent upon broad alliance support involving Germany and other European allies, as well as the United States; Poland does not want to stand alone as a forward U.S. base in a Russo-American war. There is a possibility, however, that a strong and forceful U.S. response could rally Poland. (326–329)

* * *

This prognostic scenario should not be left without at least a brief commentary. For starters, I wish to note that the book about possible conflicts was published in 1998, and the texts included were submitted most likely in 1997. The scenario described last – war between Russia and Ukraine – takes place in the year 2000. This forecast failed to materialize, fortunately, and not surprisingly. The failure of this very short-term forecast bears evidence to the scientific level and quality of the prognosticators. Since they are unable to foresee the situation three years in advance when writing about such an important event as a war between Russia and Ukraine, they are worthless. It proves that the authors don't know the real situation in Russia or Ukraine. They are also ignorant of regularities in international relations. That's why they are compelled to present a wide range of possibilities in the hope that one of them becomes a reality. Anyone can make "forecasts" on this level, even someone with unknowledgeable about the sphere of international relations.

I presented here excerpts from this book so that certain Russian admirers of the "civilized America" know that America would not hesitate to go to war if Russia engages in "bad behavior," that is, behavior that is at odds with U.S. national interests that now include even Ukraine. At least America is prodded toward this course of action by certain unprofessional prognosticators who reflect the attitudes of certain academic circles in the USA. The Pentagon is ready for these kinds of scenarios without any prodding. It is not surprising, since Russia was and still remains a strategic adversary to all of the West. This notion is actively, persistently argued, and promoted by the associates of the Heritage Foundation.

The Heritage Foundation: U.S. Leadership Based on Strength

Associates of the Heritage Foundation hold conservative views akin to those of the Republican Party, and it is to this party that they present the results of their scientific research in the domestic and foreign policy spheres. They collect their views in annual publications, which include their recommendations to politicians and government officials.

Heritage Foundation papers used to start with harsh criticism of President Clinton's policies on every single issue because the Clinton administration had no strategy, only "a vague set of slogans intended to justify existing policies."[1] The American president took a particularly large amount of flak for his policy toward Russia. For example, Kim R. Holmes, one of the chief editors of the annual collection, *Issues '98*, writes: "Take his (Clinton's) statement that the Russians have retargeted their missiles. There is, of course, no way to verify the truth of this statement. In any event, even if it were true, it would be strategically meaningless. Missiles can be retargeted in a matter of minutes. The nuclear threat, therefore, has not been reduced at all." (361)

Equally energetic criticism is leveled against U.S. military programs on account of their being insufficiently funded. The Heritage Foundation's ideal is Ronald Reagan, or rather Reagan's policy of peace through power—the policy that brought the Soviet Union to its knees without a single shot being fired. (418)

In Holmes's view, U.S. foreign policy must unfold along the following lines: "The purpose of U.S. foreign and defense policy should be to make America safe and prosperous. *(N.B., To make just America safe and prosperous, not the entire world.)* To fulfill this purpose, the U.S. government must protect and defend the people and territory of the United States of America; preserve and defend the freedom of Americans and the U.S. Constitution; and promote the longterm material prosperity of the American people." (365)

1 Butler and Holmes, eds., Issues '98: *The Candidate's Briefing Book*, 364.

Holmes goes on to formulate principles or pillars on which the conservative U.S. foreign policy must be based after the Cold War. They are strength (meaning military strength); freedom (freedom from tyranny and foreign domination; from excessive constraints imposed on America's sovereignty, policy, and economy by the United Nations; freedom to trade and engage in commerce; freedom of peoples around the world to build democratic institutions, foster the rule of law, and promote free markets); and leadership.

Holmes specifies that American leadership "should be based on a vigorous assertion and defense of American interests. It should never subordinate these interests to the national interests of other nations, some of which do not share Western values and hide their selfishness behind a facade of multilateralism."

The United States must act together with its allies when possible and unilaterally when necessary. U.S. policy must be decisive, firm, clear, and constant. Mixed signals, oscillations, and indecision erode trust in American leadership both at home and abroad. (365–366)

In the pages of the Heritage Foundation's periodicals, even more harsh criticism can be found of the previous administration's foreign policy, coming from prominent Republican politicians. For example, former Vice President Dan Quayle lambastes the Clinton administration for wasting all the advantages in domestic and foreign policy inherited from the previous administration.[1] Most importantly, U.S. leadership itself was put in a critical situation. The list of accusations encompasses practically the entire spectrum of foreign policy, including policies toward Russia and China. Talking about the financial crisis in Russia (August 1998) and her problems with democracy, he puts the question squarely: "Who lost Russia?" The answer is Clinton, of course. And why is the USA calmly watching as China unfolds a program of building up "a blue water navy?" Naturally, Quayle is against preserving the anti-missile defense treaty with Russia, which was signed "in a completely different era—with a second party that is now literally nonexistent." (3)

He is especially indignant about the state of U.S. military strength. In his opinion, "The Clinton administration is giving us defensive politics, not defense policy." (4) The end goal of nor-

1 Quayle, "The Duty to Lead: America's National Security Imperative," Heritage Foundation, *Heritage Lectures*, no. 630, (January 21, 1999).

mal defense policy is containment of future enemies. "The means, frankly, is not just to stay ahead of our competitors. We should aim to be so dominant that no one can possibly compete with us." (3) He warns against mistakes in foreign policy that take entire generations to correct.

Leadership is the duty of the United States. This is precisely the essence of America's national security, thinks Quayle and also the majority of the Republican leadership.

Russia as Seen by the Heritage Foundation

In January 1998, the Heritage Foundation organized a conference, *The State of Russian Foreign Policy and U.S. Policy Toward Russia, which was attended by experts on Russia.*[1]

All the participants, with the sole exception of Stephen Sestanovich, were critical of Russia's foreign policy and U.S. policy toward Russia. The direction of their criticism is of interest. Stephen Blank, the MacArthur professor of research at the Strategic Studies Institute of the U.S. Army War College, emphasized the gap between Moscow's foreign policy goals and Russia's real status in the world. In his opinion, Russia still views security problems in terms of military capabilities and a zero-sum game, which seems to put Russia on an equal footing with the United States. Russia's military programs are oriented toward preserving the traditional structures of armed forces, corresponding to a strategic role and missions that do not reflect Russia's actual status. Because Moscow still holds on to "neo-imperialist and hegemonist goals," NATO's expansion to the East is entirely justified, especially because, as former Foreign Minister Andrei Kozyrev noted: "Weakening NATO serves only those who wish for empire and autocracy."[2]

Blank presents an excerpt from an article by Sergei Rogov, director of the USA–Canada Institute, that says: "Washington should recognize the exceptional status of the Russian Federation

1 Heritage Foundation, *Heritage Lectures*, no. 607 (April 6, 1998).

2 See Kozyrev, "NATO Is Not Our Enemy," *Newsweek* (February 10, 1997), 31.

in the formation of a new system of international relations, a role different from that which Germany, Japan, or China or any other center of power plays in the global arena." (15) This pretension to a unique status coincides fully with the mystique of "Derzhavnost (*powerness*)," notes Blank ironically. "From a government that is essentially a ward of the International Monetary Fund and World Bank, and which lost the Cold War, these demands are not only undeserved, unacceptable to Europe, and fantastic, but worse, are also unrealizable. As Talleyrand would have said, it is worse than a crime; it is a blunder." (15) "Policy is now based on the premise that Russia must be seen as a great power equal to the United States based on its potential, not its real power, which is steadily declining both absolutely and relatively." Blank continues: "That Russian power in all these areas is declining or becoming more irrelevant to the modern world while the government dithers and becomes less relevant to international issues eludes virtually all those involved in foreign policy. Russian invocations of multipolarity serve more to gain status or inhibit solutions than to assume responsibility or offer a positive agenda for multilateral action abroad. Tragically, Russia still pursues objectives and policies in Europe that its power does not merit, that are unsustainable, and which ultimately endanger its own security."(15) Can such a state be trusted?

Other participants of the conference respond to this question with a well-argued *no*.

Angela Stent, professor of government at Georgetown University, draws attention to the phenomenon she calls "the Privatization of Foreign Policy." She writes about it with some surprise, because it's Russia she is dealing with. But there is nothing surprising about it, really, because in the last ten years Russia has become a capitalist state, adequate in its internal organization to state-monopolistic capitalism of the Russian type. In any SMC country, two foreign policies coexist: the state's policy and the monopolies' policy. (I have written about this previously, using the example of Japan.)[1]

Stent confirms this banal truth, using the example of contemporary Russia. She writes: "Russian foreign policy is also becoming increasingly 'privatized'; that is, energy companies and

1 See Aliev, *Japan's Foreign Policy*, 23–35.

industrial-financial groups are pursuing their own commercial interests, which do not always coincide with the agendas of the Russian Foreign or Defense Ministry—or even the Kremlin." (24) She notes, however, the "specifics of the Russian variant," meaning that the big companies (Gazprom, Lukoil, etc.) have close ties with government officials. As examples, she mentions the names of Boris Nemtsov and Anatoly Chubais, "whose interests lie more in economic integration with the West than geostrategic influence." (ibid.)

This is all somewhat amusing because this kind of "intertwining" of interests can be found in any capitalist country and not necessarily of the state-monopolistic type. But the American researcher is used to expecting from Russia only foreign policy of the singularly stratified kind, fitting the old Soviet standards, and she is sincerely amazed by what she describes as "deviations" in Russia's current foreign policy.

Be that as it may, the presentations of other conference participants (including Mark Gage, professional staff member for East Europe and the New Independent States Committee on International Relations, U.S. House of Representatives; Robert O. Freedman, president of the Baltimore Hebrew University; Paula J. Dobriansky, the vice president and Washington director and Kennan Fellow for Russia, at the Council on Foreign Relations) contained an urgent appeal to the Clinton administration to revise Washington's policy toward Russia because Russia's foreign policy contradicts U.S. national interests. Stephen Sestanovich, ambassador at large and special adviser to the Secretary of State on the New Independent States, U.S. Department of State, was the sole voice of dissent. Not denying the presence of a multitude of problems in American-Russian relations, he nonetheless expressed optimism about the possibility of their resolution. His evaluation in this area is close to that of Strobe Talbott. This is not surprising because every government official in every country is always an optimist.

Russia "Presents a Threat to the United States, to the West, and to the Russian People."

This sentence was uttered by another conference participant, Ariel Cohen, a senior Russia expert whom I would list among the best Russia analysts in the United States. As befits a representative of the Heritage Foundation, he criticized the Clinton administration for its inadequate approach to Russia, following up on his criticism with recommendations about what to do about Moscow. His views reflect the approach of those circles in the USA who view Russia as "neither friend nor foe," but a state that must be made subordinate to U.S. interests at all costs.

Cohen attempts an appeal to realism. "The Clinton administration and Congress," writes Cohen, "need to realize that today's Russia with a gross domestic product only slightly higher than Indonesia's and lower than Mexico's, and a living standard like Brazil's—is not the global power its predecessor, the Soviet Union, was."[1] At the same time, under the leadership of Primakov (Russia's minister of foreign affairs in 1997), Moscow was forming a strategic alliance with Beijing and Teheran. The idea of a "multipolar world" and a "coalition of equals" may potentially be transformed into an anti-American Eurasian coalition. This introduces a serious threat to the security interests of the USA and its allies in Europe, in the Middle East, and the Pacific Ring. According to Cohen's information, "During 1996, over 3,000 Russian nuclear scientists moved to China to work on modernization of the PRC's strategic nuclear program. Russia signed agreements to transfer to China its advanced gas centrifuge technology, used in uranium enrichment, and nuclear missile technology to build multiple independently targeted re-entry vehicles (MIRVs), which can arm a single missile with up to twelve warheads. Russia also has agreed to sell the technology to build Sukhoi-27 fighters with mid-air re-

1 Cohen, "A New Paradigm for U.S.-Russian Relations: Facing the Post-Cold War Reality," Heritage Foundation *Backgrounder*, no. 1105 (March 6, 1997).

fueling capabilities, as well as advanced missile-armed destroyers, to the Chinese navy."

Cohen believes that in this kind of "strategic partnership," Russia is doomed to be the junior partner. Besides, Russia won't receive adequate repayment from China. His sole consolation is the fact that not everyone in Russia approves of this policy (Primakov's policy) toward China.

As for the USA, it "must pressure Russia to make her curtail the transfer of nuclear technology to China" or even to put an end to this process ("U.S. must stop it"). In his other writings, he also keeps emphasizing that a partnership between Russia, China, and Iran "presents a threat to the USA and its allies."[1]

In one chapter of Issues 2000: The Candidate's Briefing Book,[2] Cohen criticizes the Clinton administration in his usual style for its inadequate approach to Russia. In particular, he quotes the figure of $27 billion—money transferred to Russia through the IMF since 1992 that was not used as intended, i.e., for the rebuilding of the economy. Part of it was stolen in the bowels of the Central Bank of Russia and the Ministry of Finance; part of it was "possibly" used to fund the war in Chechnya. According to Cohen's information, since 1992 the Bush and Clinton administrations gave Russia financial aid to the tune of $4 billion, and helped in providing another $48 billion as multilateral aid in the form of loans from the IMF, the World Bank, and the Group of Seven industrial nations (G-7). (707)

Cohen considers it ridiculous that such help was provided against the background of anti-Western rhetoric that was characteristic of Yeltsin during the last year of his presidency. He lists Russia's anti-Western deeds, mentioning again the military-technological cooperation with China, Yevgeny Primakov's idea of a "three-member block" (Russia, China, and India), the sale of missile technology and nuclear reactors to Iran, limitations placed on religious freedoms, and the killing of civilians in Chechnya. (709–710)

1 Cohen, The *"Primakov Doctrine": Russia's Zero-Sum Game with the United States*, Heritage Foundation FYI, no. 167 (December 15, 1997).

2 Butler and Kim R. Holmes, eds., *Issues 2000: The Candidate's Briefing Book*..

Cohen thinks that the Clinton administration's main mistake is the illusion that Russia will become a democratic, market-economy country of the Western type. It is not happening, which means that the desired result requires a different approach and a different policy.

Here is what Cohen, i.e., the Heritage Foundation, suggests:

First, if the IMF is to make loans, it must have full control on how the monies are used. If Russia is to receive these loans, she must agree to a long list of conditions, including the demonopolization of the natural gas, power-generation, fuel, and transportation sectors of the economy, the liberalization of agriculture (i.e., adoption of the law on private ownership of land), and reduction of defense expenditures, etc. Second, the USA must dump the ABM Treaty of 1972. Third, it must force Russia to stop providing technological assistance to Iran and Iraq. Fourth, the USA must give more effective support to market reforms in Russia. Fifth, it must support the sovereignty, independence, and civil societies of the New Independent States, including Ukraine, the Trans-Caucasus, the Baltic countries, and the states of Central Asia. (713–716)

To the question of whether Russia is "a threat to America," Cohen gives this answer: "Russia was dangerous in its strength and can be a danger in its weakness. Its arsenal of weapons of mass destruction and the technologies to produce them is leaking to countries that are hostile to America. Russia still has the largest nuclear arsenal outside the United States and is the only country that is capable of obliterating the United States." (719) Elsewhere, he writes: "Russia is emerging as a potentially troubling actor in world affairs." (703)

It is symptomatic that, unlike many Western observers and scholars who pin their hopes on Putin as a president capable of suppressing corruption and stabilizing the Russian economy, Cohen confidently predicts the opposite. He writes: "Instead, the people Putin has selected for his cabinet may serve only to exacerbate the problems that encumbered Russia under Yeltsin. As huge insider business deals and the war in Chechnya continue, President Clinton should be under no illusion that he will find a 'reformist' Russian president coming to the summit table."[1] And further: "Given Putin's decisions and appointments, the new Kremlin appears unlikely to veer far from the path carved out by the Yeltsin regime. This means that the Clinton administration should not confuse its need to establish a working relationship with Putin with its desires to help Russia develop democratic institutions and a free market." (ibid.)

It is something worth underscoring that, though many in the USA are skeptical about Russia in general and Putin in particular, Cohen is one of the few who voices their skepticism directly. Most importantly, his evaluations are correct and will certainly be confirmed by the subsequent course of events.

1 Cohen, "Summit Rhetoric Aside, Putin's New Cabinet Makes Russian Reforms Less Likely," Heritage Foundation *Executive Memorandum*, no. 675 (June 1, 2000).

The Nixon Center: talk softly, carry a big stick

I was about to send this manuscript to the publishing house when I came across a number of writings from the Nixon Center that is starting to acquire a certain weight in the scientific-political centers of America. The Center is rather close to the Republican Party in its ideology, but its evaluations of China and Russia are more balanced than, say, those of the Heritage Foundation. For example, David M. Lampton and Gregory C. May argue quite justifiably that rather than an "arms race," North-East Asia is experiencing an "arms modernization race." It suffices to analyze the dynamics of military expenditures growth relative to GDP in the 1990s[1]. In the same vein, they advise against exaggerating China's military potential. China's armed forces may be the world's biggest in terms of manpower, but in quality, they are far inferior to the Japanese Self-Defense Forces, to say nothing of the American armed forces (ii).

Nonetheless, they do find grounds for disquietude, but unlike the many authors who usually mention in this connection the situation in the Taiwan Strait and the strengthening of China's nuclear arsenal, these two add "deep and lingering Sino-Japanese animosity" (iii). The latter is fuelled by Tokyo's intentions to become a "normal power" in defense; Beijing is opposed to that. On the other hand, Japan shows its unease in connection with China's possibility of turning into the world's biggest military-political power. Therefore, there are objective reasons for mutual suspicions and hostility.

Among other recommendations, the authors suggest engaging China in bilateral and multilateral negotiations on arms control: between the USA, China and Russia on the global level and between the USA, China and Japan on the regional level (vii). The regional-level talks must be institutionalized as a Forum on North-East Asia (NEA). The authors also recommend reducing the numbers of front-line American troops in East Asia (currently numbering about 100,000 men) (ix).

---

1 Lampton and May. *A Big Power Agenda for East Asia: America, China, and Japan*, iii.

Rather curious are their evaluations of the Russian military strength in the Far East. The authors write: "The Russian military presence in the Far East is a shell of its former self. Towards the end of the Cold War, the Soviet Union stationed 56 divisions, 1,420 combat aircraft, 73 surface combatants, and 112 submarines in its Far Eastern Strategic Theater and Pacific Fleet. Now, Russia's presence is down to 17 divisions, 415 combat aircraft, 10 surface combatants, and 17 submarines" (28). They also note: "For the 17 divisions that have remained in the region, long periods of unpaid salaries and disappearing benefits are the norm, as they are in many parts of Russia."

The economic situation in the Far East doesn't look any better. Some 800,000 people have left the Far East. Those who remain feel themselves very uncomfortable. One former border guard and resident of Vladivostok pessimistically told Time magazine, "Between the masses of China and the wealth of Japan, our days are numbered. The only question is to whom we surrender" (ibid.).

The authors believe that despite the proclamation of "strategic partnership," China and Russia are not likely to help each other substantially in connection with NATO expansion on the one hand and the Taiwan Strait situation, on the other hand. Also, one shouldn't overestimate Russia's military assistance to China. A more serious cause for worry is the Russian scientists' eagerness to work in Chinese military laboratories and production facilities.

At the same time, it would be foolish to discount Russia altogether when analyzing East Asia. Should Russia's economy be resurrected, the natural riches of Siberia and the Far East can play an important role in the region's economy. Therefore, the goal should be "to have more productive relations with both Russia and China than they have with each other" (30).

In another collective work, we find this recommendation: to avoid Russia's becoming "a spoiler," America must try to avoid actions that provoke Russia and push it toward close relations with China and other countries (India, Iran, Iraq, North Korea) that seek to limit U.S. nuclear strength.[1]

In the Caspian Sea region, a two-layer policy must be implemented: on the one hand, Russia's legitimate interests should be

1 *What Is to Be Undone? A Russia Policy Agenda for the New Administration*, 3,7.

acknowledged to contain its expansionist behavior; on the other hand, friendly relations should be established with other post-Soviet states, without giving them promises of support, since the U.S. likely won't be able to deliver it. Especially since this region, even though it is important to the USA, is not included in the sphere of "vital interests" (11).

Generally speaking, these recommendations are a little different from those of the Heritage Foundation, except for the tonality and hierarchical precision. The essence is the same: more efficient, more profitable ways to establish U.S. leadership in the world, enabling them as the sole superpower to ensure both their own and international security. This desire is very natural when your country is superior to all the rest almost by order of magnitude. The question is, how long will this superiority last?

Condoleezza Rice: Geostrategy Without Illusions

I think the Americans got lucky. The position of national security adviser is currently occupied by Condoleezza "Condi" Rice, senior fellow at the Hoover Institution and professor of political science at Stanford University. It appears to me that she is the one who formulated the most optimal variant of Washington's foreign policy, corresponding to U.S. national interests. (I emphasize U.S. interests, not those of, say, Russia or China.) A detailed exposition of her views was published in *Foreign Affairs* before she assumed her important government post.[1]

At first sight, it would appear that she lists the same U.S. "interests" that were included in the "interest list" of the Clinton administration. But close comparison shows that Rice's list does not include "humanitarian issues" (human rights, democracy, etc.). The military aspect features more strongly. Finally, she emphasizes interaction with the big powers like Russia and China first, rather than the entire "world community."

This approach, theoretically derived from different concepts of power, is based on the realities of the geostrategic situation in the world, rather than on ideological differences between states. Rice justifiably believes that Americans should first defend the national interests of the USA, not "humanitarian causes" or the interests of "the international community" (as the Clinton administration was in the habit of doing). Rice qualifies her statement, saying that these latter interests, of course, should not be discounted absolutely. She simply emphasizes that they are realized through the process of securing national interests within the framework of a geostrategic (power) approach. In this connection, she cites the eloquent example of Russia. The introduction of democracy in the USSR (a favorite topic of Jimmy Carter) was accomplished thanks

1 Rice, "Campaign 2000: Promoting the National Interests," *Foreign Affairs* (January/February 2001).

to Reagan's geostrategic pressure. The Soviets lost the power struggle, and right away they embraced democracy and other freedoms. This accomplishment was the result of harsh play on the geostrategic field.

Equally deserved is her criticism of the Clinton administration for signing different multilateral agreements she claims are useless for at least two reasons: Either they do not involve some states on which the functioning of the agreement depends, or the fulfillment of the agreement's terms cannot be controlled. The Kyoto treaty on global warming is of the first kind because it does not include China and a number of underdeveloped states that do considerable damage to the environment on the global scale. The second kind includes, for example, the Comprehensive Test Ban Treaty.

In general, Rice is skeptical (I am entirely in agreement with her on this point) about all kinds of "norms" of international behavior. They are nothing but illusions. "Norms" are defined by the interests of great powers, not by abstract notions of justice or other humanitarian considerations. She is absolutely right when she says: "The reality is that a few big powers can radically affect international peace, stability, and prosperity." Norms, values, democracy, and so on may be good topics for discussion in academic circles, but not in real politics. Proceeding from this assumption, Rice strongly promotes the idea that it is necessary for the USA to be strong, first of all in the military sense. This military strength must be used to attain geostrategic goals, not for "realization of our values," say, in the framework of a "humanitarian intervention," though even these cannot be ruled out a priori. (In this regard, she criticizes U.S. interventions in Haiti and Somali.)

Rice disapproves of the Clinton administration's excessive attention to "humanitarian" aspects in its policy toward China. She believes these issues should be resolved through other, non-intrusive methods (student exchanges, support of private enterprise, etc.). However, her main point is something different: "This means that China is not a 'status quo' power but one that would like to alter Asia's balance of power in its own favor. That alone makes it a strategic competitor, not the 'strategic partner' the Clinton administration once called it." She suggests: "U.S. policy toward China requires nuance and balance. It is important to promote China's internal transition through economic interaction while containing Chinese power and security ambitions. Cooperation should be pursued, but we should never be afraid to confront Beijing when our interests collide."

One may disagree with such forcefulness, but this approach stems from the laws of international relations, where power rules rather than good intentions.

Please note how clearly Rice ties real national interests of the USA with its security policy. Politics is money, and money should be spent on real interests rather than imaginary or ill-defined ones. If the declared goal is the accomplishment of real interests, one must go all the way, using military means if needed, instead of sticking to empty rhetoric about "peace in the entire world." That is the main thrust of the political realist Condoleezza Rice.

Rice is considered an expert on Russia. Indeed, she has studied the military policy of USSR/Russia for a long time. This proved to be insufficient, though, to properly evaluate the prospects of the domestic political and economic situation in Russia. In this area, she makes the same mistake as almost all U.S. political scientists. She describes the current situation in critical tones, calling Russia's economy a "mutant" with "leftovers of the Middle Ages." She is also critical of the IMF loans to Russia, the quality of the country's leadership, and other negative things. In this area, her evaluations coincide word for word with those of the Heritage Foundation. But it seems to her that to overcome these negatives, what is needed is time and the advent of a new generation; then everything will be okay, like in the West. All these Russia experts do not understand that Russia will never digest capitalism of the Western type, nor will it ever have democracy or markets in the Western sense. No American expert will ever understand this—never. That is their strategic mistake about Russia.

Nonetheless, Rice believes there is no need to pay much attention to all these things; one must proceed from the knowledge that Russia "still has many of the attributes of a great power: a large population, vast territory, and military potential." She takes leave of logic at this point because only a page earlier she wrote that "India is not a great power yet, but it has the potential to emerge as one." But she ought to know that India's population is almost seven times greater than Russia's, and its territory is pretty big, too. It follows that Russia only has one attribute of a great power: strategic nuclear might.

So what is to be done about Russia? Rice suggests concentrating first on security problems. She writes: "First, it must recognize that American security is threatened less by Russia's strength than by its weakness and incoherence." The subtext is that a weak Russia may be unable to control the proliferation of nuclear weapons and military technologies. In this connection, she appeals for a full-scale realization of the Nunn-Lugar program (funding for the implementation of the SALT-2 Treaty). Second, it is necessary to concentrate on negotiations about nuclear threats. In her opinion, Russian military leaders started paying too much attention to nuclear weapons because of the shrinking of their conventional arsenal. "The Russian deterrent is more than adequate against the U.S. nuclear arsenal, and vice versa." Her idea is that it needs to be reduced. This is followed by a noteworthy but: "But that fact need no longer be enshrined in a treaty that is almost thirty years old and is a relic of a profoundly adversarial relationship between the United States and the Soviet Union."

She means the Anti-Ballistic Missile Treaty of 1972. It should be scrapped because new nuclear threats exist now (for example, North Korea and Iran), as does the possibility of proliferation of nuclear technologies from Russia and their falling into bad hands. Therefore: "It would be foolish in the extreme to share defenses with Moscow if it either leaks or deliberately transfers weapons technologies to the very states against which America is defending." In other words, the USA must rely on itself and not have its hands tied by the ABM Treaty because Russia continues to cooperate with "rogue states."

"Finally, the United States needs to recognize that Russia is a great power, and that we will always have interests that conflict as well as coincide."

In my opinion, Rice is justified when she suggests scrapping the ABM Treaty of 1972 because it was signed in a different historical situation, when the arrangement of geostrategic forces was different. Everything has changed since then; therefore, treaties should be changed or renewed—especially because any international document only reflects the real balance of powers in the world without changing it. I think Russia's leaders will be forced to put up with the United States's rejection of the ABM Treaty, just as the Soviet Union's leaders put up with the violation of the Yalta system proclaiming the inviolability of borders in Europe. The events of the late 1980s and early 1990s showed that borders can indeed be violated.

On the whole, one has to admit that Condoleezza Rice has logically formulated certain principles and foundations of the current Republican administration's foreign policy, suggesting a more optimal way of realizing national interests than the Clinton administration.

Chapter III

Official U.S. Strategic Doctrines: A View of the World and of Russia

All aspects of U.S. international activity are usually described in a number of official documents prepared by the National Security Council, the Department of State, the Department of Defense, and the Central Intelligence Agency. The most general kinds, intended for the general public, are published as annual reports or strategic documents. At the NSC, the corresponding document is titled *A National Strategy for a New Century; at the Department of Defense, Annual Report to the President and the Congress; at the Department of State, The United States Strategic Plan for International Affairs; and at the CIA, Annual Report for the United States Intelligence Community (Director of Central Intelligence).*

I will be using the latest editions of all these documents, referring, if necessary, to previous editions. I will consciously avoid detailed commentaries, limiting myself to making some remarks, so that readers can draw appropriate conclusions themselves.

It makes sense to start with the Strategy as the primary document because it is considered presidential and, in general, reflects Washington's official view of the world. The Twenty-First Century: The World Without Russia

A National Security Strategy for a New Century[1]

In the foreword, supposedly penned by the president, the status of the USA is defined right away: "The United States remains the world's most powerful force for peace, prosperity, and the universal values of democracy and freedom."

The objectives of U.S. strategy are to enhance America's security, to bolster America's economic prosperity, and to promote democracy and human rights abroad.

The strategy indicates that the main characteristic of the twenty-first century will be globalization, which is defined as "the process of accelerating economic, technological, cultural, and political integration." At the same time, it is noted that globalization will be accompanied by different kinds of "challenges" and risks that will affect the security of the USA. The most important risks are weapons of mass destruction (WMD), terrorism, drug trafficking and other international crime, resource depletion, rapid population growth, environmental damage, new infectious diseases, pervasive corruption, and uncontrolled refugee migration.

The document clearly defines U.S. national interests, divided into three categories: vital interests, important national interests, and humanitarian and other interests. The vital interests are those that relate "to the survival, safety, and vitality of our nation." "Among these are the physical security of our territory and that of our allies, the safety of our citizens, the economic well-being of our society, and the protection of our critical infrastructures—including energy, banking and finance, telecommunications, transportation, water systems, and emergency services—from paralyzing attack. We will do what we must to defend these interests, including, when necessary and appropriate, using our military might unilaterally and decisively."(1)

1 *A National Strategy For a New Century* (The White House, December 1999).

"The important national interests are those that do not affect our national survival, but they do affect our national well-being and the character of the world in which we live. Important national interests include, for example, regions in which we have a sizable economic stake or commitments to allies, protecting the global environment from severe harm, and crises with a potential to generate substantial and highly destabilizing refugee flows, such as the conflicts in Bosnia and Kosovo, etc."

"The humanitarian interests are promoting human rights and seeking to halt gross violations of those rights; supporting democratization, adherence to the rule of law and civilian control of the military; assisting humanitarian demining; and promoting sustainable development and environmental protection."

Curiously enough, threats to U.S. interests include threats originating from so-called failed states. These latter include, among others, the countries that "though possessing the capacity to govern—may succumb to the inflammatory rhetoric of demagogues who blame their nation's ills on and persecute specific religious, cultural, racial, or tribal groups. States that fail to respect the rights of their own citizens and tolerate or actively engage in human rights abuses, ethnic cleansing, or acts of genocide not only harm their own people, but can spark civil wars and refugee crises and spill across national boundaries to destabilize a region." (2) Anyone knowledgeable about the situation in Russia understands that this "bit" of the document is dedicated specifically to Russia.

Let us note the following: The main characteristics of the twent-first century are: (1) globalization; (2) multitude of "challenges" and risks; and (3) leadership of the USA as the greatest power in the world. The three strategic goals (security, prosperity, and democracy) practically coincide with the three categories of interests (vital, important, and humanitarian). Now let's move on to Russia.

Russia. In the document we are analyzing, we are interested only in Russia, or rather, the context in which Russia is mentioned or not mentioned. As was to be expected, Russia is represented in the part about arms control, where the START II Treaty between USA and USSR is mentioned, as well as the Helsinki (March 1997) agreement between the presidents of USA and Russia about the possibility of negotiations on a START III agreement.

Regarding initiatives for nonproliferation of WMD, we read that: "We are purchasing tons of highly enriched uranium from dismantled Russian nuclear weapons for conversion into commercial reactor fuel, and working with Russia to remove 34 metric tons of plutonium from each country's nuclear weapons programs and converting it so that it can never be used in nuclear weapons. We are redirecting dozens of former Soviet WMD facilities and tens of thousands of former Soviet WMD scientists in Eastern Europe and Eurasia from military activities to beneficial civilian research." (9)

It is important to identify Russia's role in U.S. policy's regional directions. In the part dedicated to Europe, Russia is discussed not as a separate power but together with Ukraine and other CIS countries. The document expresses satisfaction with the process of NATO development and NATO cooperation with Russia (and with Ukraine) on the basis of the 1997 NATO–Russia Founding Act. The U.S. goal is to help "deepen and expand constructive Russian participation in the European security system." (30)

In the sub-chapter dedicated to the CIS, it is stated that U.S. vital security interests are best served by the evolution of Russia, Ukraine, and other CIS countries into democratic market economies integrated into the world community. There are many qualifications, though, implying that the road to democracy is thorny and difficult—in short, far from completion. Yet, "It is in our national interest to help them build the laws, institutions, and skills needed for a market democracy, to fight crime and corruption, and to advance human rights and the rule of law." (32) Naturally, as soon as human rights are mentioned, the authors remember Chechnya, and in this connection they are sad that "the means Russia is pursuing in Chechnya are undermining its legitimate objective of upholding its territorial integrity and protecting citizens from terrorism and lawlessness." (32)

The strategy also indicates: "We are working aggressively to strengthen export controls (meaning armaments) in Russia and the other NIS and to stem proliferation of sensitive missile and nuclear technology to countries of concern such as Iran." (ibid.)

The strategy expresses satisfaction at the fact that although Russia was dissatisfied with NATO expansion and the Kosovo conflict, Russian units served shoulder-to-shoulder with NATO troops in Kosovo and Bosnia. In this connection, "The United States remains committed to further development of the NATO–Russia *re-*

lationship and the NATO–Ukraine *distinctive partnership*." (ibid.) Note the words I italicized: distinctive partnership for Ukraine, but plain relationship for Russia. The authors have no doubt there is nothing Russia can do—no matter how loudly its leaders oppose NATO expansion to the East. As for the other sub-regions (East Asia, the Pacific Ocean, Southeast Asia, the Western hemisphere, the Middle East, South Asia, Africa), *Russia is not mentioned at all in any capacity.*

From all this, the conclusion follows that in U.S. strategic policy, Russia only enters into consideration in two issues: the reduction of nuclear weapons and the imposition of the NATO concept of security in Europe. Moreover, it is stated directly that America's positive attitude toward Russia is dependent on the latter staying on the course of capitalist reforms, i.e., the course toward democracy and market economy, which suits U.S. national interests. The other important thing to note is that in all regions except Europe, Russia has ceased to be taken into consideration by the USA.

United States: Strategic Plan for International Affairs[1]

Let us now pore over the State Department document. Not only Russian readers but even some American readers are unable to figure out the difference between this document and the one analyzed previously. At first sight, both appear to address the same set of issues.

The *National Security Strategy* singles out the administration's priorities in terms of policy and the tools used to deflect principal threats to U.S. international security. It refers to the functions of the Department of Defense and the intelligence community under the direction of the president. The State Department's document, on the other hand, develops a complex, systematic vision of U.S. national interests. Moreover, the *Plan* formulates U.S. goals in the international arena and defines the activities of government agencies abroad. This Plan is not a strategic plan for foreign policy. Note this difference: "International affairs is a big tent that covers the full range of U.S. national interests. These range from traditional high policy issues related to ensuring national security and maintaining international economic stability, to protecting American citizens abroad and responding to global challenges to health and the environment. In contrast, foreign policy as used here is the integral part of international affairs that focuses on the conduct of relations with other nation states and international organizations in pursuit of these national interests." (4)

The *Plan* also explains the difference between national interests and strategic goals. Strategic goals reflect intentions that are realized through strategy, programs, and actions, while national interests are formulated in order to explain why these things are

---

1 *United States. Strategic Plan for International Affairs* (Department of State, Washington, D.C., First Revision, February 1999). In September of the following year, the next edition of the State Department's Strategic Plan came out, but it is no different in content from the previous one, except for some organizational details.

done. "To illustrate, the United States spends about $900 million each year on programs that support democracy around the world. Although our democracy goals are similar across countries, the interests we pursue vary greatly. Our investment in Russia's democracy stems primarily from our national security interests, whereas in Haiti it is our concern over immigration, and in Sri Lanka our values lead us to support democracy for its own sake. This logic applies to all seven of the national interests and goals in the Plan. We have also introduced the general principle in the IASP of linkages among multiple strategic goals and national interests. Thus, in Russia the democracy goal supports not only our interests in national security, but in human rights, democracy, and law enforcement as well. In the IASP, these general linkages are identified in the national interest statements."

The English language has many words that are rendered in Russian by one and the same word, "цель", pronounced tsel; therefore, it is necessary to know the nuances of meaning and the specific uses of these English words. In the State Department's *Strategic Plan* of 1997, for example, the difference is clearly specified between the words goal and objective. Thus, the *Strategic Goal* is the reduction of threats to the United States and its allies, stemming from weapons of mass destruction or destabilizing conventional weapons. The *Operational Goal* is the strengthening of the multilateral regime in support of nonproliferation of nuclear weapons, control over exports of these weapons, and nuclear self-defense in the international arena. The *Objective* or *Performance Goal* involves multilateral negotiations on a Fissile Material Cut-off Treaty by the first quarter of Financial Year 1999. (9) In other words, *objective* is a concrete goal with a set time frame for its accomplishment, while *goal* is a matter of principle, with no definite time set for its accomplishment. The following *Plan* for U.S. foreign policy should be perceived precisely in the light of the above-described nuances.

According to the *Plan*, U.S. national interests can be summed up in the following seven items:

- Protect vital interests, secure peace, deter aggression, prevent and defuse crises, halt the proliferation of weapons of mass destruction, and advance arms control and disarmament.

- Expand exports, open markets, maintain global growth and stability, and promote economic development.
- Protect American citizens abroad, manage the entry of visitors and immigrants, and safeguard the borders of the United States.
- Combat international terrorism, crime, and narcotics trafficking.
- Support the establishment and consolidation of democracies, and uphold human rights.
- Provide humanitarian assistance to victims of crisis and disaster.
- Improve the global environment, achieve a sustainable world population, and protect human health.

The realization of these interests should result in "a more secure, prosperous, and democratic world for the benefit of the American people." (2)

The following items are the international affairs strategic goals:

- *Regional Stability:* Strengthen the security of the United States and prevent instabilities from threatening the vital and important interests of the United States and its allies.
- *Weapons Of Mass Destruction:* Reduce the threat to the United States and its allies from weapons of mass destruction (WMD).
- *Open Markets:* Open world markets to increase trade and free the flow of goods, services, and capital.
- *U.S. Exports:* Expand U.S. exports to $1.2 trillion early in the twenty-first century.
- *Global Growth and Stability:* Increase global economic growth and stability.
- *Economic Development:* Promote broad-based growth in developing and transitional economies to raise standards of living and lessen disparities of wealth within and among countries.
- *American Citizens:* Protect the safety and security of American citizens who travel and live abroad.
- *Travel and Migration:* Manage fairly and effectively the entry of

immigrants and foreign visitors into the United States.

- *International Crime:* Minimize the impact of international crime on the United States and its citizens.
- *Illegal Drugs:* Reduce the entry of illegal drugs into the United States.
- *Counter-terrorism:* Reduce the number and impact of international terrorist attacks, especially on the United States and its citizens.
- *Democracy and Human Rights:* Open political systems and societies to democratic practices, the rule of law, good governance, and respect for human rights.
- *Humanitarian Assistance:* Provide humanitarian assistance to victims of crisis and disaster.
- *Environment:* Secure a sustainable global environment, and protect the United States and its citizens from the effects of international environmental degradation.
- *Population:* Achieve a sustainable world population.
- *Health:* Protect human health and reduce the spread of infectious diseases. (10)

Russia. Once again, we are interested in knowing where and in what context Russia is mentioned in this document.

In the section *Strategic Goal: Regional Stability*, we find: "Russia and China present potential long-term security challenges. However, the likelihood of a direct military threat to United States vital interests is limited." (12) It is also worth noting that in the section about U.S. exports as a strategic goal, by necessity, the focus is on emerging markets such as Argentina, Mexico, Brazil, Poland, Turkey, South Africa, India, China, Taiwan, Korea (South), Indonesia, Thailand, Malaysia, and other ASEAN countries. Russia is not even mentioned.

At the same time, in the section called Strategic Goal: International Crime, mentioned first among the countries and regions to concentrate on in this connection are the former Soviet Union, Nigeria, and East Asia.

Russia is mentioned one more time in the section about the environment.

Annual Report to the President and the Congress[1]

Let us now move on to the *Annual Report to the President and the Congress* by the Secretary of Defense. We will take up the report prepared by William Cohen in the years 2000 and 2001. We are interested in the general statements, assessments about the world, and the Pentagon's military policy, presented in the first part of the Report, called "The Defense Strategy."

The document states that though a global war is not expected in the twenty-first century, "challenges" to U.S. security will remain and even multiply. Foremost among these challenges is the possibility of aggression or threats from Iraq and North Korea. There is the reminder that: "In East Asia, for example, sovereignty issues and several territorial disputes remain potential sources of conflict. Many instances of cross-border aggression will be small-scale in nature; but between now and 2015, it is entirely possible that more than one aspiring regional power will have both the motivation and the means to pose a military threat to U.S. interests." (2) In general: "Even when important U.S. interests are not threatened, the United States may have a humanitarian interest in protecting the safety, well-being, and freedom of the people affected." (ibid.) Therefore, every Russian citizen whose security and well-being cannot be protected by his country's authorities has the opportunity to ask the USA for help.

Listed among "challenges" are the spread of potentially dangerous technologies, international terrorism, organized crime, information wars, etc., that can directly threaten the United States. Mentioned among threat sources are failed states because of their inability to resolve domestic problems.

Subsequently, the *Report* repeats the theses of the Presidential *National Security Strategy* concerning U.S. national interests in the international arena. Curiously, the Pentagon's reformula-

1 Cohen, Secretary of Defense, *Annual Report to the President and the Congress* (Department of Defense, 2000).

tion of vital interests adds one important line that is absent in the Strategy, namely: "Preventing the emergence of hostile regional coalitions or hegemons." (4)

U.S. defense strategy to the year 2015 proceeds not just from the *Strategy's* theses but also from the 1997 report known as the *1997 Report of the Quadrennial Review,*[1] also prepared in the name of the Secretary of Defense. This strategy consists of three elements: shaping, responding, and preparing; each section describes in detail the Pentagon's activities for ensuring U.S. military security. The analysis of purely military aspects of Washington's policy is outside the scope of this work, so let us proceed directly to the place and role of Russia in U.S. military strategy.

Russia. In the section on states that may potentially challenge U.S. security, in the subsection "A Global Peer Competitor," the following is said about Russia and China: "The United States faces no global rival today, nor will it likely face one through at least 2015. In the period beyond 2015, however, there is the possibility that a regional great power or global peer competitor could emerge. China and Russia appear to have the most potential to be such competitors, though their respective futures are quite uncertain. China's economy has been growing rapidly, and the People's Liberation Army continues to modernize and increase its capability. China already has a strategic nuclear arsenal that, while not large, can reach the continental United States. China is likely to continue to face a number of internal challenges, however, both economic and political, that may slow the pace of its military modernization.

"Russia could, in the coming years, re-establish its capability to project large-scale offensive military forces along its periphery, but this would require substantial preparation that would be visible to the United States. While Russia continues to retain a large nuclear arsenal with both tactical and strategic weapons, its conventional military capabilities—both in terms of power projection and combat sustainability—have weakened significantly. Russia's future will depend in large measure on its ability to develop its economy, which in turn is dependent upon a stable internal political environment. Should Russia's political system fail to stabi-

1 This document is one of the national defense reviews published every four years under the Defense Secretary's name, under different titles.

lize over the long term, disintegration of Russia as a coherent state could pose major security challenges for the United States and the international community." (2–3) Thus, Russia is listed among the factors that comprise "the uncertain future."

In the section "Regional Components of U.S. Strategy in Europe," Russia is mentioned in the context of its relations with NATO, and in more detail about its relations with CIS countries. In connection with U.S. defense goals, the following is said: "The United States seeks the development of Russia, Ukraine, and the other New Independent States into stable market democracies fully integrated into the international community and cooperative partners in promoting regional security and stability, arms control, and counter proliferation. Integral to this goal is U.S. support of efforts to secure and stem the proliferation risk posed by former Soviet NBC weapons, weapons materials, and associated delivery systems or technologies, and to eliminate any former Soviet nuclear delivery systems remaining in the New Independent States other than Russia. ...The United States wants to further develop the NATO–Russian partnership, as well as the NATO–Ukraine partnership promoting Ukraine's integration into European and Euro-Atlantic institutions." (10)

It is worth noting some nuances of the similar Report of 2001.[1]

First, the section on proliferation of dangerous technologies now includes this line: "Moreover, the possibility of an accidental or unauthorized launch from Russia or China remains a concern, albeit an unlikely one." (2)

Second, while the previous Report said that a global rival to the U.S. is unlikely to emerge before 2015, the Report of 2001 replaced the date 2015 with the words "the foreseeable future." That is, the authors decided to be cautious about time frames. The subtext is that they expect such a rival to emerge before 2015. The same section contains a noteworthy addition: "It is not clear, however, whether China will pursue a path that is inimical to U.S. interests." (ibid.) The section on Russia now contains the phrase that U.S. security may be threatened by "the inability of central authorities to maintain a coherent state [that] could pose major security chal-

1 Cohen, Secretary of Defense, *Annual Report to the President and the Congress* (Department of Defense, 2001).

lenges for the United States and the international community." (3)

Third, the section on relations with New Independent States now mentions the Caucasus and Central Asia: "The United States also seeks a peaceful resolution to the ethnic and regional tensions throughout the NIS." (13)

The most noteworthy fact is this: In the discussion of all other regions—East Asia and the Pacific Ocean, the Middle East and South Asia, Latin America and sub-Saharan Africa—Russia is not mentioned in any context. This is true of all Reports since 1995. Therefore, we can safely say that in official U.S. military documents, Russia is viewed as a regional power only in the European context.

The CIA Writes About the World and Russia

The CIA's *Annual Reports*[1] differ from the documents discussed above in that they are brief, clear, and frank (at least the part not intended for the general public). Due to the nature of its function, the CIA doesn't use the category "challenges" and operates instead with the category "threats."

The 1999 *Report* points out right away, without undue "philosophizing": "There are two categories of threats that will occupy the Intelligence Community's attention[2] in the foreseeable future: threats from our strategic rivals—China and Russia—as well as from regional worries such as North Korea, Iran, and Iraq; and the transnational threats—organized crime, narcotics trafficking, proliferation, information warfare, and terrorism." Accordingly, U.S. strategic priorities must be ranked in this order: China, Cuba, Iran, North Korea, and then Russia.

This means that in the terms of the documents discussed previously, Russia and China fall into the category of "rogue nations," i.e., the group of countries that are regarded at the official level in the USA as the countries most dangerous for the security of the United States and the entire world. Curiously enough, in the preceding *Report* of 1998 that reviewed the situation in 1997, the above-mentioned countries were listed among so-called "Hard Target countries," i.e., countries subject to the heightened attention of U.S. intelligence. In this context, Russia was characterized as a country experiencing serious social and economic difficulties, including rampant crime and corruption, and China was described

1 *Annual Report on FY 1997 Intelligence Community Activities*, Director of Central Intelligence, Annual Report for the United States Intelligence Community (May 1999).

2 The Intelligence Community (IC) is a widely branching, informal intelligence organization consisting of many government and nongovernment departments, agencies, and associations. Along with the CIA, it includes the FBI, the NSA, and certain bureaus of the Departments of State and Defense.

as a state that intends to become a superpower in the next century. The CIA Report of 1999 mentions that the CIA had analyzed the impact of the financial crisis in Russia on WMD programs and identified Russia's increasing dependence on Western financial aid to dismantle nuclear and chemical weapons. In the CIA director's opinion, this information provided the administration with a motive to continue financing WMD programs, and could be used by top U.S. officials to assess subsequent Russian requests for financial assistance. The CIA also supplied additional information on two occasions when governments were changed in Russia, and on the occasion of the Clinton–Yeltsin summit.

The *Report* indicates the CIA was implementing a program for improving the quality and speed of translation of materials from the Russian press. The Department of State Bureau of Intelligence and Research also managed the $4.6 million Research and Training Program on Eastern Europe and the NIS, which seeks to build U.S. expertise on those regions by providing assistance to more than 1,200 graduate students and senior scholars annually.

When CIA Director George Tenet presented to the Senate his report, *The Worldwide Threat in 2000: Global Realities of our National Security*, on February 2, 2000,[1] Russia was discussed in the context of different "threats." First, Russia was mentioned together with China and North Korea in connection with supplies to Iran of components for ballistic missiles and corresponding technology. Second, Russia was recognized as one of the hotbeds of international organized crime, with references made to Russian officials (no names mentioned). It is stated that in Russia itself, organized crime has infiltrated important sectors in the economy, including those that dealt with strategic resources such as oil, coal, and aluminum.

In its discussion of regional problems, the CIA started with Russia. Describing the possible shifts in policy in Russia, Tenet declined to state which of them was most likely to occur, citing the uncertainty of Putin's conduct as president. At the same time he "suggested" to Moscow some "more positive directions" that amount to support for the final resolution of the matter of START II and

1 Tenet, "Statement by Director of Central Intelligence before the Senate Select Committee on Intelligence on the Worldwide Threat in 2000: Global Realities of Our National Security" (February 2, 2000).

transition to the next phase of arms reduction through START III; and expressed the desire that Russia's leaders would go in for a deeper integration of their country into the world economy, be it through continuing cooperation within the G-8 group or through WTO membership.

At the same time, regardless of all this, the USA is primarily concerned about the storage of nuclear weapons and their components in Russia. In Tenet's words: "Russia's economic difficulties continue to weaken the reliability of nuclear personnel and Russia's system for securing fissile material. We have no evidence that weapons are missing in Russia, but we remain concerned by reports of lax discipline, labor strikes, poor morale, and criminal activities at nuclear storage facilities."

John Gannon, chairman of the National Intelligence Council (NIC), has a somewhat different view of international relations and Russia's place in the world.[1] He believes the USA is currently the sole superpower, but it will not be a hegemon because other states will attempt to change the future of the world. These "others" include the European Union (EU), Japan, Russia, and China.

Above all, shifts in power alliances are caused by the growing economic and political power of the EU and East Asia, and also by the possible (after some time) shrinking of the sphere of American internationalization (i.e., shrinking of the sphere of U.S. international influence). It is unclear how this process will unfurl, due to the uncertainty about the development of several key states. In Gannon's opinion, the EU gives no cause to worry, for it will maintain close ties to the USA through NATO, one way or another. The same applies to Japan and South Korea.

As for Russia, its pretensions of maintaining the status of a great power are based solely on its stockpile of nuclear weapons. In the next fifteen years, Gannon thinks, Russia will likely concentrate on rebuilding its economy. At the same time, it will be troubled by the contradiction between its shrinking possibilities and the passionate desire of a part of the elite to preserve great-power status.

---

1 Remarks by Gannon (Chairman, National Intelligence Council), "The CIA in the New World Order: Intelligence Challenges Through 2015" (February 1, 2000).

China will modernize and grow stronger, though the direction of its development will depend on domestic policy and economic progress.

Most importantly, "the risk of conflict between great powers remains low." In the event of a return to multipolarity as U.S. influence in the world shrinks, the biggest dangers will be ethnic conflicts in East Asia and possibly Europe.

Gannon concludes that in the period up to 2015, no country, ideology, or movement will become a threat to U.S. interests on a global level. On the regional level, however, the policies of certain countries may clash with U.S. interests, and international threats, such as terrorism, are to be expected. Some unfortunate "if" scenarios may become reality. For instance, China may fail to resolve the problem of Taiwan by peaceful means. Russia may turn toward authoritarianism, or, on the contrary, it may be consumed by anarchy and disintegration. By the way, Gannon makes a prediction about Russia: "And Russia's population is likely to shrink—perhaps substantially—as a result of declining life expectancy, which is linked to poor health care, as well as declining birth rates."

Gannon develops these ideas in more detail in his report dedicated specifically to Russia.[1] He argues that by now, Russia has "elements of the market system," but on the whole, "Russia is neither a command economy, nor a market economy." The political transformation in Russia is possibly turning toward "renewed authoritarianism."

Gannon is not much concerned about the relations between Russia and China because: "We do not see the emergence of a full-blown alliance with coordinated positions and actions on all issues." From the strategic perspective, more concern may be caused by sales of arms and technologies to China; this will happen out of purely mercantile motivations, not any strategic considerations.

His main conclusion is that Russia's future is so uncertain that it is impossible to forecast. He is personally quite skeptical about this future, as evidenced by the "old Russian joke" he recounts in his two reports. It goes like this: "What is the difference between a Russian optimist and a Russian pessimist? The pessimist

1 Gannon, *Russia in the Next Millennium* (National Intelligence Council, DFI International & Henry L. Stimson Group, December 9, 1999).

says, "Things cannot possibly get any worse.' The optimist, on the other hand, says, 'Oh, yes, they can!'"

The CIA director's *Report* garnered some attention in Russia; its section dealing with Russia was even translated and published in *Nezavisimaya Gazeta* (February 9, 2001). Actually, this Report reproduces in a milder form the truly unflattering assessments contained in a paper prepared under the auspices of the National Intelligence Council (December 2000), Global Trends 2015: *A Dialogue About the Future With Nongovernment Experts.*

I want to start with that document's section dedicated to China.

All experts note that it is difficult to forecast China's development for a period of more than fifteen years due to a multitude of variables. "Some projections indicate that Chinese power will rise because of the growth of its economic and military capabilities. Other projections indicate that the array of political, social, and economic pressures will increasingly challenge the stability and legitimacy of the regime. Most assessments today argue that China will seek to avoid conflict in the region to promote stable economic growth and to ensure internal stability. A strong China, others assert, would seek to adjust regional power arrangements to its advantage, risking conflict with neighbors and some powers external to the region. A weak China would increase prospects for criminality, narcotics trafficking, illegal migration, WMD proliferation, and widespread social instability.

"China's People's Liberation Army will remain the world's largest military, but the majority of the force will not be fully modernized before 2015. China could close the technological gap with the West in one or more major weapons systems. China's capability for regional military operations is likely to improve significantly by 2015.

"China by 2015 will have deployed dozens of missiles with nuclear warheads targeted against the United States, mostly more survivable land- and sea-based mobile missiles. It also will have hundreds of shorter-range ballistic and cruise missiles for use in regional conflicts. Some of these shorter-range missiles will have nuclear warheads; most will be armed with conventional warheads."

"It should be stressed that while experts are in agreement about China's military potential, their opinions differ widely about the strengthening of China as a great power in general. Some think that China will acquire that status; others believe that it will not, due to many problems of a domestic nature."

Now let's see what the document says about Russia. I want to point out right away that the experts' forecasts about Russia are much more accurate than those about China. They conclude: "Russia will remain the most important actor in the former Soviet Union. Its power relative to others in the region and neighboring areas will have declined, however, and it will continue to lack the resources to impose its will. The Soviet economic inheritance will continue to plague Russia. Besides a crumbling physical infrastructure, years of environmental neglect are taking a toll on the population, a toll made worse by such societal costs of transition as alcoholism, cardiac diseases, drugs, and a worsening health delivery system. (Russian experts predict that the country's population could fall from 146 million at present to 130–135 million by 2015.) Russia's population is not only getting smaller, but it is also becoming less and less healthy and thus less able to serve as an engine of economic recovery. In macroeconomic terms, Russia's GDP probably has bottomed out. Russia, nevertheless, is still likely to fall short in its efforts to become fully integrated into the global financial and trading system by 2015. Even under a best-case scenario of 5 percent annual economic growth, Russia would attain an economy less than onefifth the size of that of the United States."

"The centrality of Russia will continue to diminish, and by 2015 Eurasia will be a geographic term lacking a unifying political, economic, and cultural reality. Russia and the western Eurasian States will continue to orient themselves toward Europe, but will remain essentially outside of it. Because of geographic proximity and cultural affinities, the Caucasus will be closer politically to its neighbors to the south and west, with Central Asia drawing closer to South Asia and China. Nonetheless, important interdependencies will remain, primarily in the energy sphere."

"Russia will focus its foreign policy goals on reestablishing lost influence in the former Soviet republics to the south, fostering ties to Europe and Asia, and presenting itself as a significant player vis-à-vis the United States. Its energy resources will be an important lever for these endeavors. However, its domestic ills will frustrate its efforts to reclaim its great power status. Russia will maintain the second largest nuclear arsenal in the world as the last vestige of its old status. The net outcome of these trends will be a Russia that remains internally weak and institutionally linked to the international system primarily through its permanent seat on the UN Security Council."

Regrettably, it is precisely this forecast that is most likely to become reality, unless a miracle comes to pass—or a revolution.

* * *

A brief summary. The main official documents of the USA make the claim that the United States is the world's sole superpower, and it will maintain that status until 2015. Despite this, the United States will face many "challenges" and threats of an international scope (terrorism, drug trafficking, corruption, etc.). Russia is not regarded as a great power capable of rivalry with the USA; it is, however, listed among "threats" to U.S. security on account of Russian authorities' suspected inability to control the storage of nuclear and other weapons and to operate nuclear power stations.

As for Russia as a whole, it is the only country whose future is not forecast in any official U.S. document.

Chapter IV

National security: methodological and terminological aspects

In the previous chapter, we examined Washington's official stance on U.S. foreign policy, the country's role and place in the world. It is now worthwhile to address the methodological and terminological aspects of policy, as well as the mechanism and procedure of formulating the security strategy. For "texts" we shall use the already familiar documents: *A National Security Strategy for A New Century* (May 1997), and *U.S. Department of State. Strategic Plan* (September 1997).

The general "national security strategies" of the USA

The first part of the *Strategy* is titled *Leadership Today For a Safer, More Prosperous Tomorrow.*[1] It starts with the definition of the country's fundamental national interests, which include sovereign-

1 By the way, in the USA very important official documents, doctrines, etc. are written in lively conventional English, with quotes from classics inserted in the text or placed in the margins as captions in pretty frames. Appendixes contain statistical data and/or graphs. In other words, creative literary work goes into these documents, unlike Russian texts written in unreadable bureaucratese, for example, that same Russian national security concept.

ty, political freedoms and independence of the USA, its values, institutions and territorial integrity. Next are identified the "challenges" to national interests and the possibilities for their neutralization. It is explicitly pointed out that previous U.S. strategies must be updated due to changes in the international situation.

In the second part—"*Advancing U.S. National Interests*—suggestions are made for improving the security policy in connection with different kinds of threats to national interests, as well as for new approaches toward implementing military-political security that is ensured by enhanced capability.

The third part—"*Promoting Prosperity*"—emphasizes the foreign-economic-relations aspects of national interests, safeguarded by a set of means from the arsenal of economic security policy. All this is closely tied to support for the spreading of democracy (i.e. market economy), seen one of the main instruments of achieving economic goals abroad, in particular in "countries in a period of transition."

The final part—"""*Integrated Regional Approaches*" - deals with the specifics of regions; suggested for each of them is a different set of measures of national security policy.

The entire text is built on a three-link chain: national interest—"foreign challenges—"responses or measures through national security policy. It should be pointed out that all these "challenges and threats" are regarded as external. In other words, the *Strategy* is a foreign policy doctrine, not a document that mixes foreign and domestic policy.

The State department doctrine is even more structured. The preamble states clearly that "the purpose of United States foreign policy is to create a more secure, prosperous, and democratic world for the benefit of the American people." This strategy is presented after the following scheme:

Firstly, the directions of national interests are defined. Included in this circle are: National Security (military aspects with emphasis on non-proliferation of WMD, etc.); Economic Prosperity (open foreign markets, expand U.S. export to $1.2 trillion by 2000, etc.); protection of American citizens abroad; tightening of immigration policy; perfecting of legislation (to deal with international crime, narcotics business and terrorism); promotion of democracy (increased pressure on foreign governments to embrace democracy and respect for human rights); humanitarian problems (in connection with natural disasters); global problems (environment, diseases, population growth).

Next, national interests are identified, and after that national security policy is formulated through the definition of its goals. The next step is to present a strategy for its implementation, after that—concrete actions to be taken, and, finally, the objective to be achieved in each case. In brief, the logical chain looks like this: national interests - national security - goals - strategies - assumptions - indicators.

Naturally, this variant of policy also describes national interests and national security of the USA in the context of external threats and U.S. international activities.

U.S. experience in ensuring economic security

Essentially, until the early 1990-s the theory and practice of economic security policy was preached by only one country in the world —the USA. It is ascertained that neither West European countries or Japan singled out "economic security" in their general foreign economic policy, although the foreign-economic block was sometimes present as a separate component in the more general doctrine of "comprehensive national security," for example in Japan's foreign policy practice in the early 1980-s. In this same capacity, this block is included in each of China's three concepts of national security; in combination, they add up to what is called in China the Deng Xiaoping theory.

The only country to adopt the economic security concept in its Americanized variant is Russia in the 1990-s, i.e. in the period when the country started implementing capitalist reforms. As a result of these reforms, introduced by President Boris Yeltsin and his lieutenants (Yegor Gaidar, Victor Chernomyrdin, Anatoly Chubais, and others), a great power turned into a third-rate country with a dying-out population. At present, the threat is very real that the Russian Federation will fall apart.

It is perfectly natural, then, that in these conditions the concept of security, including its economic components, has become the commonest topic in Russian political science circles. It grew so popular that it has practically ploughed under all other approaches and theories, turning into a dimensionless doctrine that "explains" all aspects of our society. The concept of economic security got particularly "lucky" in this sense; Russian scholars managed to squeeze into it all spheres of the economy, politics, social life, etc. For proof of this, one only needs to pick up any collection or official document dedicated to "economic security."[1]

1 For example, see special issue "Ekonomicheskaya bezopasnost'" in "*Bezopasnost'*," no. 10–12 (October/December 1997).

In spite of this, scholars and politicians do not have an agreed position on the very term "national economic security,"[1] nor on the components of this concept. Since most Russian authors borrow their ideas from American authors, it is worth looking at the sources, in order to clarify for ourselves once again: (a) what do Americans mean by the term "economic security"; (b) which agencies and institutions participate in the preparation of documents that deal with this topic; (c) by whom and how are the approved documents implemented.

Definitions of "economic security"

Of all kinds of security, the biggest confusion surrounds economic security. It suffices to take a look at the structure and contents of the government document titled "*On the most immediate measures for implementing the Russian Federation's State Strategy of Economic Security (Main Theses)*" of December 27, 1996 (№ 1569). It touches on all aspects of economic and social life—a typical mincemeat of a document in which it is impossible to identify "threats" or the government bodies responsible for their neutralization or prevention. This confusion stems, in my opinion, from an unskilled compilation of American doctrines of economic security, and from a lack of understanding of the meanings of American terms. Particular confusion is introduced by the term "social security"; even some American scholars who are not theorists often treat it as synonymous with "economic security." Still, when they are formulating the concept of economic security in the broad sense of the word, they clearly distinguish social security from economic security in the narrow sense (having to do with external influences). "The narrow variant" is related to International Economic Security, as well as External Economic Security, which in turn consists of many subdirections; of these, the most important ones currently are industrial safety, industrial espionage, economic espionage. Let us take a brief look at the definitions of the domestic and external aspects of U.S. economic security.

1 For example see Korzhov, *Ekonomicheskaya bexopasnost' Rossii* (M., 1996), 7–9.

Social security. Of all kinds of security, social security is paramount; the federal government carries most of the responsibility for it. 70% to 80% of all literature on security is dedicated to this topic; most government officials deal with it. Those who specialize in these problems define the term in this way:

"Economic security, which is a part of our total welfare, can be defined as a state of mind or sense of well-being by which an individual is relatively certain that he or she can satisfy basic needs and wants, both present and future. Economic insecurity consists of loss of income, additional expense (e.g. health care), insufficient income (e.g. low wage or intermittent work), or uncertainty of income (even for a highly paid worker). Economic insecurity can be caused by premature death of the family head, old age, poor health (i.e. disability), unemployment, substandard wage, inflation, natural disasters, or personal factors such as divorce, alcohol and drugs, gambling and domestic violence."[1]

For the sake of variety, let us reproduce here the definition given by the Canadian Security Intelligence Service: "Economic security is the maintenance of those conditions necessary to encourage sustained long-term relative improvements in labor and capital productivity and thus a high and rising standard of living for a nation's citizens, including the maintenance of a fair, secure and dynamic business environment conducive to innovation, domestic and foreign investment and sustainable economic growth."[2]

These kinds of definitions of social-economic security and insecurity encompass almost all aspects of individuals' existence, and the responsibility for each individual is borne by the governments of the USA and Canada and also by the society as a whole. That's why the lion's share of the U.S. federal budget is earmarked for ensuring the needed level of social security. The article labeled "social security" alone accounts for 23% of the federal budget expenditures in the 1999 fiscal year—the single biggest item by far. If one adds together all other budget items related to social (economic) security (communities and regional development, education, health

1 Reida, *Social Insurance and Economic Security*, 5.

2 Foreign spy agencies threaten Canada's economic security, warns new study. Canada News Wire CSIS/SCRS 1996.

care, Medicare, social insurance, veterans' affairs, justice), the total amounts to over 60% of the budget.[1]

To all these expenditures, one should add the monies flowing to the social security sphere from the private sector; at the very least, they match in scope the government's outlays. One should also keep in mind that in Canada and West European countries, the shares of "social security" items in their budgets exceed those of the USA. For instance, in the United Kingdom's 1998 budget the items "social security and health care, social services" amounted to 60% and 16%, respectively, of the total budget.[2]

It should also be clearly remembered that the responsibility for social security is borne by the government, the President or Prime Minister, and not by any "external enemy."

International economic security. It is defined as "a state of the world economy that suits to the maximum degree the economic interests of the USA as a whole." Despite the undisputed leadership of the USA in the world economy, they believe in Washington that the efforts being undertaken by the USA to ensure the country's national interests, including the economic aspects, are insufficient. Actively debated at the present time is the idea of forming a special Council on Economic Security, either within the framework of the United Nations (analogous to the Security Council), or as an independent international organization, intended to bring some order and coordination to all international economic institutions such as the G-7, WTO, IMF, OECD, etc. Since the USA will be the main source of funding for such an organization, its purpose will be determined primarily by U.S. economic interests.

Technological security. Although the USA has no laws on technological security, the enforcement of this security can be clearly traced along several dimensions. Firstly, the U.S. Department of Defense in recent years has been constantly emphasizing the closest connection between technological and national (meaning military) security, demanding stricter controls over means and ways of pro-

1 U.S. Government Printing Office, *A Citizen's Guide to the Federal Budget*, Fiscal Year 2001, 13.

2 The Economist, May 30, 1998, 35.

duction and sales of "defense technology." Secondly, it succeeded in including stricter conditions of selling "technological information" in the Law on Economic Espionage of 1996 (it will be discussed a little later). Thirdly, it increased substantially investment in military industry controlled directly by the Pentagon. The latter fact is confirmed by the following figures that originate from military specialists. Back in 1965, the Department of Defense purchased 60% of the semiconductors it used in the "free" domestic marketplace. At present, it buys only 1% of semiconductors in the open market. Only a few years ago, the open market accounted for almost 100% of multi-chip modules purchased by the Pentagon; today, the figure is only 40%. This means that, on the one hand, the Pentagon seeks to place the "defense marketplace" under its firm control; on the other hand, it increases own investment in military technology and information. This policy is in sharp contrast with the trends observed in today's Russia.

In order to differentiate the measure of responsibility for economic damage to the country inflicted by "domestic and foreign enemies," American and Canadian documents contain definitions of several important terms.

Section 809 of the Intelligence Authorization Act for Fiscal Year 1995 required that the President report to the Congress on foreign industrial espionage targeted against US industry. The Act defined foreign *industrial espionage* as "industrial espionage conducted by a foreign government or by a foreign company with direct assistance of a foreign government against a private United States company and aimed at obtaining commercial secrets."[1]

Canadians came up with a definition that fits "domestic spies" as well, just in case: "*Industrial espionage* is the use of, or facilitation of, illegal, clandestine, coercive or deceptive means by a private sector entity or its surrogates to acquire economic intelligence."

Canadians also define *economic espionage* in a broader context, not limiting its sphere to the private sector. In their interpretation *Economic espionage* is defined as "illegal, clandestine, coercive or deceptive activity engaged in or facilitated by a foreign government designed to gain unauthorized access to economic intelligence, such as proprietary information or technology, for economic advantage."

1 Annual Report to Congress on Foreign Economic Collection and Industrial Espionage, July 1995.

Finally, "***Economic intelligence*** is policy or commercially relevant economic information, including technological data, financial, proprietary commercial and government information, the acquisition of which by foreign interests could, either directly or indirectly, assist the relative productivity or competitive position of the economy of the collecting organization's country."[1]

One can't help noticing that Americans—unlike Canadians, not to mention Europeans or the Japanese—are concerned in the past two-three years with giving ever more detailed definitions to different subspecies of "economic security." This is due to the fact that a wide spectrum of legislation is currently being drafted, designed to protect all spheres of U.S. economic activity inside the country and abroad. Involved in this process are practically all the structures that deal, however indirectly, with U.S. foreign economic activity.

Participants of U.S. economic security policy

In order to understand which structures are involved in the protection of the country's economic security, it is worthwhile to list the authors of the document titled *Annual Report to Congress on Foreign Economic Collection and Industrial Espionage* of 1995. The National Counterintelligence Policy Board (NACIPB), acting on behalf of the National Security Council, tasked the National Counterintelligence Center (NACIC) to draft a community-based response to this Congressional requirement. The NACIC solicited input from the relevant Executive Branch agencies, including the Federal Bureau of Investigation (FBI), National Security Division; the Central Intelligence Agency (CIA), Counterintelligence Center; the Department of State, Bureaus of Intelligence and Research and Diplomatic Security; the Director of Counterintelligence and Security Programs in the Office of the Assistant Secretary of Defense for Command, Control, Communication, and Intelligence; the Defense Intelligence Agency (DIA); the U.S. Army Intelligence and Security-Command; the Naval Criminal Investigative Service

1 Foreign spy agencies threaten Canada's economic security.

(NCIS); the Air Force Office of Special Investigations (OSI); the Defense Investigative Service (DIS); the Personnel Security Research Institute; the National Security Agency (NSA); the Department of Energy (DOE), Counterintelligence Division; the Department of Commerce, Office of Export Enforcement; the Department of Treasury, Office of Intelligence Support; and the U.S. Customs Service, Office of Intelligence. Input from each of these agencies has been incorporated into this report. This many organizations took part in preparing one single document!

In a general kind of development, the U.S. administration has created a so-called Counterintelligence (CI) structure that is charged with creating something called the Counterintelligence Community (CIC) for the purpose of protecting American industry from foreign espionage. Here is some information about the organizations included.

The FBI is the central U.S. Government agency for collecting, analyzing, and investigating foreign threats to U.S. industry. Within the Bureau there functions the FBI's Development of Espionage, Counterintelligence, and Counter terrorism Awareness (DECA) Program which provides an interface with the U.S. corporate community through which the FBI not only conveys information but also obtains investigative leads from corporations concerning foreign government and corporate attempts to illicitly collect U.S. economic and technological information.

The CIA informs the FBI and other appropriate U.S. Government agencies when it learns, in the course of its broader foreign CI and economic intelligence gathering activities, about a to reign government or company targeting U.S. industry.

The U.S. Customs Service is the U.S. Government's primary border enforcement agency with responsibility for enforcing several categories of laws that relate to illegal economic activities. For example, Customs is responsible for enforcing the Arms Export Control Act and the Export of War Materials Act, which involve munitions control and trafficking activities.

In the Department of Defense, each department has a division responsible for foreign economic and industrial intelligence, related to military programs and systems. It works closely with the FBI. One should keep in mind that the Service of the Undersecretary for Economic Security was divided in 1998 into two divisions:

the Service of the Assistant Undersecretary for Commercial and International Programs, and the Service of the Assistant Undersecretary for Industry and Innovation. This is more confirmation of the above-mentioned trend toward more narrow specialization in the sphere of foreign economic activity.

The Department of Justice has a division dealing with economic espionage. The Department of Energy has a similar division. The Department of Commerce has no special programs within the CI; its cooperation is supposed to be purely informational.

The National Aeronautics and Space Administration (NASA) is not itself a participant of the CI program, but it has access to information from the FBI and Special Access Programs and keeps its workers informed about the situation in this area.

The Department of State, apart from special divisions dedicated to foreign economic activities, has the State Department's Overseas Security Advisory Council (OSAC). It is a joint venture of sorts, comprised of State Department officials and American businesspeople. OSAC is administered under the State Department's Bureau of Diplomatic Security (DS). About 1,400 private organizations are members of this Council. There is also a powerful non-government organization called the American Society of Information Security (ASIS) that presents reports on a regular basis to the FBI itself. CI programs describe clearly the roles of each of the actors listed above, the forms and methods of espionage to be dealt with, etc. One of the fruits of the CI initiative is the Economic Security Act of 1996.

Economic Security Act of 1996

On February 1, 1996 two bills were debated in the U.S. Senate, sponsored by Senators Specter and Kohl; one is known as the Economic Security Act of 1996, the other as the Economic Espionage Act of 1996. President Clinton was present at the debates. On February 28, FBI Director Louis J. Freeh testified before the Senate in detail about the need to approve both these bills. It should be stressed that the bills had been initiated by two federal agencies—the Department of Justice and the FBI. It is worthwhile to take a closer look at them.

In Part 2 of the Economic Security Act it is stated:

1. economic security is an integral part of national security;
2. the development of new ideas and technical innovation is critical to sustaining a healthy and competitive national economy;
3. encouraging innovation and creativity requires adequate protection of vital economic proprietary information, both tangible and intangible;
4. over 50 countries have covertly tried to obtain advanced technologies from United States industries;
5. the theft, wrongful destruction or alteration, misappropriation, or wrongful conversion by foreign governments or their agents of vital economic proprietary information belonging to United States owners directly and substantially threatens the health and competitiveness of critical segments of the United States economy and, consequently, the Nation's security; and
6. current laws are inadequate to protect against economic espionage by foreign governments or those acting on their behalf.

(b) PURPOSE: The purpose of this Act is to protect the national security by preventing economic espionage and furthering the development and lawful utilization of United States vital proprietary economic information by protecting it from theft, wrongful destruction or alteration, misappropriation, and conversion by foreign governments and their agents or instrumentalities.

This Act is intended to protect the vital proprietary economic information of the United States Government and United States firms, businesses, industries, and individuals both domestically and abroad by punishing individuals, corporations, and institutions that engage in economic espionage with the intent or purpose of aiding foreign nations or governments and their instrumentalities and agents. [1]

The Senators presented the following arguments for approving their bills: American companies have estimated that in 1992, they lost $1.8 billion from the theft of their trade secrets. A 1993 study by the American Society for Industrial Security found a 260-percent increase in the theft of proprietary information since 1985. And the theft of these secrets is not random and disorganized. The press has reported that one government study of 173 nations discovered that 57 of them were trying to get advanced technologies from American companies. The French "intelligence" service has even admitted to forming a special unit devoted to obtaining confidential information from American companies. (France was the only country to be mentioned openly.)

FBI Director Freeh added the following information from a special report titled "Trends in Intellectual Property Loss": 325 U.S. corporations responded to a double-blind survey—the third in a series. For 1995, 700 incidents of proprietary loss were cited by respondents, which reflected a 323% increase in this activity between 1992 (9.9 incidents per month) and 1995 (32 incidents per month). Of these incidents, 59% were attributable to employees or ex-employees, and 15% were attributable to those with a contractual relationship with the company. In all, 74% of the incidents were committed by those who were in a position of trust with the company. In 21% of the incidents, foreign involvement was identified. The loss claimed for the 700 incidents was $5.1 billion, approximately 9% of the U.S. GNP. [2]

---

1 Senate of the United States. Comment on the *Economic Espionage Act* of 1996 and the Economic Security Act of 1996 by senators Kohl and Spector, 1 February 1996, S1557 IS 104th Congress, 2d Session.

2 Senate Select Committee on Intelligence and Senate Committee on the Judiciary. Subcommittee on Terrorism, Technology and Government Information, *Hearing on Economic Espionage*, Statement by Freeh, Director of FBI, 28 February 1996.

David E. Cooper, Associate Director, Defense Acquisitions Issues, National Security and International Affairs Division, in his report described in detail the mechanism used for stealing U.S. defense information by five allies of the USA. These allies were not named, but three of them can be deduced from their "mode of operation": France, Israel and Japan.

In previous FBI reports of 1996 and 1997 it was stressed that U.S. economic security was starting to be negatively affected by Russia in connection with total corruption at all levels of power and economic structures, as well as organized crime structures, some of them operating on U.S. territory.

Originally the two Acts were supposed to be included as amendments to the National Security Act of 1947. In the end, however, in October 1996 they became the new Chapter 90 to Title 18 of the United States Code, consisting of seven sections: Section 1831—Economic Espionage, Section 1832—Theft of Trade Secrets, Section 1834—Criminal Forfeiture, Section 1835—Orders to Preserve Confidentiality, Section 1836—Civil Proceedings to Enjoin Violations, Section 1837—Extraterritorial Investigations, Section 1838—State Laws.

Section 1831 that deals with punishment for economic espionage lists the following maximum penalties: for individuals—15 years imprisonment, a $500,000 fine, or both; for an organization—a $10 million fine. Theft of trade secrets performed not on behalf of a foreign state carries lesser penalties: for individuals, 10 years' imprisonment, a fine, or both; for organizations, a fine of $5 million.

Almost two years later, on 28 January 1998, Louis Freeh testified before the Senate again, giving a report of sorts on the performance of the Economic Security Act. He said that 23 countries were continuing to conduct economic espionage on U.S. territory, with 12 of them being particularly active. However, within the framework of the FBI National Security Division's Awareness of National Security Issues and Response (ANSIR) Program, FBI agents were providing warning information to 25,000 corporate directors. Similar warnings were sent as briefing materials to American companies operating abroad, in particular in Austria, Ireland, New Zealand, Panama, South Korea and the United Kingdom. Referring to the already mentioned American Society of Industrial Security (ASIS), Freeh declared that in 1996 alone, American intellectual property worth in excess of $30 billion was at risk. He quoted no less than ten cases of trade secret thefts prevented by the FBI on the basis of the Economic Espionage Act.[1]

Measured against the scale of the hunt for industrial secrets, the number of cases quoted should be regarded as miniscule, which apparently testifies to the imperfection of either the Act itself or the entire system for protecting the American industry.

Conclusions

The American experience shows that even in a seasoned market economy, problems of economic security retain their urgency and require that the mechanism of ensuring this security is constantly perfected. Although all aspects of economic security are interconnected, nonetheless different economic spaces of their functioning are clearly defined. The domestic field—social security—is clearly the government's responsibility. The external field—foreign economic security—is the responsibility of not only government bodies, but also private businesses and organizations, and every member of the American society. This sphere of economic security protection is getting to be defined by the policies pursued previously by the Soviet Union and currently by China.

It should be stressed that the American security strategy is not only intended to protect U.S. own economic interests from external threats. It aims for a directed development of the world economy and the economy of any country in the world, including the advanced economies of America's military-political allies. The end goal is to have them all "work for the USA."

1 Senate Select Committee on Intelligence. *Hearing on Threats to U.S. National Security*, Statement by Freeh, Director of FBI, January 28, 1998.

Chapter V

Funding for U.S. International Policy

Overcome your opponent by calculation.

Li Tsang,
ancient Chinese military thinker

Marinka, the bitch, keeps count of every penny.

From a conversation between
two Russian girls

Current U.S. strategic theory was ... born of a marriage between the scientist and the accountant. The professional soldier was jilted.

Richard Pipes

All discussions of national interests, national security, and foreign policy goals are empty talk if the costs of implementation and the sources of funding are not determined in advance. Marx said somewhere that ideas inevitably discredit themselves as soon as they become detached from real interests. To an even greater degree, the very interests or goals discredit themselves as soon as they become detached from funding. A telling example is the experience of foreign policy implementation in the USSR and in Russia today.

The USA appears to be the only country in the world where detailed calculations are done for every activity needed to secure national interests or implement the national security strategy. These calculations are The Twenty-First Century: The World Without Russia performed by government agencies, legislative bodies, and specially created ad hoc groups (like the Overseas Presence Advisory Panel established in 1999 on the Secretary of State's initiative). Every U.S. citizen may participate through his/her congressional representative. This participation is guaranteed by the law and facilitated by the fact that detailed budget information is published and disseminated free of charge, in particular, through the Internet (http://www.gpo.gov/usbudget).

For an analysis of the structure and mechanism of the funding of U.S. international activities, we will examine a number of documents: *105 th Congress Report*. House of Representatives First Session 105–94. (For purposes of brevity, let us label this document as Act 1997.); *Foreign Policy Reform Act,* May 9, 1997; U.S. Department of State, *Strategic Plan*, September 1997 (SP 1997); *United States Strategic Plan for International Affairs*, First Revision—February 1999 (SP 1999); *Summary and Highlights*. International Affairs (Function 150) (*Summary*); *Fiscal Year 2001 Budget Request,* February 7, 2000; *The Budget-inBrief*—Fiscal Year 2001, February 7, 2000 (BiB). (Note: All these documents were downloaded from the Internet.)

Procedure and Terms

Funding for international affairs is included in Function 150 of the Federal budget. The Office of the Secretary of State Resources, Plans, and Policy initially puts this part together. It is then passed on to the president's administration, where the Office of Management and Budget (OMB) plays the main role. After presidential approval of the entire budget, the documents are submitted to Congress for debate. The international policy part is discussed in subcommittees: foreign operations, commerce, justice, state, judiciary and related agencies, agriculture and rural development, and labor, health, and human services. It is then returned to the administration for finishing and signing. The whole process follows a prescribed time frame and deadlines.

Funding for international affairs is spread over programs administered by four Departments (State, Treasury, Defense [Defense Security Cooperation Agency], and Agriculture); seven independent agencies (U.S. Agency for International Development, Export–Import Bank, International Trade Commission, Overseas Private Investment Corporation, Peace Corps, Trade and Development Agency, and U.S. Institute of Peace); and three foundations (African Development Foundation, the Asia Foundation, and the Inter-American Foundation).

Keep in mind that although the international affairs section contains the funding item "international security," it only encompasses part of national security. As explained by Ambassador Craig Johnstone, director of the Office of Resources, Plans, and Policy within the Department of State, national security activities encompass the spheres of interaction with allies, the Middle East peace process, prevention of proliferation of chemical, biological, and nuclear weapons, support for peacekeeping forces (in particular in Kosovo and Bosnia), and also "what we do with respect to the former Soviet Union and the states of the former Soviet Union, in terms of trying to encourage their transition to democracy."[1] By the way, this item accounts for almost 44 percent of the entire international affairs budget. The lion's share of the funding for international security is channeled through the national defense budget (Function 050). Several national security items are also included in the Department of Energy budget.

To understand what exactly is funded under the label International Affairs, one should know the difference between it and the term foreign policy. This difference is pointed out, in particular, in SP 1999; excerpts from this plan have been quoted in the previous chapter.[2] It also contains a list of U.S. national interests.

1 See U.S. Department of State, On-the-Record Briefing on FY 2000 Budget as Released by the Office of the Spokesman (Washington, D.C., February 1, 1999).

2 This document also specifies the differences between the terms "interests" and "strategic goals." It should be stressed that in general, Americans like terminological clarity, especially in their official documents.

The Structure of Funding for International Affairs[1]

Right away, it is worth noting (indeed, State Department officials never tire of reminding us about it) that in 1949, expenditures on international affairs amounted to 16 percent of the Federal budget; today, this share is just above 1 percent. As late as 1985, $35 billion was spent on these activities (in 1997 figures). During 1987–1996, funding for International Affairs dropped by 34 percent (from $25 billion to $16 billion). Then, it started growing slowly: $18 billion in 1997; $19 billion in 1998; $23.4 billion in 1999; $24 billion (estimated) in 2000. It should be kept in mind, though, that the dynamics of these expenditures are somewhat different in the Historical Tables,[2] but the important thing is that in recent years, the international affairs item amounts to roughly 0.2 percent of GDP, and just over 1 percent of the Federal budget. I shall revisit this topic; for now, let's note that in the 2001 budget, Function 150 expenditures were approved by the president to the tune of $22.8 billion, less than in the previous two years.

Function 150 is divided into four unequal parts. The biggest sub-function is for foreign operations. In the draft for 2001, it amounted to $15.1 billion; of the thirty-two items the biggest ones were Multilateral Development Banks ($1.354 billion); Sustainable Development ($2.141 billion); Economic Support Fund ($2.313 billion); and Foreign Military Financing ($3.538 billion). There is also an item called Support for Eastern European Democracy, amounting to $610 million. This sum went up again after a dip in 2000, probably because democracy in Eastern Europe is experiencing problems again.

The second biggest sub-function is Commerce, Justice, and State; included here is funding for the Department of State itself. It grew to $6.816 billion in 2001 compared to $6.532 billion in 2000, but is still below the 1999 level ($6.951 billion). The other two

1 Budget years mentioned are fiscal years that start on October 1.

2 See *Historical Tables, Budget of the United States Government: Fiscal Year 2000.*

sub-functions are relatively minor: Agriculture (food aid) amounts to $837 million, and Labor (funding for the U.S. Institute of Peace) takes just $14.45 million.

It is worthwhile to take a look at the outlays for running the Department of State itself. The data about its staff numbers are rather contradictory. The "PS 1997" document says it is approximately 23,000 people (p. 85); another State Department document from the same year gives the number 22,209, with 9,508 career diplomats serving abroad, 7,724 diplomats in the U.S., and 4,977 other personnel. In total, 64% of State Department employees were working abroad.

Through the efforts of Madeleine Albright, the situation started changing for the better already in the following year; this is evidenced by the Foreign Policy Reform Act of May 1997 (Section 1321). It set new staff levels for the 1998 fiscal year-end. By September 30, 1998 the numbers of the External Service staff (meaning employees on U.S. soil) were to be as follows:

1. for the Department of State, shall not exceed 8,700, of whom not more than 750 shall be members of the Senior Foreign Service;
2. for the United States Information Agency, shall not exceed 1,000, of whom not more than 140 shall be members of the Senior Foreign Service; and
3. for the Agency for International Development, not to exceed 1070, of whom not more than 140 shall be members of the Senior Foreign Service.

For the following year; the Act provided for a small increase. The following figures were set for September 30, 1999:

1. for the Department of State, shall not exceed 8,800, of whom not more than 750 shall be members of the Senior Foreign Service;
2. for the United States Information Agency, not to exceed 1,000 of whom not more than 140 shall be members of the Senior Foreign Service; and
3. for the Agency for International Development, not to exceed 1065 of whom not more than 135 shall be members of the Senior Foreign Service. (Act 1997, p. 52).

One should remember that the Department of State serves 160 countries through over 250 embassies, consulates and other representative offices abroad (over 30 of these offices have been closed since 1995).

The outlays for the functioning of the Department of State were $4,679 million in 1998, $6,683 million in 1999 and $6,243 million in 2000; the sum requested for 2001 was $6,512 million approximately 28% of the total sum slated for International Affairs. If the Foreign Aid items (migration and refugee issues) are included, the actual totals were: $5,379 million in 1998, $7,784 million in 1999, $6,879 million in 2000, $7,191 million in 2001 (BiB).

Maintenance of the administrative apparatus (both at home and abroad) accounts for most the outlays—65.5%; international organizations and international conferences use up 23.4% of the total. Wages amounted to $354 million in 1999. In the year 2000 this item was joined with State Programs expenditure items, and the total was set at $2,584 million. The sum requested for Administrative Activities overall was $4,708 million. Footnotes to these figures detail the channels through which these monies are funneled.

It is curious that China is entered in the list as a separate item; for instance, in 2000 it "cost" the U.S. $1.6 million. This amount includes Chinese-language training programs, trips through China, support for American citizens living in China, fine-tuning of the information system, modernization of equipment and tightening of security at the U.S. Embassy. (BiB, 2000) I draw your attention to this matter to contrast it to the Russian Embassy's conduct toward Russian citizens in China. Without advance consultations, the latter may not even freely enter the premises of their own embassy.

The Purposes of Money Spending

The budget includes the item "Funding for the National Endowment for Democracy (NED)". In 1998 $30 million was spent on this Endowment, in 1999—$31 million, in 2000—a little under $31 million (estimate), in 2001—$32 million.

Explanation Of 2001 Request: "The FY 2001 request will provide funding for the National Endowment for Democracy (NED) at $32 million, which represents an increase of $1.128 million above the FY 2000 level. This increase is targeted equally among the following five areas: Africa, Middle East, Newly Independent States, Latin America, and Multi-regional programs to sustain the following activities:

- support countries in transition to more open democratic systems, through measures that strengthen the rule of law, protect individual liberty, and foster social pluralism;
- foster liberal democracy by strengthening civil society, including assisting the development of emerging non-governmental organizations (NGOs), and strengthening independent trade unions, free communications media, and domestic election monitoring organizations that not only discourage electoral fraud but also mobilize citizens to participate in the political process;
- provide assistance to democratic activists in authoritarian countries such as China, Cuba, North Korea, Congo, Sudan, as well as in Central Asia, the Middle East and the war-torn Balkan region;
- encourage free market reforms and develop institutions that promote political accountability, economic transparency and responsible corporate governance;
- engage new democracies in Central Europe to advance pluralism and democratic change throughout the former Soviet bloc, including strengthening counterpart groups in the Balkans, Be-

larus, the Caucasus, and Central Asia;

- provide democratic activists with access to new information and communication technologies; and
- develop strong regional networks that bring together democratic leaders in Africa, Latin America, the Middle East, and the former Soviet Bloc for mutual collaboration and assistance.

Purpose Of Program: NED is a private, non-profit organization created in 1983 to strengthen democratic institutions around the world through non-governmental efforts. An independent, bi-partisan board of directors governs the Endowment. With its annual federal grant, NED makes hundreds of grants each year to support pro-democracy groups in Africa, Asia, Central and Eastern Europe, Latin America, the Middle East, and the countries of the former Soviet Union. The mission of the Endowment is to support peaceful and stable transitions to more open political and economic systems characterized by effective governance and legal systems, an engaged and responsible civil society, and open markets.

Program Description: The National Endowment for Democracy is primarily a grant-making organization. Programs in the areas of labor, open markets, and political party development are funded through four core institutes: the American Center for International Labor Solidarity (ACILS), the Center for International Private Enterprise (CIPE), the International Republican Institute (IRI), and the National Democratic Institute (NDI). NED also annually funds scores of programs in the areas of human rights, civic education, independent media, rule of law, strengthening non-governmental organizations, and other aspects of democratic development.

Benefits: The National Endowment for Democracy's programs advance long-term U.S. interests and address immediate needs in strengthening democracy, human rights, and the rule of law. NED's support for free market reforms encourages regional trading opportunities and helps foster economic growth. Promoting democracy through the National Endowment for Democracy is vital to U.S. national security since democracies typically do not sponsor terrorism, proliferate weapons of mass destruction, or create destabilizing flows of refugees" (BiB, p. 119–120).

Here is one more illustration of International Affairs expenditures (original format preserved):

REPRESENTATION ALLOWANCES
Program Activities Summary
Summary Statement
(dollars in thousands)

Activities	FY 1999 Actual	FY 2000 Estimate	2001 Request	Increase or Decrease (-)
Promotion of U.S. National Interests	$3,790	$3,871	$3,955	$84
Protection of U.S. Citizens' Interests	$90	$90	$100	$10
Promotion of Economic Activities	$250	$250	$260	$10
Commemorative and Ceremonial Requirements	$220	$215	$230	$15
Public Diplomacy		$1,400	$1,428	$28
Appropriation Total	$4,350	$5,826	$5,973	$147

*FY 2000 and FY 2001 include public diplomacy activities previously funded by the United States Information Agency International Information Programs (IIP) appropriation.

Explanation Of 2001 Request: The FY 2001 request will support U.S. national interests, economic activities, and other diplomatic functions by providing resources for representational events. The increase of $147,000 (2.5%) is required to partially cover the cost of overseas inflation.

Purpose of Program: This appropriation provides reimbursement to diplomatic and consular personnel for officially representing the United States at functions overseas and at missions to international organizations.

Program Description: The activities funded by this appropriation typically include:

- promotion of the U.S. national interests through formal and informal interactions with knowledgeable foreign officials and long-term residents, usually at receptions, small working luncheons, and informal dinners;
- protection of U.S. citizens' interests by developing and maintaining personal relationships with foreign officials, which facilitates providing assistance and solving problems of Americans abroad;
- promotion of economic activities by establishing and maintaining relationships with foreign and American officials, business persons, labor leaders, and others who may be helpful in performing duties connected with promoting and protecting American trade;
- fulfillment of commemorative and ceremonial requirements such as Fourth of July celebrations or the laying of a wreath at the tomb of a local national hero;
- interaction with influential individuals and organizations, including the local media, key political elites, academics and members of non-governmental organizations to assess the overseas public affairs climate and convey and reinforce acceptance of U.S. policies and values; and
- promotion of peaceful relations between the U.S. and other countries by fostering mutual understanding through academic, professional, and cultural activities.

Benefits: Activities performed under this appropriation facilitate the effective conveyance of U.S. foreign policy goals and objectives, the gathering of information central to the formulation of our bilateral and multilateral foreign policy, and the cultivation of and support for U.S. policies and values (BiB, p.65).

By reproducing here in their entirety certain items of International Policy—and minor ones at that—I intend to demonstrate this simple fact: when requesting this or that sum, the Department of State must justify its needfulness from the perspective of U.S. national interests. Not in general, mind you, but in concrete detail for every U.S. action in the international arena.

Funding of Policies Toward CIS Countries and Russia

In chapter two of the *1997 Act, Development Assistance*, Section 511 is dedicated to CIS countries; it states the necessity to support "a growing class of small businessmen in the twelve New Independent States seeking to plant the seeds for the emergence of a true middle class in those fledgling states." (p. 95) These sums amounted to $625 million in 1997, $839.9 million in 1998, and $789.9 million in 1999.

Let's examine a passage, bureaucratized in style, that directly concerns Russia: "The Committee is troubled by growing evidence of Russian actions in the other New Independent States intended to undermine their sovereignty and reassert Russia's historical dominance over those states. In this regard, the Committee is concerned with rationales provided by this administration that the United States cannot oppose any surrender of sovereignty by any of the New Independent States if such a surrender is 'voluntary.' (*The Committee goes on to express its doubt that the process is voluntary rather than caused by Russian pressure—A.B.*) The Committee specifically notes evidence of Russian arms supplies and support for separatist ethnic movements in other New Independent States; allegations of Russian support for coup attempts in other New Independent States; use of economic pressure by Russia against the other New Independent States to gain political and military concessions from those states; and Russian manipulation of energy exports by several of the other New Independent States employing the Russian-controlled pipeline system to limit those states' hard currency revenues. The Committee is disappointed with this repeated rationalization by the administration of the Russian effort to 'reintegrate' the former Soviet states." (p.96)

The Ukraine comports itself differently. The Committee points out that: "The Ukrainian government has demonstrated a high degree of consideration for America's foreign policy interests at a time when Russia, in contrast, flaunts those interests." (p. 96–97)

There are some peculiar "concerns" about Belarus in connection with Russia: "The Committee strongly endorses the actions taken by the President to oppose the growing dictatorship of President Alexander Lukashenko in Belarus." (p. 97) (*The paper goes on to mention human rights violations, absence of democracy, etc.—A.B.*). "The Committee calls on the President to coordinate with other democratic states in Europe to support the reintroduction of democratic government in Belarus. While the Committee supports continued aid to nongovernmental organizations, independent media, democratic movements, and humanitarian needs in Belarus, it recommends that aid (including international loans to Russia) be curtailed if top officials of the Russian government continue to support the activities of Alexander Lukashenko. The Committee believes that the fate of democracy in Belarus will have consequences for the other New Independent States." (p.98)

Apparently, Mr. Lukashenko has good reason for his verbal attacks on the West: "Support at the highest levels of the Russian government for the dictatorship of President Alexander Lukashenko in the New Independent State of Belarus and ongoing efforts to 'integrate' Russia and Belarus should be strongly challenged and opposed by the administration." (p.107)

Regarding mass media in Russia, "The Committee notes the trend in Russia towards increasing control of the larger broadcast media and print publications by profitable monopolies with close links to top levels of the Russian government. The Committee views this trend as both a potential threat to true freedom of speech in Russia and a potential support for corrupt activities that might otherwise be publicized by a truly free press. The Committee strongly encourages the Agency for International Development to take this trend into account and to review its programs to redouble efforts to promote truly independent media. Because the sustainability of a non-state-controlled media is critical during this period of transition, the Committee supports continued assistance for independent broadcast media.

"...The Committee is encouraged by the progress of the Agency for International Development's media assistance work in Russia, and specifically by the progress being made in the print media through the Russian American Press and Information Center ("RAPIC")." (p.100)

Criticism of Washington's Financial Policy in the Sphere of International Affairs

Many American experts, particularly those involved in some way in the foreign policy process, criticized the Clinton administration and especially the Congress for insufficient financing of U.S. activity in the international arena. There are many papers on this topic,[1] but let's look at an article by Richard Gardner, former U.S. Ambassador to Spain and Italy, currently a Columbia University professor, in which he analyzes U.S. expenditures on international affairs in fiscal year 2001.[2]

It turns out that the State Department's initial budget request for international affairs for 2001 (made during the tenure of Madeleine Albright) amounted to $25 billion. The Clinton administration cut it down to $22.8 billion (as quoted above), and the budget subcommittees in Congress trimmed it down further to $20 billion, according to Gardner. The professor notes with indignation that at the same time, the defense budget in 2001 grew by $4.5 billion to $310.8 billion. Even though protests from Clinton and Albright persuaded the Congress to increase the Function 150 budget eventually by $1 billion, it is still insufficient for achieving U.S. foreign policy goals.

Gardner is also unhappy about future prospects. Following the president's proposal, Function 150 expenditures will grow to $24.5 billion by 2005, but taking inflation into account, this will actually mean a 20 percent decline against the 2000 level. Meanwhile, the military budget will grow to $331 billion by 2005, and the proportion of military expenditures to international policy expenditures will reach 16:1. Gardner reminds the reader that in the

---

1 See Halperin, Korb, and Moose project directors, *Financing America's Leadership: Protecting American Interests and Promoting American Values. An Independent Task Force*, The Council on Foreign Relations, Inc., cosponsored by The Brookings Institution (January 14, 1998).

2 Gardner, "The One Percent Solution," *Foreign Affairs* (July/August 2000).

1960s, Function 150 accounted for 4 percent of the Federal budget; in the 1970s, 2 percent; now its share has dropped to just over 1 percent.

The former diplomat believes this careless attitude toward international policy is due to failure to see these expenditures as part of the outlays on national security. In his opinion, it is precisely this budget item that actually encompasses a wide spectrum of national security issues tied to the country's seven fundamental national interests.

Gardner goes on to show what kind of money is actually needed to realize these interests. For instance, the 2001 budget allots $6.8 billion to the Department of State, with $3.2 billion from this total earmarked for administrative activities. Because of the destruction of certain embassy buildings in Eastern Africa (those in Nairobi and Dar-Es-Salaam), $1.1 billion is earmarked for rebuilding and modernization of security systems, though the actual need is $1.4 billion. Although the actual need is $330 million, only $17 million is set aside for the creation of a communications infrastructure. Not a penny was allotted to continuing training for the Senior Foreign Service personnel (700 people). Thus, the Department of State alone is underfunded to the tune of $500 million; this sum is needed to cover minimal needs.

The situation is similar regarding funding of international organizations. The budget includes $946 million for assessed contributions to international organizations, of which $300 million is for the UN itself, and $380 million more is for UN-affiliated agencies, such as the International Labor Organization, the World Health Organization, the International Atomic Energy Agency, and the war crimes tribunals for Rwanda and the Balkans. Other bodies such as NATO, the Organization for Economic Cooperation and Development (OECD), and the World Trade Organization (WTO) account for the rest. (Note: Richard Holbrooke, the able American ambassador to the UN, found himself deep in difficult negotiations to reduce the assessed U.S. share of the regular UN budget and the budgets of major specialized UN agencies from 25 percent to 22 percent at a time when many conservative politicians and scholars [for example, those at the Heritage Foundation] simply suggested telling the UN to go to hell.)

Gardner calculates that the Department of State needs another $1 billion to function normally, i.e., the expenditure total for the item *Commerce, Justice, State* must be $7.8 billion.

All this concerns Gardner from the consequences of globalization perspective, which leads to further impoverishment of poor countries. According to his figures, half the world's population lives on less than $2 per day; two billion people have no access to electricity; 1.5 billion people have no access to pure drinking water; more than a billion do not have access to education, health care, or modern birth control methods. His forecast is that at the current growth rate of 75 million people per year, the world's population will reach nine billion people by 2050, with the majority living in the poorest countries. If the current trend continues, "We can expect more abject poverty, environmental damage, epidemics, political instability, drug trafficking, ethnic violence, religious fundamentalism, and terrorism." All these problems are becoming items more important in the list of threats to national security than intergovernment conflicts. Gardner believes that at least $1.6 billion should be added to the foreign operations budget. The decision to spend only 1 percent of the budget on international affairs is not a "solution," concludes the former American diplomat.

* * *

On many occasions, I have analyzed the budgets of the Russian Federation and other countries, but I have never seen such an attention to detail as found in U.S. budgets. I want to stress in particular the Americans' respect for each cent spent on any state activity, whether inside the country or abroad. Finally, it appears that only Americans connect foreign policy goals and interests to expenditures needed for their implementation. I regard this as one of the most important advantages the USA enjoys over other countries of the world; it is the bedrock of its leadership.

As for Russia: Until Russians learn to count every penny, like "the bitch Marinka," and learn to connect talk about being a great power to their country's financial capacities, Russia will remain, in Zbigniew Brzezinski's expression, a "client" of the U.S., begging the IMF on bended knee for yet another extension of credit.

Conclusion: Public Opinion on U.S. Foreign Policy

At one of the Round Tables, Mikhail Gorbachev made this pronouncement: "I have just returned from America.... The Americans themselves, their public opinion, tend to believe they don't need thisthe world policeman role and world domination. They feel that they have enough of their own problems. Public opinion, though, is often ignored, same as in many other states. Public opinion remains just that—an opinion, while real politics moves in a different direction."[1]

This statement, characteristic of many Russian political leaders and scholars, is curious in two respects: First, Mr. Gorbachev deliberately uses the wrong term here. No one in the United States talks about being a "world policeman" and about U.S. domination of the world. The essence of these terms is conveyed through other phrases, namely, the active role of the United States in the world, U.S. leadership, and benevolent hegemony of the United States. These words don't change the essence of the phenomenon, but as propaganda tools they work effectively to win support for U.S. foreign policy. Second, what grounds does Mr. Gorbachev have for speaking on behalf of U.S. "public opinion"? Did he take the trouble of talking to each individual American? Some Russian politicians, though, aim even higher and presume to speak for "the entire humankind and all peoples"; we'll deal with this later in the chapter on Russian scholars.

Because I have never heard of public opinion polls on the scale of entire peoples and humankind as a whole, let us look into the matter of American public opinion about the role of the United States in the world and its relations with Russia and China. This is easy enough to do with access to the data from the polls conducted by the Chicago Committee on Foreign Policy. The committee has

---

1 Russia's Foreign Policy: *What is Possible, and What is Desired?* (April 1997), 28.

conducted these polls regularly once every four years, from 1974 onward. The last poll was conducted in 1998; its results were published in 1999.[1]

Polled individuals are separated into two categories: the public (ordinary folk, so to speak) and the leadership (people involved in one way or another in the U.S. foreign policy process).

The world in the twenty-first century. The majority of the public (53 percent) believes that the twenty-first century will be bloodier and more violent than the twentieth century. Among leaders, this view is shared by only 40 percent of those polled. This means that the public has fewer illusions about the future than the leaders. This disagreement is quite natural because leaders in all countries attempt to embellish the future. One has only to recall the pie in the sky that Russia's leaders used to promise to their people.

Role of the United States in the world. Sixty-one percent of the public and 96 percent of the leadership supported an active role for the United States in the world. Fifty percent of the public believes that America is currently playing a more important and powerful role as world leader than it did ten years ago; 79 percent of the public and 71 percent of the leadership are certain that in another ten years, this role will become even stronger.

Fifty-nine percent of the public and 58 percent of the leadership considered the superiority of U.S. military might in the world arena a "very important" goal.

Asked about the main factor in maintaining the country's superior might and influence in the world, 63 percent of the public said economic might, and 28 percent said military might; among the leaders, 89 percent chose economic might, and 8 percent chose military might. In other words, the proportion of those who rely on military might is much higher among the general public than

1 Reilly, ed., *American Public Opinion and U.S. Foreign Policy, 1999*, The Chicago Council on Foreign Relations (Chicago, 1999). In some cases, for verification purposes, material was used from the article by Reilly, "Americans and the World: A Survey Century's End," *Foreign Policy* (Spring 1999).

among the leaders. The people turn out to be more belligerent than their politicians.

China. The "feelings thermometer" measures the attitude toward a particular country and its leaders (neutral attitude equals 50 degrees Centigrade). On this scale, China rates 47 degrees. The majority of the public and the leaders (57 percent and 56 percent, respectively) view China's transformation into a world power as a "critical" threat to American vital interests. Despite this, 69 percent of the public and 97 percent of its leaders believe that in the next ten years, China will be playing a bigger role than now. At the same time, only 27 percent of the public, as opposed to 51 percent of its leaders, consider U.S. military intervention necessary in the event of China's invasion of Taiwan.

Russia. The "feelings thermometer" shows that between 1994 and 1998, the public's feelings toward Russia grew colder—from 54 to 49 degrees. "Feelings toward Yeltsin" underwent a similar change.

Public support for economic aid to Russia remained low: 38 percent of the public wanted it decreased or stopped altogether, while 35 percent wanted Russia to solve its economic problems on its own. Only 17 percent of the leaders polled supported this latter position. At the same time, 44 percent of the leaders preferred that Russia rely on Europe rather than America in its attempts to emerge from its crisis.

On the list of major foreign policy problems, Russia occupies fifth place in the leadership's view and eleventh place in the public's view. The vast majority of the public (77 percent) and its leaders (93 percent) still regard Russia from the perspective of U.S. vital interests, even though their concern about a potential Russian military threat is negligible. Only a third of the public continues to view Russia's military might as a critical threat to the USA, and only 17 percent of leaders feel the same way. Among these latter, 46 percent of administration members don't see Russia as an "important" threat at all. Still, 49 percent of the leaders do see Russia as a threat, but as an "important" one, not a "critical" one.

The majority of the leaders (54 percent) believe that Russia's role will become smaller in the next ten years; 42 percent believe that it will become bigger. The general public's opinion is evenly split on this issue (44 percent either way).

An interesting difference between the attitudes of the public and its leaders was revealed by their answers to this question: Should the United States use military force against Russia in the event of its invasion of Poland? Fifty-eight percent of leaders said "yes," but only 28 percent of the public. It appears that the American public, unlike its leadership, is hardly concerned about the fates of other countries.

* * *

As these polls demonstrate, U.S. public opinion is at odds with the assessment voiced by Mr. Gorbachev. It is high time for him and for other Russian leaders to start revising their perspective by basing it not on their personal experience but on scientific analysis. Otherwise, they will continue coming up with foolish pronouncements that have tragic consequences for their country.

PART II

Russia's Strategy: A Course Toward Multipolarity

Chapter I

Official Doctrines and Concepts

The National Security Concept of the Russian Federation, or the Immediate Tasks of the Party and the Government

The National Security Concept of 2000[1] is a new edition of the national security concept approved by a Presidential Decree of December 17, 1997. I have already performed an analysis of the Concept-97.[2] It is worthwhile doing the same with the 2000 edition.

Right away, I want to state that I don't regard such documents as something that affects citizens' lives or Russia's place and role in the world. This concept, just as the Constitution of the Russian Federation, constitutes a declaration of intent not backed by any real capabilities of the state to realize them. A phrase contained therein appears to hint as much: The concept is a "system of views on the provision," etc. "Viewing" can be done any way you like, especially because there are more than enough "viewers" in Russia. An analysis of this kind of document can be interesting only from the perspective of exposing the competence level of the people who

1 See the full text in Independent Military Review, *Nezavisimaya gazeta*, January 14, 2000.

2 See Arin, *Russia on Roadside of the World*, 133–41; Battler, *The Twenty-First Century: The World Without Russia (1st ed.)*

formulate and shape the country's political course. Sometimes it suffices for predicting the outcome of that course.

Just like the previous variant of the concept, the current one is not a concept of national security (CNS) but rather a compilation of assessments of all (or almost all) aspects of domestic and foreign policy, as well as instructions/demands about what needs to be done to have security triumph in a "kingdom" consisting of "person, society, and state."

Like any nonworking document, it starts with empty phrases like "the national security of the Russian Federation is understood as the security of its multiethnic people as the subject of sovereignty and the sole source of authority in the Russian Federation." This reference to "the people" is a standard cliché used by demagogues. In fact, this entire document is not any different from the CPSU documents of the "stagnant socialism" era titled "The Party's immediate objectives in the area of domestic and foreign policy." Therefore, let's examine its content, preserving the structure of the "report."

Russia in the World Community

"The world community is defined by two trends: the trend toward multipolarity, which Russia will be aiding along, and the trend toward domination of the developed Western nations led by the USA."

This assessment is deeply erroneous because the second "trend" is no trend at all, but an actual fact, and the first trend is simply not in evidence; there is no plurality of "poles" in sight beyond "the domination of Western nations." China is shaping up to be a "pole," but should it truly become one, the world will be bipolar rather than multipolar.

The concept's authors state that Russia "continues objectively to play a large role in world processes due to its significant economic, scientific, technological, and military potential and its unique strategic position in the Eurasian continent." This phrase is pure demagoguery; the fact is that Russia's economic potential is smaller than that of Australia (population 20 million), or South Korea, or Mexico, or Brazil, etc. Its science and technology potential has been destroyed and is now inferior to that of any developed country; its military potential is insufficient even to guarantee security on Russia's own territory, as in Chechnya. As for Russia's geographical position on the "Eurasian continent," it is merely a statement of geographical fact; it gives no grounds for pronouncements about the state's greatness.

The document does express a concern: "At the same time, a number of states are stepping up their efforts intended to weaken Russia's position in the political, economic, military, and other areas." Which states are included in that number? USA? Germany? Japan? By the logic of the preceding passage about two trends, these are all "developed Western nations," i.e., the very same nations from which Russia expects and actually receives economic and financial aid from time to time. How exactly are they "weakening" Russia's position?

To sum up: "Russia and the world community" consists of nothing but claptrap and assessments that have nothing to do with the realities of international life.

Russia's National Interests

The definition of Russia's national interests as "the aggregate of balanced interests of the individual, the society, and the state" in all spheres of social life is a pretty but absolutely empty phrase, for a reason that didn't even occur to any of the authors. The interests of the individual, the society, and the state cannot be balanced in principle because it is precisely their "imbalance" that makes these phenomena distinct. Furthermore, all talk about state, society, and individual is an empty abstraction until definitions are given: *what* state, *what* society, and individual in *what* system? Which kind of democracy is to be strengthened, out of a dozen different historical types? What in the world is a "social state"? Can you name even one "nonsocial state"? Apart from everything else, all this has nothing to do with national security; these are matters of a country's domestic policy.

Now let us proceed to the foreign aspect of national interests. It too is formulated in a silly fashion. “Russia’s national interests in the international sphere lie in the protection of sovereignty; in the strengthening of Russia’s position as a great power and one of the influential centers of a multipolar world; in the development of equal and mutually profitable relations with all countries and integration entities, including CIS member states and Russia’s traditional partners; in the universal observance of human rights and liberties, without allowing the use of double standards in that area.”

How can Russia possibly strengthen its position “as a great power” in a multipolar world if that world doesn’t exist? (The authors themselves mention it in the beginning as only a trend.) What is a “great power”? Give us the parameters for one. As for “human rights and liberties,” this phrase must have been inserted as a joke, considering that in Russia itself, these same rights, especially the right to life, and liberties are restricted as in no other country in the world.

The authors demonstrate their complete lack of understanding of the subject in the following sentence: “Russia’s national interests in the military sphere lie in the protection of its independence, sovereignty, state and territorial integrity; in the prevention of military aggression against Russia and its allies; in the securing of conditions for a peaceful, democratic development of the state.” The authors don’t understand that independence, sovereignty, and state and territorial integrity are not national interests *in the military sphere*; rather, they are describing the military *policy* of securing national interests that consist of such-and-such. They are missing the logic (or structure) of interconnections between national interests and the policy of securing them. This is why they start listing national interests in the “borders sphere,” in the “ecological sphere,” and so on. I would advise them to include the “sexual sphere” and especially the “brains sphere” for completeness of the package. Let us not waste any more time on empty talk.

Threats to the National Security of the Russian Federation

This part of the document is truly unique. The authors don't understand elementary things. The logic of national security concepts is that when they talk about threats, they mean threats from foreign hostile forces. The "threats" that result from mistakes and idiocy in domestic and foreign policy are called crimes of the country's leaders.

Consider this: Almost half the text in this chapter is dedicated to the sorry state of the "national economy." In this sphere threats are "complex in nature and are caused (sic!) in the first place by the considerable shrinking of the gross domestic product, the decline in investment and innovation activities, in the science and technology potential," and so forth.

Exactly. So who is responsible for the collapse of the USSR, for these "failures" and threats? Who "managed" the economy and politics in those years? Wasn't it Yeltsin and his team? Wasn't it Chernomyrdin and the "young reformers"? It turns out that all the "threats" listed in this chapter were created, initiated, and provoked by the country's previous leadership. Because all these listed "threats" are still present under the new leadership, it too bears responsibility for them. In that case, isn't this leadership the most important threat to Russia's national interests and its people? The essence of the current regime hasn't changed, after all. How can one expect it to change the situation?

The international affairs part of this chapter repeats phrases from chapter one, only through the prism of the "threats" category. Here's an example: "Threats to the national security of the Russian Federation in the international sphere are manifested in the attempts of other states to counteract the strengthening of Russia as one of the centers of influence in a multipolar world, to hinder the realization of its national interests, and to weaken its position in Europe, the Middle East, Trans-Caucasia, Central Asia, and the Asia-Pacific region." One might add, how can anyone weaken Russia's position in, say, the Middle East and the Asia-Pacific region, where they have been in a "weakened state" for the past ten years?

Or maybe someone can prove that Russia's position was never "weakened" in such countries as Chili, Mexico, Australia, New Zealand, Papua New Guinea, Indonesia, and others that are included in the "APR" (Asian-Pacific Region)?

Mentioned among the threats are "territorial demands made on the Russian Federation." Right, but who is making these demands? Isn't it Japan—a country with which Moscow is trying to build a "strategic partnership"?

In reality, all the above-listed "threats" are nothing but the result of Russia's own domestic and foreign policy.

Ensuring the National Security of the Russian Federation

This part in particular reminds me of the papers titled "The immediate tasks of the CPSU." It consists from beginning to end of phrases with words "has to," "should," "must"—verbal garbage undeserving of comment. For example, it's hard to argue with the statement that "the spiritual renovation of society is impossible without preserving the role of the Russian language as the factor of spiritual unification of the peoples of multinational Russia and the language of interstate communication of the peoples of the CIS member states." So what? The democratic-minded mass media in Russia is currently corrupting the Russian language, turning it into Anglo-newspeak with a Brighton Beach accent. This Anglicization of the Russian language has audaciously invaded all the main television channels. "Programming that promotes violence," taken from the trash heaps of Americanized culture, has taken over nearly 90 percent of all screen time. How does this fit with the achievement of the goals outlined in the National Security Concept?

All these wishes of the "has to—should be" variety will not be fulfilled, just as the wishes in the previous *Concept-97* were not, and just as those in the next *Concepts* won't be, for the reason that they are formulated by one and the same regime. It is the authority of stateoligarchic capital that is specifically Russian; it has other goals and objectives. The submitted *Concept* is nothing but camouflage, intended for a dumbed-down populace which still nurtures illusions about the possibility of their lives getting better and about the current rulers' ability to protect Russia's national interests. But these illusions will have to be discarded anyway. The elite is incompetent and illiterate, unable even to formulate the concept of the country's national security professionally.

To be fair, it should be mentioned that even some adepts of the current regime have subjected the concept in question to some cautious criticism. Some have criticized it for its structural imperfections;[1] others, for the vagueness of certain definitions. Valentin Rog suggested improving the definition of national security with the following addition: "A country's national security is its ability to maintain and defend its sovereignty, territorial integrity, national interests in the military sphere and the economic area, its cultural and moral-spiritual heritage, historical traditions and norms of social life; to ensure the strengthening of Russian statehood, the improvement and development of federalism and local self-government, as well as security in the ecological sphere."[2] This formulation, too, contains a lot of stuff that doesn't belong there, but the direction chosen is the right one. There are other critics, though, whose suggestions, if adopted, would turn the working document into captivating reading about Russian life. Ramazan Abdulatipov, for example, complained that the Concept says nothing about the security of "ethno-national communalities"; it only mentions the security of the "multinational people."[3] Valentin Rog proposed including in the Concept the national idea, so that it would turn into a "concept of the Russian soul."[4] Considering how unique this soul is, one can imagine that many volumes would be needed to contain the document intended to guide the country's policy. But then, that's not what the Concept was written for.

* * *

1 See Grishin, "National Security of Russia" (interview with Ozerov), *Profi*, no. 3–4 (2000), 64–7.

2 *Nezavisimaya gazeta*, February 11, 2000.

3 Ibid., January 29, 2000.

4 Ibid., January 14, 2000.

After analyzing the *National Security Concept* (NCS), I intended to examine critically the *Military Doctrine of the Russian Federation*, approved by a presidential decree of April 21, 2000. However, after examining this Doctrine, I lost the desire to criticize it, for, unlike the NCS, the *Military Doctrine* looks like a proper document, logical in structure and thematically justified. The approved variant is actually an improvement on the draft military doctrine of October 1999, due to the "removal" of the most vulnerable generalities about the international community. The silly declaration about Russia's commitment to the model of a multipolar world is still there, though. On the other hand, the document contains a realistic evaluation of Russia's situation in the world, and it lists the real threats to the country's national security. It contains a good deal less propaganda confetti than the NCS, which makes it a working document. Quite timely are the corrected formulations of certain terms (for example, "military conflict" in its different varieties), as well as the structural hierarchy of threats: challenge – risk – danger – threat – aggression. In this connection, it is important to underline that the threats mentioned here are threats precisely to the national interests of Russia, not to the "world" or "mankind" in general, as political and diplomatic documents say all too often. To my surprise, military theorists proved to be better prepared for the task of formulating a doctrine than the people who worked on the NSC.

Even though I cannot agree with some purely military aspects of this doctrine, I have no intention of discussing them here. First, the doctrine is, as the authors themselves say, "a document of the transitional period." 72[1] Second, it will not be implemented anyway due to the lack of funding. Third, this book is devoted to the place and role of Russia in the world, not to the problems of Russian military reforms.

Let us now examine the theoretical level of the organization that spearheads Russia's foreign policy by definition, the Ministry of Foreign Affairs (MFA).

1 See *A Military Doctrine of the Russian Federation*, the full text in Independent Military Review, *Nezavisimaya gazeta*, April 28, 2000.

Primakov – Ivanov – MFA: Demagogy – Idealism – Utopia

Before we proceed with the analysis of the MFA's official document, the *Foreign Policy Concept of the Russian Federation*, it is worthwhile to hear out Russia's two main idea generators in the area of foreign policy and international relations: Yevgeny M. Primakov, former Minister of Foreign Affairs, and Igor Ivanov, the current minister. Let us start with the former.

Yevgeny M. Primakov. Among the many causes of the Soviet Union's defeat in the Cold War and its subsequent collapse, one should pay attention, in particular, to the inability of its leaders of that time to evaluate realistically the international situation and the place and role of their country in the world. The most concentrated manifestation of their wishful thinking was the philosophy of so-called new thinking, where two of the main components were the much-touted "universal values" and deideologization of international relations. All this philosophy was built on utopian ideas and projects, e.g., the fifteen-year program of step-by-step liquidation of nuclear weapons by the end of the twentieth century.

Back then, I made public statements against this "new thinking" at the Institute of the World Economy and International Relations (Russian acronym: IMEMO), where Primakov was director at the time. In 1987 I wrote the article "'New' Philosophy in Foreign Policy from 'Deficit of Idealism' to Concessions to Common Sense." It was supposed to be published in the Institute's journal, *World Economy and International Relations*, but the editorial committee rejected it on the grounds that the author's position was at odds with the decisions of the XXVII CPSU Congress and, in general, with the policy line of the Party and the government. On the initiative of either the editorial board or Primakov personally, the article was subjected to preliminary discussion at the Director's Council, involving leading research associates of the Institute. They all criticized me for deviating from the Party line on international policy issues. (All these critics later became the most rabid of anti-Communists.) The essence of my article was criticism of the main ideas of the "new thinkers," of the utopianism and idealism of the very concept of new political thinking.

The only reason I recall this episode here is that despite the complete failure of all the utopias of the Gorbachev period, at present noless-utopian plans are being proposed again and again in order to bring about "peace in the twenty-first century." Their authors suggest humanizing the world—proceeding possibly from good intentions, supposing evidently that the world consists entirely of "doves" desiring world peace. One concrete manifestation of this childish utopia is the *Plan-Synopsis of the Concept of the World in the 21st Century*. Before analyzing this plan, I want to take a look at the current views of Primakov, whom I consider to be one of the politicians responsible for the collapse of the USSR.

More than ten years ago, Primakov was promoting the ideas of "new thinking" that went on to bankruptcy. In 1996 Mr. Primakov became Minister of Foreign Affairs, replacing the perfectly grotesque figure that was Andrei Kozyrev. Primakov's anti-Western position found support in certain political circles in Russia, and the West even appeared to take some fright. It need not have. Primakov's vision of international relations and, accordingly, of Russia's foreign policy preserves the same idealism and inadequacy characteristic of him ten and even twenty years ago. Anyone who would look up his writings from those times would find my words justified.

Let us, for instance, take Primakov's article "A Multipolar World on the Horizon."[1] What do we see there? The academician-turnedminister states: "After the end of the Cold War, the trend developed of transition from a *confrontational bipolar world to a multipolar world*" (italics mine). He either fails or deliberately refuses to notice that a unipolar system had replaced the bipolar one. His conclusion is either proof of complete professional incompetence or pure propaganda claptrap served to a starving population. The proper thing to say is this: "Regrettably, the system currently in place is unipolar, with the USA on top. But this kind of world is not to our liking, and we shall try to change it into a mul-

1 *Nezavisimaya gazeta*, October 22, 2000.

tipolar one." It is necessary also to show what means are needed to achieve this goal and where they will come from.

Primakov's statement is followed by his assessment of the international situation: "The countries of Western Europe have started demonstrating a greater independence than before, now that they have stopped being dependent on the American 'nuclear umbrella.' Their gravitation toward a 'Eurocenter' is gradually overcoming their trans-Atlantic orientation. Against the background of Japan's rapidly expanding position in the world, its military-political dependence on the United States is weakening."

On what grounds are these conclusions drawn? Just two years after the publication of this article, they were refuted by the NATO countries' joint action in Kosovo. In the following two years, AmericanJapanese military ties have become even stronger through the modernization of military cooperation. Who needs a forecast that fails to calculate the developments of the next two to three years?

Returning to the topic of a multipolar world, the academician starts listing the "conditions" that will make this "world" happen. The "conditions" often change into "suggestions." Primakov "suggests" that the mentality that divides the world into "leaders" and "followers" be eliminated. Do you really believe that Americans are dying to hear the suggestion that they free themselves from the idea of being a "leading" power? Moreover, Primakov says: "This mentality is fed by the illusions that some countries emerged victorious from the Cold War, and other countries emerged defeated. This is not true. The peoples on both sides of the Iron Curtain have combined forces to rid themselves of the politics of confrontation. The mentality of 'leaders' and 'followers,' meanwhile, directly works to support the trend toward a unipolar world. This model of the world order is *unacceptable today to the majority of the world community*." (italics mine —*A.B.*).

This guy wouldn't blink if you spat in his eyes. This kind of logic supposes, evidently, that the Soviet Union is also counted among the "victors." The academician is not perturbed by the fact that the USSR has been replaced by a shrunken Russia, squeezed along all the geostrategic vectors. I will not even mention the "fruits" of this victory on the economic and social fronts.

The appeal to a "world community" or to the "peoples of the world" who "don't accept" something or other is elementary demagogy. Politicians use this trick when they have nothing to say on the essence of the matter. "The world community" is a chimera, just as the notion that peoples make some kind of effort in the sphere of international relations. "Peoples" don't play the game of big-time politics; the leaders of their states do it for them.

The third condition, "democratization of international economic relations," is just as utopian as everything the academician writes or talks about. Not one of his postulates works in principle, not one of his forecasts comes true, and not one of his analyses can be approached from a scientific perspective because the academician has never worked on the conceptual level. He offers nothing but words (utopia – demagogy, demagogy – utopia), and nothing more.

Igor Ivanov. Regrettably, the next minister of foreign affairs, Igor Ivanov, inherited this style and approach. His assessments of the international situation are more realistic, though, proving that sometimes life does sober one up.

In his article "Russia in a Changing World," Ivanov writes: "Mankind is once again facing a choice of principle: either a multipolar system of the world order, based on the primacy of international law and strengthening of the existing international institutions, or a unipolar model with domination by a sole superpower."[1]

It is hard to understand what moves politicians to speak for all of mankind. Besides the fact that 99 percent of mankind doesn't even suspect the existence of this choice between a multi- or unipolar world, perhaps as many as 90 percent don't even know that the country called Russia exists.

Equally touching is the appeal to strengthen international institutions. This wonderful appeal suggests, supposedly, the strengthening, among other things, of such an international institution as NATO.

Yet, I repeat that reality adjusts idealists' assessments. Just one year later, Ivanov was compelled to state: "Also disappointed were the hopes that bipolar confrontation would automatically be replaced with partnership in the interests of international stability. Moreover, the power factor has not lost its significance; it only changed its orientation. A number of new areas of tension have

1 *Nezavisimaya gazeta*, June 26, 1999.

flared up, some of them near Russia's borders."[1]

The hopes were "disappointed" precisely because these policies were built on "hopes," on "faith," and on "if only," instead of relying on knowledge of the surrounding world and understanding of the Western "mentality." Otherwise, there would be no need for expressing another "regret," as Ivanov does. He continues: "Regrettably, the policy of Western states, especially in the last two to three years, has been manifesting the intent to build a unipolar model of the world order based on domination by a limited circle of the most developed states led by the USA." (ibid.) This begs the question: Why would this same USA work to create a multipolar world, closing off its own opportunities to make the world work for the USA?

On one hand, Ivanov appeals for strengthening "international institutions"; on the other, he laments: "In European affairs, the logic of unipolarity manifests itself in NATO-centrism, in the intent to build the system of European and international security around a single militarypolitical bloc." (ibid.) So where's the logic here?

The Concept of the World in the Twenty-First Century. Now we return to "The Concept of the World in the Twenty-First Century"—a pinnacle of utopianism, towering even over the utopianism of Primakov's ideas. The grounds offered for this concept are curious. Ivanov says in his article: "Promoting our *Concept of the World in the TwentyFirst Century*, we are not seeking a pretext for rivalry; we offer to seek together ways to increase manageability of world processes and to ensure stability in the world, these things being equally necessary to all states." (ibid.) Right away, the utopian touch is in evidence: What kind of rivalry can we talk about today? Rivalry between whom? Can anyone believe that the USA is seriously regarding Russia as a rival—with its GDP of only $330 billion and an impoverished population? How can a country manage a world course of action when its rulers cannot manage elementary domestic issues?

Mr. Ivanov emphasizes without irony: "The novelty of the concept consists, first of all, in taking the realistic approach to assessing the world situation and our own foreign policy resources."

1 See Ivanov's presentation at MGIMO, *Kremlin Package* (Federal News Service), May 23, 2000.

It is possible to agree, more or less, with the first part of this statement (see above), but its second part can only be perceived as a joke. It turns into a farce when you read the following: "Another important thing is the necessity to conduct a multivector policy, balanced in the geographical aspect. Considering Russia's unique geopolitical location, it must have a proper place for relations with all key regions of the world." (ibid.)

First, it is desirable to have at least a hint as to which regions are not "key" ones. The subsequent text makes it clear that Russia will be acting in all regions of the world. Moreover: "The importance of Asia is climbing up the scale of Russia's foreign policy priorities." I've been reading and hearing this phrase for more than thirty years now, and still Asia hasn't "climbed up." Second, are there enough foreign policy resources to cover all the "key regions"? Third, this variant of the concept practically doesn't differ from all the previous variants in its allencompassing nature. It does, however, differ substantially in "content"—in the direction of utopianism. Judge for yourselves from these following examples:

Claim #1: The Charter of the United Nations Organization is the foundation of the *Concept of the World in the Twenty-First Century*; the UN ensures security and stability in the world.

First, neither the UN, nor the Organization for Security and Cooperation in Europe, nor any other similar organization in all the time of its existence has ensured any stability in the world, nor is it capable of ensuring it.[1] Why on earth would they suddenly start ensuring it in the twenty-first century?

Second, these organizations are funded for the most part by the USA and its allies. Don't the authors know that Russia's share in the funding of the UN is close to 1 percent, while the USA's share is more than 22 percent? Japan, which is not even a member of the Security Council, has a share of about 20 percent. For this reason alone, the UN is an instrument for realizing precisely the

1 It seems that of all scholars of international affairs, Rogov alone understands this obvious truth and expressed it in delicate diplomatic form: "At the same time such mechanisms of ensuring international security as the UN and the OSCE see their role decreasing, their functions are supplanted by NATO and other Western institutions." Independent Military Review, *Nezavisimaya gazeta*, January 12, 2000.

interests of "the golden core" of the capitalist world. How silly in this light is Ivanov's statement that: "We see one of our main tasks in the year 2001 in working to strengthen the role and authority of the UN in international affairs, including the resolution of the remaining crisis situations in different regions of the planet."[1]

Third, in order to make these above-mentioned organizations serve "the cause of peace," Russia must acquire dominant financial and leadership position in them—something it simply doesn't have resources for.

Claim #2: The world is experiencing globalization, and the world is interconnected.

The world is indeed undergoing globalization (just one of several trends, by the way, and by no means the dominant one), but definitely not for the benefit of the entire world; this process clearly benefits the "core" group of developed countries. That's why, in most countries, this globalization process is viewed negatively as Americanization or, in the softer variant, as Westernization. The world is not interdependent; the fact is that the larger part of the world is "dependent" on the smaller part. Is it really necessary to prove these axioms?

Claim #3: Multipolarity is the world order of the twenty-first century.

Even if one agrees with this statement, there is still no proof that multipolarity is better from the perspective of international security than, say, bipolarity. Doesn't the history of international relations bear evidence that of the three states (multipolarity, bipolarity, and hegemony), it is precisely multipolarity that is most unstable, inevitably producing wars? In the twenty-first century, the world will experience all three states, and the most durable and stable one will be precisely the bipolarity that will be established in the second quarter of the century and will last for about fifty years.

Claim #4: "The law of civilized international relations."

This law does not exist. What has existed for centuries and

1 *Nezavisimaya gazeta*, December 30, 2000.

will exist always is the law of power, which itself defines what is "permissible" and what is "not permissible."

The various objectives proposed on the basis of these claims are in advance doomed to failure, as they have no objective foundation. The pinnacle of utopianism (a stronger word would be more appropriate) is the objective of "creating a new culture of peace." Throw in the slogan: "To be the light of the world!" and the expected result would then be "happy people on a happy Earth." (This is a quote from the program of the Ethical Movement, "Native Land.")

Finally, it is clear to anyone who can see that nearly all of the theses of this "Concept for the Twenty-First Century" were taken from the propaganda arsenal of American foreign policy, as evidenced even by the terminology: "preventive diplomacy," "control-and-implementation mechanisms," "international monitoring," and the much-touted concept of "sustainable development."

Conclusion: On the basis of the submitted "plan synopsis," it is possible to invent a fable about the twenty-first century that would only be believable to people who don't read books or newspapers but believe in the Ten Commandments.

Speaking seriously, Russia's strategy in the twenty-first century must be built on the realities and regularities of the development of international relations. Otherwise, all we have is just more "if only" claptrap about conquering the entire world with "Russian spirituality."

The Russian Federation's Foreign Policy Concept: The Goal Is Nothing; the Process Is Everything

The current official *Foreign Policy Concept of the Russian Federation*, approved by the president in early July 2000, is definitely an improvement over the previous *Concept* of 1993. At least it contains no illusions about the stability of the world, it identifies directly the "authors of challenges" (the USA), and it features for the first time an appeal to proceed from the state's capabilities in working toward specific foreign policy objectives.

Nonetheless, I must state that not one single goal or objective included in this *Concept* will ever be accomplished. The main reason is that it presents a distorted picture of the world and betrays a lack of understanding of the financial mechanism for implementing foreign policy. It's not surprising because the *Concept* was written by people clearly unfamiliar with theories of international relations. This means that they are used to working with words, sometimes terms, but not notions and categories. For the Russian frame of mind, it is a natural type of thinking that probably can't be escaped. I will attempt to point out some incongruities in this *Concept* and develop my arguments in subsequent chapters. Let me start with one "detail" related to the "concept of a Concept." In the beginning, it says: "The highest priority of Russia's foreign policy course is protection of the interests of the individual, society, and state." This silliness is repeated, as noted above, in almost all official documents. The individual, the society, and the state as political phenomena actually find themselves in different political fields. The foreign policy course cannot possibly protect the individual's interests because this course and the individual's interests are not directly interconnected. Related to these interests are social policy, legal policy, and economic policy, but not foreign policy.

Protection of society through the state's foreign policy course is even worse nonsense. This thing is only possible in "real socialism," when the state and the society are in natural harmony and, at some stage, simply become one. Under a capitalist system, when the society is split into classes, as in Russia, or into strata, as in the West, in the system of "the golden billion"—state and society are in a state of constant struggle. Therefore, the state's interests most of the time don't coincide with the interests of at least part of the society. This is especially true of foreign policy. It is embarrassing even to have to repeat these ABCs.

It follows that the foreign policy course can only reflect the interests of the state. In the case of contemporary Russia, they are the interests of the state-oligarchic capitalism. It is no use trying to pass off black as red. The above quote should read like this: "The highest priority of Russia's foreign policy course is defense of the state's interests." These foreign policy interests should then be detailed.

The Concept presents a distorted picture of international relations. In one of the paragraphs, it says that the process is under way of developing "regional and sub-regional integration in Europe, the Asia-Pacific region, Africa, and Latin America." In fact, apart from Western Europe, there is no integration anywhere; there is only a trend toward integration in North America (through the mechanism of NAFTA) and in East Asia. The "APR" as an integral region simply doesn't exist in the economic or the political sense. Talk of integration in Africa or Latin America is evidence of either complete lack of understanding of economic trends in these regions or failure to understand the difference between the notions "integration" and "internationalization." Judging by the Concept, the authors don't know what globalization is, either.

What do the authors have to say about the USA and the already tiresome subject of multipolarity? "The trend is strengthening toward the creation of a unipolar world structure, with economic and power domination by the USA." In reality, as I have already said above, this is not a trend at all, but an established objective fact. This fact is not camouflaged in any way; it is openly stated in all of Washington's strategic documents. This is reality, not just words; it will be demonstrated with figures below.

Here's another remarkable sentence: "Russia will act toward forming a multipolar system of international relations that will realistically reflect the many facets of the modern world with its diversity of interests." Some progress can be seen here compared to the assessments of the previous Concept that maintained that we already live in a multipolar world. In reality, it matters not at all whether Russia, China, or any other nation strives for multipolarity because the world is evolving toward geostrategic global bipolarity. The multipolar periods in history came to an end after World War II. Should anyone try to restore multipolarity artificially, one should be prepared for more frequent regional wars and military conflicts because multipolarity is the least stable system of international relations. A perfunctory glance at the history of the last two centuries suffices.

The intent to counteract the USA by helping form a multipolar world in reality will amount to helping Washington preserve its hegemony in the world because the "struggle" for multipolarity will lead to further waste and fragmentation of the "combatants'" resources, weakening them. The waste of resources is implied in the choice of foreign policy directions; they encompass all regions and subregions and all world problems. What is the rationale for developing economic relations with Africa, Latin America, and ASEAN countries thousands of kilometers away from Russia? We are unable to exert influence on them because trade with us accounts for no more than 1 percent of their foreign commerce. Those regions' shares in Russia's foreign trade are equally minuscule (about the same 1 percent) except for imports from Brazil (2 percent). The benefits of this trade are negligible when compared to the costs of conducting it (even the transportation costs alone, with fuel costs over enormous distances).

More on this topic: Why does Russia participate in 2,000 international organizations? What benefits did it ever acquire from participation in APEC? What is the payback for the annual PACE dues of $35 million? And so on, and so forth.

What objective is the state pursuing when it sends its "peacekeeping forces" to Africa (Sierra Leone, for instance), to Kosovo, and other hot spots? Is "enlightenment" the only goal? What is the price of this enlightenment? The answer offered is this: "It makes economic sense for Russia to send its peacekeepers to hot spots. First, it reduces the country's UN dues. Second, our servicemen get to make some money for themselves."[1] The latter reason is probably the main one. What is the developed countries' approach? The

1 *Nezavisimaya gazeta*, August 4, 2000.

same newspaper reports: "The USA, France, and Great Britain responded negatively to the UN Secretary General's request that they send their troops to help resolve the conflict in Sierra Leone. They referred to the spending limitations of their state budgets and their reluctance to get involved in conflicts of insignificant scale." What a paradox: Americans have "budget limitations," while Russia, whose budget is about the size of a large city's budget in America, has no such "limitations."

Speaking in principle, one can include any kind of goals and objectives in a *Concept*. But they will remain empty talk if one doesn't indicate the cost of implementing these plans. Actually, the *Concept* itself contains a most reasonable appeal: "A successful foreign policy of the Russian Federation must be based on maintaining a reasonable balance between the objectives and the means for their accomplishment. The concentration of political-diplomatic, military, economic, financial, and other means for accomplishing foreign policy objectives must be commeasurable with their real importance to Russia's national interests, and the scope of participation in international affairs must be adequate to its actual contribution to the strengthening of our country's position." Exactly. Unfortunately, these thoughts were not reflected at all even in the formulation of objectives and announced goals. To accomplish these, the sums allocated in the state budget must be increased not just by one order of magnitude, but by two.

Such is Moscow's official view of itself and the world. It evidently has problems either with its eyes or with its brains.

Preliminary Conclusions

The failures in the formulation of the official *National Security Concept* are due to the absence of methodical skills in the preparation of this type of political document. The concept of national security is a phenomenon of American political science, not the Russian one. It was developed after World War II by such scholars as H. Morgenthau, G. Kennan, A. Wolfers, S. Hoffman, and others. Even before the idea of national security started acquiring doctrinal forms, American scholars of international affairs had intense discussions over such key terms of foreign policy as "national interests," "vital interests," "fundamental interests," "national security," the category of "goal" in its different nuances (goal, aim, objective), as well as the complex category of "national power and strength," trying to define the differences between phenomena expressed by different term-words: might, power, force, capability, strength, etc. Even though debates on these topics continue to this day,[1] U.S. political science has nonetheless developed a general understanding of the basic categories of foreign policy and international relations. This simplifies the task of formulating well-structured political documents with a more or less clear concept apparatus.[2]

At the same time, Russian political scientists, having borrowed the very idea of national security from Americans, still remain embroiled in the confusion of unfamiliar terms and are not even clear about the difference in the scientific content of the words "term," "notion," and "category." Clearly testifying to this fact are discussions around the concept of "national interests."[3]

The other problem in developing the Concept of national security has to do less with methodology than with the developers'

1 See, for example, Atwood, "Towards A New Definition Of National Security," *Vital Speeches of the Day* (December 15, 1995), 135–138.

2 See *Contemporary U.S. foreign policy: documents and commentary*, compiled and edited by Elmer Plishke, 33–56.

3 See "The Concept of National Interests: General Parameters and Russian Specific Character," *MEMO*, no.7–9 (1996).

world outlook. It is perfectly obvious that the content of concepts or doctrines depends on the developers' views. In this case, I consciously avoid using the "class approach." But even in the milieu of one class—say, the ruling bourgeois class—there exist different views of Russia's foreign policy. It is perfectly obvious that those developers who are paid by compradors will talk about the necessity to join the "world marketplace" in close union with the West, while those developers who are tied to the national bourgeoisie will promote protection of "genuinely Russian state interests" that must be defended from "the predators of world capitalism," and also promote greater orientation toward "Asian countries," primarily China and India. There is nothing surprising about this, considering that in the USA, too, the general strategies of foreign policy are outlined differently, depending on which group of capitalists is currently in power. A number of international affairs scholars in the USA are working on the theoretical foundations of this set of problems; most prominent among them is Charles E. Snare, who even invented untranslatable terms for the two groups of writers I mentioned above. He calls the intermediaries "Developmental," and advocates of the national state "Active Independent."[1]

In light of everything said above, it must be clear how difficult it is to formulate a national security or foreign policy concept for Russia. An analysis of the works of leading Russian experts on foreign policy and international relations will show us where these difficulties lie.

1 Snare, "Defining Others and Situations: Peace, Conflict, and Cooperation," *Peace and Conflict Studies* 1, no. 1 (December 1994).

Chapter II

Russian Scholars: In the World of "If-only-ism," or How to Take a "Worthy Place" in the World

Very few Russian scholars work on the level of notions. This is not surprising at all, considering that the Russian type of thinking is from the outset irrational, feminine, intuitive, and steeped in mysticism. For anyone who is not Russian it is practically impossible to understand what Russian scholars mean when they write of a "worthy place" in the world for their country, of integration into the world economy, of world globalization, of Russia as a great power. Attempts to find out what all this means induce in Russian scholars incomprehension or accusations that one is trying, with evil intent, to "stretch" the discussion and get it "bogged down in arguments over concepts that cannot be defined in principle." (A.M. Salmin)[1]

In one of my books, I attempted to show, in a provocative form, the difference between the concepts "integration" and "internationalization," to prove that the "Asia-Pacific region" does not exist as an economic or political integrity. The readers of this book and even those reviewers who gave positive reviews did not respond in any way to the theoretical chapter; they either considered it unworthy of their attention.

1 *Memo*, no. 9 (1996), 77.

It should be clear by now what the consequences of inattention to the concept apparatus are from what was said above. The rare exception is perhaps the term "national interests"; the discussion about it was published in the magazine *World Economy and International Relations* (1996, No. 7–9). Although some debaters (e.g., B. G. Kapustin and D. E. Furmanov) attempted to demonstrate that this concept is impossible to define or is "heuristically low-productive," others (in particular, A.A. Galkin, Yu. A. Krasin, and A. P. Logunov) gave important and clear definitions. One may agree or disagree with them, but one can work with them.

Russian scholars of international affairs concentrate in their discussions on some key topics, the most popular of which are globalization, the structure of international relations (unipolarity vs. multipolarity), and whether Russia is a great power.

Let's examine each of these topics in turn.

Globalization, Globalization Everywhere

All scholars of international affairs recognize that the process of globalization is under way in the world, although they understand it differently. Thus, A. V. Zagorsky writes of a "rapidly increasing internationalization (sic) of economic reproduction processes on a world scale, the result of which ... is *the forming of a united, closely interconnected world-economy complex* that is the core of the modern economy." (Emphasis added by the author.)[1] This statement means that a whole, integrated world economy has been formed.

Although most authors simply state the fact of globalization, and some (like Zagorsky) perceive globalization as world economic integration, giving no thought to the term they use, V. Mikheyev analyzes this process in detail, offering his own definition of the term "globalization." He writes: "The ***globalization*** of the world economy means:

- First, the expansion of national economic interests beyond national state boundaries, the creation and expansion of transnational economic and financial structures.
- Second, the raising of "private," national economic issues to a global, world level of vision, a level that requires, for these problems to be solved, attention to world economic interests and the mobilization of world resources. In other words, the world must be viewed as a single economic space.
- Third, the influence of the situation in some segments of the global economy on other segments that are not necessarily directly associated with the first.
- Fourth, the need to coordinate on a global scale national economic and financial policies, and to create a single global set of rules as a condition for stable global economic development. This is particularly important in the light of the latest Asian

1 *Cosmopolis. Almanac* (Moscow: Polis, 1997), 162.

financial crises, which has directly or indirectly affected nearly all of the world's financial markets."

- It can be said that *the globalization of the world economy involves a critical level of economic interdependence in our world*, based on:
- Economic integration and increasing movement of capital, goods, and labor throughout the world;
- Technological integration, spurred on by world scientific and technological progress;
- The modern information and communications revolution, associated with the creation of high-speed transport and ultramodern means of communication, the increasing popularity of personal computers and the Internet." (Italicized text by Mikheyev.)[1]

I am deliberately reproducing such a lengthy fragment here in order not to distort the author's idea. The content of this quote is intended to suggest the idea that it is not just the countries of "the golden billion" that are obsessed with ideas of globalization; indeed, the message is that all the countries in the world are possessed of such "transnational economic and financial structures" that seek to function outside their nations' borders. I must note, though, that in the lists of transnational companies that are published traditionally in Fortune, to date I have failed to spot any TNC from India, China, Russia, Brazil, or Mexico, etc. In other words, the TNCs in question can only be those of the capitalist core, and I will go on to show later that even with those, everything is not so simple.

It is also unclear how to measure the "critical level of economic interdependence." The author does not elaborate on this "level" in any way, save for stating the obvious banality about "increasing movement throughout the world of capital, goods, and workforce"—a phenomenon observed throughout the twentieth century. My doubts about this specialist's professionalism are deepened when I read this: "But the conditions for this are not yet ripe. The *contradiction* between the need, born of globalization, for the peo-

1 Mikheev. "The Globalization of the World Economy and Asian Regionalism—Challenges for Russia?" *Far Eastern Affairs*, no. 2 (1999), 10.

ple of this planet for a single world economy and the *supremacy* of the national state form of economy could be described as the *main contradiction* of the contemporary age—the age of globalization of the world economy and the personification of international relations." (italicized text by Mikheev.) (11)

I, too, number myself among "the people of this planet," but for some reason, I don't feel any need for globalization. The author fails even to see that "personification of international relations" is not possible in principle because all international relations would then turn into interpersonal relations, and this would bring about a state of relations called tribal, i.e., a primitive society. In other words, this author claiming to be an expert on globalization fails utterly to understand the essence of this process; therefore, all his pronouncements are meaningless. There is even less point in addressing the writings of nonspecialists who promote the ideas of globalization.

Unlike the eager champions of globalization, Andrey Kokoshin is more cautious in his evaluation of this phenomenon because he proceeds from Russia's national interests. That tie-in is entirely justified, and I will dwell on it later. To start with, we should determine what Kokoshin means by "globalization."

Like most Russian scholars, he goes ahead and describes the phenomenon's manifestations without first defining the term, which naturally leads him into a common fallacy. He writes: "In the economy, globalization manifests itself in the sharp growth of the scale and speed of capital movement; in international commerce growing faster than the GDP of all nations; in the creation of networks of international manufacturing businesses with a fast placement of facilities for making standardized, uniform products; in the forming of global financial markets where many kinds of transactions are performed practically around the clock and in real time."[1]

Most of these manifestations were actually observed as early as the start of the twentieth century; these phenomena are described within the framework of the theory of internationalization. The only one which is directly related to globalization is the scale of financial transactions. Kokoshin is correct here when he says that the financial sphere "is becoming a self-sufficient force, determin-

1 *Nezavisimaya gazeta*, May 26, 2000.

ing the development possibilities for manufacturing, agriculture, infrastructure, and services." Today the financial sphere itself is becoming "the real economy." But this sphere is still in the process of establishing itself; it is an important aspect of globalization. It is nevertheless only a trend. At the present moment it is still too early to speak of "the emergence of a new system of international economic and political relations that has replaced first of all the system that existed from 1945 to the early 1990s."

Two different approaches are mixed up here, the geostrategic one and the geoeconomic one. The transition from a bipolar world to a unipolar one happened not as a result of globalization but as a result of the changing balance of geostrategic powers in the world. What happened in the geoeconomic sphere is that the internationalized fields and integrated fields were joined by a new phenomenon—globalization—that is "at war" with both earlier ones. Therefore, the author's basic premise is false, i.e., at present "not only the long cycle of world history that started in 1945 has reached its conclusion, but also the super-long cycle several centuries deep" (i.e., going back to the 1648 Treaty of Westphalia). According to Kokoshin, "a new super-long cycle" is now under way.

The term "cycle" itself is misused in this context; otherwise, the author would be compelled to tell about the previous cycle's regularities and the repetition of these regularities in the future. Kokoshin only wants to say that during the Westphalian era, the main subjects of international relations were states, whereas in the new cycle, the state loses its dominance to other players in international relations (for example, the TNCs). But even if this were so, one should talk of phases of historical development rather than cycles. It is no accident that Kokoshin simply lists the ***events*** of the Westphalian era rather than ***regularities***.

All this, however, is incorrect in principle because even in the era of globalization (should it become the dominant feature of international life), the state will keep getting even stronger through acquiring new functions. Instead, the question is: What kind of state will it be, of the First, Second, or Third World type? The world economy consists today of three overlapping layers, closely intertwined yet each possessing its own regularities.

Russia is being affected by all kinds of economic interaction—in a negative key in each instance, as acknowledged by Kokoshin himself. How can this be counteracted? Kokoshin believes it is necessary to close the economic gap separating Russia from "the golden billion"; this requires achieving a GDP growth rate of about 10 percent annually in the near future. This seems logical, but only at first glance. At second glance, it does not make much sense because Kokoshin admits that even after thirty or forty years, Russia will not manage to acquire a status comparable to that of the USSR. In other words, Russia will not be transformed into a great power even over decades of development, while its citizens will not settle for anything less. At third glance, the GDP growth rate matters not at all from the perspective of dependency on "the golden billion." Let me remind you that many ASEAN countries have been increasing their GDP very rapidly (by about 10 percent annually) for a fairly long time, but this has not made them "independent" of "the golden billion." Besides, these growth rates failed to improve the well-being of the majority of the population in several

ASEAN countries, for example, Indonesia and the Philippines. In other words, it is not just economic growth that matters; what matters is the character of foreign and domestic policy which, in turn, determines the character of authority. In the early years of Soviet power, Russia's economy was weaker than the economies of all its enemies, yet Soviet Russia managed to escape becoming an object of exploitation for "the world imperialism," as was said in those times.

"Russia's basic interests," as formulated by Kokoshin to include "the creation of a modern post-industrial market economy," are an illusion, a utopia, because market economy in the Western sense has never worked on Russian soil and never will. In order to create a "postindustrial economy," one must learn to rob "industrial economies" the way it is done—quite skillfully—by the "golden billion" countries. The Russian bourgeoisie can only rob its own population. Therefore, the threat to Russia really does exist, but it does not come from globalization; it comes from the capitalist system formed in the recent yearsugly as always, as everything Russian is.

Unipolar World or a Multipolar One

The theoretical basis of the polarity problem is provided by scholars of the "realist school" (H. Morgenthau, et al.); their key concepts are "pole," "power," "strength," and "national security." From this school's perspective, analysis of the international situation is performed on the geostrategic plane. The so-called globalists tend to reject this approach because they see the above-listed terms as "outdated concepts" (A.V. Zagorsky) and claim that "attempts to build the model of a uni-, bi-, or multipolar world lose their meaning."[1] However, this criticism doesn't seem to bother the geostrategists, and their internal debates center precisely on this issue of "uni-, bi-, or multipolarity." It should be pointed out right away that because the idea of "multipolarity" is embraced by the higher echelons of power, most of its proponents are scholars working for the Ministry of Foreign Affairs or structures closely tied to Russia's foreign policy agencies. There are exceptions, though, due among other things to the fact that some specialists simply are not aware of the difference between the geostrategic and the geoeconomic approaches. In any case, not one of them has combined these two approaches in a more general theory.

Be that as it may, the debates center on the issue of whether the world is unipolar or multipolar, and which of these two variants serves Russia's national interests better. A group of Russian scholars has been attacking the concept of unipolarity lately, provoked by the article written by Ira L. Straus, "Unipolarity: The Concentric Structure of the New World Order," published in Cosmopolis magazine. Although Straus has drafted a relatively complex construct of a "unipole" with the USA in the center, the idea itself is quite simple; that is, a unipolar international system has emerged. A number of well-known international affairs scholars have voiced their disagreement; for example, A.G. Volodin and G.K. Shirokov are convinced that "the trend toward a polycentric world order is becoming increasingly clear." (169) They justify this statement by first bringing up the factor of globalization, but not in the absurd fashion of Mikheyev; rather, they see it as a process that involves not just beneficiaries (the industrially developed countries) but also losers

1 *Cosmopolis*, 164.

(the underdeveloped South that is capable in certain circumstances of opposing the North). They also point to such countries as China, India, Brazil, and Japan, which supposedly also reject the unipolar world concept. (170) The authors add to this number the geoeconomic integrated groups: EU, ASEAN, and MERCOSUR. (*Until reading this, I was unaware that ASEAN was "integrated."—A.B.*) Finally, the USA itself has too many problems in trying to manage the "unipole" role. (ibid.)

The latter topic was most vividly presented by K. E. Sorokin, who described a bunch of "illnesses" inside the USA. Because Mr. Sorokin is either a Europe expert or an employee of the Institute of Europe, he reminds the reader that Europe is quite significant; by many aggregate parameters, it is "comparable or superior to the U.S." (180) A number of analogous arguments support his conviction that the concept of unipolarity is wishful thinking and that multipolarity exists already.

This scholar, being a Europe specialist, ought to know that today's Europe has at least as many "illnesses" as the USA. But this is just a quibble; the important thing is this: No matter how one puts together the macroindicators of European economies, no matter how advanced European economic integration is, Europe doesn't have a single world strategy or a single decision center; it doesn't have a single *Weltanschauung* (as Germans would say), meaning world vision; therefore, Europe is not any kind of pole or center. In current circumstances, Europe can be classified as an economically integrated zone without global geostrategic ambitions, i.e. without those *Sehnsucht und Streben* (desires) for global strategic domination that are so obviously manifested by the "ill" United States.

V.B. Tikhomirov presents even more curious arguments against "unipolarity." Being a scholar of the technological persuasion, i.e., being closer to the laws of nature, he believes that "unipolarity" is impossible by definition because one conventionally does not talk about poles in the absence of "opposites." (181) From this perspective, all talk about a multipolar world makes even less sense because even the planet Earth has only two poles. Therefore, "on the global level, the world social system has always been and remains approximately bipolar; this is manifested in its *structure-invariant.*" (182) The collapse of the USSR only changed the *structure-state* of this system; the world still stays bipolar. "Simply the place of the latter (USSR) as a "superpower" was taken by China (PRC), since

Russia proved to be noncompetitive." (ibid.)

I wouldn't much object to Mr. Tikhomirov if he had offered a measure of "superpower-dom" and an explanation for the fact that in the history of Europe, for example, there were periods of multipolarity, bipolarity, and unipolarity. Henry Kissinger, by the way, gave a qualified account of that history in his book *Diplomacy*. As for the words "polarity" and "pole" themselves, they are but metaphors of political science, replaceable by other words, e.g., "center of power," and there are four different kinds of "power" known in nature.[1]

1 I will explain in the corresponding chapter the real meaning of "pole" and "center of power"; those are different categories.

The Gorbachev Foundation: Idealist-Realists

My analysis centers on two reports prepared by a group led by G. Kh. Shakhnazarov (the chapters on foreign policy were edited by K. N. Brutenz). The first report was published in 1997 (henceforth referred to as R-1), and the second one in 2000 (R-2).[1]

I want to note the merits of these papers. First, the authors make an effort to avoid using annoying Americanisms such as "samoidentifikatsiya" (self-identification). This term's content is conveyed just fine by the Russian word "samoopredeleniye" (self-determination), and this is the word they choose to use. Second, they strive to work on the level of concepts; at least they explain the key terms such as "national interests." No surprise here, because Shakhnazarov and his school have always striven for conceptual clarity and definiteness.[2] One may agree or disagree with their definitions of particular concepts, but the important thing is that they can be used as a starting point. Regrettably, they do hang on to some established clichés, such as "take a worthy place in the world community," or the term "Asia-Pacific region." I, for one, sincerely fail to understand what place should be considered "worthy." Take the USA, India, Iran, Brazil, the Netherlands—which of these states is occupying a worthy place, and which is not? And what does this "APR" term mean? Ask any scholar of international affairs to define the Asia-Pacific region or list the countries it includes, and you will get a different answer in each case. That would be natural because this region has never existed and never will as I have shown in my already mentioned monograph about the "APR."

Third, no fewer than a hundred experts of different politicalideological persuasions took part in discussions of the problems summarized in these reports. I myself have witnessed serious disagreements on certain problems, having twice been a participant

1 *National Interests and Security Problems of Russia*; *The Self-determination of Russia*.

2 See, for example, Shakhnazarov, *The Future Worldorder*; *International Order. Political-legal aspects*.

of Round Tables. The *Reports* are presented as some sort of median line toward which these discussions tended. In reality, the ideas and conclusions contained in these *Reports* reflect the views of the Gorbachev Foundation; they do not reflect the country's public opinion or the opinion of the majority of Russia's "political class" (an expression currently in fashion). These are the views held by the authors of "new political thinking" (NPT) and "de-ideologization of domestic and foreign policy," who provided the theoretical basis for Gorbachev's practical political course. The Reports' authors still maintain the same position, and I shall now proceed to examine them.

It is amazing that the authors continue to champion the ideas of NPT and de-ideologization of policy because the utter insolvency of these ideas has been proven by the course of events over time. They should have been convinced by now that policies untainted by ideology do not exist in principle. Warning others against "wearing ideological blinkers," they go on to confirm this banal thesis by promoting democracy and market economy, which in the context of "free-market" reforms in Russia means nothing other than the capitalization of the country. That is, they speak from the platform of bourgeois or socialbourgeois ideology.

Considering themselves pragmatic realists and referring to the Biblical commandments repeated by Kant ("Do unto others as you would have them do unto you"), they proceed from the assumption that "Russia's national interests are served by the trend of globalization, by the forming of a new, more just international order in which our country must take a worthy place. This orientation corresponds entirely to the nature of national identity." (*R-1, On Main Concepts*) Evidently, the history of mankind that keeps proving constantly the uselessness of all Biblical commandments without exception (both those of Moses and of Christ) fails to teach anything to these naïve idealists. This in itself might not be so bad; what's bad is the learned authors' failure to understand that globalization by its nature is destined to destroy not just Russia but all states. There will be no "worthy places" left to occupy. In the understanding of globalization's theorists, the new globalized international order will be a nonstate economic and political space that I will explore in a subsequent chapter.

Fortunately, this false fundamental assumption does not interfere with the authors' concrete analysis of Russia's national interests and security. Their analysis contains a number of quite reasonable conclusions and assessments.

They define national interests as "… the most essential needs of the Russian society and state whose survival and development depend on their satisfaction; therefore, these are the most important goals of domestic and foreign policy." (ibid.) The authors go on to specify: "Ensuring the state's security is foremost among these goals as the *conditio sine qua non* of the country's survival; without it, no other goals can be attained. In other words, security can be defined as the single most important, number one national interest." (ibid.) This definition is quite workable, as opposed to "rubber definitions" which can twist and turn to accommodate all aspects of social life. The authors are then required to define other national interests. They write: "We believe that from the security perspective, the most important things are these:

- Political stability, i.e., manageability, maintenance of the order necessary for the normal functioning of all social and state institutions, protection of the Constitutional rule of law, citizens' rights and freedoms.
- Integrity of the state, i.e., the kind of state structure and political regime that exclude the threat of disintegration through the force of internal disputes.
- Defense, i.e., protection of the country's independence and territorial integrity from foreign armed aggression.
- Technical-ecological security, i.e., prevention of technology-caused catastrophes and handling of the consequences of natural disasters.
- Economic security, i.e., ensuring the country's economic self-reliance as a condition of the nation's survival and development.
- Foreign policy priorities that help create an international environment that is maximally favorable to Russia." (ibid.)

In this list the reader can already discern great confusion between the categories of interest and security, and domestic and foreign policy. This confusion is typical of almost all security experts.

Let's now proceed to foreign policy priorities. (*R-1*, Ch. VII) The authors assess without illusions Russia's real place in the world, one that has dropped dramatically over the years of capitalist reforms, especially from the perspective of economic potential. In this connection, they conclude: "*Russia certainly cannot aspire to the role of a superpower that was the Soviet Union. Russia undoubtedly remains one of the great world powers on which the future of the global system depends to a large extent.*" (Emphasis by the authors, ibid., Ch. VII.) One cannot but agree with the first of these two statements, but the second one begs the question: What is a "great world power"? If the authors mean only a country's nuclear potential, then Japan and Germany are not great world powers.

However, three years later, the second report (*R-2*) defined Russia's status in the world more modestly, saying: "Objective parameters indicate that save for its nuclear weapons and remnants of influence left over from the Soviet Union, Russia is currently a developing country, and not among the more prosperous ones of the lot." (*R-2*, p. 50) For all that, the authors just wouldn't shed their historic optimism. Though they don't foresee a superpower status for Russia, they write: "Russian society is determined *to affirm Russia's role as one of the great powers.*" (Emphasis by the authors, *R-2*, p. 51.) Thus, it turns out that even a not-quite-successful developing country may nurture the ambition to become a great power and fulfill its ambition. There is definitely food for thought here.

The structure of international relations is viewed through the prism of "two interconnected processes—globalization and "Americanization," i.e., the U.S. course toward establishing a unipolar system of international relations." (Emphasis by the authors, *R-2*, p.51.) The authors fail to notice that Americanization is the same as globalization, i.e., the world economy dominated by American TNCs and TNBs, and in a broader context the submission of the rest of the world to "the magnificent seven."

The authors fail to see this. They approve of globalization and disapprove of Americanization. They believe that not only Russia but also China, India, and "other countries" for this very reason strive toward multipolarity and oppose unipolarity. Curiously, this counteraction supposedly suits the interests of "the bigger part of the world community" and the countries of the West, including the United States. (*R-2*, p. 52) I've never heard of opinion polls administered to the world community on this topic, but I do know that opinion polls conducted in the United States disprove these claims. The authors, being steadfast followers of Immanuel Kant, sincerely believe that the building of a multipolar world is caused by the desire to limit American influence. "*Its main purpose* is the creation of a *system for coordinating interests*, essentially a *global democracy* that would develop the positive experience of the UN and guarantee the progress of civilization." (Italicized text by the authors, R-2, ibid.) Expressed here is the idea of a balance of interests, proposed by evidently the same authors during Gorbachev's rule. It didn't work then, and naturally it will not work in the future. We won't even discuss global democracy.

In the priorities list, it is said that in the short term, Russia must not allow itself to be isolated "along the main strategic azimuths (USA, Europe, Asia)." Once again the question arises: Is someone actually trying to isolate Russia along these azimuths? Russia can also be isolated on its own, by its lack of economic and other capabilities for action along all azimuths. Therefore, this foreign policy "priority" is simply devoid of meaning. For the middle term, some good intentions are expressed, as well as some intentions that could bring harm to the country if they are realized (God forbid!), such as "integration in international economic and political structures." For the long term, the authors favor "the preservation and strengthening of Russia's position as one of the leading actors in world politics while renouncing imperial and messianic pretensions; [and] active participation in the forming of a democratic global system."

Why does Russia need to be a "leading actor in world politics"? The answer given in R-2 is in the shape of a "super-dilemma": rebirth of imperial might or maximum achievable well-being of the people. (*R-2*, p.66.) The *Reports*' authors (and some scholars) believe the latter is impossible without the former. They don't appear to quite share this view themselves, but a number of factors force them to support the adherents of this approach. Perhaps they are right when speaking about Russia, but they are wrong in their generalizations. For example, Japan after the Meiji reforms proclaimed the principle "strong army, rich nation." After World War II, however, Japan renounced militarism (in word at least). In any case, it is not a leading figure in world politics, even though it has kept trying to obtain this status since the early 1970s. At the same time, perhaps precisely due to the things mentioned above, Japan has managed to raise the well-being of its people to the level of the world's richest countries. Likewise, Sweden and the Netherlands are far from being "leading figures in world politics," yet their well-being similarly leaves nothing to be desired. The point is, the connection identified by the authors is not universal, though—I repeat—for Russia it may be necessary.

As for item two in the "long-term plan," we must first sort out the issues of democracy in our own country and "democracy" on a global level. In both cases, the majority of the population gets nothing but trouble from "democracy."

Be that as it may, the *Reports*' authors (let me remind you again that they believe in Biblical commandments) hope that everything works out for the better in this world and build their priorities accordingly.

Quite curious is their definition of what is distinctive about the Russian situation as opposed to that of the West. I am prepared to agree with their definition of the term "the West." Their description of Russia, however, makes me doubtful. They write: "On one hand, in a broad historical context Russia as a European and mostly Christian country belongs to the West. On the other hand, it is home to an original Slavic culture and the Orthodox branch of Christianity, it is not just European but Asian as well, and as such it is a separate civilization." (*R-2*, Ch.VII)

I am prepared to agree that Russia has a separate civilization, but I don't understand how Slavic originality makes the country Asian as well as European. By this logic, Greece should also be proclaimed an Asian country because it is Orthodox, or perhaps Russian Siberians are Asians because they reside in the Asian part of Russia. In that case, Australians too should perhaps be considered Asians because they are located in the "Asia-Pacific region."

I will revisit the concept of "Eurasianism" in a special section and am bringing it up here only to show the absurdity of tying some patriots' anti-Western positions to our "Asianism." The real reason is entirely different, especially because these anti-Western positions can only be proclaimed but not realized. The authors are correct when they write that: "It is unlikely that Russia will again assume rigid anti-Western positions—there are no weighty material, social or geopolitical grounds for that." (ibid.) It is not just "unlikely" but simply impossible that Russia's official policy becomes anti-Western in reality. First, we are on their hook in the economic sense; second, "the new Russia is joined to the United States by its adherence to democratic values." So we are ideologically on their side, and geostrategically all we can do is criticize the "hegemonist" tendencies in U.S. foreign policy.

The Gorbachevists assess perfectly realistically our approaches to the USA as limited by our capabilities. They recommend leaning more toward Europe and developing relations with China without ignoring the problems that exist between our countries. They do, however, harbor illusions about Japan, counting on it as a "source of massive investment and know-how." One should not expect Japan to make a "massive entrance into the Russian market." To ditch pro-Japanese illusions, it suffices to analyze the trade-economic dynamics of the last ten years, or, better still, the last fifty years.

Similarly, Russia's policies in the "APR" have nothing to do with great-power status. Even the policies of the USSR—a superpower—did nothing to enhance the country's place in that region, not even with respect to ASEAN countries.

After describing other policy directions (the Middle East, Latin America, the Muslim "South"), the *Reports*' authors offer criticism of "isolationist" approaches and of a pro-Western foreign policy, inclining toward a pragmatic-realistic policy line that they believe to be receiving "universal approval." I have never heard of a poll taken on this issue, but I admit that the authors are essentially right in the sense that most analysts connected to the government or even just supportive of it really do favor this policy line. In my view, however, this line of realizing Russia's national interests is not at all pragmatic or realistic; it is quite idealistic and therefore cannot be implemented.

Russia: Ace, Six, or Joker?

The collective work *Russia and the Challenges at the Turn of the Century*[1] was written by associates of the Institute of World Economy and International Relations (IMEMO) of the Russian Academy of Science. They believe that contemporary Russia's main problem is its Third World psychology and its "loss of ability for self-assessment." (6) One can't disagree with this, considering not just the official programs for "taking Russia out of the crisis" but also the foreign policy doctrines and concepts of the country's leaders. It is quite interesting, therefore, to see how the authors themselves overcome this psychology and how realistically they assess Russia's place in the surrounding world. I have to stress that the IMEMO scientific clan was always notable for supreme self-confidence and self-sufficiency.

Almost all scholars of international affairs view the world of the future through the prism of multipolarity. But differences crop up when the authors argue that Russia should not force the shaping of such a world. The reason offered is this: Today's Russia has no chance of taking a "worthy place" in this world (apparently, everyone in Russia is bonkers over this issue of "a worthy place"). Therefore, Russia's interests are served by "*a certain kind of conservation of the current unipolarity ('one-and-a-half-polarity')*" [emphasis by the authors.], with conservation of the roles and functions of the USA and Western Europe as unqualified guarantors of relative global stability during the transition period. For the benefit of zealous anti-Westerners, the authors remark that the alternative is total destabilization and further "shrinking" of Russia as measured by size and weight in international affairs, increase of separatism, etc. (15–16). I stress: The authors regard the USA and Western Europe as guarantors of global stability. It would appear to follow that when NATO bombs Kosovo, or the USA punishes Iraq, they are stabiliz-

1 Blagovolin, head of project, *Russia and the Challenges at the Turn of the Century: A possibility of manoeuvre on conditions of limiting factors (geopolitical aspect)*.

ing the situation. Or maybe these acts should be considered the cost of stabilization?

Be that as it may, while the USA and Western Europe ensure "stability," Russia has a breather of sorts, a break that must be used to form its own "geopolitical pole." (16) This pole is not defined geographically, though.

The authors raise an important question: On which principles will the world be organized in the twenty-first century? Unlike those who believe blindly in democracy and globalization, they justifiably note the existence of opposite trends—anti-globalism, increasing influence of conservative (nonliberal) values. (17) They give no indication of which trend prevails, but the important thing is they at least see the opposite trends.

They objectively assess Russia's relations with the USA, coming to a conclusion rare for Russian democrats: "The USA has always been, still is, and always will be Russia's geopolitical opponent, including in the CIS zone and within the territory of Russia itself, not to mention the 'far abroad' and the geostrategic periphery—the regions of Latin America, the Middle East, and the Asia-Pacific region." Therefore, Russia's relations with the USA are most likely to be built on the basis of a "mature partnership." (19)

From realism they move on swiftly to idealism, offering a new "meaning of life" for the new world order: "That is, construct new worthy goals for mankind that can ensure order, minimal necessities, and possible harmony, and prevent chaos and confrontation." (27–28)

This is truly a statement in the Russian spirit: It doesn't matter that you're standing neck-deep in mud. You're still supposed to think about all mankind.

In reality, if you aren't strong enough to be an "ace" and are unwilling to be a "six," then aspire to be an honorary "joker." In the end, the authors believe this role will ensure "a worthy place and role for Russia in the conditions of a multipolar world." (ibid.)

I fear that if we follow the authors' prescriptions, we will still be denied a worthy place, even as a joker. Just look at what they have to say about the "APR."

First, even if we agree that such a region does exist, what does India have to do with it? India is in Asia, of course. But when looking at the map, I see that it is surrounded by the Indian Ocean, not the Pacific.

Second, look at what the authors suggest about relations with China. They warn against excessive optimism about possibilities for "strategic partnership" because "the current ties between Russia and China don't reach the level of broad-scale cooperation." (110) I accept the possibility that the ties "don't reach the level," but when I say such a thing, I'm supposed to explain what I mean by "broad-scale cooperation." I should perhaps offer the example of a country with whom relations have reached the level of "broad-scale" co-operation, but this isn't the whole problem. The authors forecast: "China will in the near future likely become the *main geopolitical opponent to Russia in NorthEastern Eurasia*,[1] and the formation of a multipolar security structure in the APR, with Russia as one of the poles, *suits the latter's interests much better than fixation on the forming of some rigid "Axis," even if it appears impressive on first sight*." (Emphasis mine. —*A.B.*) (124) Why and how that will be manifested, the authors don't tell. I venture to guess that just like the liberal democrats of all countries, they dislike China on account of its adherence to socialism.

Third, the authors suggest reducing "the Pacific Fleet by half its present size." (112) One wonders why they don't suggest reducing it to zero because, by their logic, security in the region is guaranteed by the USA, which has managed to entrench itself militarily in East Asia, too. (119)

Fourthly, the authors believe that "the inclusion of Russia in the ties and economic interaction in the APR isn't just desirable, it is inevitable" (112). I don't know which one of the authors wrote the part about the "APR," but he is definitely a dilettante, because this "desire" has been expressed in statement form since the times of Lomonosov (mid-eighteenth century). Since that time, there has been no progress in this matter.

Next (and this is the most curious part), the authors inform us with satisfaction, referring to several regional administrations, that the leading "APR" countries "have in fact already 'divided' between themselves the different zones of Russia's Far East (and its resources); namely: The region's northeastern sector (Kamchatka, Chukotka, Magadan region, and part of Sakhalin Island) is the object of

1 It wouldn't hurt to explain what is included in the region called "Northeastern Eurasia."

preferential [the authors evidently meant "preemptive"—*A.B.*] U.S. interest. The Primorsky and Sakhalin regions, as well as the Kurile Islands, are zones of preeminent prospective takeover by Japanese capital. Finally, certain "inland" zones of the region may become the object of an eventual takeover by China and South Korea." (114) Their satisfaction with this carving-up evidently has to do with China, because China "can be a much more restless neighbor to us than it is today." (118) They argue, therefore, that Russia doesn't trust China, but it can trust the USA and Japan. While in 1918–1922, these two "friends" had to intervene militarily in the Russian Far East, Russians today invite them to fill in their "geopolitical hollows." And some people still maintain that Russia has no "fifth column."

The authors' general conclusion is that Russia "will remain in a suspended state." For this reason, it should submit to the USA, despite the latter's confrontational policy; stay away from China; avoid using Third World countries against the West; and along the way develop and set nationwide goals ("national idea").

This suggestion of "submission" to the West is extremely rare, even among brazen pro-Westerners. But let's not forget that IMEMO wrote this paper. This organization submitted to the West back in Gorbachev's times and still lies on its back, experiencing a satisfaction both material and physical. It has no strength or desire left to get up and has been lying down for too long.

The Concept of "Selective Involvement"

In April 2000, S. Karaganov, the chairman of the presidium of the Council on Foreign and Defense Policy (SVOP), presented the collection *Strategy for Russia: Presidential Agenda—2000* (Moscow: *Vagrius*, 2000). The idea for this collection was clearly borrowed from Americans, most likely from the Heritage Foundation that annually publishes its exhortations to conservative candidates for official posts.[1] In Karaganov's words, this book was written by people "who are the pride of our country in both the intellectual and the political sense."[2] So, let us see in whom we are to take pride.

I was naturally interested in just one chapter, chapter two, "Russian Foreign Policy Facing the Challenges of the Twenty-First Century," written collectively by S. Karaganov, V. Averchev, A. Adamishin, A. Belkin, and A. Pushkov. (It is worth pointing out that apart from Karaganov and the journalist Pushkov, the rest are not scholars of international affairs but work as advisers to some commercial concerns.)

As Mr. Karaganov declared at its presentation, the collection is an "above-party program," i.e., it is above politics and does not reflect the interests of any political party. The suggestion is that it reflects the interests of the entire people. This stance is characteristic of many champions of Mother Russia, who keep stressing that they are above ideologies, above politics, and above all internecine struggles per se. May the country flourish and the people prosper! This is the old card-shark trick of all pro-bourgeois intellectuals claiming to be the defenders of the people's interests. It is still in use and works with Russia's politically backward and unsinkable people.

In actual fact, all the authors of this collection are champions of the bourgeoisie and the capitalist system; they admit it inadvertently themselves in their previous work on the same topic,

1 See, for example, Butler and Holmes, eds., *Issues 2000: The Candidate's Briefing Book*.

2 *Kremlin Package*, April 14, 2000. Federal News Service.

Strategy-3, which contains a phrase that must have slipped by the editors: "Perhaps the biggest problem of Russia's foreign policy is its remoteness from the country's concrete economic interests and *the main subject of these interests—Russian corporations and banks.*[1] (Emphasis mine.) How's that for an "above-parties platform"! In the collection, this phrase is absent; the editors must have been alerted.

What does "the pride of our country" have in store for Russia?

Right away, we notice that *Strategy-3 (Russia's Strategy in the Twenty-First Century: Situation Analysis and Some Proposals)* differs from the collection in being more optimistic in its assessment of Russian diplomacy. "We see a sharp activation of policy in the Far East; relations with China have been deepened, and relations with Japan have been improved." (ibid.) Similar interpretation is given to Moscow's diplomacy in the Persian Gulf region, in the Middle East, and in Europe. Moreover, it turns out that "strictly speaking, the problem of military security in Europe does not exist (for Russia at least)." (ibid.) This optimism is explained by the fact that *Strategy-3* was evidently written before the August 1998 financial crisis, at the time when Primakov was Prime Minister; the authors are entirely supportive of Mr. Primakov's political line. Besides, the *Strategy*'s authors, like all Russian scholars of international affairs, measure success of diplomacy by the number of top-level state visits and the number of good words said by politicians. Our learned political scientists somehow never get the simple idea of trying to calculate how much money is spent on all these endless visits and meetings, nor do they grasp the idea of a "return on investment" for our political and economic treasury. Phrases about "improved or deepened relations" don't mean a thing when they are not supported by figures showing improved international trade, economic cooperation, or savings in the security area.

Be that as it may, by 1999 all the successes evaporated. With justification, the authors discuss the crisis situation in Russia and how the West in this connection has tightened its policy toward her, having lost faith in Russian reforms (and having been put off by the war in Chechnya, of course). After that, their analysis follows the beaten path. On one hand, Russia's prestige has suffered and its image has worsened (63); on the other hand, "the external conditions for Russia's development remain on the whole favorable." (64)

1 *Nezavisimaya gazeta*, June 18, 1998.

These "favorable conditions" are connected to certain phenomena in world politics and economics. What are they?

"A global (and increasingly unified) post-capitalist system has been created, developing as a whole along unified rules." (65) The authors have made a great discovery: The *entire world* lives in the postcapitalist era! They forget to explain, however, just what exactly this "post-capitalist system" is, and what its rules are. Perhaps they are counting on leftover Marxist "mentality" to deduce that everyone is now living under socialism. This claim is certainly true of the Chinese and partly of the Scandinavians, but the North Americans, the Latin Americans (except Cubans), Europeans, Indians, Africans, and the Russians themselves can't help being surprised at the claim that we are all living in a socialist world! But if not, where are we? In postcapitalism. That sounds like a miracle!

Like many others, these authors also like to use other key expressions, such as "post-industrial society," "post-industrial system," or even "post-industrial civilization." (63) For example, they believe the common problem of all states, "including the most developed ones," is conservative bureaucrats "who try to manage things the old way, [and who] tend toward diplomacy of the Westphalian style rather than the post-industrial society style." (65) This claim is plainly ridiculous, considering that of about 200 states in the world, only fifty at most have entered "post-industrial society," while the rest still exist in the industrial or pre-industrial world. There's no reason why these latter shouldn't tend toward the Westphalian system, even though most of them, I suspect, have never even heard of it.

What is more interesting is that the authors apparently don't understand that the transition to a "post-industrial society," which has the services-and-information economy at its core, presupposes intensified exploitation of Third World countries, or, more precisely, of the industrial, raw materials, and agrarian sectors of Asian, African, and Latin American countries. This is precisely what "the magnificent seven" of post-industrial societies are doing in many countries, including in Russia; this is only natural because without this exploitation, the services and-information economy cannot exist on its own. Daniel Bell, who introduced the term "post-industrial society," hoped that society would be free of class antagonism and that class harmony would finally triumph. In part, this hope was fulfilled, but only in the First World. Class conflicts remain in the

Second and Third Worlds and, most importantly, persist between the First and Third Worlds, or, in Beijing's terminology, between North and South. In short, the term "post-industrial society" is applicable to some degree to developed capitalist states. Using this category to describe the entire world is just as silly as talking about post-capitalism.

The authors go on to say that this "post-capitalism" is rather like the reverse side of "universal globalization" that supposedly "erases the line between internal and external policy." (65) One hardly expects such an appalling level of analysis from "the pride of the nation." Don't they understand that "universal globalization" does not involve China, India, or Russia, while Africa, Latin America, and East Asia (the ASEAN countries except for China) are involved only as objects of the capitalist core's policies, i.e., as the exploited periphery of the capitalist system? Their own claims about the weakening of the state's role in the globalized space bear evidence that they haven't read a single work on interrelations between the TNCs and the state. They would have discovered, to their surprise, that the state's role got stronger precisely during the era of "globalization." Another problem is that they clearly don't understand the difference between globalization and internationalization, between internationalization and integration. Otherwise, they would not make such silly claims as this: "Moscow has no reasonable alternative to global involvement in the world process of economic integration." (65) This statement is absurd because the world is not integrated economically; rather, it is internationalized, and that is a big difference. The authors do remark two pages later that "on the other hand" and "despite this," the state's role is preserved, and so on, but on the whole, they fail to identify the dominant trend in the relations between the state and the TNCs in the present world economic space.

This is how Karaganov, et al., see the structure of international relations: "It is not a unipolar world that is being created, nor a classical multipolar world, but rather a multilevel, highly mobile international and interstate system where problems, especially economic ones, come to the foreground and require ever more strongly multilateral decisions and new international institutions." (67) First, the unipolar world is not being created; it actually currently exists. The question is about the direction of its transformation—toward bipolarity or multipolarity. Second, the "multilevel system" actually emerged in the early 1970s, when Japan reached the status of the third-biggest economic power. In those times, Russia parroted the Americans that the first level (security) consists of two superpowers—the USA and the USSR; the second level (economic) consisted of four powers—the USA, the Common Market, the USSR, and Japan; the third level (political) was also composed of four powers, but China was named in Japan's place. (It is a known fact that Japan is still struggling to realize its idée fixe of bringing its political role in line with the country's economic might.) As for "economic problems coming to the foreground," this news, too, is at least thirty years old, particularly in connection with Japan. So, from the geostrategic and geoeconomic perspectives, the authors contribute nothing new to the understanding of the structure of international relations and only repeat old banalities.

It would have been another matter had the authors raised and answered the question of how well the geostrategic (power) approach reflects the realities of the modern world in the context of an international world economy. In other words, which world trend will prove dominant in determining the structure of the world system—the one based on geostrategy, or the one based on geoeconomy? But they didn't even raise the question.

They do bring up quite forcefully the issue of ideology. "Instead of thinking about how to achieve economic growth and avoid falling out of the world economy, we still argue about ideology and theoretical models of development—liberal or ethical." (80) Indeed, they have no need to argue about ideology because they represent "the country's political class," and Russia (obviously, we are speaking here of the state) is typically capitalist in essence and Russian in form. However, even in capitalist societies, people do argue about models of development. The learned experts ought to know that there exist different models for bringing states out of crises. In Russia, the liberal model was tried, and half the country was lost as a result. The new leaders are giving the indication they will attempt to unite "dialectically" liberalism with the strong-state ideology (*etatisme*, in Western terminology). The outcome is already known, though. Therefore, one should consider other models in advance, too. Russia is "falling out" of "post-industrial development" precisely because it still cannot decide on its ideology. (S. Blagovolin's group writes about this.)

The only thing on which I can agree with the authors is the futility of discussions about "great Russia." In this connection, they criticize quite deservedly the concept of multipolarity that implies the restoration of Russia's status as a "pole" (or one of the poles) because Moscow has neither strength, funds, nor economic resources. (90–91)

On the whole, the authors' vision of international relations in the twenty-first century is built on concepts that do not reflect the real course of things in the world. They have fallen victims to terms ("globalization," "post-capitalism," etc.), the content of which they simply do not understand. It is perfectly obvious that not one of them has ever opened a book on the theory of international relations. They prefer "common sense," which Hegel recommended as a basis for talking to one's wife in the kitchen. This shows in their foreign policy suggestions in *Strategy for Russia: Presidential Agenda—2000.*

They give a pretty name for these suggestions: the concept of "selective involvement." They didn't invent it, but borrowed it, like a lot of other things, from Americans (specifically, from that group of American politicians and international affairs scholars who believe that America's hand should not be stretched indiscriminately throughout the world but only to those zones and countries where American involvement will prove to be most beneficial for the USA). This approach was initially called "selective involvement" and is now called "selective engagement"; these two expressions translate into Russian identically. This is the concept championed by J. Schlesinger, Ch. W. Maynes, B. Bradley, J. Baker, and others.[1]

Despite the plagiarism, this approach really can be considered the most rational option for Russia's foreign policy, provided that policy directions and priorities are equally rationally identified. But this did not come to pass. Judge for yourselves.

The concept exposition starts with the formulation of nine principles; several of these are not "principles" but rather foreign policy objectives and recommendations. For example, the first principle is formulated as the recommendation "to adopt the course of very rigid protection only for Russia's really vital interests." (92) The problem is in the interpretation of "Russia's really vital interests."

1 See details in Arin's *Asia-Pacific Region: Myths, Illusions and Reality,* 230–46.

But let us suppose that everyone is in agreement with this list of interests. They are realized and thus removed from the agenda.

Principles by definition are basic postulates that determine the entire system of a country's foreign policy activities. For example, one of Japan's foreign policy principles is its declaration that it will never become a military power (it is even enshrined in the Constitution). Japan has also formulated three "non-nuclear" policy principles. For Russia, one foreign policy principle could be the declaration that Russia does not intend to become a superpower. The authors also serve up this pearl called a principle: "It is necessary to restore to Russian foreign policy its systemic and scientific nature." (Ninth Principle, 93) This is not a principle at all, but simply a well-intended wish that the authors themselves are unable to fulfill. Principle Seven, another "non-principle," goes like this: "Foreign policy must serve the goal of attracting foreign investments to Russia. Without them, the country will not rise." (ibid.) If a country is unable to rise without foreign investments, it is worthless and should not bother to rise. This recommendation indicates absolute disbelief in the ability of "the country's political class" to rule the country.

Inserted in this foreign policy concept are a number of domestic policy issues (do that, intensify this, accelerate such-and-such, like military reform, for example), which turn the foreign policy document into a treatise on everything under the sun. First, the suggestion to "start implementing a *complex strategy of integrating Russia into the world economy*" (emphasis by the authors) (96), contradicts the essence of the "selective involvement" concept; second, it is in fact unrealistic because there is nothing to "integrate"; third, the world economy as an integral whole simply doesn't exist. Rather curious in this connection is the recommendation to develop a program for "gradual folding of the industries that prove unable to compete with imported products." (97) Should this recommendation be zealously implemented, at least half of our productive economy would have to be folded up, to the joy of our benefactors from the "golden billion" zone. One American acquaintance of mine was correct when he said that when dealing with Russians, you don't even need to give them the rope. They will find it themselves and hang themselves just fine.

The concept of "selective involvement" is not selective at all, except that Africa and Latin America are not mentioned as objects of Russia's foreign policy. It is just as all-encompassing, just as irrational, and just as costly as the currently implemented policy in the international arena. It is practically not any different from the suggestions of the Blagovolin group that amount in the end to "submission" to the West. In principle, Russia is already flat on its back.

* * *

The authors write: "One of Russia's main internal problems from the perspective of relations with the outside world is the incompleteness of the process of realizing the country's place in the world and the inadequacy of ideas about this world." (79) I agree entirely with this phrase. It is 100 percent applicable not only to the collection's authors but also to the entire "political class" of contemporary Russia. Evidently, they can't break free from their limitations.

Chapter III

In the Trap of "Eurasia"

The idea of Eurasianism is currently addressed from two opposite positions. Certain American scholars of international affairs, most notably Zbigniew Brzezinski, attack it as a concept contrary to U.S. national interests. On the Russian side, it is defended by a group of scholars and politicians who discern in it a new ideology of sorts that is capable of unifying Russia and saving the whole world in the bargain. Although in the USA the idea of Eurasianism arouses little interest (except among its opponents), in Russia it inspires heated discussions, represented, for instance, in the collection published by the Gorbachev Foundation, *Puzzles of Eurasia: Russia in the Emerging Global System*, as the product of its research project.

The topic itself is not new and is rooted in the arguments between the *Slavophiles* and the *Zapadniki* ("Westernizers") that continued throughout the nineteenth century, particularly in its second half. These arguments were followed in the 1920s by impassioned debates involving such major figures as N. S. Trubetskoy, V. F. Ern, N. A. Berdiaev, G. Florovsky, and others. Eurasianism is now once again the conduit for raising the subject of Russia's "identification" (a current buzzword), i.e., determination by the country of its place in the world. Today's discussions differ in that Eurasianism is tied in with geopolitics, which is supposed to impart a scientific nature to the problem.

In reality, all these discussions involving the political elite from both ends of the political spectrum reflect a struggle for power within the ruling milieu in the framework of the existing political and economical system. The proponents of Eurasianism formally appear to be championing Russia's *samobytnost'* (unique identity), the status of its civilization as distinct from and opposed to that of the West. The idea's opponents insist on the existence of universal Western values that Russia must necessarily espouse in order not to be derailed from the track of world civilization.

Behind these cultural science terms lurk simple economic truths. The Eurasians reflect the interests of Russia's national bourgeoisie, who are not disposed to share with the West the loot gained from exploiting their compatriots. The anti-Eurasians, or Westernizers, are ideological servants of that part of the Russian business community that is closely tied to Western capital; in cooperation with it, they impoverish the Russian population just as effectively. That's all there is to it! The rest is ideological claptrap, fed to an illiterate populace under the guise of caring for its interests. In that process, the ideologues of both camps feed themselves, naturally; one only has to analyze attentively the ties between them and their "sponsors."

On the surface, all these debates appear to be quite "scientific." Let us examine now how much this scientific aspect is worth.

Tavrovsky: Ill-Considered Bet on Primakov

Let us begin by examining a curious document by the journalist Yu. Tavrovsky that sparked a discussion. Tavrovsky, who currently assumes the rank of "political scientist," had misjudged the political situation and decided to bet on the ascension of Primakov, awarding to him the high title of "the teacher who would formulate the foundations of the new Eurasian teaching and head its implementation." The naïve Mr. Tavrovsky was hoping that Mr. Primakov would do that in his capacity as the country's president, naturally. Now even though Primakov is an academician and a member of the Academy of Sciences, over the course of his academic career, he has not discovered a single law or deduced a single regularity. He mixes up scientific terms like some Candidate of Science (a junior degree he earned with much greater difficulty than his later rank of Academician). Therefore, it would seem silly to expect any "new teachings" from him. Tavrovsky, however, is undeterred because he has found a unique qualification possessed by the Academician. "He (Primakov) is a Eurasian by birth, by biography, by education, and by career." Now I can comprehend, with some effort, what it means to be Eurasian by biography: Primakov was born in Kiev, lived in Tbilisi, and then made his career in Moscow. He, therefore, combined in himself different "cultures," so to speak. But "Eurasian by birth" is a real lulu. In that case, all of us who were born in either Europe or Asia are "Eurasians by birth," whether Chinese, German, Japanese, or Jewish. Despite his unique combination of cultures, Primakov has never managed to formulate anything and has never become a teacher. But now Tavrovsky doesn't make such demands on him anymore because Primakov also failed to become president. That job went to another "Eurasian," one who lacks, admittedly, a Eurasian biography, but who often repeats the phrase: "Russia is a Eurasian country." That's whom Tavrovsky should have bet on. He could have earned himself some kind of government position.

Lo and behold, his article produced replies first from V. Stupishin, an opponent of Eurasianism, and then from B. Yerasov, a defender of both Tavrovsky and Eurasianism. The former, naturally, criticizes Tavrovsky from the point of view of a *Zapadnik*, invoking critics of Eurasianism from times past (N. Berdiaev, I. Ilyin, and P. Milyukov), and concludes his article with a hymn to liberal democratic values and private property. The latter naturally seeks to protect Eurasians equally from these values, i.e., "the destructive influence of Western ideology and culture," and from "Western hegemonism," in general.

Even though the polemics in *Nezavisimaya Gazeta* are over, articles on Eurasianism continue to appear because the discussion appears to "fertilize" pronouncements from the president himself. In particular, the newspaper started publishing articles by one of the leading proponents of Eurasianism, A. Dugin, who has been expounding on this topic for many years, endowing it with scientific wording and intellectual depth.

A. Dugin: Eurasian Ventriloquist[1]

A. Dugin is considered in Communist-patriotic circles as an ideologue of Eurasianism and a geopolitical propagandist—a discipline that is seriously perceived as a "science" by the leaders of the nationalistpatriots (A. Prokhanov, V. Zhirinovsky) and the Communist Party of the Russian Federation (G. Zyuganov, G. Seleznev). As I mentioned already, his Eurasianism appears to be derived scientifically from geopolitics. For this purpose he builds, so to say, on the ideas of the English geographer Halford J. Mackinder, the father of geopolitics, and identifies operational pairs: Eurasianism—Atlantism, land—sea, continent—island. Naturally, the historical Russia (Kievan Rus, the Tsardom of Moscow, the Russian Empire of the Romanovs, and the Soviet Union) constitutes the first part of the pair, while the West is the second part. Obviously, it is assumed that the Russian part is the positive pole, while the Western part is negative. Here is how Mr. Dugin pretentiously formulates it: "The Eurasian impulse is the Unit of our system, our positive pole of historical being, our Truth and our Light in contrast to the Atlantist Zero, the pole of falsehood and alien darkness." Dugin is apparently using a metaphor here (the binary code of 1–0), but he actually does believe that Russia is indeed 1 and the West is indeed 0. He presents this idea in many other works. He does mention, though, that the West describes the same system of paired relations using "the reverse evaluation sign." This, in his opinion, is a manifestation of a regularity, "the main law of geopolitics." In other words, the law of geopolitics is the antagonism between land and sea, island and continent, and, of course, between the West and the non-West, i.e., the East. In order to make this gibberish more convincing, the wisdom-lover warns his readers that this law can only be comprehended by "a big reason" because "ordinary small reason" cannot crack this deep mystery of historical predetermination.

1 Dugin, "Eurasian platform," *Nezavisimaya gazeta* (November 15, 2000).

Dugin argues that this "law's" manifestation is so powerful because almost all political powers, no matter which terms they use ("gosudarstvennost'," "derzhavnost'," "patriotism"), turn consciously or subconsciously to the Eurasian idea. It is within the framework of this idea that he assesses the thesis about the strategic triangle of Moscow–Delhi–Beijing, as well as the Yeltsin–Putin thesis about "multipolarity." In his book, *The Basis of Geopolitics: the Geopolitical Future of Russia,* he proposes creating an anti-Western alliance of Russia, Japan, Germany, and Iran. To this end, he is prepared to hand over the Kurile Islands to Japan. As the English author Charles Clover notes ironically, Dugin ignores the fact "that they are not all land-based."[1]

All these constructs are supposed to have an anti-Western direction—against Atlantism, so to say. This is the essence of the European platform, an umbrella that "could unite in the name of *derzhavnost* the right wing and the left wing, socialists and free-marketers who agree with the main postulate: No domestic-policy differences should be allowed to cause destabilization of the Russian State, do harm to its security, weaken our strategic and civilizational sovereignty, or violate social stability." This is precisely what should constitute the national idea.

It is perfectly obvious that this kind of platform cannot unify the ill-assorted elements of society in Russia, especially those who have blood ties to the West. This is evidenced by the remarkable fact that anti-Eurasianists have created a Web site titled *Aziopa:A Site Against Eurasianism,* where they publish bitingly critical articles against Eurasianists. The utopianism of the Eurasian idea is obvious even from that fact alone that arguments on this topic have been going on for more than a hundred years with still no sign of a "consensus."

I have no intention of analyzing the ideology of Eurasianism here. I only wish to draw your attention to the geopolitical aspect of this idea in Dugin's interpretation. Its essence is the explanation of all international cataclysms through the category of *space*: sea—land, continent—island. (As the above-mentioned Charles Clover remarked sarcastically, "Victory is now to be found in geography, rather than history; in space, rather than time.") If this is not so,

1 Clover, "Dreams of the Eurasian Heartland: The Reemergence of Geopolitics," *Foreign Affairs*, no. 2 (March/April 1999), 9.

then how does Dugin explain his proposal for creating the alliance of Russia, Japan, Germany, and Iran—an alliance that includes, apart from Russia and Iran, one *island* state and one *Atlantic* state, against the United States, *a maritime Atlantic* power? There is clearly a lapse of logic here. Then again, Japan, a Eurasian country, finds itself for some reason in a geostrategic antagonism to Russia, another Eurasian country, yet maintains friendship with the USA, an Atlantic country. Or why do Great Britain and Japan, two island states quite alike in their geostrategic location, differ so cardinally in culture and civilization? Which part of the "land—sea" dichotomy dominates in the geographic profile of India, China, Germany, Portugal, etc.? If Eurasia has a certain integrity, why were there no fewer wars and conflicts within it than between Eurasian and Atlantic states?

To put it briefly, *space* explains nothing in international relations. It is not a category of politics, and neither is *time*. Both are just coordinates, the dimensions in which events take place. Attempts to insert space into the structure of international relations and (even worse) create a national idea on its basis are only explainable as mystical exercises similar to navel-gazing.

In conclusion: All these Eurasians love to repeat Kipling's line about the East and West never meeting. I have the impression that the fans of this quote never even bothered to read the ballad. For their information, it starts and ends with the same stanza:

Oh, East is East, and West is West, and never the twain shall meet, Till Earth and Sky stand presently at God's great Judgment Seat; But there is neither East nor West, Border, nor Breed, nor Birth, When two strong men stand face to face, Tho' they come from the ends of the earth!

(Having met, by the way, the two men became friends instead of destroying each other.)

* * *

Prior to closing this topic, I wish to reproduce my reaction to some no less intellectual scientists about whom I wrote in my previous book, *Russia on the Shoulder of the World's Road*. I mean the already mentioned Zbigniew Brzezinski, one of whose works had a certain resonance in our country. As a counterweight, I present M.L. Titarenko, director of the Institute of the Far East of the Russian Academy of Sciences. The latter has earned this honor with his book, Russia Facing Asia,[1] perceived by many as an apology of Eurasianism. So, let us start with it.

1 Titarenko, *Russia Facing Asia.*

"If-Only-ism," Titarenko-style

I wish to specify that this book by Titarenko is not a scientific treatise; rather, it is a collection of presentations made at international conferences. One can tell these texts are not scientific from the absence of a concept apparatus or even terminological clarity. For example, the author equates APEC with the EC and the WTO (63); his list of main countries in Southeast Asia includes China, Japan, and the USA. This is tantamount to saying that the main countries in Africa are South Africa, Nigeria, and the USA. In other words, this is a collection of politicized speeches designed to promote several ideas, primarily Eurasianism. Because these ideas are popular in certain academic circles in Russia, let us see how they are presented by one of their ideologues.

Titarenko proclaims "the new paradigm" of "the new Eurasia." (Let me remind you of the "old" Eurasianism of the 1920s and the even "older" one of the late nineteenth century.) He says: "Eurasianism is the precursor of the foundation of the future new world order of planetary intercivilization relations that secures the ecology of cultures and civilizations and preserves ethnic and civilizational diversity." (24) Later on he says: "*Eurasianism can become not only be the ideology of Russia's renewal, but also the new paradigm of Russia's rebirth, but it can also set an example of new ideas for intercivilization relations in the post-industrial information society.* The new Eurasianism enables us not only to strengthen the internal identity of the Russian people's national self-consciousness, but also to guarantee the freedom from conflict of intercivilization relations of co-operation between all peoples and their cultures in the wide spaces of Russia, as well as the deepening of cultural cooperation and interaction with fellow countrymen residing in other countries, ensuring their civilizational identity." (Emphasis by Titarenko.) (26–7)

Frankly speaking, this passage reminds me of the internationalaffairs sections of the repetitive *CPSU Central Committee Reports*, which always stated categorically that the Soviet society was marching in the vanguard of humanity; therefore, the balance of powers in the world was changing relentlessly in favor of the forces of socialism, peace, and progress.

I can't imagine what rarefied heights one must inhabit to fail to see that today's Russia displays tendencies directly opposite to those proclaimed by Mr. Titarenko. How can a country set an example "of new ideas for intercivilization relations in the post-industrial information society" when it has dropped back to the preindustrial era, when only a tiny part of the population uses the Internet, and most people don't even own a computer? How can you have a "deepening of cultural cooperation and interaction with fellow countrymen residing in other countries" when the state is unable to finance culture in its own country, not to mention its inability to reach an agreement with certain peoples living on Russia's territory, such as the Chechens?

The power of fantasy is needed to write the following: "The proximity and certain kinship of Russian Eurasianism to the civilizational value systems of China, Japan, and Korea, as well as the USA, create the prospect of broad favorable grounds for multilateral cooperation and Russia's mediating role in overcoming political, economic, and intercivilization frictions that apparently will be growing inevitably and acquire at times an acute character in connection with the struggle for hegemony and leadership in the APR between the USA, Japan, and China." (75) Seriously, who needs this "mediating" role of Russia, a state that is unable to cope with its own economic and ethnic problems and fails to perform even such elementary functions as paying salaries to its employees?

In this same vein, the author advertises the benefits to Russia that will supposedly accrue from the implementation of the Tumenjiang and "Sea of Japan" projects that are still in the argument and discussion phase ten years after they were first proposed.

Titarenko may object: Yes, at present, this is all a utopia, but should we choose to implement the concept of Eurasianism, it all may well become reality. Let us assume that it is indeed so. That still leaves the question: Just what exactly is this Eurasianism? After reading the works of its proponents (B. S. Yerasov, G. A. Yugai, A.A. Yazkova, and many others), I still don't understand what it is about. Perhaps Mr. Titarenko can help?

In his opinion, Eurasianism is an ideology that "can unite under one flag the right wing and the left wing, the progressives and the conservatives." (15) The author uses almost the same words here as Dugin and goes on to say that this Eurasian ideology is capable of absolutely everything. Indeed, the world has not yet seen such a superuniversal ideology. What is its all-powerful magic? It turns out that it is contained in the Russian nation's national character that includes "sobornost, kindness, sensitivity to other people's grief, readiness to share one's last possessions."(19)[1] Perhaps these qualities can indeed still be found in the Russian people, though I personally have strong doubts about that. But I haven't encountered these qualities so far among the politicians in power, the oligarchs, and the state bureaucrats, including the author of the quoted passage. Therefore, I get the feeling that Russia's impoverished masses (the hungry teachers and miners) can hardly be reconciled and united with the followers of Yeltsin and Berezovsky, the "new Russians." In any case, what does Eurasianism have to do with this?

Titarenko and his followers keep repeating the thesis that Russians are too fixated on Europe while ignoring Asian culture. He even called his book *Russia Facing Asia*. In this case, Russia is evidently supposed to turn her backside to Europe, assuming that Russia only has one face.

In reality, we never ignored Asia, and we know as much about it as the Asians know about us. But once again, what has Eurasianism got to do with it? Every single culture forms under the influence of both West and East. Yet, even though the Japanese have embraced many elements of European-American culture, it has not turned them into Eurasians. The Turks have also borrowed a lot from Europe, but they too did not become Eurasians. These peoples remain Japanese and Turks, respectively. So, why should the Russians turn into Eurasians? I agree that Russia has its own specialness, but how does it help to substitute the word "Eurasian" for "Russian"?

---

1 Titarenko would be well advised to read at least several books by authors who work in the West—that West to whom he proposes building a "Eurasian bridge." I recommend the book by Daniel Rancour-Laferriere, one of the few American authors who thoroughly knows the Russian language and who has talked with many Russians. After a thorough study of the works of Russian thinkers and writers, he gives a completely opposite assessment of the national traits of "the Russian people," the main trait of which figures in the title of his book. See Rancour-Laferriere, *The Slave Soul of Russia. Moral Masochism and the Cult of Suffering.*

Titarenko keeps complaining that we are not yet economically "integrated into the APR" and are overfocused on Europe; this, too, supposedly takes us away from Asia. To be real Eurasians, we must hurry up and integrate ourselves into this mythical "APR."

Indeed, we are not integrated into the "APR"; we are not even integrated with Southeast Asia. I will now express the thought (criminal to Eurasians) that we will never be integrated there. It's not because we ignore those regions but because our East Asian spaces are not fit for human habitation. The same analogy applies, by the way, to Canada's northern territories that are not integrated with Asia or with America, but also are not even integrated with the rest of Canada's own economy. Had Titarenko only bothered to analyze just the levels of Russia's trade with Asian countries over the last 200 years (to say nothing of integration-type ties), he would have discovered amazing things. Now let me do it for him.

Let's start with a few words about the present situation. In 1999, East Asia (seventeen countries altogether) accounted for just 10.2 percent of Russia's exports and 6.7 percent of its imports, while just one European country, Germany, accounted for 8.5 percent and 13.9 percent, respectively. Europe as a whole absorbs more than 70 percent of Russia's exports and provides more than 80 percent of its imports. Moreover, trade dynamics over the last fifteen to twenty years—indeed, over the last 200 years—don't confirm the hollow claims that "Asia" or the currently fashionable "APR" occupy "an ever more important place in Russian foreign trade." They do not, and they will not.

Let me remind you that in 1802–1804 (when statistics of Russian foreign trade started to be kept), Asia (including, at that time, Central Asia and Persia) accounted for 10 percent of exports and 17 percent of imports. By 1897, the respective figures were 10.5 percent and 11 percent. That is, Asia's share of imports dropped in favor of Europe and America.[1] For a multitude of reasons, Russia was, is, and will be oriented toward Europe. The only way to break this stable trend is to make Russia's Far East an area of bustling economic activity like California. This won't happen in the next century, though, due to the prosaic factors of geography, climate, and demography, plus a multitude of other reasons that stem from these three.

1 See Russia: *Encyclopedia* (on base of Encyclopedia of Brokgauz and Efron/ volumes 54 and 55/), 329.

I could go on criticizing Eurasianism in Titarenko's interpretation, but that would be pointless because Mr. Titarenko failed to define it. This mystery, though, characterizes all Russian Eurasianists. This compels me to conclude that Russian-style Eurasianism is just another variant of "if-only-ism" or simply "if-ism," i.e., another chimera or phantom. I would even call it a kind of fortune-telling that produces some dividends for its practitioners (the same as for those who use crystal balls or astrology) but has no practical, much less scientific, value.

Brzezinski's Eurasianism and the Response from Baturin and Dobrocheyev

Unlike Titarenko, Brzezinski uses the term "Eurasia" on the concept level in his geostrategic constructs, seemingly with the pretension of making it scientific. Let us see what comes from it. But first, a little prehistory.

Russia's *Independent Gazette* (issue of October 24, 1997) reprinted Brzezinski's article, "Geostrategy for Eurasia," which was clearly antiRussian in character yet received no polemical response from Russian political scientists in the international-affairs sphere. There is nothing surprising in this because the American's claims about the inevitable hegemony of the USA and the sorry fate of Russia really can't be refuted, at least not in the near future. Moreover, Mr. Sergei Rogov, director of the Institute of the USA and Canada, published a vast article in the *Nezavisimaya Gazeta – Scenario* (No. 3, 1998), in which he confirmed with very qualified figures that Brzezinski's geostrategic vision is justified as far as Russia is concerned. Yu. Baturin and O. Dobrocheyev did the same in an even more scientific form, based on the "physical and macrosocial approach," a method that is becoming quite popular in Russia and is known in the USA as the Theory of Complexity. However, this same method enabled our scholars to disagree with Brzezinski about Russia's future "in the long-term perspective." Therefore, their article may be viewed as a polemic of sorts against the American political scientist.[1] Baturin and Dobrocheyev's response is affected by the same "if-only-ism" that plagues Titarenko, albeit in a form that can be said to be more scientific.

The point is, even though Brzezinski and the Baturin–Dobrocheyev team use different methods of analysis, they utilize the same key terms; that is, they play the game on the same concept

1 Baturin and Dobrocheev, "Russia—a Link between Eurasia and the World," *NG-szenarii* (May 13, 1998). My text also makes use of the original draft of this article that Baturin gave to me for my information.

field. (I mean the main term that figures in the title of the Russians' article, Eurasia and Eurasian Geopolitics). My attitude toward this "science" has been sufficiently clear above; now I wish to concentrate on the concepts "Eurasia" and "Eurasianism" used by Brzezinski and which also serve as the starting point of the "physical analysis" by the Russian researchers.

Eurasia: Phantom or Reality?

So what is "Eurasia"? Zbigniew Brzezinski writes: "Eurasia is the continent where the countries are located that are the most stable in the political aspect and dynamic in development." In rebuttal of this claim, I could name dozens of "Eurasian" countries that are lacking in the above characteristics, but I will limit myself to just two, Russia and India. Brzezinski himself declares that Russia is "a political black hole." So, how can a black hole be politically stable? India's history similarly doesn't exhibit for some reason either political stability or, even less so, "dynamic development."

In this connection, the statement rings silly that Eurasia "accounts for 75 percent of the earth's population, 60 percent of total gross domestic product, and 75 percent of all energy resources. On the whole, Eurasia's potential might exceeds that of the USA." Baturin and Dobrocheyev second this pronouncement. But how can you compare the combined potential of dozens of different European and Asian countries with the potential of just one country? This comparison reminds me of the calculations performed to determine the combined potential of the so-called APR: Researchers squeeze half the world into this APR, then declare that its potential exceeds that of Europe.

Brzezinski then says: "Eurasia is a super-continent of the globe that performs the role of an axis of sorts." I utterly fail to understand how half the globe can be an "axis" of anything.

Finally: "The power that will become dominant in Eurasia will enjoy a deciding influence in two of the most economically developed regions of the planet: Western Europe and East Asia." As everyone knows, in the period after World War II, the USSR was the greatest power in Eurasia. Despite this, the "deciding influence" in Western Europe was enjoyed by the USA, and in East Asia by that same USA.

Thus, all the definitions of Eurasia, or at least those offered by Brzezinski, are simply not confirmed by historical practice and are, therefore, incorrect in principle. It follows that all subsequent constructs based on the Eurasian concept make no analytical sense. It is nothing but a game played with a fashionable word that eludes conceptual definition. It is no accident that the Russian authors felt compelled to remark that "Eurasia = Europe + Asia." This stipulation makes as much sense as, say, Eurafrica = Europe + Africa. This formula has no content beyond the statement of a geographic fact.

Is Russia the Same as Eurasia?

While Brzezinski sees Russia as "the political black hole" of Eurasia, to most Russian geopoliticians Eurasia is the same as Russia, i.e., not Europe nor Asia but some synthesis of the two—a unique entity. Here is where we fall into yet another trap. Russia is indeed geographically located in the territories of both Europe and Asia. But if we follow the culture-and-civilization principle, according to which Europeans and Asians belong to certain specific types of civilization, then Russians, who are neither European nor Asian, cannot be Eurasian. Just as Asians differ from Europeans, Russians differ from both. Russians share a special type of culture, thinking, and behavior, standing apart from all other types. Therefore, I absolutely fail to understand the often-used term *peoples of Eurasia*, for I have not yet encountered any such peoples. The Turks have not become Europeans or Euroturks just because part of Turkey is located in Europe. Likewise, Australians and New Zealanders have not become Asians on account of belonging to the so-called APR; they remain typical Europeans. Besides, the term "Asia" itself is quite tricky because the "Asians" inhabiting different parts of Asia are so different from each other that they form different types of civilization. It suffices to compare Arab Asians to Chinese Asians or Japanese Asians. The difference is as great as between heaven and earth. Moreover, the neighbor nations of China and Japan differ more from each other in thinking processes, culture, and *Weltanschauung* than, say, the Chinese differ from the Germans.

Therefore, in the geopolitical sense, the terms "Asia" and, to a still greater degree, "Eurasia" are empty notions, devoid of content.

The Future of Russia: Confederation or Integral Whole?

Now, a few words about geostrategy: Zbigniew Brzezinski has been saying for a long time that from the perspective of U.S. geostrategic interests, it is desirable that Russia disintegrate into a number of territories, such as a Siberian or a Far Eastern Republic. He has often spoken and written about the necessity to strengthen the independence of former Soviet Republics, Ukraine in particular, and also Azerbaijan and Uzbekistan in connection with Caspian oil. From the viewpoint of U.S. strategic interests, these recommendations are quite logical. Equally logical are Brzezinski's recipes for forming "strategic relations between America and China." He is even prepared to allow China's hegemony in the region (East Asia) while simultaneously "extracting" Japan from the confines of the region and pushing it into "world politics" to prevent a Japan–China struggle for leadership in East Asia that would be non-beneficial to the USA. It makes sense for Washington to put the question that way.

On the basis of their analysis, Baturin and Dobrocheyev delicately "dispute the main thesis about the confederate future of the country" (Russia), expressing certainty in its "stability" (or in its vital cycle) in accordance with "the lineal size of states in 2/3 degree." This conclusion is confirmed, in their opinion, by the centuries-long history of Russia. I have no idea how this law of the state's "land area" works in the case of, say, Japan, France, England, and Spain, states with land areas dozens of times smaller than Russia but with "life spans" almost twice that of Russia. When one considers that Russia became a "stable," that is, an integrally whole state, only under Peter the Great,[1] these authors' optimism may be viewed as wishful thinking.

The issue of which trend will prevail—"stability" (integrity) or instability (confederation)—will be decided not on the basis of the "land area" law but on the basis of the laws of politics and political economy.

The concrete outcome will depend on the socio-economic system that triumphs in Russia. Should capitalism triumph, Brzezinski's ideas will become reality. This is why:

Russia's history shows that every time democratic forms of government prevail (whether of the feudal or capitalist type), Russia becomes splintered and divided. Recall the period of feudal democracy (tenth to thirteenth centuries), the chaos after the death of Ivan the Terrible (late sixteenth to mid-seventeenth centuries), the period of capitalist development (starting in the mid-nineteenth century with the sale of Alaska), the period of democratization after 1905 that led to the events of October 1917, and the loss of Finland and Poland. (I'm certain, though, that the latter two would have "broken away" even without the October Revolution.) Finally, consider the single most destructive period in Russian history—the "democracy era" of Gorbachev and Yeltsin. By contrast, every time dictatorship was established in Russia by a tsar or an emperor (Ivan III, Ivan IV, Peter I, or Catherine II) or by a "proletarian dictator" of later times (Stalin), Russia expanded and became stronger.

Even if it is successful, the current capitalist way of development objectively leads Russia to disintegration, or at least economic autonomization of the oft-mentioned Siberia and the Far East, not to mention the further drifting away from Russia of former republics of the Soviet Union. This process is stimulated precisely by captialism because capitalism implies a high degree of autonomy for the economic subjects not only at the company level but also at the level of regions whose development follows the logic of market relations rather than orders from a central government. In this sense, it is just as silly to "strengthen" the Union of Independent States as it is to keep in Russia by force Chechnya and other

1 Prior to that, Russia existed as dozens of independent dukedoms, followed by "the Tartar-Mongol yoke," then by "the bringing together of Russian lands," and finally by "the Time of Troubles."

regions desiring to break away. The law of the marketplace dictates to the regions that they should strengthen their ties with those who offer the most "goodies." What goodies can today's impoverished Russia give them? The hopes that the current regime will be transforming in the direction of social-democratic capitalism are just utopian because this type of capitalism only works in countries with small territories and a huge historical experience of democracy. This type of capitalism is unacceptable in practice in either Russia or China.

Should we return to the socialist variant of development (in its modified form, naturally, close to the Chinese variant), then one could agree with the authors' optimism. A rigid socialist superstructure combined with the "soft" basis of a mixed economy can prevent the country from disintegration and maintain control over strategic resources and industries.

It is only in this case that Russia will become a "gravity center" (to use the expression of Baturin and Dobrocheyev) for the peoples of both Europe and Asia and even America. The problem is in making them "gravitate" to us on the understanding that we are a peer subject of economic interaction rather than an object whose natural and economic resources can be plundered. Perhaps then Russia will finally be able to build that bridge between East and West, between East Asia and Europe, invoked from time to time by the incorrigible optimists who believe in Russia's future.

Bipolarity Again?

By the way, the Russian authors' strongest objection to Brzezinski is made over an important point that they are unaware of themselves. This point is contained in the section of their article titled *America and Eurasia: Their Unity and Struggle—The Geopolitical Formula of the 21 st Century.* They say: "Political structurization will develop in the direction of American integration, on one hand, and Eurasian integration, on the other hand." They specify that initially America will dominate this process, and the next stage will see the emergence of "a new geopolitical entity on the Eurasian platform."

They are actually talking of the re-creation of the bipolar system of international relations. It will indeed be re-created in spite of the multipolarity concept that is dreamed of by utopians from weakened or underdeveloped states. But the shape of this bipolarity will not be America—Eurasia; it will be America—China. There is no integration in sight in the "Eurasian space" of the "axis" Europe—Russia—Asia; the real integration process is developing in East Asia around Mainland China. The People's Republic of China is becoming that "black hole" that pulls in the economies of all East Asian countries, not to mention commerce and investments from other countries around the world.

Please note: This Chinese hub of integration is systematically ideologized, attracting to its side all those who feel ill-treated by America, primarily Third World countries, but some other countries as well. Therefore, it is not just an economic integration complex that is in formation in East Asia with China at its core but also a strategic pole, with the PRC at its head, that objectively opposes the American pole. This is why Brzezinski is so concerned about the future of China and implores the leaders of his country to use any means, including sacrificing the interests of Japan, to prevent the transformation of China into a state hostile to the USA. He is absolutely right, but he isn't likely to succeed. The development of international relations doesn't follow the wishes of political scientists, even intelligent ones such as Mr. Brzezinski; neither does it follow the "laws" of geopolitics; it follows the elementary laws of economics that assert their irrefutable power every day.

Finally, I want to point out something that no one has mentioned so far, to the best of my knowledge. When talking about long-term or strategic perspectives, American and Russian scholars exhibit a curious discrepancy that reflects the difference in the thought processes of the two cultures. Americans, including Brzezinski, usually don't believe in the objective course of history or any kind of historical regularities. They believe in historical free will. That is why Brzezinski "skirts the question of the potential implementability of... the strategy," as the Russian authors write with either satisfaction or reproach. The American's thinking contains the gene of a creator of events and even history itself. The American, just like a true follower of the Russian botanist Michurin, does not wait for favors from nature; he creates both nature and history for the glory of America. He believes that such-and-such needs to be done: Russia must be squeezed; China must be won over to America's side; Japan must be directed this way; Europe must be directed that way, etc.

The Russian imbibes from childhood the belief in historical regularities and in "*Ru-ssi-a*" (in this sense he is close to the Chinese); he believes that in the end, history has preordained for Russia a great mission. So, despite the current crisis, hunger, and depopulation, Russians will not only emerge as victors but will also save the entire world with their spirituality, or whatever. He believes that in this great historic mission, even the laws of nature are on Russia's side.

It seems to me that Russians should stop counting on the objective laws of nature to ensure Russia's bright future against all odds, pinning their hopes on the designs of the Almighty who preordained for Moscow the role of the Third Rome destined to save the rest of humanity from its lack of spirituality. If Russians don't want to end up vassals to Americans or someone else, they should act like Americans; not "hope," not "count on" anything, but simply act—act with purpose and in cold blood, without Eurasian illusions and mysticism, in the name of Russia and the Russian people.

The first duty of those who would seek "ways to human happiness" is not to fool themselves and have the courage to frankly admit reality.

Lenin

PART III

The Twenty-First Century: Reality Without Illusions

In the first two parts of this book, when speaking of Russia's place and role in the world, I had to rely for the most part on the political science approach, or, rather, on one of its varieties—the theory of perception. Perceptions are quite often false or deliberately distorted. Real politics, though, can be practiced and often is practiced on the basis of false assumptions, but only for some time. The self-delusion usually comes to an end when a state begins to get results that negatively affect its national interests; these results sometimes amount to complete self-destruction or defeat in a particular historical struggle. The history of human civilization is full of such examples. The collapse of the former USSR can serve as a "fresh" example; contemporary Russia may yet provide another.

In Part III, I intend to show Russia's real place and role in the world, relying on economic and other statistical data that should serve to confirm or refute reasoning performed on the level of political scientific logic. But prior to that, I am compelled to address certain aspects of the theory of international relations that reflect in a generalized form the regularities of the real world's development. Only when we consider these regularities which indicate the trends of world development The Twenty-First Century: The World Without Russia we will be able to determine fully where Russia currently finds itself, and in which system of coordinates its importance is to be determined.

I know full well that Russian scholars dislike theories because: "All theory, my friend, is gray, but green is life's glad golden tree." Few of them seem to remember that this aphorism belongs to Mephistopheles, the perfidious devil who constantly lures man away from knowledge. I will dare to disobey the evil spirit's recommendation and attempt to prove, using "gray theory," that it is precisely knowledge that shows ways of freeing us from illusions. To be frank, initially I did not intend to address theory in this book; I was forced to do it by Russia's many Mephistopheleses in an effort to clear up the confusion they create about "globalization." That is the issue I will start with.

SECTION ONE

The Theory of Foreign Policy and International Relations

Chapter I

From Internationalization to Global Integration: Theory and Practice

So, what term best describes the world we live in? "We live in the era of globalization," scholars and politicians tell us. Other scholars and politicians object: "Not at all. Globalization is a myth. We actually live in the era of internationalization." Russian liberal democrats keep wailing: "Russia must become integrated into the world economy." That is, from their perspective, the world economy is integrated. "Nonsense, the world economy is localizing." Here you have one more term that came into prominence in the late 1990s.

All of these are not just words; they serve to build all kinds of theories and concepts of globalization, internationalization, integration, and localization that are called to explain and even forecast the development of international relations in the twenty-first century. Their emergence reflects objective processes in the world arena caused by increasingly close and intense interaction of all subjects and actors of world politics. In the language of systems experts, this means that different parts of the world (states, regions, subregions, etc.) enter in the kind of The Twenty-First Century: The World Without Russia interaction that shapes the world as an integral entity functioning according to laws that differ from the laws of a nonintegral, fragmented world, such as a multipolar or a bipolar world. The problem is the confusing choice of terms for describing all these phenomena.

Condillac used to say that languages are methods of analysis, and that the art of reasoning boils down to "a good design of language for each science." Hegel clarified later that it isn't just a matter of language; it is a matter of the conceptual content of terms and words. In his *Science of Logic*, that work of genius, he wrote: "Only in its Notion does something possess actuality and to the extent that it is distinct from its Notion it ceases to be actual and is a non-entity."[1] In other words, we must define whether globalization, internationalization, integration, and localization are simply synonyms (it is precisely in this quality that most scholars use them), or are concepts that reflect different aspects of "actuality." If the former is true, the topic can be safely left to journalists; if the latter is true, we must delve into the conceptual jungle in search of exact equivalents for realities.

The importance of appropriate terminology is shown by the fact that different analytical approaches are built depending on the definitions used; for example, within the framework of the globalization concept, Western authors usually identify five approaches (sometimes six). The first is built on the analysis of the common ecological risks; the second, on the analysis of world systems with an emphasis on economic processes; the third, the global culture approach, examines the emergence of a unified global culture; the fourth, the global society approach, concentrates on studying the planetary consciousness; and the fifth, the global capitalism approach, focuses on the activities of transnational corporations (TNCs), the international class (IC), and transnational organizations (TOs) in their relations with states or state institutions.

1 *Hegel's Science of Logic*, 50.

Internationalization and/or Globalization

Let me remind the reader once more that many researchers use the words globalization, internationalization, and integration as synonyms. This means that three different words are used to describe one and the same phenomenon. This is inaccurate because each of these words corresponds to a phenomenon qualitatively different from the others. Therefore, these are not just words but concepts.

This is how the British scholar Leslie Sklair understands the difference between "globalization " and "internationalization": "I argue that a clear distinction must be drawn between the inter-national and the global. The hyphen in inter-national is to distinguish (inadequate) conceptions of the 'global' founded on the existing even if changing system of nation-states, from (genuine) conceptions of the global based on the emergence of global processes and a global system of social relations not founded on national characteristics or nation-states."[1] What this means is that internationalization encompasses the area of international or interstate relations, while globalization covers the entire area of world relations where states are one among several types of actors.

Besides, the theory of globalization involves the analysis of phenomena born not only of that interaction of subjects and actors which creates the space of international relations but also of the transformation of states themselves into national communities that shape the world community.

Two other British scholars, Paul Hirst and Grahame Thomson, give their own definitions to the phenomena under discussion, in the same key but with some nuances. They write: "An inter-national economy is one in which the principal entities are national economies. Trade and investment produce growing interconnection between these still national economies."[2]

---

1 Sklair, "Competing Conceptions of Globalization," *Journal of World-System Research* 5, no. 2 (Spring 1999), 142.

2 Hirst and Thomson, *Globalization in Question: The International Economy and the Possibilities of Governance*, 8.

This is how it differs from the global economy: "A *globalized economy* is a distinct ideal type from that of the inter-national economy and can be developed by contrast with it. In such a global system distinct national economies are subsumed and rearticulated into the system by international processes and transactions. The inter-national economy, on the contrary, is one in which processes that are determined at the level of national economies still dominate and international phenomena are outcomes that emerge from the distinct and differential performance of the national economy. The inter-national economy is an aggregate of nationally located functions." (*That is, it proceeds from national or local interests—A.B.*)

"The global economy raises these nationally based interactions to a new power. The international economic system becomes autonomized and socially disembedded, as markets and production become truly global. Domestic policies, whether of private corporations or public regulators, now have routinely to take account of the predominantly international determinants of their sphere of operations. As systemic interdependence grows, the national level is permeated by and transformed by the international. In such a globalized economy the problem this poses for public authorities of different countries is how to construct policies that coordinate and integrate their regulatory efforts in order to cope with the systemic interdependence between their economic actors." (10)

Let us now rephrase this in plain English. In the authors' opinion, internationalization is but mere interaction of national economies, albeit in a more condensed and closely tied fashion than in the periods when national economies functioned under a more autonomous regime. Globalization, on the other hand, is a new phenomenon in which national economic borders are erased for real, and the main actors of economic interaction are no longer the national economies (though they still don't disappear altogether), but rather the TNCs or MNEs (multinational enterprises, in OECD terminology).

I want to draw your attention to Mr. Xu Mingqi, a Chinese scholar from Shanghai, who offers this definition of the term: "The so-called economic globalization is the interdependence of economic activities of nations, regions, and enterprises, and even of individuals, that has developed into a new historic stage, in which every single part becomes inseparable from the integrated world economy."[1] He is the only author I have read so far who derives globalization from internationalization—a process started, in his opinion, in the mid-eighteenth century. He believes that globalization started in the 1970s. (ibid.)

My approach differs from the approaches of all the authors quoted above—first of all in the methodology that leads me to a different type of thinking about the phenomena identified. It may be labeled Hegelian or Marxist-Leninist (the latter follows from the former); essentially, it is the dialectical approach. V.I. Lenin wrote: "The analysis of concepts, the study thereof, 'the art of operating with them' (Engels) always requires studying the *movement* of the notions, their connections, the transitions between them."[2]

In the context of our topic, this means the following: The forming of the world market since the second half of the nineteenth century gave birth to the phenomenon of *economic internationalization* that goes through certain cycles and phases (we shall revisit this topic) and continues to develop today. As a phenomenon, economic internationalization is the objective process of intensive interaction between subjects and actors of the world economy in the sphere of commerce, capital, and finance.

In the process of its development, *internationalization* gave birth to two new phenomena: *regional integration* (since the second half of the twentieth century) and *globalization* (since the 1990s). These two phenomena negate internationalization (even though it caused them), and at the same time they are antagonistic to each other. This contradiction can be resolved through a new phenomenon—*global integration*, or, in other words, a unified world economy—that would negate both globalization and regional integration. At the preliminary stage, globalization is "assisted" by localization, which works against integration, as will be shown in the corresponding section.

All these phenomena (internationalization, integration, localization, and globalization) will coexist for some time yet in a "mutual struggle" that will manifest itself in varying degrees. Globalization and localization are new phenomena in the world economy that exist, at the moment, only in an embryonic form.

1 Xu, "Economic Globalization, Defects in International Monetary System and Southeast Asian Financial Crisis," SASS Papers, no. 8 (2000), 229.

2 Lenin, *The Complete Works of Lenin. Fifth edition in 55 volumes*, 29: 227.

Manifested today are mainly internationalization and regional integration.

One should keep in mind that global integration, or a united world economy, implies a united world government, while internationalization, integration, and globalization do not destroy the power of national governments, though the latter play different roles in each of the three phenomena. Governments are most important in integration processes and least important in globalization processes.

Note also that the main economic actors in the integration processes are national economies and regional TNCs, while in the economic spaces of internationalization, TNCs have more importance than national companies. In globalized spaces, the leading role is played by international companies, multinational enterprises, and international banks (INCs, MNEs, and INBs).

After a concrete analysis of realities, I shall return to these definitions in order to fine-tune them, and I shall show currently prevailing trends.

Manifestations of Economic Internationalization

If one takes economic internationalization to mean sharply increasing flows of goods, capital, and labor across national borders, one can't help noticing right away that this is "yesterday's news," to use an American expression. This process was observed throughout the second half of the nineteenth century and up to World War I; the political thinkers who wrote about it include Marx, Engels,[1] and especially Lenin, in particular in his work *Imperialism as the Highest Stage of Capitalism.* At the turn of the twentieth century, internationalization was stimulated by the weakening of trade barriers and the decrease of transportation costs due to the development of railroads and the merchant marine. Between the start of World War I and the end of World War II, world trade shrank due to raised tariffs and limitations imposed on the movement of capital. Internationalization was relaunched soon after World War II, facilitated by the General Agreement on Tariffs and Trade (GATT) of 1947 that was transformed in 1995 into the World Trade Organization (WTO), and by the collapse of the Bretton Woods system in the early 1970s that was replaced by floating currency exchange rates. This was followed by Reaganomics, Thatcherism, and the administrative-financial reform in Japan—neoliberal policies that affected, among other things, the sphere of foreign economic activities. It wasn't only trade that benefited but, more importantly, the movement of capital; controls over capital flows were removed in Great Britain in 1979, and in Japan in 1980. After a considerable delay, France and Italy followed suit in 1990.

Apart from liberalization, the objective process of the emergence of new technologies was an enormously important factor, especially in the area of communications. Let me remind you that a three-minute phone call between New York and London cost about

1 Already in the Communist Manifesto of 1848, Marx and Engels wrote: "The need of a constantly expanding market for its products chases the bourgeoisie over the surface of the globe. … The bourgeoisie has through its exploitation of the world market given a cosmopolitan character to production and consumption in every country. "Marx and Engels. *Selected Works*, 38.

$300 in 1930 (at 1996 prices) and just $1 in 1996. The spreading of personal computers (PCs) together with their Internet connections had a revolutionary influence in accelerating the internationalization process, giving birth simultaneously to globalization.

As a result of technological innovation and the liberalization of terms of trade and capital movement, the growth rate of international trade in 1986–1996 exceeded the growth rate of GDP by a factor of two; the flow of direct investment grew faster than GDP by a factor of three; and trade in securities grew by a factor of ten. The physical volume of trade increased in that period from $2 trillion to $5.2 trillion. Taking a longer stretch of time, we see that since 1950, the volume of world trade has grown by a factor of 16, while GDP grew by a factor of 5.5. The proportion of world exports to world GDP grew from 7.7 percent in 1950 to 15 percent in 1995.[1]

The explosive growth of financial capital is illustrated by the following: In 1985, the combined transaction volume for currency traders of New York, London, and Tokyo averaged $190 billion per day; in 1995, this volume reached $1.2 trillion. In 1990, a total of $50 billion of private capital of all kinds was invested in emerging markets (China, East Europe, and some other countries); in 1996, this figure reached $336 billion (including the republics of the former Soviet Union).[2]

Now let's talk about the process of world migration. In Peter Stalker's paper, The Work of Strangers, published by the WTO, it is said that about 80 million people currently reside outside their own countries. Another 20 million people are living abroad as refugees. Every year about 1.5 million people emigrate, and approximately one million seek temporary refuge abroad. The countries considered most attractive for immigration are the USA, Canada, Germany, Australia, and New Zealand. In 1995 alone, 720,000 people migrated to the USA (far short of the peak figure of 2,000,000 achieved in 1991), and 800,000 migrated to Germany. More than 200,000 people arrive annually in Canada. Most immigrants come from underdeveloped countries; for example, in 1995, 90,000 people migrated to the USA from Mexico, 55,000 from CIS countries, and 51,000 from the Philippines.[3]

1 *The Economist* (November 8, 1997). Ibid. (October 25, 1997).

2 Ibid. (November 1, 1997).

3 Ibid.

Internationalization Cycles in the Twentieth Century

Despite the impressive figures, many more of which could be quoted here, one shouldn't exaggerate the process of internationalization. To clarify the reasons for this caution, let us look at the period just before World War I.

Usually the degree of involvement in the world market is determined through the proportion of foreign trade volume to GDP. Well, consider that between 1913 and 1996, this proportion hardly increased at all in the United Kingdom, Germany, and France—just by 2 percent to 5 percent, to reach 47 percent, 41 percent, and 38 percent respectively. In Japan, it actually dropped from 30 percent to 17 percent. Only in the USA did it rise substantially, from about 10 percent to 20 percent.[1]

Similar trends were observed in foreign direct investment (FDI). In 1914 its proportion to GDP in the Netherlands, the United Kingdom, France, and Germany was 85 percent, 60 percent, 18 percent, and 18 percent respectively (rounded figures); in 1996 the respective figures were 42 percent, 32 percent, 16 percent, and 15 percent. Only in the USA did this proportion grow from 7 to 8 percent to 13 to 14 percent. Today, FDI averages 6 percent of domestic investment, while in 1914, in the United Kingdom, its share was about 50 percent.

It's the same story with workforce mobility. In the nineteenth century, population migration was much greater than today. It suffices to say that between 1850 and 1914, about 60 million people left Europe.[2]The reasons for this are many, but note that today, even in Europe, where judicial barriers to migration are formally practically absent, there are no workforce flows to be observed. Linguistic, cultural, professional, and other factors produce this outcome.

1 Ibid. (October 18, 1997).

2 See details in Hirst and Thomson, 22–26.

Let us specify once again the indices used for measurement. Trade internationalization is the whole world's exports (the sum total of all countries' exports) divided by the whole world's production (the sum total of all countries' GDP). Investment internationalization is the sum total of all FDI in the world divided by the world's total GDP (less services).

When using this method, we discover that the degrees of trade internationalization and investment internationalization are different, and their phases are not simultaneous. Besides, it turns out that the degree of investment internationalization in 1913 was higher than in 1991, or at least as high as in 1991, while trade internationalization was lower in 1913 than it is now.

Proceeding with such comparisons, we find out that the first wave of trade internationalization took place in 1900–1929, followed by a decline until 1950.[1] The second wave started in the 1970s and continued into the early 1990s. Currently, the third wave is starting in trade internationalization, as well as in investment internationalization; these two are becoming synchronized.

One more indicator of economic internationalization is the correlation between national GDPs and the internationalizing world economy. In other words, the higher the degree of the world economy's internationalization, the more synchronization we expect between the growth and fall periods of national GDPs. This synchronization is not in evidence, however. According to Grimm's data, between 1860 and 1988 consistency (or synchronization) of GDP growth and fall was observed only in two periods, in 1913–1927 and after the 1970s. Prior to 1913 and in the time between the two peaks, synchronization was practically nonexistent. This indicates that the internationalizing world is still far from economic globalization, and internationalization itself is not a phenomenon of, say, the 1980s and 1990s ("the recent years," as we say here); it has a long history that exhibits certain cycles or fluctuations. Trade internationalization, for example, dropped dramatically during the depression in the 1930s. Investment internationalization exhibits

1 There is a different approach to division into periods. For example, Arrighi places the first stage of globalization in the period of "the global market under British hegemony" (second half of the nineteenth century to the early 1930s); he calls the second stage "the period of the global market reconstruction under U.S. hegemony" (after World War II). Arrighi, "The Global Market," *Journal of World-Systems Research* 5, no. 2 (Spring 1999).

cycles with two "peaks," one prior to World War I and the other starting in the 1980s. The synchronization level of economic growth indicates cyclical fluctuations with one peak in the 1920s and another in the 1970s (according to analyses performed before the 1990s).

It should be stressed particularly that in the 1990s, the process of internationalization continued to develop not only quantitatively, as China, India, Mexico, and other states joined in, but also qualitatively. In this latter respect, two developments stand out. First, financial capital started playing a much larger role in the context of economic internationalization. For example, the daily volume of foreign currency transactions zoomed from $15 billion in 1973 to $1.2 trillion in 1995. Sales of stocks and bonds by American investors grew from 9 percent of the U.S. GDP in 1980 to 164 percent in 1996.[1] Second, economic internationalization is stimulated by falling communication costs, just as in the past it was stimulated by falling transportation costs. Moreover, modern information technologies enable people to transact business without physical communication (through the Internet, for example); this helps propel the internationalization process to the level of globalization.

1 *The Economist* (October 18, 1997).

Preliminary Results of Economic Internationalization

There is nothing surprising in the fact that assessments of internationalization effects depend on the ideological stances of particular authors or groups of scholars. In particular, two schools of economists tend to clash over issues of economic globalization. One is the socalled Manchester school of the liberal persuasion (it counts among its founders David Ricardo, Jeremy Bentham, and Richard Cobden); the other is the theorist-globalist school[1] (sometimes called adherents of the Theory of Dependency). Ideologically, the latter lean toward the social-democratic or plain socialist camps. Best known among them are Immanuel Wallerstein, Giovanni Arrighi, Christopher Chase-Dunn, Leslie Sklair, Ranveig Gissinger, Nils Petter Gleditsch, and Warren W. Wagar.

The liberal school maintains that the more dependent a country is on the global economy, the higher its economic growth, its level of wellbeing, its degree of democracy, and the stronger its domestic peace. The globalist theorists reach the opposite conclusion. A high degree of economic dependency on foreign markets (i.e., a high level of foreign trade and FDI) exacerbates inequality of incomes, leading to domestic conflicts.

The paradox is that both the former and the latter are correct and incorrect at the same time. It all depends on the object of analysis and the type of economic internationalization, and also on the time period chosen for examination.

When speaking of results of internationalization's "second cycle" for the "core" countries, the liberals are almost 100 percent correct (I will explain this "almost" later). As for the "periphery," the globalists' assessments are correct. Statistical data indicate that

1 I want to reiterate that though they call themselves "globalists," they are actually analyzing and discussing the problems of internationalization. In this section, I am constrained to preserve their terminology when quoting.

between 1960 and 1990, the incomes of the richest one-fifth of the "core" grew three times faster than those of the poorest one-fifth of the "periphery." As a result, the latter's share of the world economy dropped from 2.3 percent in 1960 to 1.4 percent in 1990. During that same period, civil wars became much more frequent in the "periphery" countries. As the globalist Joke Schrijvers wrote in this connection: "The gap between a small, wealthy elite and the impoverished masses has grown to such astronomic proportions due to so-called development that many former "Third World" countries are in a state of endemic civil war."[1]

Here are more statements from the globalists:

J. Galtung (1971): "According to dependency theory, the penetration of foreign capital into peripheral economies leads to the exploitation of local human and natural resources, and to a transfer of profit back to the imperial centers. This process results in impoverishment, inequality, and injustice."

H. Hveem (1996): "The production of raw materials in poor countries serves to prevent competence-building, and the economy remains export-oriented."

T. Boswell & W. Dixon (1990), E. Muller and M. Seligson (1989), and R. Rubinson (1976) all reach the same conclusion: "Ties are created between the local power elite and foreign interests, in turn increasing income inequality in the poor countries."

Finally, F. Bourgignon and Ch. Morrison (1989), and A. Wood (1994) state bluntly: "The production of raw materials will keep inequality high and the level of welfare low." (ibid.)

To verify the trends indicated above, the globalists undertook in late 1998 and early 1999 one more wide-scale analysis of internationalization effects on ninety-six countries over the years 1965 to 1997. Their analysis confirmed the trend noticed long ago of Third World enclaves being recreated within the "core" itself (this is precisely the meaning of "almost" applied to the liberals' assessments of the "core"). They write of the emergence of a new group called

1 Quoted from Gissinger and Gleditsch, "Globalization and Conflict: Welfare, Distribution, and Political Unrest," *Journal of World-Systems Research*. 5, no. 2 (Spring 1999), 280.

"working poor" in their own countries due to the weakening of the labor movement and companies' attempts to compete with countries having lower labor costs. The TNCs constantly threaten their workers, demanding that they "understand" why their wages are being lowered, because otherwise they would have to move production abroad, which they often do. For example, between 1990 and 1994, the Swiss–Swedish company Asea Brown Boveri (ABB) terminated 40,000 jobs in Europe and North America while creating 21,150 jobs in Eastern Europe, mostly in Poland. Keep in mind that the average hourly wage in Western countries is about twelve times higher than in Poland, and Polish workers toil 400 hours more per year than, say, German workers.[1]

Observing these trends, even such liberal-minded scholars as Luttwak (1994) started writing about Third World standards that are invading the life of Americans, pointing out that 15 million of them, or 6 percent of the U.S. population, live in conditions close to those in the world's poorest countries. Gerd Junne of Amsterdam University shares the same opinion: "With about 30 percent of the U.S. population living below the poverty line, and about as many being illiterate, the North-South divide does not so much separate Mexico and the United States; rather, it goes right through the United States itself."[2]

Writing about the "periphery" countries, most authors point out the increasing inequality of incomes there, based on their own research and the Report on Human Development of 1997. They note that the share of the poorest 20 percent of the population in total incomes is decreasing in Argentina, Chile, the Dominican Republic, Ecuador, Uruguay and Mexico. In sixteen of the eighteen countries of Eastern Europe and in the former USSR, the distribution of incomes has become more asymmetrical, with poverty growing alongside the process of liberalization. It is also worth noting that the average income in the twenty richest countries exceeds the average income in the twenty poorest countries by a factor of 37, and this gap has widened over the past forty years.

1 Thurow, *The Future of Capitalism*, 168.

2 Junne, "Global Cooperation or Rival Trade Blocs?" *Journal of World-Systems Research* 1, no. 9 (1995), 17.

For greater fullness of the picture, let us look at this table from the *Report on World Development* of 2000/2001.[1]

Percentage of Population Subsisting on Less than US $1 per Day

Region	1987	1998*
East Asia and the Pacific (except China)	26.6	15.3
Eastern Europe and Central Asia	0.2	5.1
Latin America and the Caribbean	15.3	15.6
Middle East and North Africa	4.3	4.3
South Asia	44.9	40.0
Sub-Saharan Africa	46.6	46.3
TOTAL	28.5	24.0

* Preliminary estimates.

This figure (24 percent) represents 1.2 billion people. We may also add that another 2.8 billion people subsist on less than $2 per day. That is, four billion people out of the total of six billion in the world live in poverty. Although East Asia clearly exhibits positive dynamics of incomes, in South Asia, Latin America, and sub-Saharan Africa, the numbers of the poor keep growing. Especially striking is the fact that in Eastern Europe and Central Asia, the numbers of the poor grew more than twenty times. Such is the price paid for capitalist reforms.

The authors explain the high level of inequality in the poor countries through the penetration of their markets by large foreign companies that hire the best-educated part of the local population and effectively "separate" them from the rest of the population.

The authors' conclusions contain several important observations. First, FDI has a bigger negative effect on distribution of incomes and political unrest than trade, though the effect of investment and trade depends to a large degree on the economy's structure. Second, exports of agricultural products by developing coun-

1 The World Bank, *World Development Report 2000/2001: The Struggle Against Poverty: A Review*, 13.

tries lead to decreasing economic well-being, inequality of incomes, and political unrest, while exports of manufactured goods lead to higher levels of economic development, equality, and political stability. Third, countries that export raw materials tend to reproduce (with rare exceptions) poverty and weak government. *The general conclusion is this: The globalization process affects rich countries positively, while poor agrarian societies can be affected negatively.*

These conclusions are no revelations to Russian scholars. However, it is important that experts on globalization in the United States and the United Kingdom are now arriving at the same conclusions made by Russian Marxists during the first wave of internationalization.

How Can Internationalization Be Made Fair?

These same globalist theorists ask this question, and they give different answers. Certain sociologists, for example, those in the American Sociological Association, recognize only one "correct" answer. In Warren Wagar's interpretation, their solution lies in choosing "the third path of partnership, of mutual multiculturalism, a future in which radical feminism, fundamentalist Islam, populist libertarianism, militant Hinduism, Marxian socialism, born-again Christianity, megacorporate capitalism, Bosnian nationalism, Serbian nationalism, and all the other colliding forces at work in our whirling world somehow lie down together like lions and lambs in the New Jerusalem and agree to eat grass, or better yet, develop the capacity to feed themselves by photosynthesis."[1] A truly "beautiful" prospect, notes Wagar ironically, but a fundamentally wrong answer.

The answer he offers sounds quite Marxist. He proposes replacing "predatory global capitalism" with a "socialist world commonwealth." (ibid) He is also not alone in suggesting this solution. Chase-Dunn appeals for "socialist relations on the level of the entire world system." Wallerstein champions "a socialist world government." Amin speaks of forcing out the reactionary utopia of "globalization through the marketplace" and proposes a humanist globalization project "compatible with the socialist perspective."[2] They justify the socialist solution by arguing that otherwise, "the regressive and criminal scenario will most likely determine the future." Wagar himself believes that: "The next fifty years—and more—are likely to produce a reasonable facsimile of hell on earth, a time compared to which the last fifty years may survive in memory as a veritable golden age." (3) He goes on to describe in detail the mechanism of creating a "world party" (in 2035) and having it function to the year 2050.[3]

---

1 Wagar, "Toward a Praxis of World Integration," *Journal of World-Systems Research* 2, no. 2, (1996), 1.

2 Ibid., 2.

3 For details, see his work, *A Short History of the Future.*

In the end, all of them propose to establish a world state through global communications. In Chase-Dunn's opinion, the core of this world-state can be constituted by a system of "semi-peripheral democratic socialism" that includes Russia, China, India, South Africa, Brazil, and Mexico. Proponents of this idea (surprisingly many among globalist theorists) are convinced that all types of "globalization" give the opportunity to organize not only world capitalism but also those who are exploited by this capitalism. In other words, global capitalism can be counteracted at the same global level by an equally global socialism, naturally of the democratic type.[1] It is remarkable that their goals and methods are almost identical word for word to those proposed by the academician N.N. Moiseyev in a number of his recent works.[2]

It is no less amazing that similar proposals originate from scholars far from left-wing ideologies and movements. For example, the German scholar Dirk Messner wrote a big article in which he mentions the names of Yehezkel Dror (Israel), Ralf Darendorf (German), Richard Haas (USA), and Peter D. Sutherland (USA), former director general of GATT in 1993–1995. All of these authors propose setting up institutional foundations for governing the world economy.[3] This solution is forced by "the wild and merciless globalization that follows only the laws of competition and therefore is capable of removing substantial numbers of people from society in many countries." (Darendorf) Therefore, it is time to assert "the primacy of politics over the self-contained dynamics of marketplace regularities, and institutions for shaping globalization so that national societies and institutional systems in the North, South, and East are prepared for new demands." (Sutherland)

In this regard, Messner himself addresses the issue of creating a Global Governance Architecture that is, in his opinion, one of the most urgent demands of the twenty-first century. He goes on to

---

1 I remind you about the mass protests by globalization opponents in Seattle during the WTO meeting in November 1999. The protesters' favorite slogan was "The WTO kills people. Kill the WTO." See The Economist, December 4, 1999. It would seem that antiglobalism is turning into a mass worldwide anticapitalist movement.

2 For example, see N.N. Moiseyev, *The Fortunes of Civilization. The Way of Reason.*

3 Messner, "Globalisierung, Global Governance und Enwicklungspolitik," *International Politics and Society*, no. 1 (1999).

describe the laws and objectives of global governance in the spirit of the American globalists mentioned above. Instead of hegemony politics, he writes, it is necessary to create a world order of cooperation; solve the problems of poverty; give assistance to China, India, Brazil, and South Africa; solve population problems; implement the ideas of rule-of-law; and assist the development of different cultures, etc. The accomplishment of these objectives will require reorganizing national politics to connect it to global politics. Messner also describes in detail the hierarchy of tasks that global governance must address. Thus it turns out that utopian dreamers are just as abundant in the West as in Russia.

In actual fact, all concepts and proposals by the globalist theorists are utopian, at least for two reasons. The first is that "globalization" (as they understand it) has not only failed to reduce the role of the state within countries or in the international arena but, on the contrary, has increased that role. The second reason has to do with the process of integration that they simply omit from their analysis, possibly because they see it as identical to "globalization." Let us examine in this connection first the role of TNCs and then their relationship to the state.

Transnational and Multinational Corporations (TNCs and MNCs)

In the mind of the general public, MNCs, TNCs, and globalization are closely interconnected. They are called, with good reason, the main actors in the process of globalization. Many weighty arguments are offered to confirm the importance of TNCs, including statistical data.

So, what is their might? According to UN data, by the mid-1990s there were 45,000 parent TNCs in the world, controlling some 280,000 subsidiaries. Of that number, 37,000 (about 82 percent) were based in the fourteen developed countries of OECD. Ninety percent of all TNC headquarters were located in the developed world.

According to UN data (1997 World Investment Report), in 1996 TNCs sold through their subsidiaries goods and services worth $7 trillion in total (i.e., more than all the exports in the world, worth a total of $5.2 trillion). The total amount of FDI in production facilities, equipment, and private property equaled $3 trillion. Seventy percent of international technology royalties were paid out within related firms and their foreign subsidiaries. This is evidence of the key role played by the TNC in spreading technologies across the globe.[1]

About 80 percent of U.S. trade was carried out by TNCs, a proportion typical of developed countries as a whole. Approximately 40 percent of total trade took place between TNCs themselves. They are also the main accumulators of FDI. The one hundred biggest TNCs controlled about 20 percent of all foreign assets, accounting for $2 trillion of foreign sales and employing six million workers (in 1995).

In actual fact, there aren't all that many companies that are truly global. Some of the best known are Royal Dutch/Shell, Ford, General Electric, Exxon, GM, Volkswagen, IBM, Toyota, Nestle

1 Hirst and Thomson, 68.

(food), Bayer (chemistry), ABB, Nissan, Mobil, Daimler-Benz, Coca Cola, and Kodak. Their capacities are truly impressive. According to World Bank data, in 1995 only seventy countries out of a total of 200 had GDPs in excess of $10 billion. Meanwhile, Fortune reported that of 500 biggest TNCs, 440 had sales of more than $10 billion.[1]

The share of TNCs in the national products of developed countries (except Japan) is quite high and tends to grow higher still. According to OECD data for 1996 (the latest year for which comparative statistics were given) quoted in The Economist of January 8, 2000, foreign firms accounted for 15.8 percent of all production in the United States, while in 1989 that figure was 13.2 percent, and in 1985, 8.8 percent. In Canada, foreign firms' share was more than 50 percent in 1996 and about 46 percent in 1989; in the United Kingdom, 33 percent and 24 percent, respectively; in France, 29 percent and 28 percent; and in Germany, about 13 percent. The one exception is Japan, where the share of foreign firms in the national product is negligible; in 1996 it was 1 percent, less than in 1989 (2 percent).

The share of the domestic workforce employed by foreign firms is also somewhat high; in the United States it was 10.8 percent in 1989 and 11.4 percent in 1996. Statistical data indicate that, on the whole, foreign firms create more jobs than local ones. This is certainly true of the United States and the United Kingdom. Besides, foreign firms pay higher wages than domestic ones. In 1996 the gap was 6 percent in the United States, 36 percent in Japan, 30 percent in the Netherlands, 29 percent in the U.K., and 12 percent in France.[2]

It is also noteworthy that foreign firms spend huge sums on research and development. In 1996 they accounted for 12 percent of all R&D outlays in the United States, 19 percent in France, and 40 percent in the U.K. Also, their R&D outlays are proportionally higher than those of local companies. Thus, in the U.K. foreign firms spent 2 percent of their revenue on R&D, while local firms spent 1.5 percent.

Finally, foreign firms export proportionally more than domestic ones. The gap is impressive in some instances. In 1996 TNCs

1 Sklair, 143.

2 *The Economist* (January 8, 2000), 85.

exported 89 percent of their output in Ireland, while national companies exported only 34 percent of theirs; in the Netherlands, the figures were 64 percent and 37 percent, respectively; in France, 35.2 percent and 33.6 percent; in Japan, 13.1 percent and 10.6 percent. The exception is the United States, where domestic companies exported 15.3 percent of their output in 1996, while foreign companies exported 10.7 percent.[1]

Similar trends are observed in foreign firms' actions in the developing world. For example, in Turkey wages paid by TNCs are 124 percent higher than the national average, and the number of TNC jobs grows by 11.5 percent annually, while in local companies, the growth rate of jobs is only 0.6 percent. The picture is similar with respect to R&D expenditures. It is another matter that the Turkish worker's wages are lower by an order of magnitude (at least) than those of an American or European worker. That is a separate topic.

No one disputes these figures, but they beg one serious question: Is the influence of TNCs really so huge that it exceeds the influence of the state, which starts losing its importance in the era of globalization? Important conclusions depend on the answer. If the answer is yes, conjectures are in order about the disappearance of state sovereignty, a world without borders, and even about the disappearance of the state from the world arena.

1 Ibid., 86.

TNCs and the State

Though the theme "the state is dying away" is not new (the pillars of Marxism-Leninism wrote volumes about it), it is being reborn today in connection with globalization issues.[1] Those who believe unreservedly that globalization is the dominant phenomenon in the world economy claim that the state (or state sovereignty) has lost (or is losing) its importance, ceasing to be "a meaningful political unit." For example, the English scholar Evan Luard believes that: "More than in any earlier time, the state within which political activity has traditionally been concentrated, is not a self-sufficient political or economic unit, but only a fragment of a much wider entity: the world-wide political system, the international economy, world society."[2] He notes that this development is due not only to economic globalization but also to the globalization of politics.

The Portuguese scholar Jaime Nogueira Pinto writes directly of a crisis of state sovereignty. The cause, he thinks, is that "markets have tended toward integration, economic 'globalization,' the creation of a 'one-world' market."[3] He notes with some surprise that integration of markets does not lead directly to political integration, and thus "a united, economic world-market can co-exist with a still more fragmented political world." (3) The sole exception, he believes, is the European Union. It is clear from this passage that the Portuguese scholar doesn't understand that Western Europe is actually integrated both "from the bottom" (economically) and "from the top" (politically). The rest of the world's economic space

1 For example, see Kosterlitz, "Sovereignty's Struggle," *National Journal*, November 20, 1999; and Mazrui, "Globalization and Cross-Cultural Values: The Politics Of Identity and Judgment," *Arab Studies Quarterly* (ASQ) 21 (Summer 1999).

2 Luard, *The Globalization of Politics: The Changed Focus of Political Action in the Modern World* (L.: Macmillan, 1990), 3.

3 Pinto, "The Crisis of the Sovereign State and the 'Privatization' of Defense and Foreign Affairs," Heritage Foundation *Heritage Lectures*, no. 649 (November 19, 1999), 2.

is not integrated, but internationalized; that is a major difference. This is precisely why "the rest of the world" cannot be integrated politically.

Nonetheless, Pinto justifiably points out the narrowing of state sovereignty in a number of Third World countries (Sierra Leone, Liberia, Angola, Congo, Lebanon, Afghanistan, Peru, Colombia, Indochina, and the Balkans). Some of these countries are torn apart by civil war or guerrilla activities, while others are partially controlled by drug lords' private armies. In all of them, the state-run police and armed forces are unable to provide security to the citizens. That is why large corporations are forced to create their own "private security armies." (5) This results in the shrinkage of state power, i.e., loss of these states' sovereignty. But all this is not directly related to globalization as such, unless we take that word to mean the spreading of the phenomena described above over wider geographical spaces. (I can't help noticing the constant confusion of causes and effects and the ungrounded generalizations of local phenomena. Evidently, it is not only Russian scholars who are plagued by this disease.)

One example of radical globalization orthodoxy is in the presentation made by professor Kimon Valaskakis of the University of Montreal at the OECD Conference in Hamburg, Germany, in March 2000. He argued that the international system had ceased to be controlled by governments, that the Westphalian system was crumbling (Russian scholars, too, love to expound on this topic), and pointed out the European Union as an example of this trend, claiming a loss of state sovereignty in that organization.[1]

Similar ideas are presented and argued in more detail in the lectures by Anthony Giddens (1999).[2] These lectures drew a response from English scholars Colin Hay and Matthew Watson, who cast doubt on all his "arguments" in their article. They note, in particular: "The quantitative evidence makes clear that the corrosive impact of capital flight on European social models, labor market institutions, and social democratic possibilities is frequently exaggerated."[3]

1 *The International Herald Tribune* (March 30, 2000), 6.

2 See the *BBC Online Network* Web site.

3 Hay and Watson, "Globalization: Skeptical Notes on the 1999 Reith Lectures," *Political Quarterly* 70 (October/December 1999).

Although these two authors refute the globalization radicals' claims in a tactful manner, the well-known American journalist William Pfaff of *The International Herald Tribune* casts away scholarly diplomacy. He reminds the readers, in particular, that the USA, just as Albania, China, Russia, the U.K., France, Austria, or Denmark, pursues its own national interests rather than global ones. He writes: "We see the illusion rather than the reality of dissolving national power and sovereignty. The modern forces of the market and the Internet challenge established forms of national authority but do not alter the political reality that each is ultimately subject to state power, even if the mechanisms of that power have to be changed."[1] Moreover, Pfaff assesses the role of international organizations perfectly correctly: "The international institutions, including the UN and the new war crimes courts, have no independent legitimacy. None are 'democratic.' They exist because nations signed treaties giving them existence. Serbia was not attacked by the 'international community,' which has no political expression. It was attacked by a coalition of governments, each with its own motives." (ibid.)

Pfaff reminds us with perfect reason that all this uncontrolled international business is immediately brought under control as soon as it starts to threaten national interests. Even the movement of money can be controlled, if need be, through classical politics or the politics of force. There you have it—a rare case of a journalist who has a deeper understanding of a phenomenon than many scholars with academic titles aplenty!

In actual fact, the answers to these questions depend on the criteria used to determine the state's role and functions. For the time being, no one doubts the state's role in politics and in the military-strategic sphere. Already we have perspectives from which all talk of the state's disappearance is meaningless, but there might be some point in using this expression when speaking of the state's economic role. The state's huge economic role in socialist countries and authoritarian-type countries is obvious to all. The state of affairs is not so obvious in "democratic" countries, i.e., in "the golden core."

One of the main criteria of the state's involvement in the economy is public spending, as it is a measure of the state's con-

1 Pfaff, "Despite Global Changes, National Sovereignty Remains King," *The Herald International Tribune* (March 30, 2000), 6.

trol over the economy. Here are some figures from the analysis of seventeen countries done by *The Economist* with reference to IMF materials and a paper by Nicholas Crafts:

Government Expenditures as Percentage of GDP, 1870–1998[1]

	1870	1913	1937	1960	1980	1990	1998
Austria			15.2	35.7	48.1	48.6	
Belgium			21.8	30.3	58.6	54.8	49.4
Great Britain	9.4	12.7	30.0	32.2	43.0	39.9	40.2
Germany	10.0	14.8	42.4	32.4	47.9	45.1	46.9
Spain		8.3	18.4	18.8	32.2	42.0	
Italy	11.9	11.1	24.5	30.1	41.9	53.2	49.1
Canada			18.6	28.6	38.8	46.0	
Netherlands	9.1	9.0	19.0	33.7	55.2	54.0	47.2
Norway	3.7	8.3		29.9	37.5	53.8	46.9
USA	3.9	1.8	8.6	27.0	31.8	33.3	32.8
France	12.6	17.0	29.0	34.6	46.1	49.8	54.3
Switzerland		2.7	6.1	17.2	32.8	33.5	
Sweden	5.7	6.3	10.4	31.0	60.1	59.1	58.5
Japan	8.3	9.1	18.3*	28.5	43.3	46.1	....

* The average does not include Germany, Japan, and Spain, which were waging war at the time or preparing for war.

This table shows clearly the dramatic growth of public spending relative to GDP in the developed countries in the twentieth century, primarily due to growing social spending, especially since the 1960s. This dynamic refutes claims about the state's loss of sovereignty.

Naturally, the struggle to balance the budget requires bringing revenues in line with expenditures. In other words, the state exercises its huge power of collecting taxes, including taxes on corporations. Research shows that while theoretically TNCs are capable of avoiding taxes or "escaping" to countries with low-tax regimes

1 Data for 1870–1990. See *The Economist* (September 20, 1997), 11. For 1998, see Crafts, *Globalization and Growth in the Twentieth Century*, IMF Working Paper (March 2000), 41.

(such as the "tax havens" of the Caribbean), in practice, tax revenues continue to climb, even now in the Internet era. According to OECD data, between 1965 and 1998 the proportion of taxes to GDP grew from about 26 percent to 37 percent in OECD countries (combined) and from 28 percent to 42 percent in the European Community (fifteen countries). Between 1975 and 1997 corporate income taxes grew in all developed countries (except the Netherlands), ranging from 5 percent to 15 percent of GDP and averaging 9 percent of GDP in the OECD.[1] In other words, the state is capable of controlling TNCs through the fiscal system.

In the time of globalization, the state has more freedom in borrowing money because it need not limit itself to domestic banks. It can borrow from foreign TNCs, TNBs, or international financial organizations (IMF, World Bank, etc.). The state's power is in evidence even in the fact that the relatively weak Russian state showed itself capable of "penalizing" dozens of foreign TNCs and TNBs to the tune of billions of dollars by defaulting on its debt (short-term bonds).

Let's not forget that the state has an economy of its own, i.e., it owns a lot of property and effectively acts as a powerful corporation in its own right. It usually owns the strategic industries. We can cite the examples of France and the Scandinavian countries.

Nonetheless, though these proportions and forms of interdependency have a certain meaning, a more important type of interaction emerges on the political economy level. State-monopoly capitalism (SMC) has been established in all major countries of the West since the early twentieth century. Its structure and functions have definitely undergone some changes over the past hundred years. Yet, its purpose has remained unchanged: to strengthen the position of the "core" in the world arena and preserve capitalism. Therefore, for all the natural contradictions existing within each SMC and between national SMC (SMC differs in substance from country to country; compare the SMC of Japan and that of the USA or Germany), in the end they exhibit an enviable unity in their actions to strengthen the position of "the golden billion." That is why the state not only preserves its old functions but also renews them in the area of helping their TNCs in the world arena.

1 "The Mystery of the Vanishing Taxpayer," Survey. *The Economist* (February 24, 2000.

By the way, the very process of internationalization, especially in its second phase, was initiated precisely by the state, exemplified by the Thatcher government in the U.K., the Reagan administration in the United States, and two prime ministers in Japan (Zenko Suzuki and Yasuhiro Nakasone). It was these governments that launched neoliberal policies in the late 1970s and early 1980s, removing a multitude of limitations in the spheres of trade and especially investment. This type of organized policy bears evidence of the important role played by the state in the process of internationalization and globalization, pointed out constantly by American scholars such as Giovanni Arrighi. (216)

John Borrego offers this explanation: "...Global capital will locate in a country only if the state can guarantee certain conditions of production of goods, the reproduction of labor of a certain quality and price, and effective management. Competition by states in the world economic field has shifted from geographically specific advantages (such as raw material endowments or even labor costs) to less tangible elements (access to technology, flexible management techniques, marketing strategy, closeness to consumers, speed of response to changes in the marketplace, etc.)."[1]

A group of authors from Princeton University belligerently claims: "The global corporation, adrift from its national political moorings and roaming an increasingly borderless world market, is a myth."[2] This is a myth created primarily by Americans, I would add. After analyzing the TNC structures of the USA, Germany, and Japan, they reach the conclusion that "compared to many American corporations, German and Japanese firms retain a much clearer sense of their distinct national identities, a clearer commitment to national and regional prosperity in a changing international environment, and a much more realistic sense of the capacity of the rest of the world to adapt to the internal behavioral norms of their homelands." (10)

Using many examples, they demonstrate equally convincingly the well-coordinated actions of European countries to determine foreign producers' prices in their markets. Moreover, they don't

---

1 Borrego, "Models of Integration, Models of Development in the Pacific," *Journal of World-Systems Research* 1, no. 11 (1995), 13.

2 Doremus, Keller, Pauly, and Reich, "The Myth Of The Global Corporation," *Current History* (July 14, 1997), 2.

rule out disintegration processes in already integrated regions. (16) This is an extremely important idea that I shall revisit: *Globalization acts against integration.*

Let us now draw some preliminary conclusions about internationalization and globalization:

First, the process of the internationalization of the world economy is nothing new. It started in the second half of the nineteenth century. Moreover, some authors believe that "in some respects, the current international economy is less open and integrated than the regime that prevailed from 1870 to 1914."[1]

Second, MNCs truly deserving of the name are apparently not so many in number. Most of them are based on national soil, i.e., they are properly TNCs, and their trade and investment policies in the international arena depend on the strength of their national facilities.

Third, investment capital (FDI) concentrates mostly in developed industrial states, while "the Third World" (about 120 countries in all) remains peripheral in the areas of both trade and investment. The exception to this rule is constituted by certain countries of East Asia, including China.

Fourth, the world economy is far from being "global." It is actually concentrated in the triad of Western Europe, Japan, and North America, and this triad will stay dominant for a substantially long period of history.

Fifth, the coordination of these developed countries' actions (for example, through the mechanism of "the Big Seven") enables them to exert powerful directed pressures on the financial markets and on other economic trends. Therefore, global markets in no way transcend the borders of regulation and controls, even if currently the scope and objectives of economic governance are limited.

1 Hirst and Thomson, 2.

Localization and Glocalization

It is appropriate to touch here on one more interesting idea in connection with the erosion of state borders. Associates of the World Bank have published the *1999/2000 World Development Report under the title Entering the 21 st Century*, in which they focus much attention on the concept of "localization." To better explain what it is about, they first give the definition of globalization: "Globalization, which reflects the progressive integration of the world's economies, requires national governments to reach out to international partners as the best way to manage changes affecting trade, financial flows, and the global environment. Localization, which reflects the growing desire of people for a greater say in their government, manifests itself in the assertion of regional identities. … Localization has generated political pluralism and self-determination around the world. One of its manifestations is the increase in the number of the world's countries, which have climbed as regions to win their independence."[1] Let me remind you again that as late as 1974, there were still only 140 sovereign states in the world, and by 1998 their number had climbed to almost 195.

The idea of localization served as the basis for the concept of "glocalization," i.e., the process of interconnected globalization and localization. This is how its essence is defined by Thomas Straubhaar, President of the Hamburg Institute of Economic Research: "Glocalization means a world in which the natural contours of state borders are determined through the local economic area but not on the drawingboard of policy in Vienna, Versailles, or Yalta."[2]

The idea is that globalization cannot take place unless the economic infrastructure is first prepared in a particular locality. Therefore, globalization actors have need of the state that is in the business of clearing economic ground for the activities of TNCs. It

1 World Development Report 1999/2000, *Entering the 21 st Century*, 2, 8.

2 *Neue Zürcher Zeitung* (December 31, 1999), 79.

also follows from this that not only is the integration process closely tied to state power (more about that later) but also that subjects of globalization cannot manage without it, either. This follows quite logically from the inseparable ties between economics and politics at every level. Joseph Stiglitz, vice president of the World Bank, identified globalization and localization (glocalization) "as the two most important trends in the twenty-first century."[1]

(Please note that the authors don't use the term "internationalization." Perhaps they see globalization and internationalization as synonyms, or maybe they really do perceive globalization as an emerging trend. Importantly, even in this latter case, they still accord big importance to political mechanisms, i.e., government or even the state.)

Again, I stress that localization is not identical to integration. As a phenomenon, it is more closely tied precisely to globalization, though occasionally it can also manifest itself in the integration space. In the latter case, it enters into a conflict with the integration character of that space because it is oriented toward all kinds of economic subjects, no matter whether they are "our own" or "alien." One example is the penetration of Japanese companies into the European Community with the help of "local powers," which causes constant economic trade wars in Europe and within the USA–EC–Japan triad. Therefore, not only the integration process, but internationalization and globalization, as well, objectively lead to the strengthening of the state's role, not to its weakening.

Granted, everything said above relates primarily to the states of "the golden billion." But consider this statement by R. Barnet and J. Cavanagh: "The most disturbing aspect of this system (*of globalization—A.B.*) is that the formidable power and mobility of global corporations are undermining the effectiveness of national governments to carry out essential policies on behalf of their people. Leaders of nation-states are losing much of the control over their own territory they once had."[2] Clearly the authors are referring to Third World countries, which can now be said to include Russia. They go on to say: "In much of Asia, Africa, and Latin

1 *Entering the 21 st Century.*

2 Barnet and Cavanagh, *Global Dreams. Imperial Corporation and the New World Order*, 19.

America, the state is collapsing under the weight of debt, bloated bureaucracy, and corruption." (ibid.)

In other words, when talking of states collapsing under the pressure of globalization and internationalization (the difference doesn't matter in this case), we should clearly understand which states are being discussed. Globalization does not work inside "the golden billion" in the same way as it does in developing countries.

Integration

The second reason for the globalist-theorists' utopianism is rooted in their underestimation or misunderstanding of the integration process. The problem is that most analysts not only confuse the concepts of integration, internationalization, and globalization, but they are also unable to agree on the meaning of the very concept of integration. As an example, let me quote a passage from *The Economist* that arrives at a skeptical conclusion about globalization: "Nonetheless, the world economy is still far from real integration." For convincing proof, the authors use these "killer" arguments directed at the USA and Canada: "Product markets are still nowhere near as integrated across borders as they are within nations. Consider the example of trade between the United States and Canada, one of the least restricted trading borders in the world. On average, trade between a Canadian province and an American state is 20 times smaller than domestic trade between two Canadian provinces, after adjusting for distance and income levels. For all the talk about a single market, the Canadian and American markets remain substantially segmented from one another. For other countries, this is truer still."[1]

The authors of this passage write of globalization while actually using the criteria of integration. Some authors simply go ahead and "combine" globalization with integration in the term "global integration"—a phenomenon that at this moment in history is nothing more than a "global dream," to borrow an expression from the title of the authors' own book.[2] Of course, it isn't all one and the same thing. Keep in mind there are no fewer problems with the concept of integration than with the concept of globalization. Polemics between Western economists give an idea of how complicated this topic is.

How do American scholars define integration? Patrick M. Morgan, for example, laments: "What is integration? Surprise! There is no generally accepted definition of integration. ...Some

1 *The Economist* (October 18, 1997).

2 *Global Dreams*, 15, 22.

consider integration to be a *condition* (as when we say a community is 'integrated'), but it is equally plausible to think of it as a *process* (as when we say Western Europe is 'integrating' via its Common market)."[1] He then attempts to systematize different definitions of the term "integration." For diversity, let us look at some other definitions, like this one given by Robert Grosse and Duane Kujawa: "Regional integration is expansion of commercial and financial ties among countries in a regional group, leaving the rest of the world outside of the group."[2]

Grosse and Kujawa identify five types of regional integration: The first level of economic integration (the free trade area) involves the elimination of tariffs on trade among the countries in the regional group (EFTA, ALADI [Latin American Free Trade Area], U.S.-Canadian FTA). The second level (the customs union) involves the elimination of tariffs among member countries *plus* the establishment of a common external tariff structure toward nonmembers (the Andean Pact, CARICOM). The third level (the common market) is characterized by the same tariff policy as the customs union plus freedom of movement for factors of production (i.e., labor and capital) among member countries (EC). An economic union is characterized by harmonization of economic policy beyond that of a common market; specifically, an economic union seeks to unify monetary and fiscal policy among its member countries (Belgium-Luxemburg Economic Union). The highest level of economic integration is political union, under which all economic policies are unified. Countries that unite under a common government lose their national identities and become parts of a single state (United States, Soviet Union, and Canada)."[3]

Peter C.Y. Chow defines the concept of economic integration in almost the same key, with some minor nuances for the purpose of determining the integration zone in the "APR." He identifies several levels of integration: "The lowest level of integration is a preferential trading arrangement, under which member countries reduce their trade barriers for one another yet determine their own sepa-

1 Morgan, *Theories and Approaches to International Politics. What are we to think?* Second edition, 211.

2 Grosse and Kujawa, *International Business: Theory and Managerial Applications.* Second edition, 715.

3 Ibid., 273–6.

rate trade policies toward nonmember countries. The next level is a free trade area (FTA), under which participating countries eliminate trade barriers within the area but maintain their own trade policies toward nonmember countries. A more cohesive trading group is a customs union, which, in addition to the functions of the FTA, also decides a common commercial policy toward non-members. A common market further integrates the economies among member states by extending the dimension of free trade policy to factor markets, allowing, for example, free capital and labor flows across national boundaries. The most comprehensive integration is an economic union, which maintains common economic policies as well as a common currency for all members."[1]

Some proponents of the "Pacific era" idea understand that such definitions of integration, even of just its first level, don't let them single out the "APR" as some kind of integration zone. To somehow resolve this conundrum, they started "reinventing" the concept of integration to save the "APR" concept.[2] The essence of their innovation is this:

To begin with, the concept of regional integration is divided into market integration and institutional integration. In the words of the Korean scholar Ha Jong Yoon, "Market integration primarily involved trade movements of merchandise, while institutional integration entailed legal and institutional matters aimed at enhancing trade, with both functional and institutional integration."[3] He only speaks of trade here, but the idea is clear: The governance mechanism "above" regulates the spontaneous market flows "below." In this case, it was important to Yoon to convey the idea that integration must not result in an "egoistic bloc" that discriminates against outsiders while simultaneously isolating itself from "the global economic system."

Though these considerations appear reasonable, they not only fail to rescue the "APR" idea but also push the whole concept into an even more hopeless dead end. This becomes obvious when we analyze the same considerations as expressed in a more complex form by Peter Drysdale, the father of the whole Pacific idea.

1 Chow in Hsiung, ed., *Asia Pacific in the new world politics*), 196–7.

2 By the way, it was precisely the "APR" problem that provoked debates about the concept of "integration."

3 Yoon. *Asia-Pacific Community in the Year 2000: Challenges and Perspectives,* edited by Chung, 75.

Drysdale realized some time ago the "unwillingness" of the "APR" to shape itself into an integrating region. Apparently following the dictum that "regions are inevitably the construct of analysts and decision-makers,"[1] he decided, together with Ross Garnaut, a businessman and scholar who was his old "APR" companion-in-arms, and Richard Cooper, another scholar, to create a new theoretical construct for the "APR." The key concepts here are the terms "institutional integration," "market integration," "open regionalism," and "discriminatory regionalism."

Their definitions of the first two terms are practically identical to those given by Ha Jong Yoon, so I will not reproduce them here. The nuance, according to R. Cooper, is this: "A region can be integrated in the first sense (i.e. institutional—*A.B.*), but not in the second (in the market sense—*A.B.*)."[2] Moreover, markets "of course cannot be fully integrated either, at least in the sense of equal product and factor prices." (ibid.)

This twist really does enable one to do away with the problem of "APR" borders. In this subtext, an organization or group of organizations is created, e.g., the Asia-Pacific Economic Cooperation (APEC) that builds its policy on coordinated (integrated, so to say) principles and governs the marketplace process (the flows of goods, capital, and people between the member countries of this organization). It doesn't matter, then, in which part of the globe the state is located. The important thing is, it should be a member of the organization, which amounts already to institutional integration. In this case, institutional integration can become so detached from market integration that the meaning of the economic integration concept can become lost. But even in this obviously difficult spot, there is a way out.

According to Drysdale and Garnaut (coauthors of the chapter), "institutional integration" functions within the framework of "open regionalism," which means, first, flows of "public goods," i.e., goods from the public sector. Secondly, "institutional integration" precludes discrimination against external subjects (those lo-

1 Mack and Ravenhill, *Pacific Cooperation: Building Economic and Security Regimes in the Asia Pacific Region*, 6.

2 Cooper, "Worldwide Regional Integration: Is There an Optimal Size of the Integrated Area?" in *Asia Pacific Regionalism: Readings in International Economic Relations* by Garnaut and Drysdale, with Kunkel, 12.

cated outside the region); and third, these flows are directed by the governments of the member countries of the "open regionalism."[1] The authors specifically stress that "discriminational regionalism" is directed against outsiders, concentrating only on the members' own benefits. They oppose in principle uncontrolled "market integration" that is based on flows of private-sector goods and recognizes no borders. To them, therefore, "the optimum region is the world."[2] They continue: "There are the first two elements of Asia Pacific 'open regionalism': recognition of the power of market forces in promoting high intensity in ultra-regional trade; and acceptance in principle that there is a role for governments in provision in public goods to promote regional trade expansion."[3]

To sum up the authors' ideas, "open regionalism" primarily means a system of regulation through the mechanism of "institutional integration" of economic flows originating from the public sectors (state-owned property) of countries included in a certain region, combined with a policy of good will toward the functioning of "market forces" both inside the region and outside its borders. Drysdale personally is being "super-dialectician" here: On the one hand, he demonstrates his loyalty to the laws of free markets; on the other hand, it seems to him that he "rescues" his favorite concept of the "APR." This is not entirely his personal position, though; it is the theoretical basis for the entire APEC policy that attempts to implement this theory in practice. This approach contains a number of theoretical incongruities.

First, market forces embodied by TNCs or MNCs are so powerful that they are not likely to embrace the interests of regionalism, be it even of the "open" kind. Their own interests are more important to them. Second, even members of an "open regionalism" will not always desist from "discriminational regionalism" if it is needed to protect their own economic benefits, as evidenced by the activities of almost every state in the APEC zone, whether Japan or South Korea, to say nothing of Malaysia. The essence of institutional integration would amount precisely to protection of self-interests against those of outsiders. Otherwise what would be

1 Garnaut and Peter Drysdale, "Asia Pacific Regionalism: The Issues" in *Asia Pacific Regionalism*, 2.

2 Cooper, 18.

3 Garnaut and Drysdale, 6.

the purpose of integration? Finally, how can an "open region" be integrated? If "all countries are welcome," what regionalism are we talking about?

As a result, all formulations dissolve: "Open regionalism" in the "APR" extends to include the whole world, and "integration" transforms into elementary economic cooperation of everyone with everyone, i.e., internationalization. In short, we are confused, a natural result when attempts are made to construct reality out of theory instead of creating theory from reality.

Europeans are more consistent in their treatment of this issue because they proceed from their own experience of the Common Market.

Jacques Pelkmans, the author of a classical textbook on European integration, formulates it this way: "Economic integration is defined as the elimination of economic frontiers between two or more economies." But this does not necessarily mean the elimination of borders (territorial and political ones) between states.[1] The textbook goes on to describe different stages of integration (similar to those described above) and the means European integration uses to set itself apart and defend itself from "newcomers," though not always successfully.

By now, it should be clear from everything said above that integration is not only different from globalization but also different from internationalization. It is obvious that the first concept stands for a certain entity, while the latter phenomena reflect diversification.

From this systemic perspective, the concept of integration means the following: *Economic integration is the highest form of internationalization of economic life, reached in the process of joining different national economies together in a single economic complex having a specific institutional structure and functioning on the basis of coordinated economic policy on both the inter-state and the super-national basis.* So far, such phenomena are only realized on the regional level.[2]

1 Pelkmans, *European Integration: Methods and Economic Analysis*, 2.

2 My definition of economic integration owes much to the research performed by Borodayevsky. See *Crisis of World Capitalist Economy in 80s.*

The definition is comprehensive, but it requires substance.

First, the "joining" goes through different development phases: The growing economic interdependency of states evolves into mutual penetration of their economies, and national reproduction processes become intertwined and eventually fused.

Second, of the three phases of the social capital circuit in the countries that participate in integration, it is not only the first and third phases (taking place in the circulation sphere) that get integrated; the central second stage—production itself, the technological process of creating goods—also gets integrated. What results is "the interweaving of the circuits of combined national capitals as a whole."

We need to devote some attention to this phrase, for it marks precisely the divide between the integration and preintegration processes in the course of internationalization of economic life. A. D. Borodayevsky writes: "Therefore, it is not so much the large-scale, intensive and stable trade exchange between two or several neighbor countries in the region that expresses in itself the essence of their economic rapprochement and growing interdependency within the framework of the forming integration complex, as the interweaving of national production processes that stands behind it..." (163)

Third, it is important to keep in mind that so-called partial integration in different links of the integration process does not in itself constitute integration. It is only in their synthesis (in the systemic sense) that these *fragments* are capable of giving birth to an essentially new state of the regional economy—an integration system in the form of an economic complex. This is not the same as a simple sum of national economies.

Fourth, the integration net of economic interconnections gives birth, as its density increases, to a specific "crystalline grid" (to use Mr. Borodayevsky's fortunate expression) that serves as the inner construction of the integration "crystal." In other words, the complex acquires its own institutional structure in the form of different mechanisms that have economic and political functions. As Jacques Pelkmans writes, "In the real world, economic integration is always to some extent political." (3)

Mechanisms of the EC type give certain strength to this "grid" and help maintain and develop the integration process, setting it ever further apart from the surrounding nonintegrated milieu. The latter is especially important for understanding the essence of one complicated phenomenon. Thus, A. D. Borodayevsky makes a claim that first seems strange: "Regional integration constitutes the dialectic negation of the global, universally capitalist nature of this process; it expresses the desire to confine it to the limits of a group of states." (157)

This isolation from the rest of the world alarms champions of global integration, such as Bruce Russet.[1] But that is a separate topic. It is important to remember that regional integration isolates itself from the rest of the world. This thesis captures the dialectics of relations between integration and internationalization. Special attention must be paid to this aspect because, for example, most of the "APR" experts don't see the difference between integration and internationalization. Ci Yunji, professor of economics at Jilin University in China, writes: "The so-called world economic integration is actually the internationalization of the process of production and reproduction of all countries in the world, and the alliance, integration, and incorporation of economic movement of the world."[2]

This is not an isolated opinion. Many "APR" experts share it. I don't think it merits any logic-based refutations. Let's just say that the economic interaction of the professor's country (China) with, say, Japan or the USA somehow doesn't resemble the character of integration cooperation in Common Market countries. In any event, any analysis loses meaning if we fail to differentiate clearly between these two important notions. *Internationalization (economic) is the objective process of global economic interaction in the spheres of trade, capital, and finance.* Therefore, it is not governable and is not institutionalized.

Integration emerges on the basis of internationalization as its highest form. From the start, it doesn't follow the principle of coexistence with the foundation that gave birth to it, but enters instead into a struggle with it. A direct analogy suggests itself here

1 Russet, *International Regions and International System*, 227–33.

2 *The Shaping of Economic Cooperation in Southeast Asia,* Special Publication of the Southeast Asia Research Center of Jilin University (July 1993), 24.

with the interrelations between monopolies and markets. While internationalization as an objective process expands its geographic boundaries, integration, on the contrary, narrows them while its intensity and depth grow substantially. Integration, therefore, is antagonistic not only to preintegration economic forms but also to internationalization itself. Internationalization and integration cannot exist without each other; yet their existence has the form of an objectively contradictory interaction. Integration actually separates economic spaces not only between economic systems of different types, as it did in the period of confrontation between socialism and capitalism (represented in Europe by the competition of the two blocs, the EC and the CMEA), but also between systems of the same type.

This manifestation of the integration process is due to the fact that while internationalization reflects the objective course of the world economy's development, integration is an objective-subjective process in which the subjective side often plays a bigger role than the objective side. It is no accident that you often hear talk of integration politics and never any talk of internationalization politics. Politics means governance and choice of partners that take into consideration the objects' parametric properties (their alliance affiliation, their interests, their might, power, etc.).

Given the definition above, the only economically integrated region in the world is the European Union. NAFTA is in the initial stages of integration, mainly because of its weak Canada–Mexico link. East Asia is showing a trend—only just a trend so far—toward integration, with unknown consequences due to a possible change of the structural configuration. In other words, the economy of China may become its center. At the same time, it is far too early yet to speak of integration processes between the three economic centers, USA–Western EuropeJapan, much less of any "integration processes" in the nonexistent "APR."

Globalization, or the Theory of Global Capitalism

Now is the time to examine the economic essence of globalization—a subject analyzed usually within the framework of the theory of global capitalism. This theory has been created by some of the most outstanding scholars in the West, such as Giovanni Arrighi, Jacques Attali, B. Ballasa, Walden Bello, John Borrego, Bruce Cummings, Harriet Friedmann, Alain Lipietz, P. Tayler, Nigel Thrift, Robert Wade, and Immanuel Wallerstein. I will now use their reflections to describe the economic mechanism of the globalization process. The following text is to some degree a brief summary abstract of the works of several American scholars, primarily Cummings, Wallerstein, and especially Borrego.

* * *

The capitalist world economy of the 1990s and 2000s is a highly complex interweaving of production, capital, information, technologies, labor markets, and all other links in the process of extracting maximum profits, controlled by the three centers of economic might and the transand international corporations and banks. On the whole the world economy has become more mobile, changeable, complicated, and interconnected. In this new system any kind of economic activity has meaning only in the global context. This system gave birth to a new global division of labor. The prosperity or decline of this or that economy, this or that state, even this or that region depends on the sources and structure of capital accumulation, and it also matters who controls the capital within the world economy.

Global Accumulation of Capital: Its Structure and Dynamics

In the system of global capitalism, the organization of production and economic activity vary from standardized mass production to production oriented toward the individual consumer. Also, vertically integrated large-scale production organizations or enterprises are replaced by a vertically disintegrated or horizontal network of connections between production operations. The transitional state in the world economy from Fordism to post-Fordism began in the mid-1970s.

It is common knowledge that Fordism relied on a system of mass production and mass consumption. This system was based on a stable, well-paid workforce in First World countries and on the intensive exploitation of labor and resources in Third World countries. Production processes were concentrated in relatively large enterprises.

The distinctive trait of post-Fordism is lessening rigidity and increasing flexibility of production. Though this trend is accompanied by many other processes, the most important thing therein is minimization of limitations on free movement of capital and acceleration of its turnover. In the 1980s, interrelationships between business and capital led to the weakening and shrinking of the state's ability to regulate the process of capital accumulation. New forms of interaction, reflected in Reaganomics, Thatcherism, and the administrative-financial reform in Japan, accelerated the processes of economic deregulation that led to many important victories for capitalism. To a large degree, these were accomplished at the expense of the lower classes of society. Most importantly, post-Fordism became established on a worldwide scale, becoming a nourishing environment for the process of capitalism's globalization.

The development of global capitalism is closely tied to the strategy of maximizing process flexibility. Four major processes are usually mentioned in this context:

First: Production becomes decentralized and fragmented. Within the framework of global capitalism, the Ford-type company splits into many subdivisions and subprocesses, organized into small firms spread widely throughout the world across communities, regions, and states. The benefits of this splintering and dispersion are obvious. For example, in the process of dividing certain aspects of the production process, a firm can sever ties with the parent company and start cooperating with other producers, and exploit the cheap labor or resources of other firms located elsewhere, even in other parts of the globe. Capitalism is also comfortable dealing with the state. Small, decentralized operations are more flexible and free in their choice of location; they prefer places with lower overhead costs and lower costs of living for workers, as well as places where labor is poorly organized. The workers must "understand" that demands for higher wages and/or unwillingness to agree to lower wages "force" the enterprise to relocate. Local authorities are also compelled to show "understanding" for activities of such firms (on account of job creation), especially when making decisions about taxation. The reverse side of global decentralization of production is the increasing centralization of financial holding companies that are more profitable and secure.

Second: With production dispersed through many communities, regions, and states, the R&D and financial structures, as well as the institutions of control, clearly become concentrated inside the great cities of the world and First World countries. Global flexibility with wide branching on a world scale depends on establishing a rigid interconnected net of points of control that supplies the greatest financial and intellectual resources facilitating the accumulation of capital. These points of control (the great cities and the major states) "orchestrate" and control production and perform R&D work throughout the world. For example, certain global corporations, i.e., TNCs and TNBs, conducted mass surveys among professional workers from the research institutes of the former Soviet Union involved in the development of new technologies, as well as among college/university students. These surveys are links in the chain of activities having to do with global research and global information gathering for the purpose of maximizing capital accumulation. Though these types of activities are performed for the most part in more or less developed states, they are now being introduced in enclaves in so-called semi-peripheral states such as Hong Kong, Singapore, India, and Mexico. Global capitalism's most urgent problem is that increasing flexibility requires rigid coordination within the framework of "the three economic centers," i.e., the USA, Western Europe, and Japan, or within the system of "the Group of Seven" of the leading First World countries.

Third: The space-time compression in the conditions of global capitalism facilitates maximal expansion and acceleration of the production process. Geographic dispersion and decentralization of production in combination with centralized ownership and control require new forms of communication, transportation, credit, and innovative technologies that would connect production facilities and other "remote" operations to controlling institutions. The global system of interaction is becoming more complex and dependent on extremely complicated and flexible informational and financial ties. These new technologies are also accelerating the movement of material goods across the globe. In the words of one theorist, "we obtained a world economic order that sentenced itself to knife-edge existence. It is a world economic order tied to speed." In addition, global corporations, armed with new technologies and organization forms, have benefited from low production costs and a more favorable legislative climate in Third World countries. The spacetime compression is simultaneously reducing the importance of political borders, which helps accelerate the flows of goods and information. This aspect of global capitalism is supported theoretically by the neoliberal concepts and is championed quite fanatically, for instance, by "the Chicago School" of economics. The proponents of neoliberalism insist on the opening of markets and on corporative strategies; both of these measures are intended to overcome protectionist barriers. By the way, the policy of neoliberalism is one of the main reasons for the impossibility of organizing an economically integrated bloc in the socalled "APR," or even anywhere in East Asia.

Fourth: The space-time connection between the state and the economy characteristic of the early phase of capitalist development is currently in the process of disintegration. The state's ability to mediate between the marketplace and the society is declining. Global capitalism has narrowed substantially the state's local, regional, and national control over the economic and even non-economic spheres of society.

Post-Ford-type companies seek places with "a good climate for business." These firms are capable of ensuring quality by using a well-trained workforce and a highly developed, well-organized infrastructure. At the same time, their activities lead to falling wages and decreasing organization of labor, ultimately resulting in a lower standard of living for the population. Despite this, the state uses tax breaks and other incentives to lure or simply to keep businesses. "Economic development" often means that the state stimulates competition between enterprises for the right to set up activities in a particular area, with communities turning into "war zones."

Fifth: Within the framework of global capitalism, the number of First World industrial workers is dropping dramatically, and the essence and quality of their work is changing. Full-time employment is replaced with part-time and temporary work; manufacturing and agriculture are crowded out by the services sphere. Part-time and temporary workers are hired and fired in accordance with market conditions, while necessary production levels are maintained without additional labor costs. Simultaneously, benefits are cut and promotions slowed. Also, the workday schedule is becoming more flexible. On the whole, this new work regime reduces full-time workers' bargaining power when negotiating with employers for better working conditions. Older workers realize they would be unable to find equivalent-level jobs if they lose their current ones. Accordingly, they are more inclined to make concessions in order to keep their jobs. The post-Ford system thus brings worse working conditions, lower wages and benefits, and removes security guarantees, i.e., guaranteed jobs for the vast majority of workers. In this connection, the economic theorist, A. Lipietz, makes the archcurious "discovery" that the post-war concord between labor and capital is gone, and employers now view workers one-sidedly as goods to be "utilized or cast away at the employer's discretion." This definition of "the pliable worker" is at the heart of post-Ford-era flexibility.

Governance and Global Capitalism

New forms of governance have emerged under global capitalism that are qualitatively different from those of multinational capitalism of the Fordist type. Intensifying economic activity now only has meaning in the global context, be it the car-making industry, electronics, textiles, or garment manufacturing. In global capitalism, maximum flexibility means approaching the limits of what is possible. It has the following characteristics:

First: Global capitalism demands a fundamental revision of the concept of state—a concept attached to this day to the functions of a national government. The emergence of global corporations has made it necessary to consider the idea of a global state. The establishment of global firms capable of avoiding the controls of national bureaucracies has historical importance. The rapacious pollution of the environment with industrial wastes by uncontrolled international corporations is now moving to the foreground environmental problems that transcend national borders. The emergence of new kinds of problems creates a growing need for civilized solutions to them that can only be achieved through global institutions and organizations.

Second: The hegemony of global capitalism is reflected in the forming of international bureaucratic alliances that govern and regulate the movement of capital throughout the globe. The WTO, the IMF, and the World Bank are the watchdogs of global investment. They have the power to increase or reduce investment flows in accordance with the class interests of global capitalists, keeping a sharp watch over the whole process of global capital accumulation. The process of global regulation has given a new impulse to liberal ideology in support of global capitalism. (This ideology itself is now relying on so-called modernization theory.)

Third: Global capitalism can only function and flourish under weak states or open borders for free movement of capital and goods. Weak states are forcibly distracted from developing their national economies and are made to concentrate instead on open-door economic policies, luring supermobile global capital at any cost. This leads to the creation of chaotically heaped production enclaves throughout the world, with the pattern of economic development being different inside a state's national borders than outside them.

Fourth: Another integral part of global capitalism is the intense utilization of women in the world labor market. Young women in the Third World are a huge source of cheap labor for global corporations. In the 1990s they became global capitalism's strategic workforce. For example, in the 100 or so free-trade zones around the world, 80 to 90 percent of light-assembly workers are women. Women are preferred by the global corporations because they are viewed as obedient, easily manipulable, and prepared to do dull work.

* * *

Thus, within the framework of global capitalism, investment and financial capital, production, management, markets, work processes, information, and technology are organized on a worldwide scale. Economic and organizational changes have occurred as a result of the greatest technological revolution in the history of mankind. Its core is information technology—computer science, microelectronics and telecommunications—surrounded and supported by scientific discoveries in other areas, such as biotechnology, new materials, lasers, and renewable energy sources. The information technology revolution has created supernational organizations that function in the interests of the global capitalist system based on a global division of labor.

Based on everything said above, I would define *economic globalization as the process of controlling and governing all kinds of economic activity on a worldwide scale in the interest of the countries of the West.* In the geoeconomic space, this process manifests itself in the West's economic might growing relative to the rest of the world (the West vs. the Rest). In the geostrategic space, economic globalization furnishes the material basis of the West's dominance over the rest of the world.

I'll reiterate the main distinctive characteristics of the economic processes analyzed to distinguish them better. Internationalization is a process that supposedly unfolds in the mutual interests of all countries. Integration works mostly in the interests of the group that is integrating. Globalization is implemented and managed in the interests of the West alone.

General Conclusions

Four trends are currently observed in the world economic space at different degrees of intensity and advancement: internationalization, regional integration, globalization, and localization. Various authors interpret these trends differently. Some concentrate on localization and globalization, believing these trends will dominate in the new century, merging into "glocalization." Others place the emphasis on globalization, while actually talking about internationalization. Still others, like Hirst and Thomson, indicate two types of economies that are "not inherently mutually exclusive." They maintain that "rather in certain conditions the globalized economy would *encompass and subsume* the inter-national economy," i.e., internationalization will become part of globalization. They qualify their claim: "It is our view that such a process of hybridization is not taking place, but it would be cavalier not to consider and raise the possibility."[1]

My approach is different, as I stated at the beginning, and it amounts to the following:

The first phase of internationalization (late nineteenth century to the start of World War I) encompassed the whole world, forming "the international community of capitalists." Certain trends emerged at this stage that V. I. Lenin formulated in the shape of a universal law: "The development and increasing frequency of all kinds of contacts between nations, the breaking down of national borders, the creation of an international unity of capital, of economic life in general, of politics, science, etc. —this is all a universal law of capitalism, characteristic of the mature stage of this formation."[2] Historically, the process went like this: Initially monopolies "merged" with the state, forming StateMonopolistic Capitalism (SMC); from this entity grow the TNCs that together with domestic SMCs form the world economic relations of the capitalist world. As a result, the development of capitalism "moves in the *direction*

1 Hirst and Thomson, 16.

2 Lenin, *The Complete Works of Lenin*, 24: 124.

of just one universal trust that swallows all enterprises and all states without exception."[1]

This phase was interrupted by World War I and resumed after World War II, reaching maximum development in the 1970s and 1980s. The socialist world (USSR, Eastern Europe, China, and several East Asian countries) broke away from this trend and started building rather successfully its own economic zone with an intensive integration pull (at least in Eastern Europe). At the same time, the capitalist world's internationalization started producing integration enclaves within its zone; this integration is most advanced in Western Europe, medium-level and incomplete in North America (through the mechanism of NAFTA), and still only in embryonic form in East Asia (in the system USA–Japan–Asian NIC). Within the triad USA–Western Europe–Japan, internationalization started coming into conflict with the integration processes; this conflict was scaled down somewhat through switching the mechanisms of internationalization over to Third World countries. Please note: This second phase "gave birth" to regional integration; the latter's relations with internationalization were described above.

The third phase of internationalization started in the 1990s. It produced two new phenomena: globalization and localization. The former was helped along by the collapse of the socialist system. The territories of the former USSR and the countries of Eastern Europe are now labeled "emerging markets." Also usually classified together with this group of countries are China (on account of its policy of openness), India (for the same reason), and Mexico. I call this group of countries the Second World.

All four economic trends that I analyzed work differently in each of the Three Worlds. Internationalization encompasses all Three Worlds. Integration continues within the First World ("the golden core"). In East Asia, the integration enclave is being wound ever tighter around China. Localization is confined mostly to the First World, where it works against integration and aids globalization because local authorities are interested in luring in capital regardless of nationality.

Globalization, now in full swing, works mostly out of the First World and is spreading to the Second and Third Worlds. The latter two are objects of globalization, not its actors.

1 Ibid., 27: 98.

In the future, internationalization will yield to integration and globalization. The integration sphere encompasses certain regions, while the globalization sphere includes the whole world. Contradictions between these processes will grow more acute as globalization develops, when economic possibilities for regulating integration processes will become exhausted, and at the same time integration will start clashing with globalization in the same economic fields. While these two groups will still be able to arrange some kind of deal in the Third and Second World zones, it is nearly out of the question in integration zones because states/governments will still play a huge role in the latter. Uncontrolled market forces embodied by MNCs and MNBs will come into conflict with the states/governments of the integration zones, which may result in the disintegration of these zones. (Some economic analysts agree that this cannot be ruled out.) On the economic level, the contradiction will be resolved through absorption of the weak by the strong, and the forming of global integration, i.e., the forming of a united world economy.

But this economic trend is counteracted by geostrategic factors, i.e., the system of relations on the level of states proper, where the law of power works inevitably in world politics. In other words, the merging of economic globalization with regional integration into global integration requires political globalization, i.e., liquidation of political borders—that is, eradication of states' sovereignty. This is not likely to happen in the foreseeable future, though historically it is inevitable, as V.I. Lenin wrote back in the early twentieth century. He believed that the universal historical trend of capitalism was leading "to the breakdown of national borders, erasure of national differences, assimilation of nations, manifesting itself more powerfully with each new decade, constituting one of the greatest engines that will transform capitalism into socialism."[1]

"Socialism again" will likely be the irritated reaction of some liberal democrats. "Yes, socialism again!" will be the response of quite a few American scholars whose opinions I quoted above, even though I call their ideas utopian. They don't comprehend the complexity of the geostrategic struggle on the global level, of the inter-civilizational and religious conflicts in the world that cannot be resolved by a capitalist world government and, under current

1 Ibid., 24: 125.

historical conditions, a world government can only be capitalist. At the same time, I agree with their thesis that global integration is only possible under world socialism. This means that socialism must first triumph on the national level, starting in the First World and resurrecting in the Second. How soon will this come to pass? I don't know. But I do know that it will happen inevitably unless mankind loses its sense of self-preservation; this latter eventuality cannot be ruled out.

In conclusion, two perspective trends exist in the world to-day-globalization and regional integration. The merging of these trends into a single process would mean the formation of a world state with a world government. This is possible in principle but not inevitable in the foreseeable future. There are too many uncertain variables woven into this process for us to forecast their effects.

Chapter II

The Contours of the World in the First Half of the Twenty-First Century and Beyond (Theory)

The contours of the world and the general structure of international or world relations depend on the method chosen by the researcher for his analysis. It seems evident that a world outlook based on a class-and-ideology approach differs from worldviews based on, say, civilizational or technological approaches. In other words, the geostrategic and geoeconomic approaches that I explore in my study are but varieties of the structural method, i.e., just two of many methods used to analyze international relations. Like any single method, they don't cover the entire spectrum of international realities. Nonetheless, the three laws of international relations I have uncovered by using these approaches make it possible for us to accurately forecast the structure of international relations for at least fifty years into the future, and probably a little further.

The Geoeconomic Structure of the World

The geoeconomic structure of the world is defined by the different states' economic weights that reflect their economic potential; the latter is customarily estimated on the aggregate level through the GNP/GDP/GNI[1] indicator. A comparative analysis of these potentials enables us to determine a state's economic might that can be assessed as a "pole." This is how I formulate my law of "poles": *In geoeconomic space, a global or regional pole is a subject whose economic might exceeds the economic potential of the next mightiest state by a factor of at least two.* Therefore, economic potential is not synonymous with might. It is precisely the phenomenon of might that gives birth to the phenomenon of a pole.

GNI figures for the year 2000 indicate that in Latin America there are no poles, as Brazil's GNI of $610 billion is close to that of Mexico (the next-biggest economy) at $497 billion. In Africa the South African Republic is a pole with a GNI of $129 billion, followed by Nigeria ($33 billion). In the Near and Middle East, Turkey can be considered a pole ($202 billion); it is followed by Iran ($107 billion). In East Asia, Japan is a pole (about $4.5 trillion); it is followed by the People's Republic of China (about $1 trillion). Eastern Europe, like Latin America, has no poles due to the fact that Russia's GNI amounts to a small figure ($241 billion); it is followed by Poland ($162 billion). The same situation exists in Western Europe because Germany, with its GNI of $2.1 trillion, is insufficiently ahead of the second-place United Kingdom ($1.5 trillion).

With its GNI of about $10 trillion (more than double of that of second-place Japan), the USA is the world pole. Note that the proportions stay practically the same when we recalculate the GNI figures at Purchasing Power Parity (PPP) prices, with the exception of China. Moreover, PPP is a tool mostly used for comparisons of countries' internal economic situations rather than for analysis of international relations. Thus, some regions have their own "pole," but on the global level, there is currently only one pole, the USA.

As for Russia, its economic potential enables it to form a "pole" in Eastern Europe (with Poland in second place). But Eastern Europe is in itself a specific economic subregion that is more closely tied to Western Europe than to Russia or the CIS as a whole; therefore, it is more logical to view Russia as a "pole" among CIS countries. In any case, Russia's pretensions, often voiced in Moscow, to be a

1 Gross national income (GNI), formerly referred to as gross national product (GNP), measures the total domestic and foreign value added claimed by residents. GNI comprises GDP plus net receipts of primary income (compensation of employees and property income) from non-resident sources. The World Bank began to use this indicator in 2002.

global or even just a regional "pole" are dubious, considering that its economic potential (GNI) in 2000 was only the nineteenth biggest in the world, and its per capita GNI was 114 th in the world (seventy-ninth when measured at PPP). Russia's place is in the local CIS space, after all.

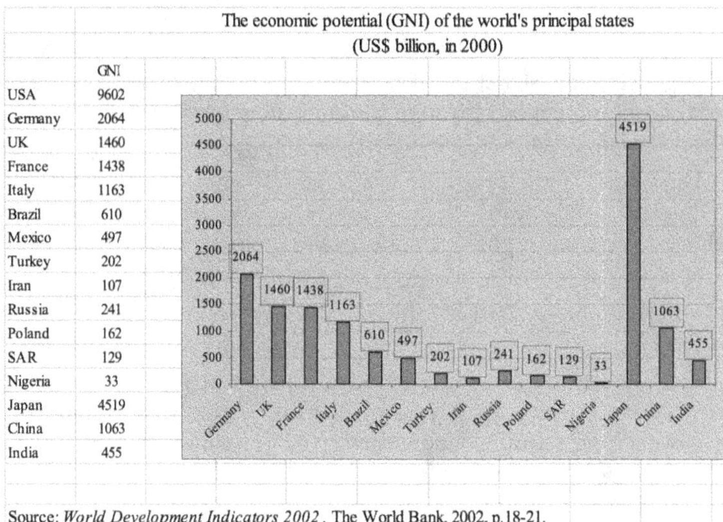

The economic potential (GNI) of the world's principal states (US$ billion, in 2000)

	GNI
USA	9602
Germany	2064
UK	1460
France	1438
Italy	1163
Brazil	610
Mexico	497
Turkey	202
Iran	107
Russia	241
Poland	162
SAR	129
Nigeria	33
Japan	4519
China	1063
India	455

Source: *World Development Indicators 2002*. The World Bank, 2002, p.18-21.

The Geostrategic Structure of International Relations

The geostrategic structure of international relations is determined not through poles but through the concept of a "center of power."

A center of power is capable of subjugating the activities of other subjects or actors of international relations to its own national interests. Depending on the sphere over which this control is exercized, a center of power can be local, regional, or global.

Hegemony is power directed toward subjugating all actors of international politics for the purpose of realizing the hegemon's interests.

What is the difference between a *pole* and a *center of power*? A pole is not necessarily engaged in the system of international relations. For example, Japan during the Tokugawa Shogunate period (the period of self-isolation) was comparable in its economic parameters to the great powers of Europe, but it was not a center of power because it had no foreign policy; that is, it was not a subject of international relations. The same is true of China prior to the nineteenth century; it surpassed every European country in economic mass but did not conduct an active foreign policy, i.e., did not try to impose its control in the system of international relations. In other words, a pole becomes a center of power when it conducts an active and aggressive (assertive) foreign policy directed toward subjugating other actors to its external and internal interests. On the basis of such reasoning, we can formulate the law of the "center of power": *The transformation of a subject that is a pole into a center of power presupposes the presence of a foreign policy potential (FPP), the volume of which exceeds the competitor's foreign policy potential by a factor of at least two on the regional level and four on the global level.* This proportion defines the law of the "center of power."

FPP itself is formed through the sum of outlays on foreign policy. This resource is composed of revenue streams contained in the country's budget and realized through the foreign policy apparatus (FPA). It is sometimes difficult to define clearly what belongs to foreign policy and what belongs to domestic policy, yet there do exist certain institutions that are unequivocally built into the foreign policy process. These include the ministries of foreign affairs, defense, information and propaganda services, foreign-economic organizations, external security, and intelligence services, etc. The problem is that foreign policy outlays in national budgets are not always assigned to specific institutions of the state. More often than not, they are contained in items labeled according to sphere of activity: e.g., "International Affairs," "National Defense," "Assistance to International Economic Development." Although every single ingredient of a power center's FPP works toward the defence of national interests, the volume of resources committed to each of the main foreign policy directions depends on the type of the "center of power," which can be economic, political, or militarystrategic. For example, in 1997 Japan spent about $29.5 billion (about 0.7 percent of its GNP) on the item "Assistance to International Economic Cooperation" (it includes official development assistance [ODA]). In the same year, the United Kingdom and Germany spent $19.6 billion and $19.7 billion, respectively, on similar items (1.5 percent and 0.95 percent of their respective GNP).[1] Obviously, the difference of $10 billion gives Japan an advantage in the world economic arena, conferring traits of an economic "center of power" on the Japanese pole.

Usually the lion's share of the foreign policy potential is included in the item "National Defense." This item determines the country's military potential that can theoretically be used in the event of aggression. Currently, because direct attacks between nuclear powers are practically out of the question, this potential actually determines the function of containment, while also influencing the type of the state's conduct in the world arena. At the same time, non-nuclear components of the military potential can be used against non-nuclear powers in the defense of "national interests."

In the system of international relations, the item most actively used for financing activities is called "international affairs." It is precisely this "dynamic" item that defines the scope and depth of the country's activities in the international arena.

1 See *Japanese Statistical Yearbook, 2001*, table 25–12.

I repeat: While the economic potential turns into a might-pole when it is at least double the next largest potential, FPP turns a pole into a global center when it is at least four times the size of the next largest potential. This is due to the fact that FPP must cover the four main regions of the world: Europe, East Asia, Latin America, and Africa together with the Near and Middle East.

Calculations show that Western Europe does not have a center of power because the total foreign policy potential of each of the main powers in this subregion (Germany, the United Kingdom, France, and Italy) is in the range of $40–50 billion (in 1999). Japan's FPP exceeds $50 billion, allowing us to classify this country as a regional center of power. (China's FPP is about $10–12 billion, according to its official statistics.)

The FPP of the United States in fiscal year 1999 (excluding the budget item "International Economic Cooperation") was approximately $300 billion, or almost five times the FPP of second-place Japan. Therefore, we currently have only one center of power on the global level—the USA.

Japan is the center of economic power in East Asia. The temptation to classify China as a center of military power in that same region should be resisted because China's potential is neutralized by the USA. Western Europe has no centers of power of any kind because of the approximate equality of the main states' foreign policy potentials. Russia, of course, does not deserve any mention in this context.

The Theory of the Three Worlds and Their Characteristics

Let's look at our definitions again. The "center of power" is a political category, or a geostrategic category—the superstructure to the structure of international relations. The "pole" is an economic notion that reflects certain phenomena fundamental to the structure of international relations. Both of these phenomena shape only the structure of international relations, not their content. That is determined by the goals pursued by states, international organizations, TNCs or MNCs, nongovernmental organizations (NGO), blocs, or alliances of states. To simplify, on the system level, these goals (and ultimately the whole content of international relations) are defined by the struggle for power (interstate level) and the struggle for world markets (states plus TNCs and MNCs). Both are born of the uneven economic development of states.[1]

For convenience of analysis, let us also simplify the categories: internationalization, integration, and globalization. The motivation for internationalization is access to markets for trade and investment. The essence of integration is the forming of closely interconnected economic enclaves, i.e., the unification of all cycles of economic activity in one entity. Globalization is the spread of financial-investment and information activity across the entire world for the purpose of establishing control over everything.

I will further simplify by dividing the world into three groups of countries on the basis of their economic development level. Scholars of international affairs habitually do this when they speak of the Three Worlds (which are not to be confused with poles).

---

1 I won't delve here into the deeper causes of this struggle, a topic that has been debated for centuries now. Of all modern interpretations, I will briefly refer to Wallerstein, who deduces this struggle from the "endless" accumulation of capital that is the main engine of the capitalist world economy. See Wallerstein, "The Modern World-System and Evolution," *Journal of World-Systems Research* 1, no. 19 (1995), 4.

The First World (developed countries) is the so-called golden billion comprising three zones: North America, Western Europe, and Japan, with their established forms of capitalist economy and democracy.

The Second World (countries of medium-level development) consists of the CIS, Eastern Europe, the Baltic countries, China, and India. They all pursue reformist policies in the economic sphere, i.e., they reject the previous models of socialism or state capitalism and attempt to embrace new models that are close to Western models of capitalism.

The Third World (developing countries) is traditionally seen as consisting of the countries of Africa, Latin America, the Near and Middle East, East Asia (except China, Taiwan, and South Korea), and South Asia (except India). They all have in common a low level of socialeconomic development and the fact that almost all of them are objects of world policy, not subjects.

The Three Worlds are neither poles nor centers of power. The phrase just suggests a conventional division of the world into parts according to levels of economic development. It is just a coincidence that the First World is simultaneously a center of power and the sole economic pole.

How do we characterize each of the Three Worlds?

The First World works in all three economic spaces, albeit with varying degrees of intensity. Each of the three subregions within the First World has its own integration zone: Western Europe has the European Community, North America has NAFTA, and Northeast Asia has the subsystem (not shaped institutionally) of Japan– USA. In the first case, we see an advanced integration; in the second, a budding process; and in the third, a trend. All three sub-regions are quite actively involved in internationalization. In the field of globalization, the USA is the leader all by itself. To achieve true global leadership, the USA must "open up" regional integration and combine it with globalization—in other words, arrive at "global integration." Then U.S. geoeconomic leadership will turn into global leadership. This is precisely why the USA is interested in world globalization, i.e., the subjugation of not only the Second and Third Worlds but also the First. This is also precisely why European states use localization as one of the forms of resistance; it involves the inclusion in the local economic space of companies and investments from any country (although, objectively, localization works toward globalization).

On the whole, from the perspective of economics, the First World is an economic enclave that is integrated or tends toward integration. As a center of power, it is opposed to and, therefore, is inevitably antagonistic to the forming of other centers of power.

Economically, militarily, and politically the First World is the most powerful, dominating the other two Worlds. On this account, the system of international relations can be viewed as a unipolar world with a single center of power—the USA.

The Second World is not integrated. It functions in the field of internationalization and is an object of globalization. Certain attempts to integrate among the countries of this World exist (for example, integration around Russia within the CIS and around China in Southeast Asia). In the field of internationalization, too, the Second World is an object, not a subject, except for China, South Korea, and Taiwan; the foreign economic activities of these three countries are now felt in the markets of other countries, including in the markets of "the golden billion."

Among Second World countries, there are two challengers for great power status: Russia and China.[1] This is indicated by their official strategy for forming a "multipolar world," i.e., their intention to destroy the existing structure of international relations.

The Second World is weaker in all respects than the First World and has a love-hate relationship with the latter. On one hand, it desires economic cooperation; on the other, it jealously guards its independence. There are no indisputable poles in this world, though China comes closest to being one. The Second World is less integrated than the First and less interconnected in the economic sense. It has no united policy or alliance relationships. It is in flux, part of it attaching itself to the First World, and part of it to the Third World. In any case, the Second World cannot be currently viewed as a pole; it is simply a geographic zone.

1 Some scholars of international affairs also mention India in this context. I exclude India from the number of pretenders to great power status on account of its lack of will for this purpose. In other words, this country's strategy is not directed toward acquisition of great power status.

The Third World has no fields of integration, unless we count the attempts of Latin American countries toward closer, more coordinated interaction within the economic confines of the Caribbean area. It functions as an object of internationalization. At the same time, it is an object of globalization, although it must be said that its lack of infrastructure makes it less susceptible to globalizing forces than, say, Southeast Asia.

Objectively, it is interested in multipolarity. To a still greater degree, it is interested in bipolarity because the latter gives it more opportunities to use the conflicts between the "poles" in its own interests. Currently, the Third World is a conglomerate of states with a sociopolitical system that is feudal in nature with elements of capitalism (Africa), or feudal-capitalistic (Southeast Asia), or criminal-capitalistic (Latin America).

Now let us explore the dynamics.

Development Phases of the Structure of International Relations

In my work, I often speak out against the concept of multipolarity and promote the concept of bipolarity, while stressing that today's world is unipolar. On this account, I am often accused of being an enemy of Russia and an inveterate protagonist of the USA. Other critics, on the contrary, approve of my unwavering support for bipolarity. I mention these personal considerations solely to stress that the formation of particular structures of international relations is determined by objective processes of a systemic character, not just through the individual efforts of a specific power or group of countries. For example, the current world leadership of the USA, the collapse of the USSR, or the rise of China cannot be explained through the great military-economic might of the USA, the incompetence of Soviet leadership, or the wisdom of China's leaders. These facts all have their place within the framework of the combination of a multitude of systemic trends in world relations. Each of these trends has its own regularities, and, in their interaction, they determine the general direction of movement for the entire system. Therefore, I cannot be a supporter of any particular concept of polarity. My task is to explain scientifically the existing structure of international relations and to attempt to forecast subsequent developments.

Let us move on to the analysis of the development dynamics of international relations. With some exceptions, a unipolar structure usually evolves into a multipolar one. The latter gives birth to a bipolar structure, which in turn transforms into a unipolar one, and so on.

If we limit our analysis to international relations within Europe, we see that in the early nineteenth century a unipolar system (under France's dominance) was replaced after the Congress of Vienna (1815) by a multipolar system (the Concert of Powers). By the end of the century, the latter had evolved into a bipolar system (the Entente and the German-Austrian bloc). In the twentieth century, following World War I, unipolarity (USA: 1918-1936) was replaced by multipolarity (USA/UK–Germany/Italy/Japan–USSR: 1937–1941). After World War II, bipolarity was established (the Soviet bloc vs. the Western bloc:

1950–1989). The Soviet bloc's defeat resulted in a unipolar world (since 1990, the USA). Following this logic, in the twenty-first century today's unipolarity will be replaced with a multipolarity, which will then transform into bipolarity, which in turn will evolve again into unipolarity. We represent this development in the following table:*Change Dynamics of the Structure of International Relations*

19th Century Europe	Unipolarity	Multipolarity	Bipolarity
	1800–1815	1816–1890	1890–1914
20th Century World	Unipolarity	Multipolarity	Bipolarity
	1918–1936	1937–1941	1950–1989
21st Century World	Unipolarity	Multipolarity	Bipolarity
	1990–2025	2026–2050	2051 + 40–50 Years
22nd Century World	Unipolarity		

The duration of each structure's life span varies over cycles, but what is important is the regularity in the sequence of structural changes. Keep in mind that the change of structures within each period is filled in each particular case with a different content (the character of the reasons for the change, the character of policies used, and so on).

Using the logic of my approach, I'll build another table for purposes of clarity:

Superstructure:	One Power Center →	Many Power Centers →	Two Power Centers
	↕	↕	↕
Basis:	Unipolarity ⟶	Multipolarity ⟶	Bipolarity

Now let's sort out the current situation using the scheme above. The world's base foundation is currently unipolar, and the corresponding superstructure has just one global center of power. This is the First World, or "the golden billion" group of countries, led by the USA. But the USA is not just the leader of this world; it is the world hegemon in both its basis and superstructure. It is precisely the USA that calls the shots in international relations as a center of power. In this connection, is the USA a hegemon, or just a world leader? And if the USA is indeed a hegemon, is that good or bad for world order and international stability?

Hegemon-leader. The Russian answer to questions like this is: "Call me a cooking pot if you like, but don't put me in the oven." Unlike the Russians, Western scholars conduct lively debates about these topics, just as they do about other things. This is natural because, according to Ludwig Wittgenstein, a phenomenon only exists when it is named. If I call someone a cooking pot, I have every right to put that "pot" in the oven in accordance with its systemic interconnection. If the USA is a hegemon, that title defines a certain policy type and attitudes toward it; if the USA is just a leader, then a completely different type of policy and corresponding attitudes are engaged. This is why American political sociologists accord such a great importance to words. Words acquire the character of concepts and categories in their use.

In Terry Boswell's opinion, being the world leader does not necessarily mean being the world hegemon. He makes it clear that leadership means economic dominance, while hegemony means military-political dominance.[1] In other words, leadership stems from economic superiority, but the leader's actions can be motivated by considerations of economic cooperation up to the point where the leader's interests coincide with those of others or the world community as a whole. This is precisely the policy of the USA as it creates "public goods" in coordination with other states, primarily those of the First World.

Referring to Charles Kindelberger, who introduced this term in 1981, the German scholars K. Hausken and T. Plumper define *public goods*, or *őffentliche Güter*, as "the type of goods that cannot be excluded from consumption, and consumption by one actor does not exhaust the good's usefulness to other actors." In international economic relations, public goods include open trade systems, well-defined property rights, common standard measure-

1 Boswell, "Hegemony and Bifurcation Points in World History," *Journal of World-Systems Research* 1, no. 15 (1995), 3.

ment units (including international money), consistent macroeconomic policies, adequate actions in the event of economic crises, stability of exchange rates, and the liberal international economic order.[1]

Clearly all these goods are defined by the First World's interests and cannot suit the interests of the Second and Third Worlds.

But even if we admit that the USA is a hegemon, not just a leader, in this case too the answers to the question of whether it is good or bad may well be different. A hegemon usually has a negative effect on the structure of international relations through the pressure it applies and the attempts it makes to impose its will on others. (See my definition above.) These are minuses, so to speak. But there are also pluses that stem from the objective character of how the hegemon functions. This is how Boswell describes this phenomenon: "Because a world leader has emerged from the global war with overwhelming military and economic power, a new world order will be enforced. In so doing, the leader reconfigures the patterns of exchange and security to its benefit, setting up the potential requirements for hegemony. The military capacity of a hegemon is thus a critical determinant of its staying power, such as the protection of global shipping lines described by Modelski and Thompson. However, this too is a double-edged sword. Military over-extension is a prime source of economic decline." (21)

In Boswell's opinion, there is nothing wrong in all of this because: "A world leader becomes hegemonic when the institutional order it enforces builds an inertia into the otherwise chaotic movement of the system. Hegemony is a period of relative peace and order in a system that is inherently competitive, dynamic, and uneven."(3) George Modelski characterizes hegemony in exactly the same way: "Order in world politics is typically created by a single dominant power," and,"the maintenance of order requires continued hegemony." Order in this context means "peace and a liberal economy."[2]

1 Hausken and Plümper, "Hegemons, Leaders and Followers: A Game-Theoretic Approach to the Postwar Dynamics of International Political Economy," *Journal of World-Systems Research* 3, no. 1 (1997), 40, 42.

2 Modelski, "The Evolution of Global Politics," *Journal of World-Systems Research* 1, no. 7 (1995), 26.

From the West's perspective, these statements make sense. The hegemon (in our case, the USA) is interested in stability and preservation of the geostrategic status quo because this stability doesn't just serve the interests of the First World. This stability also suits the rulers of the rest of the world, who can control the internal political situations in their countries when relying on the USA. It is no accident that the Russian political-economic elite is extremely interested in close cooperation with the USA despite the fact that many of Washington's actions contradict Russia's strategic interests.

At the same time, the status of hegemon is indeed a double-edged sword, and not just in the sense described by Boswell. Its reverse side is the inevitable resistance to hegemony as it structures and concentrates the struggle of all other forces against itself. If there were several centers of power with pretensions to hegemony, the forces of the states that engaged them in struggle would be dispersed. It is much easier to fight a single hegemon. Therefore, hegemony objectively nurtures many enemies against itself, and the USA will not be able to avoid this struggle.

From First-World Unipolarity to a World Community

What I've outlined above suggests the inevitability of the transition from unipolarity to multipolarity, from one center of power to many centers of power. Which will wreck the current system?

In the international arena, the main challenger to the sole leadership of the USA is China. As it increases its economic mass, China will be able to form an integration zone in East Asia while simultaneously establishing its presence in the economic territories of Third and Second World countries, and eventually in the First World, as well. This process has already started, as evidenced by the activities of Chinese state-owned companies in the USA and several European countries (France in particular). Combined with China's geostrategic strengthening (growth and improvement of its military potential plus expansion of political influence), its foreign economic activity will work to wreck the unipolar world and stimulate first the formation of a multipolar and then a bipolar world. According to some experts, this will happen by the middle of the twenty-first century. This topic is discussed in a special section that follows this chapter.

The other country aspiring to wreck the current system is Russia. More will be said about this country in subsequent chapters.

One factor working to wreck the unipolar structure (a factor mostly ignored by Russian scholars but studied diligently in the USA) has to do with the formation of workers' movements in the Third World interested in the democratization of international relations, not in the hegemony of any country or group of countries.

Most Third World countries won political independence during the period of decolonization and turned into nation-states. Economically, though, they remained dependent on their former colonial masters. Today they are dependent on all First World countries. However, in the last ten to fifteen years, the transformation of the economies of the developed countries into those based on services and information has led to the industrialization of the Third World. That is, heavy industries that consume plenty of metals, power, and labor migrate there. Accordingly, the working class is growing in these countries. In Boswell's terminology, these states that used to implement nation-state policies now are more actively implementing class-state policies. (37) In other words, the classic class conflicts within capitalist states, as described by Marx and Lenin, are transformed into interstate-class conflicts that permeate relations between the First and Third Worlds. It is especially curious that American social political scientists now claim that the working class is becoming the central actor in the democratization of the whole world (34),[1] contrary to their earlier assessments that ascribed democracy to the bourgeois class and bestowed the "democratic" label on states where the majority of the population was disenfranchised.

Therefore, the struggle of the working class in Third World countries, in combination with an increasingly worldwide anti-globalist movement, is the main factor stimulating the collapse of the unipolar world.

Another factor is domestic policy problems in the First World itself—economic, ethnic, and class problems (such as the formation of Third World enclaves inside First World states), including the amazing phenomenon of the communitarian movement growing in those countries.[2] The latter indicates that socialist consciousness is spreading through ever wider strata of capitalist societies, influencing even members in the circles of power.

From the international perspective, apart from the strengthening of countries that aspire to a new status in the world, the erosion of unity between the three zones of the First World, as well as Tokyo's oscillation between China and the USA in search of a correct strategic line that adequately serves the national interests of Japan, will become extremely important.

Each topic merits a separate discussion to be continued in my

1 See more detail in *Global Labor Movements* (Special Issue). Guest-edited by Nash, Jr. *Journal of World-Systems Research* 4, no. 1 (Winter 1998).

2 I expounded on this theme in my book, *Russia in the Strategic Trap*, 65–8. For a comprehensive coverage of this topic, read the book *Communitarianism: A New Agenda for Politics and Citizenship* by Tam.

subsequent research papers. It is important here that I just identify several factors that produce changes in the structure of international relations.

The history of international relations bears evidence that multipolarity is the least stable system, ranking ahead of other systems in the number of wars and conflicts that it generates. This thesis is confirmed by the history of Europe over ten centuries. It is also confirmed by the events of the mid-nineteenth century. In that period, the centers of power (Great Britain, France, Germany, and Russia) were busy grabbing colonies around the world and, for a time, managed to find points of contact for cooperation within Europe proper (including Russia prior to the Crimean War). But as soon as the periphery was divided into spheres of influence, all attention became concentrated on Europe, where some spheres of influence remained to be divided (the straits, the Balkans, the Saar, parts of Poland and Ukraine, etc.). The whole system of multipolarity crumbled, yielding to a bloc-shaped bipolarity poised on the threshold of a grandiose clash.

In theory, a multipolar system can be stable when the centers are equally powerful. But in accordance with the law of unequal development of states, this ideal situation is impossible in practice. Some state inevitably surges ahead of the others, and the law of power is engaged: *As soon as a state reaches a level of economic might and military potential comparable to the might and potential of leading states of the world, it starts demanding a new status for itself, which means a rearrangement of the spheres of world influence.*[1] Because the old great powers usually oppose these demands, newcomers can usually acquire a sphere of influence only through the destruction of the existing structure of international relations, including the corresponding system of security.

Therefore, the most unstable system of all is the multipolar structure of international relations with its many centers of power. It is a world in chaos and constant struggle that gives birth to frequent regional conflicts, including military ones. From the perspective of international stability, it is the worst structural variant of the international system. We can only hope now that the multipolar world will quickly (by historical measures) evolve into a bipolar one

1 The law of power should not be confused with the definition of the category of power. That definition is contained in Aliev's "Might of the State and Global Correlation of Forces" in *State and Society*.

with two centers of power (for instance, the USA and China). This time, it will not be the differences in economic development levels that will distinguish the confrontation between the two centers of power (though these differences will certainly remain, as they did during the period of the capitalism-socialism confrontation in the second half of the twentieth century). Instead, the main differences will be the geostrategic and geoeconomic contradictions fed ideologically by the ideas of socialism and capitalism or, to put it differently, equality and inequality.

On the level of polarity, two economic integration fields connected through internationalization will yield to globalization. The latter will be filled to a much greater degree than today with the problems of environment, demography, joint mastery of outer space, etc. All these things will tie the two blocs together. They will be divided by geostrategy, i.e., the struggle for resource-rich territories, cheap workforces, etc., not yet included in the bipolar system.

How will the differences between the two blocs be resolved? It follows that the inevitable collapse of bipolarity must result in unipolarity. Indeed, this is what will happen. It is a different matter that unipolarity, which first emerged on a completely different curve of the historical spiral, will now assume a global character; that is, one pole will cover the whole world. In other words, the basis will now have the form of *global integration*, as was noted back in the chapter on globalization; a united world economy will be formed on this planet. The superstructure then can be labeled as universal political relations that correspond to the term "World Community."

It is perfectly natural that all the phenomena identified here are only possible in the event of an actual decrease in the importance of states as world actors. I don't believe they will disappear from the world arena altogether, but they will certainly lose their classical meaning by the end of the twenty-first century. The forming of a united world economy with the World Community as the superstructure will inevitably lead to the forming of a world government of precisely the socialist type, as I mentioned in the chapter on globalization. Only socially oriented governments are capable of fairly redistributing, governing, and controlling the world economy. T. Boswell and W. Wagar forecast the emergence of such a government by the middle of the twenty-first century. I hold to the idea that it will only emerge after all the phases of the structural polarity cycle run their course. In other words, the world must become convinced once again that world problems cannot be solved without resolving the contradictions in the area of social justice, be it on the level of states or of individual societies. This truth would seem to be obvious. But historical experience shows that any and all truths must be experienced individually by each country, each nation, and the entire world community. We are given one more century for this purpose, the twenty-first century.

* * *

I will now sum up the important theses presented above:

First, there are certain laws that function in the geoeconomic and geostrategic spaces, in particular, the law of might or poles, the law of power, and center of power. Using these laws enables us to identify more correctly not only a state's place or role in the world but also the possible outcomes of its foreign policy.

Second, the poles are the bases and the centers of power are the superstructure in the polar theories of international relations.

Third, the polar structures of international relations are not static; their evolution follows the scheme: unipolarity → multipolarity → bipolarity. The corresponding superstructures evolve similarly: one center of power → many centers of power → two centers of power.

Fourth, in accordance with Hegel's laws of dialectics, the unipolarity of the late twenty-first century that completes the upward spiral of history will actually mean a united world whose further evolution will follow other laws propelled by other contradictions. The structural approach that I used in this chapter will lose its meaning.

Chapter III

National interests, national and international security

Two things are needed in national security policy:
first, enemies; second, allies.

A brief history of national interests' definitions in foreign policy

The problem of national interests has been debated for almost 100 years now, but no consensus has been reached to this day. However, many Russian scholars fail to understand what all the fuss is about. It is obvious to them that national interests include the preservation of territorial integrity, independence, survival, and (better yet) prosperity of the people. How can this be difficult to understand? But no, Americans have to start "digging": What does preservation of territorial integrity mean? Does this concept include protection of allied states' territorial integrity? Does it include protection of national air space? Does it include so-called disputed territories whose status is not clearly defined or is at least questioned by one or several parties (such as the Senkaku Islands)? What does preservation of independence mean? Is independence even possible in today's world? Can Russia be called an independent state if it forms its budget on the basis of IMF recommendations, and its economy depends on whether world oil prices go up or down? If Russia's population declines by about 750,000 annually, how does that impact "survival"? If "only just" 50 percent of Russia's population subsists on just US$1 per day, is that any kind of prosperity, or just survival? The questions keep coming.

Everything is not as simple as it seems at first glance. It is no accident that the best theorists and thinkers continue debating this topic. These debates tend to produce new problems rather than revelations of truth. Nonetheless, the understanding of the category of national interests has evolved and acquired depth.

Let's start with a brief history of the definitions of national interests in foreign policy.

National interests can be examined from different directions (for example, from the philosophical perspective). We are interested in its foreign policy aspect, a topic that first came under discussion in the early twentieth century. The famous Admiral Mahan favored a militarily precise definition, championing the idea of building, expanding, and strengthening a superior Navy, not only for defending U.S. territory but also for the "defense of our just national interests, whatever they be and wherever they are."[1] Among those interests, Mahan included the defense of national territory, the extension of maritime commerce, acquisition of territorial positions that would contribute to command of the seas, maintenance of the Monroe Doctrine, hegemony in the Caribbean, and active promotion of the China trade. (ibid.) This is the classic imperial approach of "defending" national interests. In those times, national interests were expressed frankly and bluntly, in keeping with the type of thinking common in that period.

Apparently, it was Charles Beard who first introduced "philosophy" into the definition. He dedicated a special book to this topic, The Idea of National Interest (New York: Macmillan, 1934). Beard was the first one to note the evolution of the term "national interests" ("dynastic" interests—interests of raison d'ètat, and interpretations depending on the type of society).

---

1 See Olson, McLellan, and Sondermann, *The Theory and Practice of International Relations*, 59.

In the late 1930s this topic was tackled in the widely known book by E. H. Carr, *The Twenty Years Crisis, 1919–1939*, which gave an impetus to the research work of such scholars as George Kennan, Walter Lippmann, and Hans J. Morgenthau. After World War II, a lively discussion started about this topic; apart from those theorists already mentioned, it involved Reinhold Niebur, Harold Guetzkow, Arnold Wolfers, Kenneth N. Waltz, Karl W. Deutsch, Johan Galtung, Morton A. Kaplan, James N. Rosenau, and others.[1]

Different scholars build the hierarchy of interests differently.

Robert Osgood gave top priority to "national survival and self-preservation," which he defined in terms of territorial integrity, political independence, and support for fundamental government institutions.

John Chase formulated a sequence of interests: (1) Deprive potential aggressors of bases from which they might launch attacks against the United States; (2) support self-government and democracy abroad; (3) protect and advance commerce; and (4) help establish and maintain a favorable world balance of power.[2]

As you can see, ideology became important again in the early period of the Cold War and caused a heated discussion: Should "values" be included in national interests? If so, how should they be defined?

Alexander L. George and Robert Keohane formulated a contradictory interpretation of the concept of national interests, grouping interests in three general categories: physical survival (the survival of people, not necessarily the preservation of territory or sovereignty); liberty (the ability of the inhabitants of a country to choose their form of government and to exercise a set of individual rights defined by law and protected by the state); and economic subsistence (the maximization of economic welfare). It is the first category that causes some confusion, for it is unclear how survival of people can be achieved without territory or sovereignty. Perhaps the authors had some peculiar organization of society in mind they could not share. As for Morgenthau, his innovation was to tie na-

1 For more about them and about theorists' debates in other countries, see Pozdnyakov, ed., *National Interests: Theory and Practice. Selected articles*; Vasquez , ed., *Classics of International Relations*.

2 *The Theory and Practice of International Relations*, 58.

tional interests to the category of power and proceed from there to the wider category of "balance of powers."

Fred A. Sondermann grouped his criticisms into five points:

1. Formulation of interests is too general, vague, and all-inclusive as to be ultimately nonfunctional, i.e., not suited for use by politicians. Previous attempts to specify terms more precisely led only to greater confusion and complications. For example, as soon as Morgenthau introduced the category "power" into the context of national interests, every theorist "rushed" to try and define what it is. (60)

2. How do we separate goals from the means of achieving them? As Vernon Van Dyke noted: "When we use the language of means and ends, we say that means can themselves be ends and the ends can be means." (ibid.) For example, Morgenthau suggested the category of power as a measure that should be applied to national interests, thus turning it into a goal of foreign policy. George and Keohane wrote in response: "Power is ... only one sub-goal of national interest, and an instrumental goal at that, rather than a fundamental value in and of itself." (60–1) In other words, was power a goal or an instrument of foreign policy?

3. Whose interests are we talking about? Who is to determine them and how? Answers to these questions require examination of phenomena that have to do with the structure of society, the state, classes, and strata. Sondermann believes that the second question at least should be answered by "accept[ing] the definition of the national interest provided by a nation's high officials and policymakers." (62) I offer that it doesn't matter how anyone, be he scholar or ordinary citizen, understands what national interests are. In any event, only that concept of national interests will be adopted which best suits the interests of the people in power. The degree to which these interests reflect the objective needs of the nation or state depends on the character of the society, the state, and on the balance of political powers inside the country. Marx and Engels covered these topics and supplied the answers back in the nineteenth century.

4. Realization of national interests by top bureaucrats is debated within the framework of interaction (based on the feedback

principle) between the bureaucracy and the general public (a topic totally ignored in Russia).

5. Which subjects realize national interests in the international arena? Is it the state, international corporations, or social organizations (i.e., nongovernmental ones)? This topic became particularly important in the 1990s.

Sondermann himself raised the issue that is often discussed in theoretic literature: The national interests of one country must correspond to the national interests of other states. He writes: "Given the international context, given the continuing need to conduct foreign policy, to frame goals and to seek to achieve them, three qualities—modesty, restraint, and openness to change—should be cultivated by decision-makers, observers, and citizens alike." (64) In his understanding, modesty means that one can know what is best for others—indeed, sometimes what is best for one's self. There should be restraint in the assertion of one's own interests (personal, organizational, group, or national) against those of others.

Morgenthau earlier wrote this on the subject: "... The national interest of a nation... must be defined in terms compatible with [the interest of other nations]." (64) George and Keohane, though, hold other views on the concept of national interests. They give a preference to "self-regarding," while excluding "other-regarding" and "collective" interests. The latter are not excluded in principle, especially "in periods of great danger," but such periods are rare. Therefore, "to argue a priori that self-regarding interests must always be given priority over otherregarding interests is not morally tenable." Openness can mean a willingness to accept national self-interest as a fact without accepting it as a norm, or a willingness to entertain alternative forms of the national interest and national policy. (64–5)

We can support Sondermann's position from the perspective of morals and well-meaning wishes, but the categories he listed are so vague and open to interpretation that they can hardly serve as the basis for formulating national interests.

I wish to draw your attention to the Canadian theorist Kalevi J. Holsti, whose book *International Politics* is already in its sixth or seventh edition.[1] While in the first edition (1967) he still paid attention to the concept of national interests, by the fifth edition he had

1 Holsti, *International Politics: A Framework for Analysis.*

moved on directly to foreign policy proper by building a hierarchy of goals, clearly defined as fundamental, middle-term, and long-term. In turn, these goals were divided into concrete and abstract ones.

Fundamental goals reflect the values he calls "core" interests or objectives that must be protected at all times by any means. They include security, autonomy, and independence of the political unit and its political, social, religious, and cultural institutions, as well as the wellbeing of its citizens (123). On the concrete level, this means territorial integrity, national security, territorial unity, and economic well-being. On the abstract level, it means protection, autonomy, and security.

Middle-range objectives include on the concrete level weakening of opponents, support for allies and friends, development of economic opportunities abroad, regional dominance and expansion, and the creation and support of international institutions. In the abstract form, they amount to acquisition of prestige and spreading of values abroad (human rights, socialism, etc.). In his graph, Holsti uses a different word for this level: goals.

Long-range goals can be characterized as "aspirations," the achievement of which does not require all of the state's resources. Unlike "core" goals, these are selective; that is, choice is the issue here, not necessity. But a state that decides to work toward long-range goals usually makes radical demands on all the other subjects of the system, thus provoking instability. One example of such a goal on the concrete level is the building of "a new world order." On the abstract level, this would translate into world order, international peace, and security. (124)

I have no intention of examining in detail the interpretations of each level of goals, especially because Holsti himself has reinterpreted them in the spirit of post-Cold-War paradigms. The important thing here is that Holsti drafted a structure of goals. The reader may remember that goals also appear in a structured form in the official doctrines of the USA.

I also want you to note that when American theorists analyze national interests, they tie them in clearly with foreign policy. Otherwise, doctrines or concepts of national interests would turn into a treatise on all of the society's problems.

To complete this brief overview of "national interests," I yield the floor to E. Pozdnyakov, one of the few Russian theorists to be well-acquainted with the literature produced in the West on this subject, but who stuck nevertheless to his own views on every aspect of the theory of foreign policy and international relations, and on other things as well.

Pozdnyakov's understanding of "national interests" coincides on many points with my own views.

Pozdnyakov sees interests "as the expression and realization of objective needs, and thus as the general motivation of a human being's activities."[1] Only afterward do interests acquire the form of concrete goals. Pozdnyakov also maintains that interests are subjective in essence because they are formulated by people. (59)

Many years ago, I described these mutual ties in this fashion: "What we call the forming of foreign policy is one of the phases of the foreign policy process that takes place within the framework of the national system under the influence of such internal and external factors that produce in the system (state) an objective need to enter into mutual relations with the outside world. ...However, in order that these objective needs caused by the country's economic development may be realized in their interaction, they must pass through the stage of subjectivization, i.e., be realized by the social powers in the state—in other words, to acquire the form of interests. That is why interest is a subjective form of expressing the society's objective needs. But interest as such is not embodied in politics. Politics begins when interest is transformed into a goal. What interest and goal have in common is that both reflect any given society's objective need; the difference is that the former is realized and the latter implies subjective *activity* through the state's institutional mechanisms. Therefore, *goal* means interest in action. It follows that foreign policy is the law determining the character of a state's activity and its style of action in the world arena. But, at this stage, an external goal is just an idea about the necessity for action. Such ideas are usually embodied in foreign policy programs as concepts and doctrines. In the process of their formulation, particular importance is accorded to the role and place of the state in the world, and to an assessment of the ways in which this state and its policies are perceived by the international milieu."[2]

1 Pozdnyakov, *Philosophy of Politics. In two parts*, 2: 56–7.

2 R.Sh-A. Aliev, *Japan's Foreign Policy,* 15–16; see also R. Sh-A Aliev, From Foreign Policy to World Relations (M.: ION ZK KPSS, 1989), 3–4.

We differ on the answer to the question of whether "subjective interests" can be true. Pozdnyakov states: "Some sociologists and political scientists believe that an interest is objective only when it is true, and if it is false and belies the subject's true needs, it ceases to be objective. One could agree with this statement if some absolute criterion existed for determining an interest's truth or falsehood. But there is no such criterion; it cannot exist in principle; and a subject proceeds in his activities from interests as he understands them at any given moment in time. It is these interests that are true in his mind." (59)

This answer rejects in principle the cognizance of phenomena—seemingly on the basis of subjectivity. In this case, Pozdnyakov betrays Hegel in favor of Kant. Together with Hegel, he betrays all objective laws ever learned by man—laws that prove their truth in practice. In actual fact, there is a criterion of truth—practice, however banal that may sound.

If the realization of goals that reflect interests results in failure or in damage to the state's interests, it does not mean that interests as such (as a category of philosophy or political science) are false. Instead, their formulations are false, made as they are by people incapable of understanding the country's true interests. True interests strengthen the state when realized through foreign policy; false interests weaken or destroy the state. Pozdnyakov supplies the example of Afghanistan to justify his thesis. The invasion of Afghanistan by Soviet troops in 1979 did not serve the objective interests of the USSR. In fact, it actually helped destroy the USSR by proving to be the initial shock leading to the superpower's collapse. Many interests of the Soviet Union proved to be false, formulated as they were by truly incompetent leaders in the Brezhnev regime. As a result, the Soviet Union made its exit from the world arena. Russia's current interests are formulated in an equally false manner (see *Part Two*), and the results will not be long in coming.

Meanwhile, those interests that stem from the state's real needs and are connected to real possibilities for implementation can be realized, as a rule, and therefore are true. So the criterion of truth exists. The problem lies in the people who formulate interests or, rather, in the competence level of those who formulate and implement interests and goals. This is precisely why American theorists discuss so energetically the third and fourth groups of problems formulated by Sondermann.

Pozdnyakov defines foreign policy interests in the same spirit as Americans. This is quite natural because the interests they define on different levels are objectives for all states.

Turning his attention toward Russia, Pozdnyakov pronounces himself justifiably against setting Russia in opposition to Asia and to the West, and also against forcing Europe (European civilization) on Russia. (95–96) He writes: "Russia has its own destiny, determined by the whole course of its formation as a historical individuality." (99) Later he says: "If Russia wants to preserve its great future, it must remain Russia. It has no need to set for itself the goal of becoming European or joining Europe. This goal is just as absurd and unreal as if it were to decide to join China, India, or Japan. Russia is not Europe, not Asia, and not even Eurasia; it is simply Russia." (102)

I like these words because I once wrote pretty much the same thing before I read Pozdnyakov: "So where is Russia located? Not in Europe or in Asia—I'm convinced of that. Russia is located ... in Russia."[1]

With this I want to stop making comparisons. But to students of foreign policy and international relations, I strongly recommend this book by E. Pozdnyakov, as well as his other works.[2]

Next, I will touch on the problem of interrelations between national interests and national security.

1 Arin, *Russia in the strategic trap*, 69.

2 Though I disagree with Pozdnyakov's conclusions on a wide range of issues, he deserves to be read because he is probably the only scholar in Russia who works on the conceptual level.

National Interests and National Security

When formulating the category of national interests, all theorists included the category of national security, giving it a decisive importance. Subsequently, these two categories are merged somewhat. As Arnold Wolfers points out, "The trouble with the contention of fact, however, is that the term 'security' covers a range of goals so wide that highly divergent politics can be interpreted as policies of security."[1] To "divorce" these categories, an additional category had to be introduced—"values," or "core values," words used by Walter Lippmann. As he was introducing this category, Wolfers suggested: "Security is a value, then, of which a nation can have more or less, and which it can aspire to have in greater or lesser measure. It has much in common, in this respect, with power or wealth, two other values of great importance in international affairs. But while wealth measures the amount of a nation's material possessions, and power its ability to control the actions of others, security, in an objective sense, measures the absence of threats to acquired values, in a subjective sense, the absence of fear that such values will be attacked. In both respects a nation's security can run a wide gamut from almost complete insecurity at one pole to almost complete security or absence of fear at the other…." (ibid.) The problem, in Wolfers's opinion, is that the same phenomena are perceived differently not only within one state but also by other states—a "discovery" actually made by the ancient Greeks and illustrated brilliantly in Plato's *Dialogues*. In this case, Wolfers becomes fixated on the category of security and fails to show how it differs from national interests. His reasoning creates the impression that these two are the same thing. The confusion continues to this day.

To escape this vicious circle, I offer my own interpretation of interconnections between the categories.

Designing a national security concept must be done methodically: First, formulate a national interests concept; second, designate actual and potential threats to national interests. Only after

1 See *Vasquez, ed. Classics of International Relations, 151.*

that, formulate policy for preventing or neutralizing threats, e.g., a national security policy.

To understand the functional roles of national interests and national security, look at the entire chain of the foreign policy process:

Two conditions comprise a state's objective need. First, like any system, a state is objectively attuned to self-preservation, i.e., preservation of its integrity. Second, it needs to preserve this integrity as long as possible. For a number of reasons, these needs are realized through interaction with the external environment, or, to put it simply, in interaction with other states or international subjects. But this interaction itself requires *realization* of its necessity; therefore, the process is *subjective*. Its result is expressed in the form of interest. In the language of philosophy this would be called the process of subjectivization of the society's objective needs. To put it simply, a state's *interest* is the subjective form of expressing a society's objective needs. These are expressed in a cumulative form through the interests of the state; that is, they are essentially *state interests.*

State interests are divided into internal and external ones. Among the former, the most important ones are *stability and development*—two contradictory phenomena; the balance thereof makes the state-system stable, i.e., integral. I will subsequently discuss only external interests, leaving the internal ones alone, particularly because in principle they manifest themselves identically, only in different political-economic spaces.

The external environment is extremely nonhomogenous; therefore, the state's interests with regard to each subject will differ in content. Still, in interaction with any actor, the fundamental interests stay the same, always including territorial integrity; independence, or political sovereignty; preservation of the dominating system, i.e., the political-economic regime; and economic development and prosperity, which depends to a large degree on interaction with the external environment.

A country's national-cultural *originality* must also be included in its fundamental interests, a phenomenon designated in the West by the term "identity." Some Russian scholars have embraced this term in the form of the word *identichnost*, though the word *identichnost* actually has a different meaning in the Russian language (more like "similarity"). One should keep in mind that

Americans understand capitalist values to mean markets and democracy, and identity to mean the American way of life.

Apart from the fundamental interests and values, strategic and tactical interests also exist. These interests are dynamic, changing, and constantly corrected, depending on the current international situation. Ultimately, their realization is intended to expand, enlarge, and enhance the scope of fundamental interests. This can mean, for example, expansion of territory at the expense of other subjects, acquiring control over the sovereignty of other subjects of world politics, and imposing on others one's own system of governance and values ultimately for the sake of one's own fundamental interests.

But this is all theoretical because interest as such is not embodied in politics. Politics start when interest is transformed into a *goal*. What interest and goal have in common is that both reflect the society's objective needs; the difference is that the former is *realized*, while the latter presupposes subjective *activity* through a society or state's institutional mechanisms. Thus,

a goal is interest in action.

Therefore, an external goal functions as a law that determines the character of a subject's activity and courses of action in the world arena. In other words, a goal is embodied in the category *activity*, which, in turn, is described by the string of terms *action, influence, interaction, volume of relations*, and the somewhat stand-alone category *intensity*. The totality of phenomena manifested through the category *activity* is called *foreign policy*. In essence,

> ***foreign policy is the state's conscious activity directed toward achieving external goals***

in accordance with the country's national interests.

It is necessary to stress that transnational and international companies and banks, as well as any important actors in the society, such as political parties, also have foreign policies of their own, often with effects on the international environment sometimes greater than those of the country's official policy, but with activities having nothing to do with national interests. They have their own interests that are often at odds with the interests of their own countries.

Realization of foreign policy requires a corresponding foreign policy apparatus (FPA) that usually consists of the ministry of foreign affairs, ministry of defense, and ministry of foreign trade, etc. Though functionally each institution is responsible for just one direction of foreign policy, in practice they often complement (and sometimes interfere) with each other. Their main function is to implement policy, including ***security policy***. The ultimate goal of the latter is, at the minimum, the protection of fundamental interests and values; at the maximum, the unlimited expansion of their scope. In turn, security policy is divided into many different policies corresponding to different functional directions and different perceived "threats": military security, economic, technological, ecological, informational, cultural, and other security.

These categories are interconnected with another string of categories that includes ***foreign policy***. This includes the ***might*** of a state and its ***weight***, which is tied to the category of ***prestige***. Foreign policy itself is connected to the categories of the state's ***role*** and ***power***. Through this string of categories, the relationship between the state's economic potential and its ability to realize external goals is determined in practice. Analysis of all these relations invokes in turn the category of ***perception*** that spawned its own direction in theory, perception theory. It is at this level that doctrines or concepts of foreign policy are formulated, including national interests and security concepts.

Keep in mind the difference between doctrine and concept. The former is theory-and-propaganda support for state policy, and the latter is the aggregate of views and recommendations as to which policy is most expedient for the state at a particular moment in history. History knows the Monroe, Truman, and Ford doctrines, but there were no such things as a Morgenthau or a Deutsch doctrine. The latter two had offered concepts and theories of national interests and security.

This excursion into theory was needed primarily to "divorce" the category of national interests from security policy. These categories reflect different functions of the foreign policy process that is divided into two phases: the phase of forming and formulating foreign policy, and the phase of implementing it in the system of international relations. The category of interest belongs to the first phase, and security to the second phase.

Thus,

> ***interest is a category of politics that reflects the realization (subjectivization) of the state's objective needs.***

The foreign policy interests, i.e., national interests directed outward, are the expression of the state's general and particular needs that stem from its social-political nature and also from its place and role in the system of international relations.

> ***Security (national) is a category of politics that means the ways and forms of ensuring the state's national interests both inside the country and in the system of international relations.***

> ***Security (international) is a category reflecting that state of international relations which ensures the fundamental national interests of all subjects of world politics.***

Note the difference between national and international security:

> ***National security is a policy, while international security is a state of affairs.***

The answer to the question of which state of international security is preferable to a particular country depends on its understanding of its own national interests. Because these interests usually differ substantially between different powers, they are the internal sources of danger, i.e., tensions, conflicts, and wars in the world arena. This is why the formulation of the concept of national interests and the identification of threats to these interests must precede the formulation of national security policy.

The Soviet Union's International Security Concept

I draw your attention to a strange fact: Absent from the main foreign policy documents (the national security concept, the military doctrine, and the foreign policy concept of the Russian Federation) of Russia today is a clear formulation of what constitutes international security. In the Soviet Union's foreign policy documents, international security wasn't just clearly defined but was also the core around which the USSR's foreign policy developed. The concept of international security was initially formulated as a set of regional concepts of collective security in Europe or in Asia. They were then transformed into the concept of all-encompassing international security, worked out in detail during the rule of Mikhail Gorbachev. The latter concept consisted of many components but specifically contained two points. First, it was stressed that security cannot be unilateral, i.e., serving the interests of just one country or a group of countries (coalition); it can only be all encompassing, i.e., serving the interests of every country in the world. Second, all security problems, including those in the military sphere, must be resolved through political means. Finally, a grandiose program of universal disarmament was proposed to be accomplished by the year 2000.[1] In concentrated form, the concept of international security was formulated thus: "National and international security is a factor of preservation of peace, founded on the mutual dependency of *national and international security*. The ensuring of individual states' national security and international security in general is part of the general task of the current era: the preservation and strengthening of universal peace and prevention of nuclear war."[2]

---

1 See details in *Materials of the 27th Congress of the Communist Party of the Soviet Union*, 62–76; *Policy of force or force of the reason? (Arms Race and International Relations)*, 291–301.

2 *What is What in World Politics*. Dictionary–Reference, 47.

This formulation identifies two important points: the connection between international and national security, and the prevention of nuclear war as the main goal of national and international security.

The latter goal was achieved through the defeat and removal from the world political map of precisely that power that was campaigning most actively for the prevention of nuclear war. In other words, the bipolar system had to be wrecked and replaced with a unipolar system for nuclear world war to be relegated to the backyard of world politics.

The international security concept of the Soviet period did include some other components besides the nuclear weapons aspect. Professor M.D. Proector, who participated in the formulation of official concepts of international security, writes:[1] "Apparently international security is that state of international relations that creates the most favorable conditions for sovereign development of states—for ensuring their full political independence, for defending their national, or alliance, or general interests against aggression and military-political pressure, for equitable relations with other states."[2]

I draw your attention to the great importance accorded to the concept of state sovereignty less than fifteen years ago. While this concept is still mentioned today in Moscow's official documents, it does not occupy its former place of honor.

1 It should be noted that IMEMO scholars were actively involved in the development of this concept of international security.

2 Proector, *World Wars and the Fortunes of Humankind*, 252.

The Fundamental External Interests of Russia and the USA: Differences and Coincidences

The official foreign policy documents of today's Russia no longer contain formulations of international security. Neither do the official documents of the USA. The same is true of nonofficial documents. I once searched the Web for materials on international security (specifying the words *international + security*) and got 234,000 references. I browsed through hundreds of files, but nowhere did I find a definition of international security. At the same time, a huge amount of material on national security can be found in both Russia and the USA. This is indicative of what will be explained below.

But first let's consider if it's possible to construct a system of international security that would serve the fundamental interests of all countries. We must analyze these fundamental interests or, rather, their formulation by the important actors of world politics.[1] I select two countries (Russia and the USA) as examples, but to obtain a fuller picture, we must analyze the national interests of at least ten of the most important countries in world politics.

On the theoretical level, the following are usually included in fundamental interests: territorial integrity; independence, or political sovereignty; preservation of the prevailing system, i.e., the political-economic regime; and economic development and prosperity, which depend to a large degree on interaction with the external environment.

Let us see now how these interests are formulated in Russia and in the USA. We need only reproduce these formulations here in brief, using the two main documents: Russia's *National Security Concept* (approved in January 2000), and the latest version of the American *National Security Strategy For a New Century*, prepared

1 Actors of world politics should be considered important if their activities form the structural framework of the system of international relations. It is usually superpowers and great powers included in this number.

by the U.S. National Security Council and approved by the president.[1]

First, let's note where the two countries' interests coincide: concerns about international terrorism and drug trafficking, environmental problems, and proliferation of weapons of mass destruction. All of these concerns are not fundamental interests, though. Between the fundamental interests of Russia and the USA, the differences are quite substantial.

In particular, in the Russian variant we read: "The national interests of Russia in the international sphere boil down to ensuring the sovereignty…" The idea of sovereignty is also mentioned in other parts of the Concept. In the American document, the topic of sovereignty is not mentioned at all. This means that the USA doesn't accord much importance to the sovereignty of other states. Moreover, its document contains a thesis that compels the USA to violate other states' sovereignty. We will discuss that later.

The term *vital interests* is identical in content to the term *fundamental interests*. This is how the vital interests of the United States are defined: "Among these are the physical security of our territory and that of our allies, the safety of our citizens, the economic well-being of our society, and the protection of our critical infrastructures—including energy, banking and finance, telecommunications, transportation, water systems, and emergency services—from paralyzing attack."

I draw your attention to the word *our*. U.S. national security strategy is geared toward the protection and realization of the interests of America and its allies. For example, the key U.S. goals in the international arena, as stated in the *Strategy*, are the strengthening of America's security, fostering America's economic prosperity, assisting democracy, and establishing human rights abroad. It is this latter goal that gives Americans "the right" to interfere in the internal affairs of those countries deficient (in Washington's opinion) in democracy and human rights and leads to the violation of those states' sovereignty.

In the Russian variant of the national security concept, national interests are formulated in a neutral fashion—in the general

1 *A National Security Concept of the Russian Federation.* Independent Military Review (January 14, 2000); and *A National Security Strategy for a New Century.*

mode, so to say. It is never made clear that a specific national interest relates precisely to Russia and the Russians.

The most important theses of the two Concepts are also in conflict. The Russian variant states that Russia's national interests in the international sphere lie in "reinforcing the position of Russia as a great power and one of the influential centers of the multipolar world." The American variant states clearly that: "The United States remains the world's most powerful force for peace, prosperity, and the universal values of democracy and freedom." Other U.S. official documents specify in advance U.S. preparedness to counteract any power's attempts to assume a dominant position in a particular region. For example, the *Annual Report to the President and the Congress* of the U.S. Secretary of Defense for the year 2000 contains an important phrase absent from the Strategy: "Preventing the emergence of hostile regional coalitions or hegemons."[1]

To these fundamental differences, minor ones can be added. For example, Russia insists on "equal and mutually beneficial relations with all countries," while the USA specifies clearly which states should be treated "equitably" and which ones "punished."

Here we see a clear divergence in how the two countries formulate their national interests. We would have found equally substantial differences if we were to compare U.S. fundamental interests with those of India, China, etc. This divergence implies differences in understanding the category of international security, which in turn lead to contradictions and inevitable struggles. The outcome of these struggles will depend on the national security policy.

1 Cohen, Secretary of Defense, *Annual Report to the President and the Congress* (2000), 4.

National Security, the Country's Foreign Policy Potential, and the International Security

National security is policy directed toward the protection and realization of a country's national interests. This policy can take different forms and use different means: economic, diplomatic, military, etc. One way or another, all states protect their external interests when they implement national security policies. The difference between states is in the amount of financial resources allotted to this branch of policy. The funding of the state's external policy depends not only on the state's external goals in the international arena but also on the state's financial resources, which in turn depend on the country's economic potential. If, say, a state aspires to the role of a great power and allots only $1 billion to foreign policy, you could guess in advance that its attempts are doomed and the $1 billion is wasted. It takes foreign policy expenditures of at least $50-60 billion per year for great powers to acquire that status. But should a state spend $50 billion annually on foreign policy while its economic potential (measured as GDP) is about $200-250 billion, then it is ruining itself, because a foreign policy potential of $50 billion requires a GDP of at least $1 trillion.

These regularities were demonstrated "brilliantly" by the Soviet Union, a country where more than half of the economy was working toward external goals. These goals not only did not correspond to the country's national interests but were also in fundamental conflict with the state's internal needs—that is, the leaders of the USSR failed to harmonize expenditures on foreign policy with expenditures on domestic policy. The inability to count was one of the main reasons for the collapse of the Soviet empire.

All the categories are interconnected in the string: *international security – national interests – national security – foreign policy potential – economic potential*; their interrelations are defined by the laws of economic mass, center-of-power, power, and optimal proportion between expenditures on foreign and domestic policy. (See the previous section.)

Let us compare the foreign policy potentials of today's Russia and the USA on the basis of the above. The figures are clearly stated in the two countries' budgets. For our comparison, let's use the two countries' actual budgets for the Financial Year 1999. The item "International Activities" consumed $2.7 billion in Russia and $22 billion in the USA. Let us add to these figures the outlays on other kinds of activities directed toward the protection of national interests, especially defense spending. For Russia, we get a total of about $10 billion, and for the USA, about $300 billion.

The conclusion follows that when two countries' fundamental national interests are in conflict, the winner will be the country that spends more on national security policy or on foreign policy in general. Napoleon used to say, quite justifiably, that three things are needed to make war—money, money, and more money.

The foreign policy potential of the entire West, of which the USA is the recognized leader, is about $550 billion annually (rough calculation). This potential enables the West to maintain a unipolar world with the USA at the top. It makes sense for all pretenders to multipolarity to at least calculate first the amount of economic and financial resources they need to earmark to wreck the existing structure of international relations.

There is more than a simple connection or interconnection between the structure of international relations and the content of the international security system. Rather, this interconnection is defined by a constant: Whoever dominates in the geostrategic space of international relations gets to determine the content of international security. The latter then ultimately coincides with the national security of the country that is the hegemon or leader.

This conclusion is confirmed by historical practice. After the defeat of Napoleon, the context of security in Europe was determined by the victorious countries: Russia and Great Britain, until the former was defeated in the Crimean War. In the Cold War years, international security was defined by the bipolar structure of international relations or, in other words, by the two superpowers, the USA and the USSR. Since we currently have a unipolar world led by the USA, international security is defined by "the golden billion." This is why the United States has no need to formulate separately the concept of international security; it has actually already formulated it in its concepts of national interests. As a result, the current global structure of international security largely serves the interests of the Western countries. Wherever these interests are infringed upon, Western countries quickly "correct" the situation, not shying away from using military power. Examples abound in Europe, in the Middle East, in Latin America—all around the world.

I feel no need to give any moral assessment of the West's conduct because I believe that power rules the world—not morals, and not even international law.

The Evolution of the Structure of the International Security System

For some reason, it has become customary to say that during the Cold War period, security concepts, whether international or national, had military aspects in the foreground, while after the end of the Cold War, other aspects of security (economic, ecological, demographic, etc.) became more important. This is not quite true. Even in earlier times, more than just military aspects were included under the category of security. For example, Japan's policy in the early 1980s was based on the doctrine of comprehensive national security that consisted of military, political, and economic parts. The previously mentioned concept of universal security included as many as ten different aspects of security, though the military aspect was certainly the single most important one.

But the problem is that even now, after the end of the Cold War, the military aspect remains the most important in the cause of ensuring both national and international security. Just compare the funds allotted to different aspects of security in practically any influential country in the world and you will see that "defense" outlays are the biggest by far, usually by a whole order of magnitude or even more. It's no use nurturing the illusion that the military factor in world politics has ceased to matter, or at least, has lost much of its importance. It is true that we hear hardly any talk about the possibility of nuclear war. But the real probability of nuclear war has hardly decreased; on the contrary, it has increased, considering that several more states will acquire nuclear weapons in the twenty-first century.

Nonetheless, today we certainly hear more about problems relating to the geoeconomic situation in the world, i.e., problems concerning internationalization, integration, and globalization. Most of the time, the world is disturbed by problems of the world economy, finances, energy supplies, and information technology. Admittedly, at least in this moment in history, those spheres are sufficiently controlled and professionally governed by the West, which doesn't need help for solving problems in these areas.

Yet, there are certain aspects of international security where the West is interested in cooperating with everyone: international drug trafficking, terrorism, corruption, the environment, and especially the proliferation of weapons of mass destruction. The latter subject concerns the USA primarily in regard to Russia. Many experts in the USA, particularly those in the Heritage Foundation, express doubts about Russia's ability to control its own nuclear weapons. This is why the Bush administration, having cut many kinds of aid to Russia, will not only keep intact the funding for programs of liquidating nuclear weapons but also may even increase this funding. In other words, there is a large zone of international security in which the West will gladly enlist volunteers for solving problems.

There is one more area where the West, or rather the USA, is interested in Russia's participation—China.

China and the System of Collective Security in Asia

I'll start by reminding you of the idea of a collective security system in Asia proposed by the USSR in 1969. It eventually suffered an undignified demise because everyone viewed it as Moscow's policy intended to encircle, or at least neutralize, China, which at that time was conducting an active anti-Soviet policy.

In general, peace initiatives in order to establish collective security are usually needed only by weak states. Hegemons have no use in principle for multilateral organizations because these organizations' rules require endless coordination between members in pursuit of unanimity. This limits the members' freedom of action and, at the same time, reduces the set of means that can be used to achieve goals. As Stephen Blank noticed, "Hegemonist powers usually prefer to deal with potential challenges on a bilateral basis rather than face organized challenges."[1] It is no accident that the United States has always been cool toward such ideas.

The situation started to change in the 1990s. Political-academic circles in the USA started increasingly proposing all kinds of initiatives to create collective security mechanisms for East Asia. For example, in 1992, J. Nye (who later became an assistant to the secretary of defense) suddenly proposed convening a conference on security and cooperation in Northeast Asia, a quasi-organization that would include the USA, Japan, China, Russia, both Koreas, and possibly Mongolia and Canada.[2] Some scholars even suggested a variant that copied the OSCE.[3]

The reason for the appearance of such initiatives is clear as day: The intention is to engage China in these organizations and check its "hegemonist ambitions." All these American initiatives

1 Blank, "Helsinki in Asia? Towards a Multilateral Asian Order," *The Journal of East and West Studies* (April 1994), 102.

2 Nye Jr., "Coping with Japan," *Foreign Policy* (Winter 1992/93), 101, 103.

3 See *The Washington Quarterly* (Winter, 1994), 94.

coincide almost 100 percent with the previously mentioned Soviet collective security initiative of 1969. The reason is that many American experts, as well as some non-American ones, see China as a potential superpower capable of wrecking the current unipolar system. They only keep guessing whether that will happen in fifty years or in twenty, or even sooner. This is why engaging Russia in precisely the American variant of "collective security" would amount to killing two birds with one stone. First, a real strategic alliance between Russia and China would be prevented. Second, America would have a strong back in the event of a real confrontation with China in the future.

Another similar concept is the currently fashionable preventive diplomacy concept (analogous to the concept of preventive security policy). Outwardly, this decorous-looking concept is about preventing conflicts from emerging between states or inside states. Numerous enthusiasts are even proposing to create organizational structures for implementing this concept (for example, the Council for Security Cooperation in the Asia Pacific, with its headquarters in Singapore).[1] However, to function on the basis of political means, preventive diplomacy needs (in the words of Robert M. Gates) "to have recourse to powerful military forces and be prepared to use them."[2] In other words, preventive diplomacy won't work without recourse to guns. Next, it turns out that because there is no recognized leader among Asian countries, leadership must "fall on the shoulders of the USA" "because of America's wealth, military power, and pervasive political and cultural influence, the United States today still exercises a preponderance of power." (ibid.) Gates discloses "reality" quite frankly in his conclusions. Having made a polite nod toward international organizations, he concludes his article with these words: "Nonetheless, as OSCE, NATO, and the UN demonstrated vividly in Bosnia, no multilateral organization anywhere can be effective in dealing with serious potential conflict unless one country is willing to assume the responsibilities and burdens of leadership and others are willing to follow. Such leadership can be exercised through multilateral organizations (such as ASEAN), but one nation with credibility and resources appropriate to the problem at hand must take a lead. Further, consultation among

1 See *PacNet Newsletter*, no. 44 (November 1, 1996).

2 Gates, "Preventive Diplomacy: Concept and Reality," *PacNet Newsletter*, no. 39 (September 27, 1996).

nations is ever more important, but it is of value in preventive diplomacy only if action—not endless debate—is the result." (ibid.)

Gates is right, of course. Practice has shown already that all the organizations listed here never could and never will stop conflicts and ensure international security. The OSCE, which failed to stop conflicts in both Yugoslavia and Russia, is a particularly good example of such futility.

To a large degree, this is because all these organizations (UN, NATO, APEC, IMF, WTO, etc.) don't serve the interests of international security; instead, they serve obviously the interests of the "magnificent three"—the USA, Western Europe, and Japan, who fund these organizations, control them, and (naturally) use them for their own purposes. The same will be true of any international organization created with the participation of this troika. These entities don't object to these organizations. Although they are a financial burden, they perform certain useful ideological and propaganda functions, acting as international parliaments of sorts where the discontented can let off steam. However, the Western states will keep relying on their own bilateral security structures that are more reliable and less troublesome.

Conclusion

The history of international relations shows that most "peace initiatives" come from weak states. The subtext of this activity consists of intentions to use peaceful diplomacy on a multilateral basis to "bind" all the subjects of a certain strategic space with mutual obligations into some system of collective security. The idea of such systems is simple: The initiating state wants to draw the state it perceives as a threat into the "collective" security system, thus neutralizing its hegemonist aspirations with collective obligations.

But even if such a system is successfully created, it cannot last long. It lives for exactly the time needed by a state aspiring to leadership to accumulate the economic mass to turn into a center of power capable of wrecking the existing status quo. Recall the example of the League of Nations and Germany prior to World War

II. In other words, such a system is wrecked in accordance with the law of power: As soon as a state reaches a level of economic might and military potential comparable to the might and potential of the world's leading states, it demands a new status for itself, which means a redivision of spheres of world influence. Because the old great powers usually resist such demands, acquisition of spheres of influence is usually possible only through the destruction of the old structure of interrelations, including the corresponding system of international security.

Nonetheless, the idea of "peace initiatives" as such, together with collective security, makes some sense for all states, regardless of their current might. The weak seek to blend into a "collective" and become equal with everyone, including the strong. The strong seek to exercise their hegemony, while referring to the support of the "collective." The "collective" cannot avoid supporting the hegemon's deeds because the whole system of collective security is subsidized by this hegemon (much like the United Nations is currently subsidized). This system enables the middle-level powers not aspiring to hegemony to increase their military and economic potential quietly without advertising their true intentions, so that after a while they can break free of the "collective" and initiate a redivision spheres of influence.

International security is a reflection of the world's geostrategic structure. The main framework of this system is formed by the states that are mightiest economically and strongest politically. This enables them to force their national interests on the rest of the world, turning them into international interests. There are two ways toward this goal: Either become a strong state, or side with the strong states.

SECTION TWO

Russia's Place and Role in the World in the Twentieth Century

Preliminary Comments

To identify Russia's place and role in the world, we must first define the terms "place" and "role" in the context of international relations. On the concept level, they are derivative links in the whole chain of the foreign policy process and the system of international relations. But I don't intend to present here the theory of international relations; I will limit myself to defining these two words as terms, not as notions.

The definition of the term "place" depends on the field or sphere of object research. Research is usually conducted in the geoeconomic, geostrategic, or social fields. In the geoeconomic space, "place," means the ordinal number of the state's "weight," or comparative "might" calculated as the aggregate economic potential of a particular country. When this potential reaches a certain size in accordance with the law of economic might, it can become a structure-forming element of international relations.

Indirectly, the "place" can also affect the geostrategic (power) field, even when it is in a state of "inactivity" (i.e., absence of foreign policy). For example, mountains are immobile and do not initiate the flow of air currents, but the height and location of mountains cause changes in the direction of airflow and wind patterns. A state with a GDP of $5 trillion may conduct no foreign policy at all, but the international system will react in some way to the mere *existence* of such a state. In other words, even though its "space" is not built into the geostrategic space, it is objectively capable of affecting the structure and system of international relations in this field, too.

In the social field, the "place" of a state reflects the society's formational essence, if we stick to Marxist terminology. It is defined through the categories of capitalism and socialism, the struggle between which is not at all over and, in fact, appears to be just beginning. If we stick to the nonclass approach on the basis of bourgeois political science, then we define "place" by the type of state (authoritarian, liberal, democratic, dictatorial, etc.), or by the type of economy (agrarian, industrial, post-industrial, computerized, developed, underdeveloped, etc.). These aspects of international relations are not examined in this book.

A state's "role" is the subjective assessment of a particular state's foreign policy in the international arena by the participants in the international arena. What interests me is the objective side of this role, i.e., Russia's foreign policy potential, which I analyzed here in comparison with foreign policy potentials of other important countries. This concept is closely tied to the category of "center of power."

Generally speaking, I want to show in this chapter Russia's real place and role (as measured through its economic mass and foreign policy potential) at the start, the middle, and end of the twentieth century. I will also connect these objective facts to the assessments offered by politicians and scholars in the preceding chapters.

Chapter IV

Russia's Place in the Geoeconomic Space

In worldwide practice, it is customary to determine a country's economic potential (that fixes its place in the world) through a number of macroindicators, the most common of which are GDP, GNP, or GNI (an aggregate economic indicator); per capita GDP (a relative indicator of the standard of living); GDP growth rate (dynamics of the economy's development); the population's life expectancy (a reflection of several indicators, including standard of living, health care, infant mortality, quality of life, etc.); military expenditures (the degree of involvement in the struggle for geostrategic dominance); and foreign trade (the degree of involvement in the world economy).

As a nod to tradition, I'll continue to include the military expenditures indicator, which actually belongs in the geostrategic sphere, in the list of macroindicators pertaining to the Human Development Index (HDI).

In view of this book's content, the indicators mentioned above make sense only through a comparative analysis. Because Russia's leaders keep proclaiming that Russia is a great power, we shall compare all its The Twenty-First Century: The World Without Russia macroindicators to those of the great powers; by default, these include the USA, Germany, the UK, France, Japan, and China. Of the European states, I will keep here only Germany as the mightiest economic power.

* * *

A few words are in order about statistics. Forget about statistics being "lies." Let me just note that even when they do "lie," statistics still work for political purposes in the same way as do deliberately distorted assessments of the goals or conduct of particular states in the world arena. However, even among the "believers" in statistics many are confused, for example, by the "obvious" incongruities in GDP estimates. Indeed, one often reads that, say, Russia's GDP in 1996 was $360 billion, while another material contains the figure $990 billion; it would seem that one of the authors is lying. But in actual fact, both figures are correct. It's just that in the first case, the currency exchange rate was used, while in the second case, GDP was calculated using Purchasing Power Parity (PPP). The exchange-rate-based indicator is considered dependent on circumstances (exchange rates can be deliberately set too high or too low), and is therefore less objective.

But the matter is not that simple. The choice of indicator depends on the topic of research. The PPP indicator gives a more realistic picture when comparing the levels and states of economies between developed and developing countries; i.e., it is more suited for comparisons of social-economic indicators. The exchange-rate indicator is better suited for comparing "places" and especially "roles" because in the sphere of international relations, intra-country differences don't matter. I have decided to include all three indicators wherever possible: GNP, GDP at the exchange rate, and GDP at PPP. Also keep in mind that different GNP figures are sometimes given for the same year. This depends on the base year chosen for the U.S. dollar. For example, the GNP figure for 2000 can be given in current prices, or it can be given in 1990 prices. The base year is usually specified in tables.

The sources I used here are the materials of the Russian State Committee for Statistics ("Goskomstat"). The materials I used for comparisons come mostly from international organizations such as the IMF (in the area of foreign trade), the World Bank, and the United Nations. Because different methods are used to this day for calculating a particular macroindicator (even in the area of foreign trade), some resulting estimates may differ from each other. Still, the differences are not that important when speaking of the general picture.

In any case, statistics provide a more objective picture of Russia's place and role than empty, unsubstantiated claims.

Russia's Place in the World at the Beginning of the Twentieth Century

For subsequent comparisons, it would be useful to determine Russia's place in the world at the beginning of the twentieth century. I wrote a whole book on that topic and now will reproduce here, in abridged form, certain results from that analysis. Note that at the beginning of the twentieth century, the discipline of comparative statistics did not yet exist; therefore, there was no universally accepted methodology for comparisons. Relatively few macroindicators were used for comparisons at that time, and Russia was usually absent from summary tables. This was not just due to the poor statistical base in Russia itself. V. A. Melyantsev, a contemporary specialist in comparative analysis, maintains that "the problems of Russia's economic development are so complex and, paradoxical as it may seem, so poorly worked out in the aspect of practical measurements of growth dynamics, that they require a number of special research projects."[1]

I became convinced of the truth of this statement from my own experience after shoveling through a pile of statistical materials from that period. However, I did manage to compile some useful figures from Western and Soviet-Russian sources. By the way, I took a substantial amount of data from Lenin's *Notebooks on Imperialism*. This work contains a most complete summary of statistical facts from all the main countries of the world, some of which Lenin later used in his work, *Imperialism: the Highest Stage of Capitalism* (1916). Even though the body of statistical materials I compiled is still not complete, I trust that it will help answer questions that interest many people.

Relying on the indicators mentioned above, let us look at their actual values at the beginning of the twentieth century. I must specify that the GDP indicator was not in use in those times; instead, the volume of industrial production was used.

1 Mel'yanzev, *East and West in the second millennium: Economy, History and the Present*, 228.

The volume of industrial production. The following table gives a certain idea of Russia's place among the principal states of Europe together with the USA as concerns the main industries of that era.

Output of Main Industrial Products in 1913 (Annual Average Data)

	Germany	Great Britain	France	Italy	Austria-Hungary	USA	Russia
Population (millions)	64,9	45,0	39,2	34,7	52,4	97,6	132,1
Pig iron (millions of tons	14, 8	9,8	4,7	0,4	2,2	30,2	3,9
Steel (millions of tons)	15,34	6,94	4, 09	0,83	2,46	....	4,20
Coal, incl. brown (millions of tons)	251,5	292,0	39,9	....	50,7	450,2	30,2
Railroads (1913) (1,000 km)	63,7	37,7	51,2	17,6	46,2	410,9	62,2

Sources: Grenville, *A History of the World in the 20 th Century*: 16, 24–5, 33, 53–4. The data on the USA and the line on railroads come from Lenin, *Notebooks on Imperialism*, 28: 462–3, 468.

In aggregate volume of industrial production, Russia occupied fifth place in the world behind the USA, Germany, Great Britain, and France. The gap separating Russia from the leading powers was quite substantial. Kenwood and Lougheed estimate that in 1913, Russia accounted for just 4.4 percent of the world's industrial production, while the USA accounted for 35.8 percent, Germany for 14.3 percent, Great Britain for 14.1 percent, and France, 7 percent. Russia was at that time ahead of Japan, whose share was just 1.2 percent.[1]

1 Kenwood and Lougheed, *The Growth of International Economy: 1820–1990*, 171.

Per capita production. On this count, Russia's situation was much worse. According to Michael Kort's estimates, per capita income in Russia was falling behind "its European competitors." "In the fifty years between 1860 and 1910, Russia was unable to overtake even Spain or Italy, much less the real industrial powers, in that vital measure of industrial progress."[1] He also calculated that, "In 1900, Russia's per capita production had been one-eighth that of the United States and one-sixth that of Germany; on the eve of the war those figures were one-eleventh and one-eighth, respectively. In 1913, Russia produced only one-tenth as much coal and barely half as much steel as Great Britain, a country with less than half Russia's population. Over half of the empire's industrial equipment still had to be imported."[2]

Applying W.A. Lewis's special method utilizing the U.S. industrial output as the base for comparisons at 100 units, it turns out that Russia's per capita output in 1917 amounted to only nine units; that is, Russia was in twenty-second place in the world, behind its vassal states Finland (27 units) and Poland (13 units), and behind even such states as Chili and Argentina. Japan was at six units at the time.[3]

Military potential. In this area, Russia was near the top of the list. Its aggregate military budget was second only to that of Great Britain; it was number one in the number of ground troops and fourth in navy size (behind Great Britain, the USA, and France).

Foreign trade. Russia was number six in the world in the volume of foreign trade. Its share of the world trade was about 4 percent in 1913.

Education. The level of education is an enormously important indicator of a nation's potential. On this topic, there has been and continues to be a lot of speculation about Tsarist Russia; in particu-

1 Kort, *The Soviet Colossus: The Rise and Fall of the USSR*, 79.

2 Ibid., 80.

3 Kenwood, Lougheed, 128.

lar, it is claimed that almost all peasants were literate under the last tsar. The situation was actually different, though one has to admit a certain progress in this regard after 1910. In 1900, outlays on education amounted to 2.1 percent of the state budget, while in 1804, their share was 2.6 percent. *The Brockhaus and Efron Encyclopedia* contains comparative figures for the end of the nineteenth century, showing that in 1897, 2 percent of Russia's budget was spent on education. Per capita expenditures on education were 2.84 rubles in England, 2.11 rubles in France, 1.89 rubles in Prussia, 0.64 rubles in Austria, 0.55 rubles in Hungary, and 0.21 rubles in Russia.[1]

In 1896, Russia (not counting Finland) had fifty-two institutions of higher education. In 1893–94, there were 25,166 students enrolled therein; only 4 percent were women. The number of elementary school students was 3,801,133 in a country whose population was 126,369,000 people. The *Encyclopedia* states: "On the basis of these data, the elementary education indicator for Russia equaled three." For the USA, this indicator equaled twenty-one.[2]

In 1913, education expenditures started to grow, reaching 4.6 percent of the budget. According to modern corrected data, by 1900 only about 30 percent of Russia's adult population was literate.[3] At the same time, in the principal states of Europe and North America, 90 percent of the population was literate.

Population mortality and life expectancy. Average life expectancy is the ultimate indicator of a society's development level. At the end of the nineteenth century, mortality in Russia was 35 people per 1,000; in Scandinavian countries, 17; in England, 19; in France, 22; and in Germany, 24. In Russia, only 550 of every 1,000 children born lived to the age of five; in Western Europe, more than 700.

In 1893–95, in European Russia, 555 out of 100,000 died of acutely infectious diseases; in Austria (second place), 350; in Belgium, 244; in Ireland, 102.5. Russia had only 155 physicians per one million people; Norway and Austria had 275; England had 578.[4]

1 *Russia: Encyclopedia*, 206.

2 Ibid., 400.

3 *Nezavisimaya gazeta* (April 1, 1999).

4 *Russia: Encyclopedia*, 224–5.

On the whole, the average life expectancy in 1913 was 52 years in Great Britain, 51 in Japan, 50 in France, 50 in the USA, 49 in Germany, 47 in Italy, 30 in China, and 23 in India.[1] In Russia it was 30.5 years.[2] Consider that in 1896–1897, the average life expectancy in Russia was 32 years (31 for men, 33 for women).[3] That is, average life expectancy *decreased* over the years of Russia's capitalization. Curiously enough, the same thing is happening today. Why is that?

Data on emigration are useful, too, showing that as capitalism developed in Russia, emigration also grew. Russian authorities did not keep correct or complete statistics. However, we have records for certain periods. In 1861–1870, 3,050 people emigrated annually to the USA; in 1887–1891, 55,524 people; in 1892–1896, 52,969 people; and in 1897, 29,981 people left. So it turns out that in the period 1887–1897, the number of emigrants was 19 times greater than in 1861–1870.[4]

The aggregate result is that Russia's nominal economic mass was fifth biggest in the world.

1 Mel'yanzev, 145.

2 *Nezavisimaya gazeta,* ibid.

3 *Goskomstat Rossii.*

4 *Russia: Encyclopedia,* 105.

The Years of Soviet Power: The Transformation into a Superpower

It is extremely difficult to perform a comparative analysis of the USSR's place in the world between 1917 and the end of World War II, primarily because of the untrustworthy nature of Soviet statistical data from those years. This problem produced heated debates among economists who started (especially after 1991) to recalculate the USSR's economic development for those years. V. Kudrov's voluminous article in which he quotes alternative estimates, primarily those prepared in the bowels of the CIA, is an example.[1] Despite all these arguments, no one denies the fact that the Soviet economy made a colossal jump before World War II.

Kenwood and Lougheed relied on League of Nations statistics, quoting the following data in their book: Taking 1913 as 100, the world index of manufacturing activity averaged 185 in the years 1936–38, where the index for the United States stood at 167; Germany, 138; Britain, 122; and France at 118, all well below the world average. In contrast, many new countries had industrialized at an enormous pace: The Soviet Union's index rose to 774, Japan's to 529, Finland's to 289, India's to 230, and Sweden's to 223. (170) In other words, the USSR developed faster than any other country in the world.

Percentage Distribution of the World's Manufacturing Production, 1913–38

Period	U.S.	Germany	U.K.	France	Soviet Union	Japan	India	Rest of world	World
1926–29	42,2	11,6	9,4	6,6	4,3	2,5	1,2	22,2	100,0
1936–38	32,3	10,7	9,2	4,5	18,5	3,5	1,4	20,0	100,0

1 Kudrov, "Soviet economic growth: official data and alternative estimates," *Voprosyi ekonomiki*, no. 10 (1995).

This table shows that in 1926–29, the USSR's share of the world's manufacturing production was actually 0.1 percent lower than Russia's share in 1913. However, over the next ten years it grew explosively. For the first time in its thousand-year history, the Russian state acquired the status of the world's second-biggest industrial power.

After World War II, the Soviet Union's economic potential grew still more, earning it the status of the world's other superpower. See the following table:

Russia's Economic Weight Compared to Other Leading Powers in 1985

	USA	W. Germany	Japan	China	USSR
Population (millions)	239	66	121	1,040	277
GDP (in current prices) ($ billion)	3,947	625	1,328	266	1,390
Per capita GDP (dollar)s	16,492	10,245	10,993	255	5,011
Infant mortality	11	10	6	51	26
(before 1 year)					
Average life expectancy	76	75	77	69	70
Exports ($ billion)	219	184	177	27	87
Imports ($ billion)	353	159	130	42	83
Defense spending ($ billion)	258	32	26	40	277
As % of GNP	6,4	3,2	1	5,1	13,1

Sources: Russett, Starr, *World Politics: The Menu for Choice,* (Appendix B); Military Spending: *World Military Expenditures and Arms Transfers—WMEAT-95;* Foreign Trade—*WTO. Merchandise Trade Section, Statistics Division* (July 1999).

Though the USSR's economic potential was still almost three times smaller than America's, even American scholars believed on the basis of statistical calculations that the Soviet Union would be closing the gap inevitably. For example, the well-known futurologists Kahn and Wiener forecasted that if U.S. GNP was to grow at 5.5 percent annually and the Soviet GNP at 7 percent, by 2000 the gap would be much reduced, and by 2020 the USSR would almost catch up with the USA.[1] Clearly those two scholars couldn't imagine that the USSR would shortly collapse, and its GNP would shrink to the size of Australia's or even Sweden's.

Apart from the growth of economic might, one should pay attention to the important indicator of average life expectancy. In Russia, it was 31 years for men and 33 years for women in 1896–97; 30.5 years in 1913; and by 1970–71, it reached 63 years for men and 74 years for women. Thus, in little more than fifty years of Soviet power, this indicator more than doubled, which is unprecedented in world history.

The following table shows that starting from 1985, i.e., the first year of ill-advised reformer Mikhail Gorbachev's regime, the Soviet Union's indicators started falling behind those of the USA, and the gap started growing. However, even in 1991, hardly anyone expected the collapse to be so shattering that the Russian state would drop from second place to nineteenth by the end of the century.

1 Kahn and Wiener, The Year 2000: *A Framework for Speculation on the Next Thirty-Three Years*, 159.

Economic Weight of the USA and the USSR Compared

	1980		1985		1991	
	USA	USSR	USA	USSR	USA	USSR
Population (millions)	226	267	239	277	252	293
GNP ($ billion)	2 600	1 500	4 054	2 118	5 695	2 531
GNP per capita	9 810	5 730	21 140	9 475	22 550	8 639
GNP growth, %	0,2	1,5	3,2	(4,1)* 0,9	(-)0,7	(-)12,9
Life expectancy, m/f	69/77	64/74	71/78	63/73	72/79	64/74
Infant mortality	14	27,7	10,3	20,7	8,9	17,8
Exports ($ billion)	217	76	211	87	422	51
Imports ($ billion)	250	69	359	83	509	45
R&D spending (% of GNP)	2,4	....	2,8	2,2	2,6	0,6
Defense spending ($ billion)	144	198	266	277	280	260

Note: 1985 GNP is given in 1982 prices.

Sources: For 1980: *What about Russians and Nuclear War?*, 231. For 1985 and 1991; *Statistical Abstracts of the United States* (1994); International Trade Statistics (1989); IMF, *Direction of Trade Statistics Yearbook* (1995). USSR GNP growth in 1985 is given according to CIA statistics.

* *Soviet statistics.*

So, by the mid-1980s, the Soviet Union held second place in the world in GNP and in manufacturing production (its share of the latter was about 20 percent); third place in the number of school students; second place in the number of higher-school students; and first place in the number of physicians per 10,000 of the population. Average life expectancy more than doubled over the years of Soviet power. In the military sphere, "equal-weight strategic parity" was achieved between the USSR and the USA, between the Warsaw Pact Organization and NATO. The USSR's share of the world's exports was 4.45 percent, and of imports, 4.13 percent (1985). By 1990, these shares had dropped to 1.7 percent for exports and 1.9 percent for imports.

Thus, the Soviet Union was a regional "pole" in the Eurasian geographic space, with a GNP more than double that of second-place (West) Germany. At the same time, the USA remained the world "pole" on the global level, with a GDP more than double that of either the USSR or Japan.

The End of the 20th Century: Russia at the Bottom

So much has been written about the collapse of Russia's economy over the years of capitalization, there is no point in repeating it here. The analysis of the causes of this collapse is not among the topics of this book. In this section, we will just have a look at the same points of comparison used to determine Russia's place in the world at the start of this century.

Russia's Socio-economic Performance
Against the Background of the World's Leading Powers, 2000

	Measurement Unit	Years of estimate	USA	Germany	Japan	China	Russia
Population	Millions		272	82	127	1,262	146
GNI	$ Billion		9,602	2,063	4,519	1,063	241
Rank			1	3	2	7	19
GNI per Capita	$		34,100	25,120	35,620	840	1,660
Rank			7	17	5	141	114
GNI (PPP)	$ Billion		9,601	2,043	3,436	4,951	1,165
GNI (PPP) per Capita	$		34,100	24,920	27,080	3,920	8,010
Rank			3	20	12	124	79
GDP Growth Rate	%	1980–90	3	2,2	4	10,1	1,6
GDP Growth Rate	%	1990–99	3,4	1,5	1,4	10,7	-6,1
Human Development Index, Rank			6	17	9	96	60
Life Expectancy at Birth	Years		77.0	77.7	81.0	70.5	66.1

Infant Mortality Rate	Per 1,000 Live Births		7	5	4	40	22
Mortality Rate for Children under 5	Per 1,000 Live Births		8	5	4	40	22
Internet Hosts	Per 1,000 People		295.2	24.8	36.5	0.1	2.2
R&D Expenditures	As % of GNP	1990-2000	2.5	2.3	2.8	0.1	1.1
Exports	$ Billion		781.1	551.5	479.2	249.3	105.2
Rank			1	2	3	7	17
Imports	$ Billion		1257.6	502.8	379.5	225.1	45.5
Rank			1	2	3	8	28
Direct Foreign Investment	$ Billion	1990	48,954	2,532	1,777	3,487	....
		1998	193,373	18,712	3,268	43,751	2,764
Foreign Debt	$ Billion	1990				55.301	59.797
		1998				154,599	183,601
Military Expenditures	$ Billion	2000	301,7	28,2	45,8	22,0	9,7
	% of GDP		3.1	1.5	1.0	2.0	3.7

Sources: World Bank, *World Development Indicators 2002*; WTO, *International trade statistics 2001*; *The Human Development Report*, 2002; *The SIPRI Military Expenditure Database*, 2004.

Russia's GNI at the end of the twentieth century. The table above shows that by 2000, Russia ranked nineteenth in the world in GNI size and 114th in per capita GNI. The picture is not much changed when we use PPP for the per capita indicator; the rank changes from 114'h to seventy-ninth. I remind you that in 1913, Russia ranked fifth in the world in industrial production.

In recent years, among the great powers, Russia was the only one going to ruin instead of continuing to develop. (In the past decade, its manufacturing production volume fell by more than 50 percent.) The average annual GDP drop was 6.1 percent. In other words, Russia left the rank of great powers and regressed by a century or two.

Military potential. Considering only defense spending, SIPRI (2002) data show that, on this indicator, Russia ranked only behind the USA.[1] Russia does keep a nuclear potential formally at parity with that of the USA. In actual fact, this parity is most likely a fiction because a military budget of only $5 billion (official Russian budget data for 2000) makes it impossible for Russia to maintain the country's nuclear posture at the required level. The level of combat-preparedness and qualification of the armed forces is evidenced by the simple fact that, in two years, they still have not managed to finish the war in Chechnya, i.e., destroy some "bandit groups." The possession of a strategic nuclear potential puts Russia in the rank of great powers only on a formal basis.

Education and science. In 1917, a worker in Russia had only one year of education on average; in 1941, four years; in 1960, six years; and in 1990, 10.5 years (compared to 14 years in the USA). In 1990, the USSR had 5.2 million students in universities and colleges; the USA had about 13.8 million.[2] By 1999, the number in Russia dropped to four million, with almost half of the student population taking evening classes, correspondence courses, or attending private self-styled "academies" and "universities" where the quality of education is close to zero.

The financial aspect of education. Between 1991 and 1999, education spending decreased by 48 percent overall and by 38 percent per student. In 1999 and 2000, education spending amounted to 3.6 percent and 3.75 percent, respectively, of the federal budget, almost like in America; however, these percentages translate to just $1 billion and $0.97 billion, respectively.[3] Russian statistics provide no details about the use of this money, or whether any additional channels existed for financing education. Therefore, the figures quoted above should probably be regarded as "final" ones without any additions. (In reality, it is not so, but that is a separate topic.)

---

1 *SIPRI Yearbook 2002*. In this case, Russian military expenditure as an exception was converted by use of the PPP conversion factor.

2 Data from foreign sources. See *Pravda* (September 20, 1994).

3 *Goskomstat Rossii for 1999 and 2000; Nezavisimaya gazeta* (February 16, 2000).

Here is another aspect of the same phenomenon: According to data from international sources, the USSR spent about 2.2 percent of its GNP on the development of science and technology in 1985; in 1999 and 2000, this figure was just 0.3 percent, or $500 million.

According to official data, between 1989 and 1999, R&D spending in Russia grew from 10.9 billion rubles to 47.3 billion rubles when measured at current prices, but in constant prices, it fell by a factor of 3.3. According to preliminary data, in 1999 it did not exceed 30 percent of the 1989 level.[1]

According to Russian newspapers' data, about one-third of all R&D personnel have left their jobs, and academic science has lost about half its research fellows.[2] The most talented researchers have left Russia; their number is at least 180,000 to 250,000 in the spheres of science, scientific services, and medicine.[3]

Demographic situation. For the first time after World War II, the country's population shrank in 1993 by 300,000 people; in 1994, it shrank by a further 920,000; in 1995, by 164,200; and in 1996, by 475,000. In that year, the number of deaths exceeded the number of births by 60 percent.[4] The most tragic statistic is the drop in life expectancy for men. Let me quote Gundarev, a leading Russian expert on this problem, who heads a laboratory at the State Institute of Prophylactic Medicine and is the author of the book *Why People Die in Russia and How Are We to Survive?* In his interview with the newspaper *Argumenty i facty,* he said: "In order to picture the scale of our current demographic disaster, let us compare it, for example, to the 1930sthat dark period of our history with its collectivization and subsequent famine, mass exiles, and repressions. The country lost 15 million people then (those who died of the mentioned causes and those who were never born for the same causes). That is,

1 *Ekonomika i zhizn'* (April 21, 2000).

2 According to Volsky's data, since 1991 Russian research institutes have lost between 40 percent and 70 percent of their personnel, and their funding shrank by a factor of 15. See *Rossiiskaya gazeta (*January 15, 1997).

3 *NG Nauka* (January 19, 2000).

4 Other sources give these figures for population decreases: 220,000 people in 1992, 750,000 in 1993, 920,000 in 1994, and 785,000 in 1995. See *Pravda* (July 10, 1996).

additional annual mortality was 890 people per 100,000. In Russia, over the last four years, this indicator (excess mortality plus drop in births) amounted to 1,150(!) people annually per 100,000."[1] As one English economist put it, "It is hard to find a historical precedent for such mortality in a time of no war and no natural disasters."[2] *Nezavisimaya Gazeta* comes to the following conclusion: "It turns out that in their annual destruction of human potential, the current Russian reforms exceed the destructive might of Stalin's regime by a factor of two; they are comparable to World War I, and only Hitler's invasion brought bigger loss of life."[3] It follows that the current democratic regime is many times more "totalitarian" than Stalin's totalitarian regime.

In other words, Russia is exhibiting the trend of a nation dying out. This thesis is confirmed by a number of other figures. Russia ranks first in Europe in infant mortality. According to specialists' estimates, the number of children born sick is 2.3 times greater now than five years ago. Data from the Ministry of Health Care indicate that 80 percent of all schoolchildren are affected by some kind of illness. Alcoholism is a well-known scourge in Russia; unfortunately, the "reforms" have further exacerbated this problem. The American magazine *U.S. News & World Report* informed readers that the USSR had 4.5 million registered alcoholics in 1988; Russia had six million by 1996.[4] This problem partly accounts for Russia's unique feature, i.e., the world's greatest gap between life expectancies for men and woman—12.4 years in 1999.

The shrinking of the population is due to a large degree to environmental catastrophe in Russia; awareness of this catastrophe is low both in the country itself and in the West. The Ministry for Protection of the Environment and Natural Resources prepared a report in which it says that water is now undrinkable in about 70 percent of Russia's rivers and lakes, due to decades of careless industrial and agricultural practices. About 80 percent of the water supply system does not meet the standards of hygiene, and 40 percent of equipment in this system is completely obsolete. Up to one-third of all dairy products sold in Moscow are infected by fecal

1 *Argumenty i fakty*, no. 8 (February 1996).

2 *The Economist* (July 9, 1994), 50.

3 Quote from *Obzory SMI Rossii* (June 2, 1997).

4 *U.S. News & World Report* (April 15, 1996).

bacilli. The content of sulfurous gas in Moscow's air is twice as high as in New York and eight times higher than in Paris. Thirty percent of all food products in Moscow contain poisonous chemicals in health-endangering quantities. The maximum permissible norms for absorption of radioactive substances into the body, approved by the Ministry of Health Care of the USSR and in effect to this day, are ten times higher than the norms approved in the West. The annual "per capita consumption" of hazardous substances in Russia is about 400 kg.

The World Health Organization forecasts that Russia's population will drop to 130-135 million by 2015. According to WHO data, Russia currently ranks ninety-first in the world in life expectancy, and twenty years from now, it should drop to 125th place (among 188 states). In 1999 Russia ranked 130th in health care levels. Nicolas Eberstadt, a specialist on population issues, wrote an article sarcastically titled Russia: *Too Sick to Matter?*, in which he quotes data about the catastrophic demographic situation there. He concludes with a symptomatic phrase: "It looks like Russia will be bedridden for many, many years."[1]

Human Development Index—HDI. As I mentioned already, the HDI has been in use since 1990. This indicator is an aggregate of average life expectancy, the average education level of the adult population plus aggregate indicators of schooling, and per capita income in U.S. dollars, corrected to account for PPP.

By this index, the table above shows that Russia ranked sixty-second[2] in 1998 among 174 states; it was behind not only all the developed states, but even behind Cuba and Belarus (fifty-sixth and fifty-seventh, respectively), as well as a number of Latin American, Asian, and African countries. In 1995, Russia ranked fifty-seventh. In 1990, the Soviet Union (in its worst year) ranked thirty-third by this same indicator.[3] Thus, in just eight years, almost thirty states managed to overtake post-reform Russia.

1 Eberstadt, "Russia: Too Sick to Matter?" *Policy Review*, no. 95 (June and July 1999)

2 *Human Development Report 2000: Human Rights and Human Development.*

3 *Literaturnaya gazeta* (July 23, 1996).

Foreign trade. In 1913, Russia's share of the world trade was between 4 and 6 percent (sixth place in the world). In 2000 this share dropped to 1.2 percent: 1.7 percent for exports (seventeenth place) and 0.7 percent for imports (twenty-eighth place).[1] The following table helps us draw important conclusions.

Shares of Regions and Individual Countries in the Exports and Imports of Russia/USSR/Russian Federation

	1913		1980		1992		2000	
	E	I	E	I	E	I	E	I
Western Europe	89	78	29.7	26.2	53.7	48.1	39.8	34.2
Eastern Europe			46.3	46.9	23.9	16.4	22.8	7.8
North America	1	6	0.4	5.2	2.2	11.4	7.8	8.6
East Asia	2	6	5.2	5.2	13.5	15.6	7.8	5.3
Middle East	6	4	2.5	1.2	2.5	1.6	2.8	0.6

Calculated using data from the following sources: For 1913, P.A. Khromov. *Russia's Economic Development in the XIX–XX Centuries. 1800–1917* (M., 1950), 490–493; IMF, *Direction of Trade Statistics Yearbooks (DOTS),* 1984, 1997, 2001.

First, the dynamics of regional and countrywise share of Russia's aggregate foreign trade between 1913 and 2000 show that even though Europe's importance decreased by the end of the century, it still remains Russia's main trading partner. Germany's share alone is greater than the share of all of East Asia (including Japan and China). This means there is no objective ground for all the talk, conducted throughout the century and especially today by the "APR"-babblers, about Russia's need to reorient itself more actively toward the "APR." Russia was—and still is—oriented toward Europe.

Second, one can see a regularity in the low importance to Russian trade of Africa, Latin America, South Asia, the Near and Middle East, not to mention Australia and Oceania. Occasionally, some of these regions increased in importance, due to either temporary

1 WTO, *International Trade Statistics 2001.*

market conditions or massive sales of weapons, but not to any real demand that usually stems from objective economic interests.

Third, the dramatic increase in the USA's share of Russia's foreign trade in the years of the country's capitalization is also due more to political considerations than to economic interests. America's share can be expected to decrease in the future due to the inevitable deterioration in the general climate of American-Russian relations.

Fourth, the following table shows Russia's extremely insignificant share of the great powers' foreign trade. In trade with other countries of the world, this share is even smaller. In other words, Russia, on the whole, has no influence on the state of the world trade, except for three items—oil, gas, and weapons. Outside the CIS, Russia exerts no noticeable influence on the world's trade-economic situation.

Russia's Share of Selected Countries' Exports and Imports

	1993		2000	
	E	I	E	I
Germany	1.9	1.9	1.1	2.7
France	0.7	1.3	0.5	1.3
Italy	1	2,6	1.0	3.2
USA	0.7	0,3	0.30.6	
Japan	0.4	1.1	0.1	1.2
China	2.9	4.8	0.9	2.6

Calculated from IMF, *Direction of Trade Statistics Yearbooks (DOTS),* 1997, 2001.

Fifth, Russia is not a member of any integration zones or fields and does not participate in globalization. Instead, it is a passive object of internationalization. This situation reflects its weak economic mass.

Sixth, Russia has no real chances of breaking into the ranks of the world's major trading powers, either in the near- or middle-term perspective.

Faith in Russia's potential based on its truly enormous natural resources is perfectly groundless because natural resources do not define a state's place in the world.

* * *

Over the past hundred years, Russia's place—and accordingly, its status in the world—experienced some dramatic leaps. Prior to 1917, Russia ranked fifth in the world, with the status of a regional power; between 1917 and 1985, it ranked second, having the status of a superpower; after 1991, it dropped to nineteenth place and acquired the status of a state that matters only in the CIS geographic space.

Russia was thrown back not only when compared to the period of the USSR's existence but also when compared to the tsarist period of the early twentieth century. This phenomenon is unique in that this throwback was not due to wars or natural disasters, but happened in peacetime.

It is obvious that Russia's current status is not natural for a country that has been for many centuries a structure-forming element in the framework of international relations. The question of whether it has the actual potential for reclaiming great power status is a topic for another book.

Chapter V

Russia's Foreign Policy Potential

Many Russian analysts continue to call Russia a great power, or even a center of power in the military sense, pointing at the state's strategic nuclear potential that still satisfies the principle of "strategic parity" with the USA.[1] They either fail to or refuse to understand certain simple things. In today's circumstances, nuclear weapons are a force for containment; i.e., they are a static factor that cannot be used in principle and create no possibilities for acquiring influence outside the state's limits. The nuclear potential does win certain points from the perspective of the state's prestige, being indicative of the country's science-and-technology potential. But from the international perspective, influence is acquired not so much through possession of a nuclear potential but rather through membership in alliances and possession of a network of military bases, of a seaworthy Navy, and of modern non-nuclear components of armed forces that can be used abroad against specific countries without causing damage to the whole world. Remember that the Soviet Union suffered defeat in the Cold War despite having strategic parity with the USA.

1 The most sober-minded scholars are coming to realize that this is in actual fact an illusion. For example, Rogov writes: "The balance of armed forces in Europe has worsened dramatically. Today NATO has three- to fourfold superiority over Russia in the quantities of the main kinds of conventional weapons. The West's qualitative superiority is greater still, and in the coming years it will keep growing. ...The military-strategic balance is showing signs of tipping in favor of the USA due to Russia's inability to maintain parity on the levels provided for by the SALT-1 and SALT-2 Treaties." See *Independent Military Review* (January 12, 2001).

To a large degree, this defeat was also because the USSR violated the law of optimal proportions between funding for foreign and domestic policy in its budget. Expenditures on international affairs, particularly for the military component, bankrupted the USSR. Even though no one at that time calculated the Soviet Union's foreign policy potential, many experts now maintain that at least half of the economy—if not two-thirds of it—served the military sphere. Accordingly, this sphere claimed the lion's share of the budget. The result was collapse on all fronts.

* * *

How does Russia's current state of foreign policy funding compare to that of other important states? First, we need to formulate the concept of foreign policy potential discussed perfunctorily in the theoretical section. Because I am introducing this concept for the first time to the theory of foreign policy and international relations, I must elaborate on its connection to other concepts and discuss methods of calculating it.

> ***A state's foreign policy potential (FPP) is the aggregate of resources expended on the implementation of foreign policy.***

Being an aggregate of targeted uses of resources, FPP is realized through the foreign policy apparatus that consists of agencies operating in areas as diverse as foreign economic relations, military, diplomacy, propaganda and ideology, secret services, immigration and border control, etc.

The FPP is not only part of the state's economic might but also a derivative of this might. Its size defines the financial aspect of the state's role in the world, i.e., the geostrategic structure of the world depends on the size of states' FPP in accordance with the law of centers of power.

The FPP is calculated on the basis of the funding specified in the state budget for all kinds of state activities. The problem is, not all states publish their budgets in full; some states seek to conceal certain budget items from the general public. For example, in Russia's federal budget, many items related to the FPP are either presented in a too-general form or simply kept a secret. Other difficulties in making comparisons between countries are due to the fact that the distribution of budget resources between items follows different patterns. For example, the USA includes in the item "International Affairs" the maintenance of the Department of State and funding for international organizations, etc. (see *Part One, Ch. IV*), while the United Kingdom's budget separates the maintenance of the Foreign & Commonwealth Office from the funding of membership in the European Community. In Japan international activities are funded through the Ministry of Foreign Affairs, but most Official Development Assistance (ODA) is administered through other ministries and agencies. In Italy international activities are included in the item "foreign ties." It's not always easy to find out which items contain funding for other aspects of international activities.

Also, keep in mind that three spending items account for most of the FPP: (1) national defense; (2) international activities (diplomacy); and (3) foreign economic activities. These three components usually account for 85 to 90 percent of the FPP total. I have to limit my analysis to the first two components of the FPP because the third component, foreign economic cooperation, is not clearly stated in Russia's budgets for the fiscal years 1998-2000. For the purposes of this book, though, it is more than enough because it is primarily "defense" and "international activities" that define the power segment of the geostrategic field.

To better understand the following table, one should keep in mind that the item "International Affairs" in the U.S. budget means the Function 150 Account (see *Part One, Ch. IV*); in Japan it is funded through the Ministry of Foreign Affairs (MFA); and in the U.K. it is likewise the MFA (called Foreign and Commonwealth Office), which funds "international affairs" and makes net payments to EC institutions. In Russia it is the budget item "international activities," which includes international cooperation; participation in peacekeeping activities; implementation of interstate treaties within the CIS; international cultural, scientific and informational ties; and economic and humanitarian aid to other states.

Foreign Policy Potential of the USA, Japan, United Kingdom, and Russia (FY 2000, US$ billion)

	USA	Japan	UK	Russia
International Activities	22.6	7.0	6.1	1.8
Share of Budget, %	1.2	0.9	1.1	6.6
National Defense	304.1	44.7	34.7	5.0
Share of Budget, %	16.7	5.8	6.2	16.5

Sources: Russia: On the Federal Budget for FY 2000 (Goskomstat); the USA: The Budget for Fiscal Year 2002; Japan: The Japanese Budget in Brief. MOF, Budget Bureau, 2001; the UK: The Government's Expenditure Plans 2000–01 to 2000–02. Cabinet Office, April 2000.

The table above shows that the USA has an FPP of about $327 billion; Japan, more than $50 billion; the UK, about $41 billion; and Russia, about $7 billion. These figures tell better than words exactly who is who in the world arena. From the perspective of foreign political activities, the "international activities" item is the most important one because it is funding for *ongoing activities* in the international arena; it stands for kinetic energy, so to speak. The item "national defense" is not exactly "idle" (especially in the policies of the USA and the UK), but in the sphere of international relations it works only in exceptional cases. This item can be said to mean potential energy, though the defense potential forms part of the state's image.

It is noteworthy that the FPP of both the UK and Japan substantially exceed the FPP of Russia, though both these countries do not pursue the objective of becoming a "great power," at least not on the official level. Meanwhile, Russia lays claims to great power status, as evidenced by the *Foreign Policy Concept of the Russian Federation.* The goals set in this *Concept* include: "Ensuring the country's security and protection, and strengthening of its sovereignty and territorial integrity, of positions of strength and authority in the world community that best suit the interests of the Russian Federation as a great power, as one of the influential centers of the modern world...."[1] Apparently, Russia intends to accomplish this goal by spending just \$1.8 billion annually. With such low expenditures, it is obvious that Russia will never attain the desired status, no matter how fervently its leaders try to convince themselves and others that Russia is a great power.

FPP defines the material base of the category "role" which, in the system of international relations, means the subjective assessment of a country's foreign policy. Let us examine this category with regard to the USSR. The Soviet Union's role in the world was great indeed. It was this role which allowed it to stake a legitimate claim to superpower status. This status was acquired through raising the Soviet state's FPP practically to the level of the USA. But the U.S. FPP was based on an economic might that was more than double the economic might of the Soviet Union. In other words, Moscow had to spend colossal sums of money on its FPP in order to maintain its superpower status. This resulted in lower expenditures in the domestic arena. By the time the USSR finally achieved equal-weight strategic parity with the USA by the early 1980s, its annual GNP growth rate had decreased to 1.8 percent. (In the 1970s, it averaged 3 percent.)[2] Meanwhile, U.S. GNP growth was constantly accelerating, especially in the 1980s. In other words, a country can violate for some time certain proportions between domestic and foreign policy expenditures or, on a more general plane, between GNP and FPP, but sooner or later such violations will bring about a collapse, regardless of the role-image it projects in the world arena. For example, skillful propaganda can create a positive peace-loving image in the world arena, but the qualitative assessment of its role will not matter if the image is not supported by a real foreign policy potential proportionate to the state's economic might. For example, many countries perceive the USA as an aggressive state. Despite this negative image, the USA accomplishes its goals because its FPP is in proportion to expenditures on domestic policy, and all its policies rely on the country's great economic potential.

In this connection, the task arises of finding optimal proportions between expenditures on domestic and foreign policy. During

1 The Foreign Policy Concept of the Russian Federation Document (English translation), full text, *Nezavisimaya Gazeta* (June 11, 2000).

2 Kudrov, 106.

the Cold War until the mid-1970s, the share of FPP was about 42 percent in the U.S. budget; 31 to 32 percent in the West German budget; 20 percent to 29 percent in France; 16 to 26 percent in the UK; 9 to 15 percent in Italy; and 8 to 10 percent in Japan (where the share of "international activities" varied between 1 and 3 percent). By the early 1990s, the share of FPP decreased (primarily due to lesser defense spending) to 25 percent in the USA, 23 percent in Germany, 20 percent in France, 15 percent in the UK, 6 percent in Italy, and 7 percent in Japan.[1] By the end of the 1990s, the share of FPP in the GNP of these countries shrank even further.

The picture is different in Russia. *The optimal proportions between budget expenditures on domestic and foreign policy (and, accordingly, between FPP and GNP) are still violated, though to a lesser degree than in the USSR.* Let us examine this problem, using examples of other countries.

The USA affirms its leadership in the world, yet limits international affairs to 1.2 percent of its budget; Japan, to 0.9 percent; and the U.K., 1.1 percent. (These figures are similar in Germany, France, and Italy.) In Russia the share of this item is 6.6 percent (!).

The actual figure is much higher. The official figure does not include outlays on information-and-propaganda support for foreign policy; the process of working out foreign policy decisions (for example, preparation of concepts, doctrines, and other similar documents); the maintenance of various organizations, such as the Center for Strategic Research, etc., all items specified in detail in the U.S. budget in the section for international affairs. So, if we add the cost of these bodies (including the cost of the Ministry of Foreign Affairs), plus the cost of information-and-propaganda activities directed at foreign countries, the grand total would be approximately $2-2.1 billion, or 7.3 to 7.4 percent of the budget.

Adding together the two components of the FPP (international activities and defense), we arrive at this share of the national budget: 17.9 percent in the USA; 6.7 percent in Japan; 7.3 percent in the UK; and about 24 percent in Russia.

If we add to these sums the outlays on other areas of security having to do with external threats (state security agencies, border guards, utilization and demolition of weapons), we arrive at these

1 States budgets of leading capitalist countries (the budgets of central organs of power). *Selection of analytical reviews.*

approximate figures (for FY 2000): 19 to 20 percent in the USA; 7.5 percent in Japan; 8 percent in the UK; and 33.3 percent in Russia.

Russia's Foreign Policy Potential

	1995 Trillion Rubles	1999 Million Rubles	2000 Million Rubles	2001 Million Rubles	2002 Million Rubles
International Activities	27.3	58080.3	56119.0	22182.9	42.858
Share of Budget, %	9.9	8.7	6.6	1.9	2.2
National Defense	49.6	116127.4	140852.0	218924.7	300702.8
Share of Budget, %	18.0	17.5	16.5	18.3	15.4
Law Enforcement and State Security	20.2	55445.5	79801.0	131620.8	173863.3
Share of Budget, %	7.3	8.3	9.3	11.0	8.9
Including:					
State Security Agencies	N/A	8443.0	N/A	21191.5	31813.5
Share of Budget, %	N/A	1.3	N/A	1.8	1.6
Border Defenses	N/A	5587.4	N/A	11943.4	17558.0
Share of Budget, %	N/A	0.8	N/A	1.0	0.9

Sources: Data from the State Committee for Statistics for 1995 and data from the Ministry of Finance: *On the Federal Budget for 1997, 2001, 2002; On the Preliminary Results of the Execution of the Federal Budget of the Russian Federation for 1999*

It turns out that the USA, the center of global power, spends about 20 percent of its budget on maintaining its leadership; Japan, "simply" a great power, spends less than 10 percent; while Russia, seeking great power status, spends more than 30 percent.

In principle, there is nothing surprising in this; the state that seeks to wreck the structure of international relations always spends more than the state that has already won leadership in the world. The problem is that Russia's 30 percent of the budget is supported by a weak, unstable economy vulnerable to both external factors (such as oil prices) and internal factors (the possibility of a social unrest). Russia's foreign policy potential "devours" more important expense items in the budget—items on which the existence of today's capitalist state actually hinges. In other words, "great power" status is out of Russia's reach on account of its low economic mass. To continue to chase this phantom may cause further disintegration of the country and a wholesale dying out of its population.

Russia's current policy is a classic example of "expense" policy inherited from the leaders of the "advanced socialism" era. Everyone knows the results from the previous era. Therefore, it is easy to forecast the results of the current policy.

The main goal of any foreign policy is to cause no damage to the country's economic mass (at the minimum), but rather increase this mass (at the maximum). President Clinton put it succinctly in his report for 1999, *U.S. National Strategy in the 21 st Century*: Every dollar spent abroad must produce $10 worth of benefits to the country. To achieve such results, it is necessary not just to formulate realistic objectives but also to keep them within the country's financial or (more correctly) economic capabilities.

The international activities of prosperous states indicate that regional leaders spend no more than 10 percent of their budgets on international activities (in the aggregate); the world hegemon (USA) spends 20 percent; local powers spend less than 10 percent, while their economic mass (GNP or GDP) exceeds $500 billion. These proportions are violated only in exceptional cases, such as Taiwan and South Korea, or in underdeveloped countries involved in regional conflicts of the precapitalist type (for example, in Africa).

Russia, of course, is not in any sense typical; it always spent colossal sums on "defense of the Motherland." This is due not only to historical reasons (perpetual external threats) but also to the incompetence of the country's ruling circles, who stayed in the trap of invented, false stereotypes about the state's national interests. For example, the halfcentury-long struggle for control of the Bosphorus Strait did not serve Russia's national interests for the simple reason that the country's trade and development as a whole was not tied to Mediterranean countries. To a large degree, Russia's economic backwardness was caused by the enormous expenditures on foreign policy and maintenance of its great power status; it was actually Russia's opponents who reaped benefits from this status because the "games" played in the world arena were bankrupting tsarist Russia, just as they later bankrupted the Soviet Union in the time of Brezhnev.

This old Russian-Soviet style of thinking is alive to this day. For example, one of the journalists from *Nezavisimaya Gazeta* (July 26, 2000) accused the Ministry of Finance of blocking the appropriation of $1 million in entrance fees to the Fund for Cooperation with ASEAN. He believes that this lousy million is nothing compared to the benefits that will accrue from cooperation with ASEAN countries. Such naivety! What benefits is he talking about when the share of ASEAN in Russia's foreign trade has never exceeded 1 percent until now, in spite of having ten members? The journalist asserts that Russia stands to reap "political benefits." He obviously doesn't understand that political benefits in the world don't matter if they don't translate into economic benefits. In principle, any kind of policy is "expense-based." Policy only becomes profitable when political actions produce economic benefits. Recall Clinton's statement. I proclaim with conviction that whether Russia does pay that $1 million in dues or not, its share of ASEAN trade (and ASEAN's share of Russian trade) will not change at all as long as the country's economic mass stays below $500 billion. The same is true of Russia's participation in the much-vaunted APEC. These dues are money thrown away for nothing. The same also applies to PACE. All these are "chattering" organizations that only serve to feed bureaucrats.

I think I read somewhere that Russia has membership in almost 2,000 international organizations. Naturally, it pays dues to all of them, and no one bothers to count the total expense. It is high time somebody did the accounts in order to determine how necessary each of these memberships is. As taxpayers, Russian citizens should not be paying for some bureaucrats' free trips to different countries, trips that benefit only the bureaucrats and their families

General Conclusions. First, only those win who can count. Second, Russia is not a great power, much less a center of power. Third, all its pretensions to become one are bound to fail.

Chapter VI

Russia's Strategic Prospects[1]

I'm not naïve. I do not believe the things I say below will influence in any way the people involved in the decision making process and implementation of Russia's foreign policy. The list of my proposals rejected by political and academic officials in positions of power is already too long. Ever since 1976, when I started actively participating in situation analyses and preparing reference materials for those "at the top," I encountered complete disagreement with all my assessments of the international situation and, accordingly, complete rejection of the actions I proposed. I was not believed in 1978 when I said that the Japan-China treaty signed that year would not lead to the formation of a military-political alliance between the two countries—an alliance expected by the majority of scholars and high-ranking officials in the International Department of the CPSU Central Committee. Most colleagues, especially the "scientists" on "Primakov's team," disagreed with me categorically when I claimed in the early 1980s that the Pacific Community cannot be organized in principle, not even as an economic organization. In 1988, I asserted at a Round Table attended by the German magazine *Der Spiegel* that reunification of the two Germanys was inevitable, producing laughter from the Soviet Germany experts. They became tense when I talked about the uselessness of Gorbachev's proposal for creating "a common home in Europe." American Sovietologists from Stanford University received with mistrust my statement made at the conference in Vladivostok in June 1991; I

1 This chapter is a shortened version of the Russian original.

said then that the collapse of the USSR was inevitable, and security problems in the Far East should be discussed not with the Gorbachev administration but with the Yeltsin one. Soviet participants from the Institute for Far Eastern Studies received my statement as a provocative joke. I now encounter similar reactions in capitalist Russia. For example, at a Round Table arranged by the Gorbachev Foundation, Mikhail Gorbachev himself and many others discussed quite seriously the economic development plan proposed by Yevgeny Primakov, who had just been appointed Prime Minister. I told them that the plan could not be fulfilled in principle, and that Mr. Primakov would not stay Prime Minister for long; those claims puzzled those present. In response to my pessimism, everyone continued to express historical optimism, both in the Soviet era and in today's capitalist times.

But in all these cases I was proven right, and my opponents wrong. All subsequent events always confirmed the truth of my statements. Yet, despite the failure of all their forecasts and assessments without exception, it is still the "failures" (my opponents) who continue to "set the tone" in politics and participate in the foreign policy process. It is these people—Gorbachev, A.N. Yakovlev, Yeltsin, Primakov, and their entourages, advisers, and experts—who are responsible for the collapse of the USSR, for the failures in domestic and foreign policy that led to the country's GNI rank dropping to nineteenth in the world, resulting in Russia's virtual disappearance from the world arena as a power broker of international relations. I don't think they did it on purpose; they were simply mistaken. But those are precisely the kind of mistakes that are worse than crimes. How can this be?

This phenomenon has many causes, one of the more important of which is that scholarly and political officials are a part and parcel of established institutional structures that dictated in the past and still dictate in the present the conduct of and reasoning behind foreign policy. Can anyone imagine, say, the minister of foreign affairs championing a reduction of diplomatic activities and, accordingly, a reduction of his ministry's staff? Of course not!

Another reason, characteristic of the Russian mind-set, is the absence of the tradition of counting how much a policy costs, how much particular actions cost, and how reasonable are the objectives and the costs of achieving them.

At a press conference where Mikhail Gorbachev presented the final report of the research project, *Russia's Self-Determination,* (analyzed in the corresponding section), I asked Mr. Gorbachev how much Russia was spending on foreign policy, and how much it would cost to implement the report's suggestions. Mr. Gorbachev became confused and asked Mr. G.Kh. Shakhnazarov, the well-known scholar of politics and international affairs, to answer. Shakhnazarov declined, referring to the fact that the "international" parts of the report were the responsibility of K. N. Brutenz, who was not present at the press conference. I was prepared for this lack of knowledge. But still, I am shaken by the fact that people who used to hold such high government positions don't even know the order of magnitude of foreign policy expenditures. The same is true of the current "policymakers." Such is the level of their competence.

In Russia (this was also true of the USSR), officials in government never criticize their superiors, not to mention the country's top leaders. Can anyone imagine the director of some academic research institute lambasting the president for his disastrous policies? Never! The director would simply lose his job, or, at the very least, his institute's budget would be cut. One's "position" is more important than the "truth." Or take another example: President Putin wrote (or perhaps only signed) an article on the "APR" in which he proposed building a Common Home with this nonexistent "APR." It is hard to imagine a more illiterate article, yet not one Russian "scholar" dared to criticize it. It is not just a matter of "position" and "truth"; the problem is the slave psychology of Russian bureaucrats, especially in the higher echelons. Slaves they always were, and slaves they will remain.

Therefore, the words below are not directed at these officials (who hardly ever read anything, by the way); they are addressed to those who have not yet lost the ability to reason and accordingly assess the real world objectively.

* * *

Today's Russia finds itself in a strategic trap as a result of attempts to rebuild the country in a Western-capitalist mold. The introduction of Western models of authority and the market economy have destroyed the former socialist superstructure and substantially deformed the economic base. But instead of the expected breakthrough in economic development, the country dropped to nineteenth place in the world in the size of its economic potential; relatively speaking, it joined the ranks of underdeveloped countries of the Third World. The only remaining sign of superpowerdom is the nuclear-missile arsenal, even though its strategic capability is in some doubt.

Political degradation, economic depression, and social tensions in the country can cause at any moment a new reshuffling of forces, with new political structures inevitably emerging in the superstructure and in the base.

Under these conditions, it is extremely difficult to formulate a foreign policy concept for a country that has not yet defined for itself its ideological interest. Ideology is usually the soul and core of any doctrine and concept of national interests and national security. It is precisely ideology that determines the choice of allies and, in turn, the position of the external setting toward the championing of a particular ideology. Yet, despite the uncertainty about this particular fundamental interest-value, there exist other fundamental interests—soulless, perhaps, but no less important. They include territorial integrity, political independence or sovereignty, the need for economic development, and national-cultural originality. Because the fundamental interests reflect the state's objective needs that make its very existence possible, they are not subject to compromise and are defended by any means available, including military force. But these are general theses, applicable to all countries. We are interested in today's realities that require that we consider "the current moment." Proceeding from these realities and from all the considerations contained in this book, I now suggest my variant of Russia's conduct in the international arena, formulated in the shape of a rational foreign policy concept for Russia.

A Rational Foreign Policy Concept for Russia

This concept relies primarily on five basic principles:

1. Outlays on foreign policy must work to increase the state's GDP, not decrease it.
2. The country's foreign policy potential (FPP) must be rationally combined with outlays on domestic policy; under current conditions, it must not exceed 10 percent of the total budget.
3. Foreign policy goals must be formulated on the basis of actual financial possibilities for their achievement; i.e., they must correspond to the size of the FPP.
4. The country's place and role must be assessed on the basis of the laws of geopolitics and geostrategy.
5. The system and structure of international relations must be assessed through the prism of objective realities rather than subjective (wishful) or ideologized ideas about the world.

As we determined in the previous chapters, Russia is not a great power, or a *pole*, or a *center of power*; instead, it is a state whose sphere of influence is limited to the CIS space. Attempts to accomplish objectives outside that sphere of influence are doomed to fail. Recognizing these facts is the number one condition for rational foreign policy.

The second condition is that objectives must be changed to make them match the FPP, which, in the current circumstances, appears to be almost three times too high. The item "international activities" must be brought down from 6.6 percent of the budget to

2 percent,[1] and the item "defense" from 16.5 percent to 8 percent.[2] It should be noted that these shares would then still be higher than in Japan or in the Big Four European countries.

For the Ministry of Foreign Affairs (MFA), this suggestion translates into a narrowing of its sphere of activities in the international arena, not only in geographic space but also in involvement in international problems. Accordingly, the Ministry's headquarters staff should be cut to 2,000 people, and the staff of embassies and other offices abroad should be cut in half. The downsizing should affect the "obsolete" old-timers and the mass of officials pretending to be busy. The drop in numbers should be compensated by labor productivity growth to the tune of five to six times, i.e., reaching the volume of work performed by Japanese diplomats, for example. Naturally, this reform also presupposes a rearrangement of MFA's divisions in accordance with the new tasks, while old tasks are to be discarded.

Successful implementation of foreign policy requires, apart from other things, objective knowledge of the surrounding world. In this case, it means, on one hand, knowing how the leading actors of international relations assess Russia's place and role and, on the other hand, knowing the structure of international relations in the geoeconomic and geostrategic systems. These things would appear to be obvious, but to Russian politicians they are not. The preceding chapters make it clear that most of these people believe the geoeconomic world to be dominated by globalization or integration, and the geostrategic world to be multipolar.

In actual fact, the world economy consists of three economic interaction types: internationalization, integration (which exists in advanced form only in Western Europe), and globalization, with internationalization still being the dominant type. Russia has no economic capabilities for participation in either the integration field (outside the CIS limits) or the globalization process (which is governed by the G-7). This means that internationalization is still the only field of action for Russia. Even in this place, it should

1 Surprisingly, it was cut to 1.9 percent in FY 2001.

2 Though the armed forces are currently in the process of "reforms," I doubt their effectiveness. Nonetheless, I shall not pursue this topic any further here because this chapter mainly deals with the conceptual foundations of the country's national interests.

restrain itself from attempts to reach across the whole world but should concentrate instead on selected strategically important countries.

It should also be acknowledged that currently there is just one "pole" in the geoeconomic space and just one "center of power" in the geostrategic space—the USA. This state of affairs is likely to last for another twenty to twenty-five years. Following a brief period of "multipolarity," this system will subsequently be replaced by a stable bipolarity with two centers of power as a result of China's evolution into a superpower.

Russia must renounce the concept of "multipolarity"—not only because of unnecessary expenditures involved in the acquisition of "pole" and "power center" status but also because the multipolar system is the most dangerous variant of international relations—a struggle of all against all. Instead of "playing games" in the geostrategic field, Russia should concentrate on solving its domestic problems and on strengthening the CIS.

It is necessary to reformulate the concept of the country's national interests, proceeding from a FPP that amounts to 10 percent of the budget, the country's real place and role in the world, and an objective assessment of international relations. The concept must have a clear structure and hierarchy. National interests must be divided into fundamental ones, important ones, and less important or secondary ones. The concept must identify threats to the interests in each block, response actions, and expected results. All domestic policy topics must be removed from the concept. These topics should be discussed in other documents, such as the strategy of Russia's development for the next ten or twenty-five years. (In China, Deng Xiaoping laid out a strategy for the next eighty years!)

It is clear that ranking interests is not an easy task because politicians and experts assess differently the importance of specific interests. This problem is encountered even by Americans belonging to the same political school, as shown in Part One, Chapter II of this book. For example, the current Bush administration has substantially reformulated all blocks of interests and the means to realize them. There is nothing strange in this because no doctrine is a dogma; it must change in accordance with new objectives—"challenges"—or with changes in the international situation. Nonetheless, certain objective criteria make it possible to rank interests according to importance, especially *fundamental* interests. Hardly anyone would argue that the objective of becoming a great power can be defined as a fundamental interest. This particular goal is obviously nothing but ambition. It is not attainable in the present circumstances, and is harmful, too, because it requires additional financial resources at a time when the Russian government is currently in such a squeeze that it cannot even pay its workers in the public sector on time. An equally absurd "interest" contained in Russia's current Foreign Policy Concept is the "development of regional and sub-regional integration in Europe, the Asia-Pacific region, Africa, and Latin America." How will Russia participate in African integration when its share of world trade is just around 2 percent? Why should Russia show any interest in Africa and Latin America when it doesn't even have the resources to form an integration field within CIS limits? This is laughable, and all the more so because integration is not even in evidence in any region except Europe.

The ultimate criterion for determining a "fundamental interest's" rank is its relation to the preservation of an independent state and the security of its citizens.

In Soviet times, there used to be a section in *Literaturnaya Gazeta* titled: "If I were the director…" in which readers offered different suggestions for solving various problems. So, if I were the "director," I would say that Russia's national interests, based on the current state of the country and the surrounding world, should be defined as follows.

Russia's National Interests

The fundamental national interests are aimed at securing the conditions necessary for the preservation of the Russian state, of its sovereignty, and for ensuring its citizens' security from external threats. Russia's fundamental interests are:

1. Ensuring the country's territorial integrity and protecting the state's political sovereignty.
2. Ensuring national security, preventing attacks that use weapons of mass destruction, and preventing border violations by foreign armed forces.
3. Preventing the emergence of hostile states on Russia's borders.
4. Preventing economic damage from being inflicted by foreign states, transnational corporations, and international financial organizations.
5. Ensuring the national-cultural originality and identity of the Russian people.

Important interests are those that increase Russia's capabilities to realize its fundamental interests. They are:

1. Development of constructive relations or alliances with states whose policies suit or match Russia's foreign policy goals.
2. Prevention of proliferation of weapons of mass destruction.
3. Help in preventing regional conflicts, primarily in regions bordering Russia.
4. Participation in the struggle against international crime, terrorism, and drug trafficking.

5. Prevention of uncontrolled migration across Russia's borders.
6. Prevention of the spreading of religious extremism in any form.
7. Participation in only those international organizations whose activities touch directly on Russia's national interests.
8. Helping increase Russia's GDP through trade and other economic activity in the world arena.

The less important or secondary national interests are those that are not connected directly to the fundamental and important interests, yet indirectly facilitate (or may facilitate in the future) the realization of those interests. Among these are:

1. Gradual transformation of the current economic and political relations with CIS countries into a channel of integration relations.
2. Neutralization of the "fifth column," serving the interests of foreign states to the detriment of Russia's national interests.
3. Counteraction of cultural aggression by foreign countries.
4. Protection of the Russian population in former Republics of the USSR from infringement of their civil rights.

Threats to Russia's fundamental interests

Threats to Russia's territorial integrity include:

- In the North: encroachments by Estonia and Latvia on certain Russian territories, and by certain circles in Germany on the Kaliningrad region.
- In the Far East: Japan's territorial claims to the Southern Kuril Islands.
- In the South (Northern Caucasus): the struggle by part of Chechnya's population to break away from Russia.

Threats to political sovereignty include:

- Attempts by Western countries, primarily the USA, to interfere in Russia's internal affairs, for example under the pretext of "preventing Russia's return to totalitarianism" or "absence of freedom" for mass media.
- The forming by Japan of a pro-Japanese lobby among politicians, scholars and businesspeople to act in its interests on the issue of "returning the Northern territories."
- The activities on Russian soil of foreign mass media and others, for example "scientific organizations," as well as support by foreign countries for certain Russian mass media acting against the Russian state's interests.

Threats to national security include:

- The expansion of NATO to the north, east and south; the presence of "peacekeeping forces" in CIS countries; the strengthening of the American-Japanese military alliance in the Far East.

Threats of economic nature include:

- The uncontrolled penetration of Western companies (often through dummy firms and organizations) into the strategic sectors of Russia's economy, as well as discrimination against Russian goods in the markets of Western countries.

Threats to Russia's national-cultural originality include:

- The introduction of Western values.

Clarifications and Adequate Responses

Territorial integrity. Japan's claims on Russian territories have turned that country into Russia's strategic adversary. To a certain degree, Moscow itself provoked Tokyo into taking an adversarial stance by admitting to the existence of "territorial" problems, in particular, in the Tokyo declaration of 1993. If Russia truly intends to preserve its territorial integrity, it should proclaim that it has no territorial disputes with Japan. The Southern Kuril Islands belong to Russia and always will. No punitive sanctions could cause greater harm to Russia than ceding these islands to Japan.

With respect to the Baltic countries and Germany, an official statement must be made strongly asserting the inviolability of existing borders. After that, all discussion of this topic must cease.

The situation is different with Chechnya. By now, experience has shown that the Chechen problem cannot be resolved through military means. The current state of war may last too long; this means that evergreater resources will be directed toward Chechnya without any real return. This problem actually extends throughout the Caucasus region. "Threats" from that region come in a constant flow: the infiltration into Russia of terrorists, narcotics, and illegal immigrants, all of which are threats to both fundamental and important interests. The Chechen situation requires an analysis of the whole region from the perspective of Russia's national interests, as well as a cost-benefit analysis of interaction with this region.

How much does Chechnya cost Russia? What commercial and strategic benefits does Russia derive from its interaction with the TransCaucasian states? I remind you that in 2000, the share of Middle Eastern countries in Russia's exports (mostly weapons and military or semimilitary technology) and imports was 2.8 percent and 0.6 percent respectively. The combined share of the Trans-Caucasian states (Azerbaijan, Armenia, and Georgia) in the CIS foreign trade with Russia in the same year was 1.5 percent for exports and 2.3 percent for imports. In Russia's total foreign trade, their share was 0.2 percent for exports and 0.8 percent for imports. So, what is all the fuss about?

I suggest that the Chechens be given an opportunity to hold a referendum on whether they want to stay in Russia. Should they vote for separation, they must be granted full independence and the border sealed. A sealed border must be established, in fact, against all states of the Caucasus region. They should then be left to their own devices and ways of development.

All analogies are imperfect, of course. Nonetheless, De Gaulle did save France when he "let go" of Algeria (after having first spilled a lot of blood there). Great Britain grew stronger only after it "let go" of all its colonies and semi-colonies. By not following their example, Russia will not only be facing a constant threat from the Caucasus but will also be bankrupted.

After a while, it is obvious that this same Chechnya will start begging to be "taken back." It should not be "taken back" until Russia itself emerges from its crisis.

The so-called strategic benefits to Russia's national interests from the Caucasus are illusory. The entire history of Russia-Caucasus relations is rife with the innumerable sacrifices made by the Russian people for the sake of false stereotypes promoted by Russian leaders who were unable to determine correctly the country's real national interests.

Political sovereignty. I understand it to mean full freedom to conduct an independent domestic and foreign policy. No country is currently threatening Russia's sovereignty directly. However, Japan's efforts to form a pro-Japanese lobby among politicians, scholars, and businesspeople having access to mass media and to the decisionmaking process is a development that can be interpreted as an indirect threat. The main function of this pro-Japanese lobby is to influence the government and public opinion in favor of handing over to Japan the Southern Kurile Islands. No other state in the world allows its mass media to promote the idea of handing over its territory to another country. Freedom of the press must not turn into freedom of encroachment on the state's fundamental interests. Russia has a real problem in that most of its press is in the hands of those who oppose Russia's national interests.

Of course, Japan has the right to act firmly and decisively in defense of its own national interests and form a lobby in any country, including Russia. In turn, Russia has the right to suppress such activities as unconstitutional—and that means antinational and antistate—with appropriate consequences for the lobbyists. This certainly applies to all sorts of lobbyists working in the interests of foreign states.

Economic interests. At this moment in history, it is Russia's economy that is suffering the most. In this case, the internal and external aspects of economic security strategy coincide. The experience of recent years shows that the capitalist market mechanism does not work in Russia, even though almost 80 percent of all enterprises are in private hands. These "hands" have demonstrated amazing deftness in the cause of personal enrichment but also complete inability to manage private property in accordance with the laws of capitalism. This is quite natural because real capitalism was built on a different historical base, on a different cultural-national soil. Russian culture and the mind-set of the Russian people reject individualistic capitalism. The Russian state with its vast spaces and perpetual foreign threats is characterized by a centralized form of governance and a collective form of property, which means socialism in its original Russian variant. Unlike the previous authoritarian socialism, its current form must be based on all property forms that coexist while the state holds on to the base industries (power generation, transportation, communications, postal service), military, industry, and strategic raw materials. These industries are all unprofitable, and development of strategic resources is capital-intensive, but they provide an impulse for the development of all other property forms, and state control prevents their takeover by foreign capital that can only work against Russia's economic interests.

From the perspective of foreign economic strategy, Russia does not need entry to the world marketplace for three reasons. First, the world economy is on the brink of a protracted crisis, with signs indicating a serious system collapse. Second, the world economy is governed by international organizations led by representatives of transnational and international companies and banks from the three centers of capitalism—the USA, Western Europe, and Japan. They all possess colossal financial capabilities. Russia's economic circles are incapable of competing with them in principle, not only in their markets but also in their own Russian market. Third, Russia doesn't need to gain entry to the world economy because its own territory contains everything necessary for a self-sufficient and prosperous economy. More than half of the world's natural resources is located on Russian territory. There is nothing in the world that Russia is incapable of producing itself.

At the same time, even though Russia as a whole has no need of the world market, the Russian Far East (RFE) does have need, not of the whole world, but of Northeast Asia (NEA). Interaction with that region's marketplace can produce a certain economic effect needed for development of the RFE. Therefore, economic strategy must emphasize the development of relations with China, the two Koreas, and the western territories of Japan.

For all that, economic strategy must assert the primacy of Russia's national interests and defend them firmly, including against the excessive unruliness of Chinese businessmen in the Far East. The strategic interests that may lead to a partnership with China must not infringe on the economic interests of Russian merchants. The relations between the USA and Japan are an example to emulate: Alliance and friendship are fine, but money is not to be shared.

Transfer of technologies and construction of production facilities abroad should always be justified by their ties to Russian enterprises on Russian territory. As the example of Japan shows, this strategy pays for itself hundredfold.

Russia has no economically justified interests in Africa, Latin America, Oceania (including Australia and New Zealand), or even in the ASEAN zone. From the perspective of objective economic interests, Russia has no need of the Near and Middle East either, as was said above.

As I stated already in the previous section, it is Europe that has always occupied and still occupies the top spot in the hierarchy of Russia's foreign economic ties. Therefore, strategic emphasis should be placed on Europe. But here, too, the "all-encompassing" approach should be avoided. It is necessary to concentrate on the key states, especially on Germany. There are many reasons for this, not only economic ones. Some ten to fifteen years from now, certain geostrategic factors will come to the foreground that will start changing the configuration of both Europe and the world. It is too early to discuss them yet, but one should keep them in mind.

* * *

I have expressed here only the most general considerations about problems of formulating a rational foreign policy. The general idea is to scale down Russia's international activities and concentrate primarily on realizing the country's fundamental interests. This is actually the policy once described by A.M. Gorchakov, a wise minister of foreign affairs in tsarist Russia, in this short but pithy phrase: "Russia is concentrating." He said it after Russia's defeat in the Crimean War. Today, Russia is in an even worse situation than back in the middle of the nineteenth century. It has lost great power status. Its place and role has ceased to be of any significance to the international community. Well, similar catastrophes have happened before, and not only in Russia. It is time to "start concentrating."

Selected Bibliography

Note: Academic papers and magazine articles such as those appearing in the Nezavisimaya gazeta (Independent Gazette), *Time*, or *The Economist* are not referred to in this bibliography. Their entries are given in text notes.

Statistics, Reference Books, and Reports of International Organizations

Contemporary transnational corporations. Economical-statistical reference book. Moscow, 1983.

Direction of Trade Statistics. *Yearbooks* [prepared by the General Statistics Division of the Bureau of Statistics of the International Monetary Fund], 1984, 1997, 2001.

Goskomstat Rossii (the Russian State Committee for Statistics). Annual reports.

Nikhon Tokei Nenkan 2001 (Japanese Statistical Yearbook, 2001). Tokyo, 2001.

Russia: Encyclopedia (on base of Encyclopedia of Brokgauz and Efron/ volumes 54 and 55/) L.: Lenizdat, 1991.

The SIPRI Yearbook 2004. *World Armaments and Disarmament.* Oxford: Oxford University Press, 2004.

The SIPRI Yearbook 2002. *World Armaments and Disarmament.* Oxford: Oxford University Press, 2002.

States budgets of leading capitalist countries (the budgets of central organs of power). *Selection of analytical reviews.* M.: IMEMO, 1987.

UN DP, *Human Development Report 2002.* Deepening democracy in a fragmented world. New York: Oxford University Press, 2002.

UN DP, *Human Development Report 2000. Human Rights and Human Development 2000.* New York: Oxford University Press, 2000.

U.S. Census Bureau. *Statistical Abstract of the United States: 1994, 1995, 2000.*

U.S. Government Printing Office. *A Citizen's Guide to the Federal Budget*, Fiscal Year 2001; *The Budget-in-Brief—Fiscal Year 2001.* February 7, 2000; *Historical Tables. Budget of the United States Government.* Fiscal Year 2000; *Summary and Highlights. International Affairs (Function 150).* Fiscal Year 2001 Budget Request, February 7, 2000.

U.S. State Department. *FS Salary and Benefits.* May 15, 1996.

United Kingdom. Minister for the Civil Service and the Chief Secretary to the Treasure. *The Government's Expenditure Plans 2000–01 to 2001–02.* April 2000.

What is What in World Politics. Dictionary-Reference. M.: Progress, 1987.

World Bank. *World Development Indicators 2002.* Washington, D.C., 2002.

World Bank. *World Development Report 2000/2001. Attacking Poverty.* Washington, D.C., 2001.

World Bank. *World Development Report 2000/2001. The Struggle Against Poverty. A Review.* Washington, D.C., 2001.

World Bank. *World Development Report 1999/2000. Entering the 21st Century.* New York: Oxford University Press, 1999.

World Bank. *Global Economic Prospects and the Developing Countries 2000.* Washington, D.C., 2000.

World Military Expenditures and Arms Transfers – 95 (WMEAT-95). Washington, D.C.: Arms Control and Disarmament Agency, April 1996.

WTO. *International trade statistics* 2000.

WTO. *Merchandise Trade Section*, Statistics Division. July 1999.

Public Documents

Annual Report to Congress on Foreign Economic Collection and Industrial Espionage. July 1995.

Annual Report on FY 1997 Intelligence Community Activities, Director of Central Intelligence.

Annual Report for the United States Intelligence Community. May 1999.

Cohen, William S., Secretary of Defense. *Annual Report to the President and the Congress*. Department of Defense, 1997.

Cohen, William S., Secretary of Defense. *Annual Report to the President and the Congress*. Department of Defense, 1998.

Cohen, William S., Secretary of Defense. *Annual Report to the President and the Congress*. Department of Defense, 1999.

Cohen, William S., Secretary of Defense. *Annual Report to the President and the Congress*. Department of Defense, 2000.

Cohen, William S., Secretary of Defense. *Annual Report to the President and the Congress*. Department of Defense, 2001.

Contemporary U.S. Foreign Policy: Documents and Commentary. Compiled and edited by Elmer Plishke. USA: Greenwood Press, 1991.

Economic Security Act of 1996. S1557 IS 104th Congress, 2d Session.

The Foreign Policy Concept of the Russian Federation. Document. English translation, full text, *Nezavisimaya gazeta*, June 11, 2000.

Gannon, John C. *Russia in the Next Millennium.* National Intelligence Council, DFI International & Henry L. Stimson Group, December 9, 1999.

Gannon, John C., Chairman, National Intelligence Council. *The CIA in the New World Order: Intelligence Challenges Through 2015*. February 1, 2000.

Global Trends 2015: *A Dialogue About the Future with Nongovernment Experts.* NIC 2000-02, December 2000

Materials of the 27th Congress of the Communist Party of the Soviet Union. M.: Politizdat, 1986.

A Military Doctrine of the Russian Federation, the full text in Independent Military Review, *Nezavisimaya gazeta*, April 28, 2000.

A National Security Concept of the Russian Federation. January 14, 2000. English translation, full text, *Nezavisimaya gazeta*, January 14, 2000.

A National Security Strategy for A New Century. Washington, D.C.: The White House, May 1997.

A National Security Strategy for A New Century. Washington, D.C.: The White House, October 1998.

A National Strategy for a New Century. Washington, D.C.: The White House, December 1999.

Russia's Military Doctrine. English translation, full text. *Arms Control Today*, May 2000.

Senate of the United States. *Comment on the Economic Espionage Act of 1996 and the Economic Security Act of 1996* by Senators Kohl and Spector. February 1, 1996, S-1557, IS, 104th Congress, 2d Session.

Statement by Louis J. Freeh, Director of FBI. Senate Select Committee on Intelligence and Senate Committee on the Judiciary: Subcommittee on Terrorism, Technology and Government Information,

Hearing on Economic Espionage. February 18, 1996.

Statement by Louis J. Freeh, Director of FBI. Senate Select Committee on Intelligence. Hearing on Threats to U.S. National Security. January 28, 1998.

Tenet, George J. *Statement by Director of Central Intelligence before the Senate Select Committee on Intelligence on the Worldwide Threat in 2000: Global Realities of Our National Security.* February 2, 2000.

U.S. Congress. 105th Congress Report. House of Representatives 1st Session 105–94. Foreign Policy Reform Act. May 9, 1997.

U.S. Department of Defense. *The United States Security Strategy for the East Asia-Pacific Region.* Washington, D.C., November 1998.

U.S. Department of State. *On-the-Record Briefing on FY 2000 Budget as Released by the Office of the Spokesman.* Washington, D.C., February 1, 1999.

U.S. Department of State. *Strategic Plan.* September 2000.

U.S. Department of State. *Strategic Plan for International Affairs.* Washington, D.C., First Revision—February 1999.

Author's Books and Articles

In Russian:

Aliev R. Sh. [Alex Battler] "Might of the State and Global Correlation of Forces." *State and Society.* M.: Nauka, 1985.

———. *Japan's Foreign Policy, 1970s-80s (Theory and Practice).* M.: Nauka, 1986.

———. *From Foreign Policy to World Relations.* M.: ION ZK KPSS, 1989.

Arin, Oleg. [Alex Battler] *Asia-Pacific Region: Myths, Illusions and*

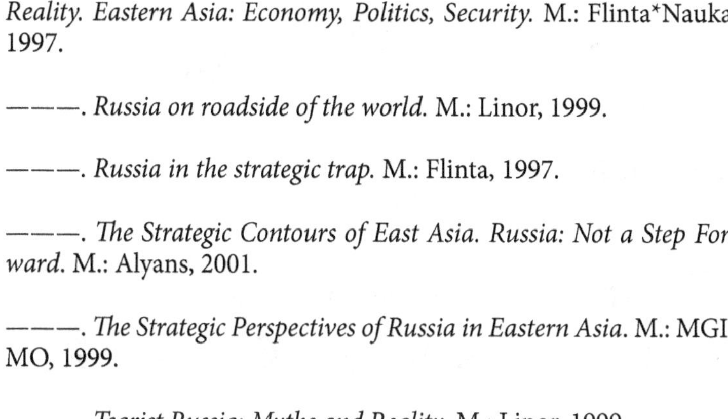

Reality. Eastern Asia: Economy, Politics, Security. M.: Flinta*Nauka, 1997.

———. *Russia on roadside of the world.* M.: Linor, 1999.

———. *Russia in the strategic trap.* M.: Flinta, 1997.

———. *The Strategic Contours of East Asia. Russia: Not a Step Forward.* M.: Alyans, 2001.

———. *The Strategic Perspectives of Russia in Eastern Asia.* M.: MGIMO, 1999.

———. *Tsarist Russia: Myths and Reality.* M.: Linor, 1999.

Contemporary political systems. Essays. M.: Nauka, 1978.

Belous, T.Y. *International industrial monopolies.* Moscow: Myisl', 1972.

Borodayevski, A.D., V.P. Trepelkov, and V.P. Fedorov, eds. *Crisis of world capitalist economy in 80s.* M.: Mezhd. otnosheniya, 1986.

"The Concept of National Interests: General Parameters and Russian Specific Character," *MEMO*, no.7–9 (1996).

Empires of financial tycoons (transnational corporations in the economy and politics of imperialism), ed. I.D. Ivanov. M.: Myisl', 1988.

Grishin, A.V. "National Security of Russia" (interview with V.A. Ozerov), *Profi*, no. 3–4 (2000).

International Order. Political-legal aspects. Ed. G. Kh. Shakhnazarov. M.: Nauka, 1986.

International Relations, Politics and Personality. Annual of SPSA, 1975. M.: Nauka, 1976.

Khromov, A. P. *Russia's Economic Development in the Nineteenth-Twentieth Centuries. 1800-1917.* M.: 1950.

Korzhov, G. V. *The economic security of Russia*. M.: 1996.

Kudrov, V. "Soviet economic growth: official data and alternative estimates." *Voprosyi ekonomiki*, no. 10 (1995).

Lenin, V.I. *The Complete Works of Lenin. Fifth edition in 55 volumes*. M.: Politizdat, 1958-1965.

Lunev, S.I., and G.K. Shirokov. *Russia, China and India in the Modern Global Process*. M.: 1998; electronic version.

Mel'yanzev, V.A. *East and West in the Second Millennium: Economy, History and the Present*. M.: Moskovskyi universitet, 1996.

Mikheev, V. Globalization of the world economy and Asian regionalism—challenges for Russia? *The problems of the Far East*, no. 2 (1999).

Moiseev, N.N. *The Fortunes of Civilization. The Way of Reason*. M.: MNEPU, 1998.

National Interests and Security Problems of Russia. M.: Gorbachev-Fond, 1997.

National Policy of Russia: Ideas and Reality. Gorbachev-Fond. M.: April–85, 1997.

Nikonov, A.D., ed. *Problems of Military Detente*. M.: 1981.

Policy of force or force of the reason? (Arms Race and International Relations). M.: Politizdat, 1989.

Political Systems of Modernity (Essays). Moscow: Nauka, 1978

Pozdnyakov, E.A., ed. *National Interests: Theory and Practice. Selected articles*. M.: IMEMO, 1991.

Pozdnyakov, E.A. *Philosophy of Politics. In two parts*. M.: Paleya, 1994.

Proector, D.M. *World Wars and the Fortunes of Humankind.* M.: Myisl', 1986.

Russia in Eurasia. Gorbachev-Fond. M.: April–85, 1998.

Russia's Foreign Policy: What is Possible and What is Desired. Gorbachev-Fond. M. : April-85, 1997.

Russia and the Challenges at the Turn of the Century: A possibility of manoeuvre on conditions of limiting factors (geopolitical aspect). S. E. Blagovolin, Head of Project. Moscow: Institute of National Security and Strategic Studies, March 1998.

Russia at the Threshold of Political Change. In two parts. M.: Gorbachev-Fond, 1999.

Russia in the Surrounding World: 1999. The Analytical Series. M.: Press, 1999.

Shakhnazarov, G. Kh. *The Future Worldorder.* M.: Politizdat, 1981.

Sokolov, Yu.V. "About myths and realities of world politics." *New Order for ever?* M.: MNEPU, 2000.

Sorokin, K.E. *Contemporary Geopolitics and Geostrategy of Russia.* M.: ROSSPEN, 1996.

State monopolistic capitalism: common features and characteristics. Moscow: Politizdat, 1975

Strategy for Russia: Agenda for the President-2000. M.: Vagrius, 2000.

The Self-determination of Russia. M.: Gorbachev-Fond, 2000.

Titarenko, M.L. *Russia Facing Asia.* M.: Respublika, 1998.

In Western Languages

Ahrari, M. E. with James Beal. "The New Great Game in Muslim Cen- tral Asia." *McNair Paper 47 (January 1996).*

Alberts, David S., and Thomas J. Cherwinski, eds. *Complexity, Global Politics, and National Security.* Washington, D.C.: National Defense University, 1997.

Aliyev, Kenan. "Security in the Caucasus: Caspian Crossroads." Interview with U.S. Lt. Gen. William E. Odom. *Caspian Crossroads Magazine* 4, no. 2 (Winter 1999).

*American Public Opinion and U.S. Foreign Policy.*1999. The Chicago Council on Foreign Relations. Chicago 1999.

America's National Interests. The Commission on America's National Interests. The Nixon Center, July 2000.

Arrighi, Giovanni. "The Global Market." *Journal of World-Systems Research* 5, no. 2 (Spring 1999).

Atwood, J. Brian. "Towards A New Definition Of National Security." *Vital Speeches of the Day*, December 15, 1995.

Barnet, Richard J., and John Cavanagh. *Global Dreams. Imperial Corporation and the New World Order.* New York: Touchstone Books, 1995.

Battler, Alex. *The Twenty-Fisrt Century: The World Without Russia.* First ed. American University & Colleges Press, 2004.

Binnendijk, Hans, with Alan Henrikson. "Back to Bipolarity?" *Strategic Forum*, no. 161 (May 1999).

Blank, Stephen J. "Helsinki in Asia? Towards a Multilateral Asian Order." *The Journal of East and West Studies* (April 1994).

Booth, Ken, and Steve Smith, eds. *International Relations. Theory today.* Cambridge: Polity Press, 1997.

Borrego, John, Alejandro Alvarez Bejar, and Jomo K.S., eds. *Capital, the State, and Late Industrialization: Comparative Perspectives on the Pacific Rim*. Boulder: Westview Press, 1996.

Borrego, John. "Models of Integration, Models of Development in the Pacific." *Journal of World-Systems Research* 1, no. 11 (1995).

Boswell, Terry. "Hegemony and Bifurcation Points in World History." *Journal of World-Systems Research* 1, no. 15 (1995).

Brzezinski, Zbigniew. "America in the World Today." In *Complexity, Global Politics, and National Security* edited by David S. Alberts and Thomas J. Czerwinski. Washington, D.C.: NDU, 1997.

Brzezinski, Zbigniew. "Living With Russia." *The National Interest* 61 (Fall 2000).

Butler, Stuart M., and Kim R. Holmes, eds. *Mandate for Leadership IV. Turning Ideas into Actions*. Washington, D.C.: Heritage Foundation, 1998.

Butler, Stuart M., and Kim R. Holmes, eds. *Priorities for the President*. Washington, D.C.: Heritage Foundation, 2001.

Butler, Stuart M., and Kim R. Holmes, eds. *Issues 2000: The Candi- date's Briefing Book*. Washington, D.C.: Heritage Foundation, 2000.

Butler, Stuart M., and Kim R. Holmes, eds. *Issues '98: The Candidate's Briefing Book*. Washington, D.C., Heritage Foundation, 1998.

Chafetz, Glenn, Michael Spirtas, and Benjamin Frankel, eds. *The Origins of National Interests*. London: Frank Cass, 1999.

Chung, Il Yung, ed. *Asia-Pacific Community in the Year 2000: Challenges and Perspectives*. Seoul: Seijong Institute, Korea, 1992.

Clover, Charles. "Dreams of the Eurasian Heartland: The Reemergence of Geopolitics." *Foreign Affairs*, 2, no. 2 (March/April 1999).

Cohen, Ariel. *The "Primakov Doctrine": Russia's Zero-Sum Game with the United States.* Heritage Foundation *FYI,* no. 167 (December 15, 1997).

Cohen, Ariel. *A New Paradigm for U.S.-Russia Relations: Facing the Post-Cold War Reality.* Heritage Foundation *Backgrounder,* no. 1105 (March 6, 1997).

Cohen, Ariel. *Summit Rhetoric Aside, Putin's New Cabinet Makes Rus- sian Reforms Less Likely.* Heritage Foundation *Executive Memorandum* (June 1, 2000).

Crafts, Nicholas. *Globalization and Growth in the Twentieth Century.* IMF Working Paper (March 2000).

Desch, Michael C. "Culture Clash. Assessing the Importance of Ideas in Security Studies." *International Security* 23, no. 1 (Summer 1998).

Doremus, Paul N., William W. Keller, Louis W. Pauly, and Simon Reich. "The Myth of The Global Corporation." *Current History* (July 14, 1997).

Eberstadt, Nicolas. "Russia: Too Sick to Matter?" *Policy Review,* no. 95 (June/July 1999).

Ellsworth, Robert F. "American National Security in the Early Twenty-First Century." *U.S. National Security: Beyond the Cold War.*

Exploring U.S. Missile Defense. Requirements in 2010: What are the Policy and Technology Challenges? Washington: IFPA, April 1997.

Foreign spy agencies threaten Canada's economic security, warns new study. Canada News Wire CSIS/SCRS 1996.

Gardner, Richard N. "The One percent Solution." *Foreign Affairs* (July/August 2000).

Garnaut, Ross and Peter Drysdale, with John Kunkel, eds. *Asia Pacific Regionalism: Readings in International Economic Relations.*

Australia: Harper Education Publishers, 1994.

Gates, Robert M. "Preventive Diplomacy: Concept and Reality." *PacNet Newsletter,* no. 39 (Sept. 27, 1996).

Gilpin, Robert. *The Political Economy of International Relations.* Princeton: Princeton University Press, 1987.

Gissinger, Ranveig, and Nils Petter Gleditsch. "Globalization and Conflict: Welfare, Distribution, and Political Unrest." *Journal of World- Systems Research* 5, no. 2 (Spring 1999).

Global Trends 2015: A Dialogue About the Future with Nongovernment Experts. NIC 2000-02, December 2000.

Goldfrank, W. L. "Beyond Cycles of Hegemony: Economic, Social, and Military Factors." *Journal of World-Systems Research* 1, no. 8 (1995).

Grenwille J.A.S. *A History of the World in the Twentieth Century.* Cambridge: The Belknap Press of Harvard University, 1994.

Grosse, Robert, and Kujawa Duane. *International Business: Theory and Managerial Applications.* 2nd ed. Richard D. Irwin, Inc., 1992.

Halperin, Morton H., Lawrence J. Korb, and Richard M. Moose, project directors. *Financing America's Leadership: Protecting American Interests and Promoting American Values: An Independent Task Force.* The Council on Foreign Relations, Inc., co-sponsored with The Brookings Institution (January 14, 1998).

Hamilton, Lee. "Changes in American Foreign Policy Over the Past Thirty Years," Institute for the Study of Diplomacy (November 18, 1998).

Hausken, Kjell, and Thomas Plümper. "Hegemons, Leaders and Followers: A Game-Theoretic Approach to the Postwar Dynamics of International Political Economy." *Journal of World-Systems Research* 3, no. 1 (1997).

Hay, Colin, and Matthew Watson. "Globalization: Skeptical Notes on the 1999 Reith Lectures." *Political Quarterly* 70 (October/December 1999).

Hegel's Science of Logic. Trans. A.V. Miller. London: George Allen & Unwin, 1969.

Hirst, Paul, and Grahame Thomson. *Globalization in Question. The International Economy and the Possibilities of Governance.* Cambridge: Polity Press, 1999.

Holmes, Kim R., and James J. Przystup, eds. *Between Diplomacy and Deterrence. Strategies for U.S. Relations with China*. HF, 1997.

Holsti, K.J. *International Politics. A Framework for Analysis*. New Jersey: Prentice Hall, 1987.

Hsiung, James C., ed. *Asia Pacific in the New World Politics.* Boulder: L. Rienner, 1993.

Huntington, Samuel P. "The Lonely Superpower." *Foreign Affairs* 78, no. 2 (March/April 1999).

Huntington, Samuel P. *The Clash of Civilizations and the Remaking of World Order*. London: Touchstone Books, 1998.

Hutchison, Kay Bailey. "A Foreign Policy Vision for the Next American Century." Heritage Foundation, *Heritage Lectures*, no. 639, July 9, 1999.

Jordan, Amos A., William J. Taylor Jr., and Michael J. Mazarr. *American National Security*. Baltimore and London: The Johns Hopkins University Press, 1998.

Junne, Gerd. "Global Cooperation or Rival Trade Blocs?" *Journal of World-Systems Research*, 1, no. 9 (1995).

Kahn, Herman, and Wiener, Anthony. *The Year 2000. A Framework for Speculation on the Next Thirty-Three Years.* New York: Macmillan Company, 1967.

Kaizer K., u. H.-P. Schwarz, Hrsg. *Weltpolitik. Strukturen - Akteure - Perspektiven.* Stuttgart: Klett-Gotta, 1985.

Katzenstein, Peter J., ed. *The Culture of National Security: Norms and Identity in World Politics.* New York: Columbia University Press, 1996.

Kenwood, A.G., and Lougheed, A.L. *The Growth of International Economy 1820-1990.* L., New York: Routledge, 1992.

Keohane, Robert O., and Joseph S. Nye. *Power and Interdependence.* New York: Harper Collins, 1989.

Khalilzad, Zalmay, and Ian O. Lesser, eds. *Sources of Conflict in the 21st Century. Regional Futures and U.S. Strategy.* Rand, 1998.

Kort, Michael. *The Soviet Colossus: The Rise and Fall of the USSR.* NY, 1993.

Kosterlitz, Julie. "Sovereignty's Struggle (Globalism)." *National Journal*, November 20, 1999.

Kozyrev, Andrei V, "NATO Is Not Our Enemy," *Newsweek*, February 10, 1997.

Lampton, David M., and Gregory C. May. *A Big Power Agenda for East Asia: America, China, and Japan.* The Nixon Center, 2000, ii.

Luard, Evan. *The Globalization of Politics. The Changed Focus of Political Action in the Modern World.* London: Macmillan, 1990.

Mack, Andrew, and John Ravenhill. *Pacific Cooperation: Building Economic and Security Regimes in the Asia Pacific Region.* Boulder: Westview Press, 1995.

Mandelbaum, Michael, ed. *The New Russian Foreign Policy.* Council on Foreign Relations (NY, 1998).
Marx and Engels. *Selected Works.* London: Lawrence & Wishart, 1991.

Maruyama, Masao. "Thought and Behavior." *Modern Japanese Politics*. Tokyo, Oxford, and New York: Oxford University Press, 1979.

Mazrui, Ali A. "Globalization and Cross-Cultural Values: The Politics of Identity and Judgment." *Arab Studies Quarterly (ASQ)* 21 (Summer 1999).

McGrew, Anthony and Christopher Brook, eds. *Asia-Pacific in the New World Order.* New York and London: Routledge, 1998.

Messner, Dirk. "Globalisierung, Global Governance und Entwicklungspolitik." *International Politics and Society,* no. 1 (1999).

Modelski, George. "The Evolution of Global Politics." *Journal of World-Systems Research* 1, no.7 (1995).

Morgan, Patrick M. *Theories and Approaches to International Politics. What Are We to Think?* 2nd edition. Palo Alto: Page-Ficklin Publications, 1975.

Nash Jr., Bradley, guest editor. Global Labor Movements (Special Issue). *Journal of World-Systems Research* 4, no.1 (Winter 1998).

Nation, R. Craig, and Michael McFaul. *The United States and Russia into the 21st Century.* Carlisle: Strategic Studies Institute, October 1, 1997.

Nye, Joseph Jr. "Coping with Japan." *Foreign Policy* (Winter 1992/93).

Olson, William C., David S. McLellan, and Fred A. Sondermann. *The Theory and Practice of International Relations.* 6th edition. Englewood Cliffs: Prentice-Hall, Inc., 1983.

Pelkmans, Jacques. *European Integration: Methods and Economic Analysis.* London: Longman, 1998.

Pinto, Jaime Nogueira. The crisis of the sovereign state and the "privatization" of defense and foreign affairs. *Heritage Lectures* (HF), no. 649, November 19, 1999.

Quayle, Dan. "The Duty to Lead: America's National Security Imperative." Heritage Foundation, *Heritage Lectures*, no. 630 (January 21, 1999).

Rancour-Laferriere, Daniel. *The Slave Soul of Russia. Moral Masochism and the Cult of Suffering.* New York and London: New York University Press, 1995.

Reida, George E., ed. *Social Insurance and Economic Security*, 5th ed. Prentice Hall, 1994.

Renwick, Nail. *Multinational Corporations and the Political Economy of Power.* Canberra: Australian National University, 1983.

Reilly, John E. "Americans and the World: A Survey Century's End." *Foreign Policy* (Spring 1999).

Reilly, John E. ed. *American Public Opinion and U.S. Foreign Policy. 1999.* Chicago: The Chicago Council on Foreign Relations, 1999.

Rice, Condoleezza. "Campaign 2000: Promoting the National Interests." *Foreign Affairs* (January/February 2001).

Russet, Bruce M. *International Regions and International System.* Chicago: Rand McNally, 1967.

Russet, Bruce, and Harvey Starr. *World Politics: The Menu for Choice.* New York: W. H. Freeman & Company, 1989.

Santis, Hugh De. "Mutualism: An American Strategy for the Next Century." *Strategic Forum*, no. 162 (May 1999).

Sestanovich, Stephen. "Where Does Russia Belong?" *The National Interest* 62 (Winter 2000/2001).

The Shaping of Economic Cooperation in South-East Asia. Special publication of the South-East Asia. Research Center of Jilin University (July 1993).

Sklair, Leslie. “Competing Conceptions of Globalization.” *Journal of World-System Research* 5, no. 2 (Spring 1999).

Snare, Charles E. “Defining Others and Situations: Peace, Conflict, and Cooperation.” *Peace and Conflict Studies* 1, no.1 (December 1994).

The State of Russian Foreign Policy and U.S. Policy Toward Russia. “*Heritage Lectures*”, no. 607, April 6, 1998.

Steel, Ronald. “The New Meaning of Security.” *U.S. National Security: Beyond the Cold War.*

Strategic *Assessment 1997. Flashpoints and Force Structure.* Washington, D.C.: National Defense University, 1997

Strategic Assessment 1998. *Engaging Power for Peace.* Washington, D.C.: National Defense University, March 1998.

Strategic Assessment 1999. *Priorities for a Turbulent World.* Washing- ton, D.C.: National Defense University, 1999.

Talbott, Strobe. “*Russia: Its Current Troubles and Its On-Going Transformation.*” Testimony before the Senate Foreign Relations Committee (Washington, D.C., Sept. 23, 1999).

Tam, Henry. *Communitarianism. A New Agenda for Politics and Citizenship.* Macmillan Press Ltd, 1998.

Thurow, Lester. *The Future of Capitalism.* London: Nicholas Brealey, 1996.

Transforming Defense. National Security in the 21st Century. Report of the National Defense Panel. Arlington, VA, December 1997.

Tzu, Sun. *The Art of War. Translated by Thomas Cleary.* Boston and London: Shambhala, 1988.

U.S. National Security: Beyond the Cold War. Carlisle: Strategic Studies Institute, 1997.

United States. Strategic Plan for International Affairs (Department of State, Washington, D.C., First Revision, February 1999).

The United States Security Strategy for the East Asia-Pacific Region, 1998. U.S. Department of Defense, Washington, DC, November 1998.

Vasquez, John A., ed. *Classics of International Relations.* New Jersey: Prentice Hall, 1996.

Wagar, W. Warren. "Toward a Praxis of World Integration," *Journal of World-Systems Research* 2, no. 2 (1996).

Wagar, W. Warren. *A Short History of the Future.* 2nd ed. Chicago: Chicago University Press, 1992.

Wallerstein, Immanuel. "The Modern World-System and Evolution." *Journal of World-Systems Research* 1, no. 19 (1995).

Ward, Hugh. "Structural Power—A Contradiction in Terms?" *Political Studies* 35, no. 4 (1987): 593-610.

What about Russians and Nuclear War? New York: Pocket Books, 1983.

What Is to Be Undone? A Russia Policy Agenda for the New Administration. The Nixon Center, February 2001.

White, Stephen, Alex Pravda, and Zvi Gitelman, eds. *Developments in Russian Politics.* London: Macmillan Press, 1997.

White, Stephen, Alex Pravda, and Zvi Gitelman eds. *Developments in Soviet and Post-Soviet Politics.* London: Macmillan Press, 1992.

Xu, Mingqi. "Economic Globalization, Defects in International Monetary System and Southeast Asian Financial Crisis." *SASS Papers [Shanghai Academy of Social Sciences]*, no. 8 (2000).

Index

I

J

K

L

M

N

O

P

Q

R

S

T

V

W

X

Also by Alex Battler

- Tsarist Russia: The Collapse of Capitalism (2020, in Russian).
- Science of God (in 3 volumes, 2019, in Russian).
- Society: Progress and Force: Criteria and First Principles (2008, 2019 in Russian and English).
- Dialectics of Force: Ontóbia (2005, 2008, 2020, in Russian and English).
- Eurasia: Myths and Reality (2019, in Russian).
- Mirology: Progress and Force in World Relations (in 2 volumes, 2019, in Russian.)
- The 21st Century: the World without Russia (2001, 2002, 2004, 2005, 2011, in Russian; 2004 in English – 1st edition; 2005, in Chinese).
- The Truth and Myths of Tsarist Russia (2010 in Russian).
- On Love, Family, and the State (2006, 2008, 2019, in Russian and English).
- The Strategic Contours of East Asia. Russia: Not a Step Forward (2001, 2003, in Russian).
- Japan: View on the World, Asia, and Russia (2001, in Russian).
- Russia on roadside of the world (1999, in Russian).
- Russia in the Strategic Trap (1997, 2003, in Russian).
- Asia-Pacific region: Myths, Illusions, and Reality. Eastern Asia: Economy, Politics and Security (1997, in Russian).
- Japan's Foreign Policy, 1970s–80s: Theory and Practice (1986, in Russian).
- Japan and the Soviet-Chinese Relations of 1931–1975 (1976, in Russian).

Alex Battler

The Twenty-First Century: The World Without Russia

Cover Design and Book Interior Layout
by V. Battler

Printed in the United States of America

SCHOLARICA®
2020

www.ingramcontent.com/pod-product-compliance
Lightning Source LLC
Chambersburg PA
CBHW062045270326
41931CB00013B/2957

* 9 7 8 1 7 3 5 5 9 8 9 1 8 *